A CONTINUING TRIAL OF TREATMENT

reviewed negatively
by Mitchell in AA
Dec 1990 p. 1061

CULTURE, ILLNESS, AND HEALING

Editors:

MARGARET LOCK

Departments of Anthropology and Humanities and Social Studies in Medicine,
McGill University, Montreal, Canada

ALLAN YOUNG

Department of Anthropology, Case Western Reserve University, Cleveland, Ohio, U.S.A.

Editorial Board:

LIZA BERKMAN

Department of Epidemiology, Yale University,
New Haven, Conecticut, U.S.A.

ATWOOD D. GAINES

Departments of Anthropology and Psychiatry, Case Western Reserve
University and Medical School, Cleveland, Ohio, U.S.A.

GILBERT LEWIS

Department of Anthropology, University of Cambridge, England

GANANATH OBEYESEKERE

Department of Anthropology, Princeton University,
Princeton, New Jersey, U.S.A.

ANDREAS ZEMPLÉNI

Laboratoire d'Ethnologie et de Sociologie Comparative,
Université de Paris X, Nanterre, France

A CONTINUING TRIAL OF TREATMENT

Medical Pluralism in Papua New Guinea

Edited by

STEPHEN FRANKEL

*Department of Epidemiology and Community Medicine,
University of Wales College of Medicine*

and

GILBERT LEWIS

*Department of Social Anthropology,
University of Cambridge*

KLUWER ACADEMIC PUBLISHERS

DORDRECHT / BOSTON / LONDON

Library of Congress Cataloging-in-Publication Data

```
A Continuing trial of treatment : medical pluralism in Papua New
  Guinea / edited by Stephen Frankel and Gilbert Lewis.
       p.    cm. -- (Culture, illness, and healing)
    Includes index.
    ISBN 1-556-08076-X (U.S.)
    1. Medical anthropology--Papua New Guinea.  2. Medicine,
  Primitive--Papua New Guinea.  3. Medical innovations--Social
  aspects--Papua New Guinea.  4. Papua New Guinea--Social life and
  customs.    I. Frankel, Stephen.  II. Lewis, Gilbert.  III. Series.
  GN671.N5C68 1988
  362.1'0995'3--dc19                                          88-12044
```

ISBN 1-55608-076-X (HB)
ISBN 0-7923-0078-5 (PB)

Published by Kluwer Academic Publishers,
P.O. Box 17, 3300 AA Dordrecht, Holland.

Sold and distributed in the U.S.A. and Canada
by Kluwer Academic Publishers,
101 Philip Drive, Assinippi Park, Norwell, MA 02061, U.S.A.

In all other countries, sold and distributed
by Kluwer Academic Publishers Group,
P.O. Box 322, 3300 AH Dordrecht, Holland.

Cover photograph: a Huli aid post orderly administering oral rehydration solution to a child.

All Rights Reserved
© 1989 by Kluwer Academic Publishers
No part of the material protected by this copyright notice may be reproduced or
utilized in any form or by any means, electronic or mechanical,
including photocopying, recording or by any information storage and
retrieval system, without written permission from the copyright owner

Printed in the Netherlands

TABLE OF CONTENTS

1. STEPHEN FRANKEL and GILBERT LEWIS / Patterns of Continuity and Change — 1
2. BRYANT J. ALLEN / Infection, Innovation and Residence: Illness and Misfortune in the Torricelli Foothills from 1800 — 35
3. JOHN BARKER / Western Medicine and the Continuity of Belief: the Maisin of Collingwood Bay, Oro Province — 69
4. GILBERT H. HERDT / Doktas and Shamans among the Sambia of Papua New Guinea — 95
5. MICHAEL W. YOUNG / Illness and Ideology: Aspects of Health Care on Goodenough Island — 115
6. ANDREW STRATHERN / Health Care and Medical Pluralism: Cases from Mount Hagen — 141
7. ACHSAH H. CARRIER / The Place of Western Medicine in Ponam Theories of Health and Illness — 155
8. CAROL JENKINS / The Amele and Dr Braun: a History of Early Experience with Western Medicine in Papua New Guinea — 181
9. PAUL ROSCOE / Medical Pluralism among the Yangoru Boiken — 199
10. ANN CHOWNING / The Doctor and the Curer: Medical Theory and Practice in Kove — 217
11. DAVID C. HYNDMAN / Gender in the Diet and Health of the Wopkaimin — 249
12. DAVID R. COUNTS and DOROTHY AYERS COUNTS / Complementarity in Medical Treatment in a West New Britain Society — 277
13. EDWARD LIPUMA / Modernity and Medicine among the Maring — 295

LIST OF CONTRIBUTORS — 311
REFERENCES — 313
INDEX OF SUBJECTS — 329

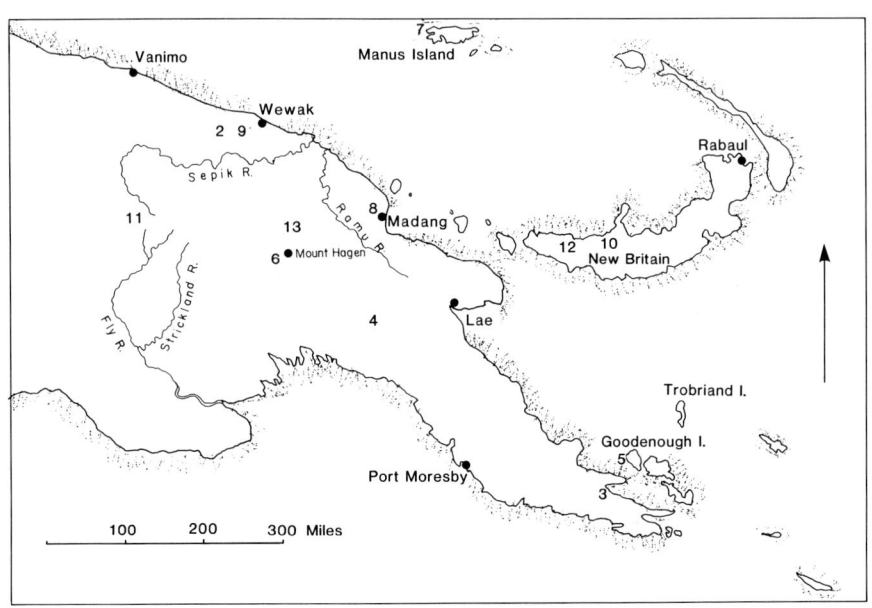

Fig. 1. Map of Papua New Guinea; numbers refer to the chapter where the area is described.

STEPHEN FRANKEL AND GILBERT LEWIS

1. PATTERNS OF CONTINUITY AND CHANGE

INTRODUCTION

How do people with their own medical traditions respond to new theories of disease causation and to novel treatments? Answers to this question are central to the study of innovation and change. The analysis of this issue also has practical relevance to those trying to influence the high levels of illness and death which characterize many of the countries where traditional approaches to illness still prevail. Medical pluralism, the coexistence of differing medical traditions, is now the common pattern in all but the most isolated areas of the world. In Papua New Guinea there are now few, if any, populations that still rely exclusively upon their traditional treatments. Despite this trend the importance of Western medicine in societies such as those in Papua New Guinea is reflected in the anthropological record only to the most limited extent. We therefore felt that a volume bringing together accounts of responses to illness in a wide range of Papua New Guinean societies would be important in correcting this imbalance (Fig. 1).

Pluralism, continuity and change: these are the subjects of this book. Papua New Guinea is a particularly rich field to study questions of changing medical practice. What has happened in Papua New Guinea? Is it like what has happened in other countries with a colonial past? Or has it been distinctive? This collection of papers with evidence from village experience offers a chance for us to consider the question.

The accounts presented in this book tackle questions raised in our first request for contributions. The contributors write from recent firsthand observation of places and settings in which they worked as anthropologists in the field. The authors were asked to provide portraits of care and change. Immediate knowledge and experience of what it is like in a village come from sharing in daily life there; obviously it takes time to get a fair idea of this. Few outsiders have the chance of doing this as anthropologists do.

The scope and focus of each anthropologist's contribution differs according to his or her main research interests and the availability of Western treatments in the research area at the time of field work, but the range of relevant questions we asked them to consider included the following: What are the common patterns of response to illnesses of different sorts? What is the relationship between traditional concepts of health and illness and the acceptance or rejection of particular aspects of Western medicine? What continuities or contrasts are there between the traditional and modern organization of health care? Is there conflict between Western and indigenous responses to illness? Where Western treatments are readily available, under what circumstances are traditional remedies applied? Are there cultural barriers to the acceptance of Western treatments, or are more mundane issues such as access and cost more important where Western treatments are not sought or persevered with? Historical analyses of the differential acceptance of aspects of Western medicine, both conceptually and in practice, were particularly encouraged.

It is difficult to reach back to the past through descriptions. Societies in Papua New Guinea were different before European contact, but they were not static and unchanging. The baseline from which we can discuss change will thus be rather arbitrary depending on the time of that first contact and the sources which are available. The time between the present and the "traditional" or pre-contact past varies and as it lengthens so, to some extent, must fade our hopes of knowing about people's previous medical ideas and practices. The prospect of following what has happened and is happening in societies scarcely affected by introduced Western medicine is of much interest because the chance of doing this anywhere in the world has all but disappeared.

In many cases these will be the memories of older people, but now there are fewer places left still with people who remember the first coming of whites and before. With the Manus, Goodenough Island, and the Collingwood Bay examples in this book, there are the observations made by earlier anthropologists and other writers but no one is left who witnessed the time before colonial contact.

Views of the past are influenced by the present. There are some sharp contrasts between past and present, identifiable by the equipment, location and people. A hospital may be frightening to strangers; requests for blood or urine possibly remind some of sorcery; the needle, bottles and sterilizer are shiny and foreign. In a place like Manus, the dramatic shifts of political events and long exposure to different people and ideas, can make it rather hard to discriminate precisely what was indigenous before, and tell, say, what was the Manus view of sin or guilt before there were any Christian influences.

There are at least two sets of ideas about the past that we may be after: one is the view held by the people about their own past, the other is the reconstruction of it to be made by the outside observer.

The people's views on their own tradition will determine what, by difference or novelty, they consider to be foreign or introduced. If there are no records and if memories are fallible, we have hardly any way of knowing how rapidly the content of that "tradition" may have changed. This will not matter much if our interest is only to describe the distinctions they make now. But if we want to understand the processes of change, we shall probably wish we could differentiate between what really happened, and stories that gild or distort or forget the past.

The local sense of pluralism in medical practice may or may not correspond to the observer's view of this. The observer may for various reasons suppose that a particular idea, for instance of germs or of sin, is not purely indigenous yet local people consider it to be so. The same goes for practice. By local standards what they do is customary, but the outsider doubts it. The people of some societies seem to be more concerned than others to distinguish their own practices and beliefs from foreign or new ones; they try to preserve custom. Or they may reject foreign introductions, or particular elements of their past, making conscious efforts at selection. Some religious movements have revived or held on to tradition as vehemently as others have rejected it. Christian conversion has often fired opposition to heathen custom. But by no means all communities are concerned with such discrimination. These issues are raised by many of the following studies when the authors discuss whether or not the people they worked with saw the mixture of native and foreign ways as contrasted or opposed.

Accommodation, assimilation, substitution, rejection; defense of ideas and practices, or attacks on them; apathy and indifference; eager innovation – many different responses are possible. Why expect consistency? People are likely to pick and choose according to their past experience, their opportunities, and the information available to them. Choices differ; Allen and Strathern in this volume draw attention to some paradoxes and inconsistencies of choice. Taken as a whole, the studies here show diverse attitudes to medical innovations. In another context of change in Papua New Guinea, the term "cargo cult" perhaps gave a misleading impression of uniformity to the movements put under that heading; in fact the content of what went on in those movements showed much variety and many shifts of attitudes to Europeans and to change. In regard to medicine and care of the sick, we find a rather similar variety, and sense the shifting views and the uneven paths of change. The people who introduced the changes, and the people to whom they were brought, and the land, all contributed.

We are observers bound by some of our assumptions about medicine. In our own societies it is a specialized distinct field. The local traditional analogues to medicine in Papua New Guinea were not organized in the same way. We readily think of a "health service" and a "medical system"; we isolate them in our minds as institutional systems and give them a singular identity and coherence as systems. There is little evidence here that care of the sick, or treatment and knowledge of illness, used to form a specialized department of social life coordinated as a system of medicine. Instead care of the sick was part of family and local obligation, ritual and religion came into it, and ideas about illness touched many activities and beliefs.

Certain elements recur in the accounts of their traditional ideas on illness and treatment: spirits, sorcery, wrongdoing, injury, poison, infection, pollution. We do not find all of them equally represented in each society; sometimes one or two elements are conspicuously elaborated. For each society explanations of illness and ways to treat it mount up; the ties of these ideas and practices with other aspects of their social lives and environment are varied. There may be people who specialize in diagnosing illness or treating it, but not a special organization for medicine as a whole or a monopoly of it.

One would not expect to find a specialized separable system of medicine without a complex division of labor and a different scale of society and technology. The treatment of illness may involve many aspects of social life, people, places, activities, ideas. We should not force "system" or "coherence" in a strong sense onto these practices; to do so would make an assumption about them that is mistaken and derives chiefly from our own experience of a clearly isolated "medical system". The unruly mixture of elements should stop us forgetting, if we run that risk, that illness always has a social context. It is a risk of specialization in medicine that the elaboration of specialized knowledge establishes a rather artificial boundary round what is technically relevant and "medical" and what has been seen as belonging outside it, not really medical, irrelevant, or lay, or unscientific. A readiness to wear blinkers, especially to shut out the social dimensions of sickness, has been a reproach sometimes merited by Western medicine.

Many elements may come into a full account of traditional practice. Some are clearly organized or show principles of procedure linked to particular domains of social life or particular interests. There is wide scope for interpretation of the ideas, their causes and effects, and they offer many examples of ways in which illness may tie into other social concerns, e.g. the link of illness to frustration and resentments over ceremonial exchange gifts (Strathern), the moral contexts in which illness is explained by sorcery (almost all the essays in this volume!) or ancestral reprimand (Carrier). Illness may be seen as a sanction for misconduct, a mystery, a sign of revenge, or a sign of the power of spirits, a natural risk, and so on. Responses to illness are informed by an assembly of ideas and practices in which there may be patches of systematic elaboration, often with the focus of attention set by other than medical concerns, but in which there is little evidence that the people of the society itself, or any special category of person in it, are concerned to unify the disparate elements into an overall coherent scheme. Such a systematizing propensity is more likely to occur when specialization develops. Certain people come to have an occupational (or professional) interest in making sense of a field of knowledge; they want to make practical use of it and, by doing it successfully, so justify their claims to hold expert knowledge. When a collection of ideas and practices is not tightly unified into a coherent system, it should be easier to introduce new practices to it and change it by subtraction or substitution without upsetting the collection as a whole. This is relevant to the pluralism we find now, the persistence of local ideas side by side with introductions. Nadel (1954) noted that the most elaborate coherently organized parts of Nupe religion were most vulnerable to change because of the possibility, by breaking or destroying faith in a single link, of damaging the whole chain. Particular ideas, patches of practice and belief, that do not belong in any crucial way to a whole grander system can be dropped or changed or kept going without having broad consequences.

An anthropologist may be tempted to make a system of the people's practice for them! A catalogue of disparate elements is less satisfactory than a neat analysis with no loose ends. We should like to have the wit to see, to reveal, a system behind their ideas, half-hidden, to find neat solutions to the puzzles of their symbolism. The risk of this is that the system we produce is our own invention not theirs.

Another problem about reconstructions of past traditional medicine is that they are usually dominated by accounts of the ideas and beliefs involved, and it is rare that a reader can get much idea of practice. Ordinary care, nursing, feeding, social support, decisions on treatment, the management of simple cases as well as serious ones, are things that can be observed but are either hard to describe or seem too trivial to bother about. Beliefs not practice are what come out of accounts of traditional medicine; and the gap between theory and practice is impossible to tell. Indeed the balance of medical anthropology in general has been tipped towards theory, ideas, semantic content, symbolic interpretation, rather than towards practice and behavior. This is surprising as it should be a particular virtue of medical anthropology to alert us to the social context in which the management of illness is set. We may understand the ideas and practices better when we are able to see them in context. One aim of this book is to provide pictures and analysis of the contemporary settings of village care which will give an immediate sense of the places and the problems faced by people in providing care and meeting needs on an everyday basis, the common problems as well as the exceptional ones, ordinary practice as well as special rituals, the real variety of care and need.

AGENTS OF CHANGE

The development of village health services

Many of the accounts in this book describe the rural health services of Papua New Guinea as these appear to the villagers of various parts of the country. Much of this analysis takes a historical perspective on this experience, and it is therefore desirable to summarize here the development of Papua New Guinea's emergence as a modern state, and the development of the rural health services which are the limit to most villagers' experience of Western medicine.

The land area of Papua New Guinea is approximately 500,000 square kilometers, and includes the eastern half of New Guinea as well as some 600 islands. In size the country therefore approaches that of Thailand. The population is approximately 3 million. The terrain ranges from lowland swampy plains, to highland valleys, to the central mountain ranges that reach 4500 meters in altitude. Besides this topographical diversity, there is considerable cultural and linguistic diversity in the present population with over 700 different language groups. Within this diversity some generalizations about the traditional societies may be helpful at this stage for those unfamiliar with the country and its societies. Political units are generally small, traditionally numbering no more than a few hundred individuals. Leadership is usually achieved rather than inherited. Economic activity is often directed towards the accumulation and distribution of pigs and shell valuables. People are usually self-sufficient in foodstuffs for domestic consumption. Staple foods differ with altitude, with the starch of the sago palm predominating in the lowlands and the sweet potato in the highlands, where 40% of the population live. Taro, and to a lesser extent yams, are grown in both lowland and highland areas.

The boundaries of the independent nation of Papua New Guinea are the product of rivalries between the European colonial powers in the nineteenth century. New Guinea was known to European explorers from the sixteenth century, but only limited interest was taken in the area until the nineteenth century. The western end of the island was claimed by Holland in 1828 as an extension of the Dutch East Indies. The Germans established themselves in the Bismarck Archipelago and the northeastern mainland in the early 1880s. Partly in response to the German settlement, Britain claimed the southeastern section, known as Papua, as a protectorate in 1884. Agreement was reached with the Germans on the division of east New Guinea in that year. Australia occupied German New Guinea in 1914 and, after the war, was granted a League of Nations Mandate to continue its administration. However Papua and New Guinea were administered separately until the Pacific War. The joint administration of the Territory of Papua and New Guinea was established in Port Moresby in 1946. Australia granted self-government in 1972, and independence was achieved by the State of Papua New Guinea in 1975.

The early health services of Papua and New Guinea concentrated their limited resources upon the needs that seemed most pressing to the administrators of the time. The priority was to supply the expatriate community with curative services as similar as possible to those available at home. Hospitals for Europeans were therefore set up in the larger centers. Nevertheless the disease problems of the general population were noted in the annual reports from the early part of the century. A number of conditions were said to be common, including yaws, dysentery and tuberculosis. Gonorrhoea reached epidemic proportions. There was considerable interest in the effects of these introduced diseases and speculation on the severity of the depopulation which was assumed to be inevitable. A particularly pessimistic note was struck by the Government Medical Officer when he commented in 1914 that "the question of the dying out or otherwise of the Papuan has an important bearing upon the future development of the Territory" (Annual Report, Papua 1913–14: 163).

The main source of simple treatments in modern Papua New Guinea is the aid post orderly (APO). These health workers serve between some 500 and 1500 people each depending on the population density of the area. Their general education is usually limited to six years' primary schooling or less. They are then trained to offer a range of treatments for common ailments, which includes the use of penicillin injections, and are also encouraged to teach aspects of disease prevention in the villages.

The modern aid post orderly has his origin in the health policies of early colonial governments. Once it had been accepted that the administration had some responsibility for the health needs of villagers, the extent of the known health problems of rural areas and the paucity of resources combined to challenge the prevailing view of the proper medical division of labor. The case is argued in the Annual Reports:

> ... Owing to the number of natives scattered over a large area of country and the relatively small amount of money available, it will always be impossible to do much for the true village native unless natives themselves can be trained up to

help as assistants. It would be an extraordinarily expensive matter to have medical men available all over the Territory .... It is therefore hoped gradually to train natives up to do something in the matter of treating ulcers, administering Novarsenobillon in the care of yaws, and in the matter of preventing dysentery, hook worm, and, perhaps malaria, and to have some idea of isolation of the sick in cases of infectious disease and if sudden epidemics occur (Annual Report, Papua 1921–22: 117).

It was also hoped that health workers of this sort would increase the people's trust in medical treatment, so that "... the native will be quite ready to trust himself to the medical officer, even for ... more severe lines of treatment, by the time it is feasible to have adequate resources for carrying them out in the villages" (ibid).

This policy was advanced much more quickly in New Guinea than in Papua. The appointment of *"Heil-tultuls"* (medical and sanitary assistants deployed in villages) was initiated by the German Imperial Government as early as 1903. By the end of the 1930s some 4000 of these workers were thought to be dispensing treatments in their home areas in the Mandated Territory of New Guinea, while only sixty paramedical workers were active in Papuan villages. There are numerous references in the Annual Reports to problems with these workers, but they continued to be deployed as there was no practical alternative means of providing simple health services. "In general, it may be said that they do effective, though primitive, work, and that their importance and their value are becoming constantly more obvious" (Annual Report, New Guinea 1925–26: 65–6).

During the Pacific War health services for the non-combatant population were largely withdrawn. When civilian administration returned in 1946 the health services of Papua and New Guinea were for the first time provided by a single department, based in Port Moresby. The main strategy for tackling the problems of health care in the rural areas was again through the use of village health workers. The rationale for the new policy was very similar to that given to justify the earlier programs in Papua and New Guinea. The diseases with high mortality were treatable with available drugs. "If native medical assistants could be trained to recognize these diseases when they occurred in the villages, and then to give the appropriate drug in a measured dose from pictorially labelled bottles, many lives would be saved .... It was postulated that even illiterates could be trained to observe, diagnose and treat .... Six ... schools were established with the aim of placing a thousand native medical assistants in a thousand villages" (Gunther 1972: 750–1). "Native medical and hygiene assistants" came to be called "aid post orderlies". Aid post orderlies are still being trained and deployed, and are still the mainstay of rural health services (Frankel 1984). The extent to which their remedies may be sought or persevered with emerges from the accounts that follow.

Concern over a possibly catastrophic decline in population was common in the health departments of both Papua and New Guinea at the beginning of the century. It was known that infant mortality was high and suspected that fertility had declined. References to infanticide as a possible cause of seemingly low birth rates are common in the reports (see Young, this volume). The early administration health schemes were run mainly by, and largely for, men. The care of women and children tended to fall to the missions; women tended to by-pass government hospitals, preferring the mission establishments (Kettle 1979: 36). This is still the case today in many areas. The first specific scheme to combat these trends contains the main features that became the conventions of Maternal and Child Health (MCH) services. The plan was to establish a chain of infant welfare clinics. The clinics would use records to follow the progress of each child. In addition they would offer ante-natal care and a midwifery service to the mothers (Annual Report, New Guinea, 1929–30: 32). The first clinic was opened in 1931 at Malabunga, New Britain. The women were "at first very shy, but soon it was found that they could not resist the offer of Novarsenobillon injections for framboesia in their children" (Annual Report, New Guinea, 1931–32: 37). As with other attempts to offer health services in new areas, treatment for yaws was the initial lure to the clinic.

The Malabunga clinic was founded on the initiative of the administration. However, developments there influenced the later structure of MCH services. The explanation for the decision to delegate this work to the missions presages recurring issues in MCH work:

> In dealing with the ultra-conservative native women, it is considered essential that a unit should, for a long period of years, be staffed by the same personnel who should be thoroughly acquainted with the native languages, as the native women with very few exceptions, do not speak "pidgin" ... The religious missions of the Territory ... have a considerable personnel fluent in the local languages, ready trained to bush conditions, and accepting the isolation as part of their obligation. In these circumstances the Administration accepted the offer of the Methodist Missionary Society of Australasia to take over the Malabunga Centre as a going concern" (Annual Report, New Guinea, 1932–33: 51–2).

The Administration provided a cash subsidy for staff and maintenance and supplied drugs and other supplies. This became the pattern for most MCH services in rural areas.

Government officers, missionaries, planters and traders

One striking thing about the changes Europeans brought to Papua New Guinea is that the country was colonized rather late in the history of European colonization. Parts of the interior had scarcely come under effective colonial administration before that rule was ended. Coastal experience of white administration may amount to a hundred years in some places, but the length of time is much shorter in the mountainous interior. The political and economic aims of colonial governments were rapidly changing during that period. In many places there are people still alive who saw the first coming of white people. Their memories of what the past was like before contact provide one kind of baseline for some areas, while reports by the first white patrol officers and by explorers may provide them for other areas. The administration of Papua New Guinea extended control to nearly the whole of the country in the end. The population involved in the territories now included as Papua New Guinea amount to about three million, but dispersed over a huge surface. The sheer size of the island, its forests and mountains, the scatter and diversity of small independent communities, so many different languages – these were difficulties for the administration. Travel was tough because of the mountains, fast rivers, forests and swamp. Transport had to be by foot, except along the coast and some big rivers. Roads for vehicles are not easy to make. Light aircraft could carry people and goods to and from inland stations when small airstrips were later cleared at new government and mission stations.

The short period of colonization brought major changes, but very unevenly. Three major sources of white influence were: government officials (*kiap*, patrol officers, and *polis*, policemen); missionaries; plantations and mining camps where men went as contract laborers. The chapters in this volume show something of the variety of village experience. Events such as contact and pacification, the Second World War, fluctuations in the prices of goods on world markets, and the introduction of cash crops, have not had uniform impact on different communities. The timing of events in relation to experience of other social changes – schooling, local government, Christianity – may give the same events differing meanings and effects depending on the place. In Manus during the war (see Carrier, this volume) the local population of a few thousand people received over the course of two years or so nearly a million USA servicemen in transit, their machines and baggage of war. Manus people by then had almost fifty years of contact with officials, missionaries and planters. Contrast that exposure to a mass of foreigners with the isolation of the Sambia or Maring who may have seen only a handful of white brief visitors in their territory.

There were not many officials to set against the size and ruggedness of the country and the walking involved to reach inland villages. "Government" from a village point of view was represented by the patrol post, *kiap* and *polis*. They exercised the power of *lo*, law, perceived (and often enough misunderstood) as demands that had to be obeyed, the power to punish, to command fighting to stop, the dead to be buried, houses to be built in certain ways, latrine pits dug, to collect taxes, do the census, to settle and judge disputes, to fine offenders or take them to jail. They also made health inspections. People will show how they had to line up, standing straight, arms stiffly by their sides, palms forward, to be inspected by the *kiap*.

Missionaries, recruiters, plantation managers, gold seekers, oil search explorers, bird hunters: these were some of the other kinds of alien strangers that people in various places encountered early on; later came airplanes and their pilots, doctors, nurses, tradestore owners, army personnel, anthropologists and others – but the list would depend on the area in question. Christian missionaries stand out; they set up stations and stayed. In some cases they came as whole families – husbands, wives and children. The churches and denominations they belonged to had different countries of origin, different styles of worship and different evangelical aims. Missionaries were often strong influences and agents of change because they settled and provided schooling, trade goods, jobs, skills and medical aid as well as religious teaching.

Work at plantations or goldfields on long contracts (two years or more) gave many men their first experiences of life outside their home areas, wage labor, white employers and towns. It brought them into contact with other Papua New Guineans and changed their views of their own local identity and of regional diversity. In towns, along roads, the evidence of change is continual and many-sided – clothes, radio, vehicles, buildings, strangers, new things, new goods, new activities. In other places inland, village life has hardly changed: the patrols used to come round annually, or roughly so; or there was a tax collection, or a census, or the vote. Or the kiap might come because of a dispute, or send a policeman to investigate. The patrol post or the mission station was the focal point to see signs of change – the airstrip, the planes and the pilot, strangers coming in, friends going off or returning, the tradestore, the market, the new road. But villagers away from the station got on with their lives scarcely disturbed. That might depend on the mission. Some missions did a lot of bush patrols and village visiting for religious teaching, health clinics or schooling.

ENVIRONMENTS AND PATTERNS OF DISEASE

Variation in the length and intensity of the contact experienced by different communities is one obvious dimension of pluralism. New Guinea has held special interest for biological and medical experts because of its relative isolation and late colonization. It contained a variety of environments, and in some areas the lure for research workers of relatively unacculturated communities of people. The attraction was the prospect of studying human adaptations in these different environments, and the patterns and variety of human diseases there, as examples of what may happen in societies little touched by the technology of the West or by the infectious disease pools of the Old World.

In order to understand some aspects of health we need to know how people adapt to a particular environment, whether or not they are much affected by European contact. This would include study of the resources, constraints and possibilities of their physical environment; the population size, composition, and density of settlement; life expectancy; their state of nutrition, the kinds and amounts of food they eat; their normal mode of life, and the patterns of disease with which they have to contend.

The geographical variety of New Guinea sets certain conditions for the survival and subsistence of human populations, their parasites, and the diseases they are prone to. The flora, soils, and other resources of the small islands, mainland coast, lowland rain forests, and central highlands differ (Brookfield and Hart 1971, Ward and Lea 1970). In the interior, high mountains and cold alter the tropical vegetation and the crops that people can depend on. Altitude and temperature limit the distribution of the mosquitoes that spread malaria. Seasonal variation in rainfall is marked in some areas and gardening practices in most parts of the country are affected in some way by it. Drought has caused famine on the small islands; frost has caused famine in the highlands. In general the humidity and heat support a luxuriant growth of plants, the richly complex flora of lowland tropical rain forest, the correspondingly rich and varied insect life, and the accompanying problems for people who live in such environments – problems of storing food, flies, insect bites, disposal of waste, fungal infections. The ecology must affect the distribution pattern of some diseases (for example by effects on diet, insect vectors); there are some obvious disease gradients (for example of malaria with altitude); and many ecological relationships that remain to be investigated.

The ecology must obviously have played its part in determining the modes of subsistence followed by different groups in New Guinea. A few areas (for example, the Simbu area of the Highlands and the Abelam area of the East Sepik) are densely settled with over 200 persons per square mile in some localities and correspondingly intensive use of the land. Soil fertility, the requirements for growing particular staple foods, techniques of cultivation and knowledge of cultivars must be combined in explanations of these population distributions. Sago, taro, yams, sweet potatoes and bananas have different water, soil and temperature requirements. The densest settlement in the whole of the Sepik occurs in the Abelam and Wosera areas where the soils are outstandingly fertile; the people have produced a yam variety called asakua which is very hardy, pest resistant and storable, and they have developed elaborate and efficient techniques for growing ceremonial long yams (Allen 1976: 14, 25). Elsewhere in the Sepik, there are societies depending primarily on wild or planted sago supplemented variably by root crops, some fishing or hunting and gathering. Settlement is thin in the Sepik plains which have very low soil fertility (Haantjens et al. 1972). In other parts of the country, lack of some resource may oblige people to organize complex exchange or trade relationships to survive in a particular swamp or river or island environment. The trading systems in the Massim area (Leach and Leach 1984), the Vitiaz Straits, and between Sepik river and plains peoples (Gewertz 1983), are examples of adaptive solutions to environmental constraints by means of trade and exchange. They redistribute resources and they may require local specialization of production or activity – a symbiosis with equal or unequal relationships of exploitation between neighbouring communities (see Chowning and the Counts, this volume, for some striking examples). Some solutions must have proved more effective than others, and movements and changes of population followed.

Archaeological findings (Strathern 1982, Golson 1982) are beginning to show how things changed over a long time span in some areas of Papua New Guinea. For example, there were complex drainage systems, presumably for growing taro, at Kuk in the Central Highlands 6000 years ago. Settlements increased and spread out in the Highlands after the introduction of the sweet potato about 300 years ago. Interpretations of these and other recent findings proliferate: likely effects on leadership and the size of populations and social units; the development of ceremonial exchange, pig rearing and the relations between communities; intermarriage and the inequality of men and women. These interpretations have drawn on observations of present day communities to help in imagining what the past was like. Stone tools, pottery and shells reveal by their distribution some of the exchange links that must have existed between coastal and island populations, as well as between coastal and inland populations in the prehistoric past (Hughes 1977). Discussions of the anthropogenic grasslands (Robbins 1960), deforestation in the highlands (Sorenson 1972), the introduction of the pig and the sweet potato, warn us not to assume that conditions in Papua New Guinea were unchanging until Europeans came.

The flora and fauna of New Guinea indicate the relative isolation of the island and its peoples. Most New Guinean mammal species are marsupial, and some of these, like many of the bird species, are distinctive to New Guinea. Dogs, pigs and rats came later, with man. The first people came presumably from South East Asia as did some of the crops now grown. Other crops, the dog and the pig, may have come with later movements of people. Languages, blood group frequencies and body features vary greatly in Papua New Guinean people (Chowning 1982b, Howells 1973). The diversity is so conspicuous that linguists, physical and social anthropologists have all commented on it and wondered how to explain it. Why are the communities so small in numbers? Is isolation the cause or an effect of this variety? What has the topography of the land done to mould the kinds of community found and the contacts they made with each other? Sparse populations and isolation spared New Guinea a number of communicable diseases, for example schistosomiasis, trypanosomiasis, leishmaniasis, measles, mumps, chickenpox and other crowd infectious diseases; tuberculosis and smallpox seem to have first come in the nineteenth century. These absences of certain infectious diseases reinforce the impression of a Papua New Guinea almost isolated from South East Asia and the wider world until the nineteenth century. European ships had passed along the coast before then, but they hardly stopped.

Colonizers are likely to bring their own microparasites with them when they come. Indeed the colonists themselves may seem to act as macroparasites on the local people when they invade and exploit a place unasked. Although terrain, climate, malaria and hostile people deterred Europeans, eventually they came. It is not possible to reconstruct for sure what the disease patterns were like before that (Maddocks 1973: 70–74), but the absence of some of the diseases mentioned above is clear, either because they are still lacking or because people have described their first occurrence. Epidemics of dysentery, smallpox, influenza and measles were linked with the experiences of early contact (for example Allen 1983, Frankel 1986: 26–8, and in this volume Allen, Barker, Chowning, Young); explanations of the cause of these diseases given locally in some areas associate them with white foreigners or the changes they made. A disease like measles, which gives lifelong immunity, needs large densely settled populations to produce enough new susceptible people to transmit and maintain the disease, and Papua New Guinea does not have dense settlement like that.

The communicable diseases that were presumably there before European colonization include: malaria, filariasis, yaws; intestinal parasites such as roundworms and amoebiasis; fungal diseases; scrub typhus and dengue. It is likely that European contact brought scabies, venereal diseases, tuberculosis, hookworm and the crowd infectious diseases; contact also led to a new mobility and speed of travel – migration, displacements for work, greater safety among strangers, town life. The new possibilities of travel have opened up communities that were relatively closed and self-contained before and have exposed them to, among other innovations, diseases they never knew before. The prevalence of tuberculosis in Melanesian populations is directly related to the degree and length of European contact they have had and to the degree of urbanization and culture change they have undergone (Wigley 1973: 179). Maddocks (1973: 70) suggests that leprosy may have first spread to the islands of New Guinea in the nineteenth century, but the disease is now widely prevalent (Russell and Bell 1973: 185–190). Its distribution in the Highlands suggests that it is longer established there than tuberculosis. In various places a distinct vernacular name for leprosy, associated with established local explanations of it and attitudes to it, might lead one to suppose that it had been endemic for a long time. But no name and a high incidence rate, a rate apparently rising rapidly in some communities (Stanhope et al. 1968), suggest that some people, for example in the Anguganak area of the West Sepik, are highly susceptible because they lack previous exposure either to leprosy or to tuberculosis.

The general question raised by these examples concerns the degree of past isolation of different communities and populations in New Guinea, and the extent to which any of them can be regarded as a "virgin soil" population which was exposed only recently and by European contact to a range of new diseases. It is obvious that contact has exposed them to new diseases, but it is not clear that isolated communities are more vulnerable to the effects of these new diseases because they are genetically more susceptible. It is plausible to suppose that infectious diseases have been significant selective agents in human prehistory and that this ought to be reflected in genetic differences of susceptibility to disease. So far the main support for this view has come from study of animal populations and experiments (Skamene et al. 1980), and from work on certain human blood groups correlated with the distribution of malaria. Other human evidence is surprisingly scant (Black 1980, Black et al. 1977, Bodmer and Cavalli-Sforza 1976, Garruto 1981, Neel 1977). What is more impressive is the interaction of human biology and social behaviors in their effects on disease patterns, the interaction of such things as diet, knowledge, environment, fertility and marriage practice, migration, epidemics, and nursing care for the sick.

The interactions of environment, biology and social behavior occur over the whole range of illness, and not just in respect of the diseases caused by germs or parasites. There are regional differences in morbidity and mortality in Papua New

Guinea (e.g. Bell 1973, Vines 1970). These are evident but it is not possible to provide strictly comparable and detailed data for all the regions because the sources of information (survey, hospital and aid post statistics) are not uniform. Nutrition and differences in mode of life and environment play an important part. The Islands region (including New Britain, New Ireland, Bougainville and Manus) has the tallest and heaviest people in the country. There is little undernutrition and less anemia than on the mainland, yet the people have had longer exposure to Europeans and this has altered their diet, responses to illness, patterns of work and employment, exposure to tuberculosis, venereal disease, alcohol and traffic accidents; they have had programs for controlling malaria, immunizations, etc. The Sepik provinces include populations exposed to hyper- and holo-endemic malaria; undernutrition is widespread and some of the lowest birth weights in the world have been recorded there; tropical polyarthritis and Burkitt's lymphoma occur; chest infections are common causes of death. Some of the population is scattered in remote communities with access to few introduced health services and they remain largely, as they were before, dependent on their own means of care for the sick. The Highlands include some relatively large densely settled populations. Altitude limits the transmission of malaria; acute infective diarrhoea, dysentery and pneumonia are prevalent; chronic chest disease is a problem in older people; there is some undernutrition especially from protein lack and injuries from traffic accidents and land disputes reflect social changes and competition for land.

These are the broad differences in disease patterns between the various regions. A number of studies allow more refined analysis of the patterns of disease that emerge in particular social and physical environments (for example Feachem 1977, Frankel 1986, Hornabrook 1977, Lewis 1975, Maddocks 1978, Sinnett 1977, Sinnett and Whyte 1973, Sturt and Stanhope 1968). There must probably be more detailed ecological demographic and medical information on the Fore of the Eastern Highlands than on any other Melanesian group of people (Gajdusek 1963, 1977, Hornabrook 1976, Lindenbaum 1979, Sorensen 1972). Of the variations that emerge from such intensive studies it is perhaps the areas of nutrition and malnutrition which provide the most powerful focus for exploring the interaction of ecology and society in Papua New Guinea.

Nutrition

Whether the diet is adequate or not cannot be told just from knowing about the kinds of food grown or collected; the association between food systems and nutritional status is complex because it also depends on how the people choose to use the food they have as well as on the quantity, seasonal availability and quality of the foods. Within a single community there may be times of scarcity in the year, differences of wealth and consumption between households, of access to land and food, and of permission to eat according to sex, age and status. Every society has customs about what to eat and how to prepare it. The conventions vary from trivial habits to strict prohibitions; elaborate systems of food prohibitions and taboos may control access to some kinds of food. Justifications for these rules lead in many directions, but the rules cannot all resist changes in social circumstances and experience. Gnau rules about the time to introduce new vegetable and meat foods into the infant's and toddler's diets are probably unsound nutritionally. A number of foods they have could serve to broaden and improve the child's diet but prohibitions stop them from doing so at a time when the small child is also likely to be exposed to malaria and other infections. The child's nutritional needs for growth suffer in competition with illness. Delays in weight gain, sometimes severe malnutrition, follow. Malnutrition weakens the young child's ability to resist further infection and to cope with infectious disease and recover from it. It would be foolish to adopt in principle a romantic or Panglossian view of local customs. From within village experience, there may be no basis for critical judgement of their own nutritional practice; customary patterns and rules enabled their parents and ancestors to survive; the heights and weights of their children seem to them normal if they have no alternative standards to use. They may have no means to make the connection between dietary practice and a particular medical problem. The Fore in the Eastern Highlands had rules that deprived women from having as much pork as men. In a chapter on the "politics of protein", Lindenbaum (1979) connects Fore views on women, female pollution and inferiority with Fore justifications for rules granting men privileged access to pork. She suggests that the lack of meat, made worse with these rules, might have made eating human flesh more acceptable to women when they first tried it. This might explain the pattern of mortuary cannibalism in the past, the peculiar epidemiology of kuru and its greater prevalence in women.

Some of the effects of customs on diet are direct and intended; others are unexpected or unrecognized and, indeed, they may be unintelligible except in the explanatory frameworks of medical or scientific inquiry. As for protein, we can see that social changes over a long time have played some part in meat consumption and availability. The change from hunting and gathering to settled gardening altered the environment; when the population increased, more land was gardened, land use became more intense, more forest had to be cut down, the habitats of wild animals were disturbed and game became scarce. Something like that probably happened in the ancient past where soils were found to be good and people clustered. The first introduction of the pig, its spread in the forests as wild pig for hunting, and the later Highlands shift from hunting to herding pigs (Morren 1977), is a sequence in Highlands prehistory, one that was to be affected by the advent of the sweet potato which made it possible to feed and keep pigs in larger numbers. The story is different in the lowlands. In the lowland rain forest of the West Sepik, hunting wild pig continued to be an important source of pork (Lewis 1975: 48–50). The quite recent consequences of administrative control over warfare, followed by the introduction and use of a few shotguns, have been to deplete the bush near villages of game that used to be there (wild pig, cassowary, goura pigeon). The men must go further to find game, further than they would have dared to go before.

More people from more villages do this now.

Protein is important for a child's satisfactory growth and development, and undernutrition is serious in some parts of Papua New Guinea. Clinical signs of malnutrition provide the most direct evidence of it: weight below the accepted standards for the child's age, with wasting and stunted growth as signs of severe insufficiency. Mild or borderline undernutrition is difficult to assess; it is easy for health workers to adjust their standards for normality to the local population of the area where they are working. Relatively few children show easily recognisable stages of malnutrition, but marasmus and kwashiorkor have been reported from some areas (Wookey 1973). Poor food can affect health, fertility, morbidity and mortality in various ways: delayed puberty, late onset of the menarche, amenorrhea, short stature, anemias, lack of body fat, rapid wasting and weakness during intercurrent illness, conspicuous loss of muscle mass with aging, vulnerability to infection, specific deficiency diseases, babies with low birth weights, women with nutritional edemas of pregnancy. The list makes it sound bad, but these effects are not found everywhere. Food scarcity in fact did not seem a problem to observers in many areas. For example, in the West Sepik in lowland forested hills around Lumi, all the gardens, the abundance of nature, a warm humid climate, the profusion of leaves, banana plants, pawpaws, breadfruit trees, palms, the seeds scattered casually that germinate, the suckers stuck in the ground that flourish – they leave one with an impression of luxuriant nature. It becomes hard to reconcile that impression with findings or reports of malnutrition. Yet the Lumi district of the West Sepik is one area which the 1978 nutrition survey found to have disturbing levels of malnutrition (UNDP 1983: 21) and from that area Wark and Malcolm (1969) reported some of the poorest growth rates recorded anywhere.

It is clearly not a simple problem of supply, or of starvation. Local people's views on whether they lack adequate food do not necessarily coincide with those of outsiders. In a very informative discussion of the nutritional status of the population of Papua and New Guinea, Wookey (1973) notes some surprising inconsistencies in foreign and local observers' conclusions about whether nutrition was a serious problem in the part of the country they knew. One reason for this is lack of information, another is variation in the standards people use. One opinion may be based on general impressions, another on long experience of a particular village and the local pride and satisfaction of someone who has worked successfully to raise and feed a flourishing family, a third on weighing and filling out the charts of hundreds of infants, a fourth on the district breakdowns from the 1975 and 1978 nutrition surveys. The weight gain of children in many parts of the country keeps pace with international standards up to about six months and then falls below those standards. Repeated exposure to malaria and other infections at the time of weaning may lead to wasting, serious malnutrition and long term stunting of growth. Malnutrition during the phase of rapid growth between six and 24 months can have long-term effects. The stunting of stature may result in low weights-for-age being recorded during childhood and adolescence because of deficiencies at a critical time, rather than because of persisting malnutrition.

The problem is to identify the causes of specific effects. This is exactly the problem which Hyndman sets out to analyze in his paper on gender in the diet and health of the Wopkaimin. Their rules and classifications of appropriate foods systematically favor the allocation of animals to adult men. As a population, the Wopkaimin are nutritionally affected by the social allocation of foodstuffs, by the pattern of food-getting behavior, by the dividing and sharing of food, and by age and sex specific food taboos. The pattern of food-getting behavior is a crucial factor in this. The serious implication is that women require, but only marginally receive, adequate nutritional returns to sustain their constant levels of energy output.

If the cause of a low weight-for-age measurement at seven years old is the stunting of growth produced by untreated malaria and respiratory infections in the first few years of life, a survey of children's weights may give a misleading impression of the prevalence of malnutrition. A sequence of measurements of weight charted in the child's *Helt Buk* at the Infant Welfare Clinic may show the striking depression of weight gain that often accompanies illness that may lead to loss, not gain, in weight and afterwards take so long to restore. Fever, lack of appetite, distressed breathing, or lack of suitable alternative foods, may all have made it hard for the sick child to suckle or eat enough and these problems also contribute to the immediate effects of the illness. The child's weakness, lack of desire to eat, infrequent or small feeds, the child's poor ability to suckle or ingest, the monotony of food offered or the alternatives, how prepared, their quality and assimilability: these may determine what the sick child actually manages to eat. It is not a simple question of food supply and quantity. And afterwards, competing demands on the mother by the rest of her family, to work in the gardens, to cook, and to make up for time she lost nursing the sick child, may leave her little time to spare to feed the child as frequently as he or she may need to make a good recovery.

Poor nutrition is not necessarily just the result of precarious supply and harsh environment. The first thing would be to find out whether there is malnutrition: where and among which people, the variation by age and sex, whether more frequent among the aged, widowed or orphaned, how affected by size of family and stage in the developmental cycle of the family. Physical and clinical findings provide direct evidence of nutritional success or failure, but the causes are indirect and have to be traced out. Some relevant factors are bound to be social and complex. When people eat in groups from a common leaf, plate or bowl, then small children may need to eat fast, be bold and grab, to get a good share. With leaves and vegetables supplying most of the nutritional needs, the child must take in a greater bulk of food to get adequate protein. Sex, birth order, size of the family, can all affect a child's chances because of rules of precedence, as can excessive burdens of pregnancy and work on the mother. Garden tasks vary in intensity; seasonal and social demands affect the times of meals, their frequency and content.

The many jobs and responsibilities which face a woman with small children become clear if you try to note exactly all she does in a day: fetching wood and water, getting the fire going, carrying food back from gardens, gathering leaves to go with the starch staple, working in the gardens, cooking, keeping an eye on her children and on her piglet, breastfeeding the baby, perhaps in the evening taking food to her widowed father in his hamlet because he cannot eat food cooked by his sons' wives, or getting up before dawn to take produce to sell at a local market. Then there are the arguments with the older children about which one will stay in the village minding the baby if the mother has to go off to work in the garden for the day, the crying of hungry babies in the village, the droning chants of their older siblings trying to comfort them or to make them shut up; and in the late afternoon, the echoing high-pitched yodelling calls from the village ridge to the mothers away in the gardens to come back because their babies are crying, and their minders are fed up and want to play.

Rules, taboos, customs: the ones for food vary in strictness, clarity and sanction. They do not apply to all or uniformly. The Gnau put much stress on birth order and seniority, and rules about food apply most strictly to the first born. In part they explain this by an idea about the inexperience of parents with their first children, in part by an idea about the child being the product of the fresh whole stock of blood of its parents, and subsequent children less so; and they wish to see the order of birth properly maintained in the order in which their children will develop, grow up, and get married. From this one might expect some difference between the nutritional status of first and subsequent children. But none are apparent. Food rules affect girls and boys differently; again it is hard to see any gross disparity in the health and nutritional state of boys and girls.

Hyndman's precise measurements have telling force. Young (also in this volume) records the finding of differences between boys and girls in regard to health and the treatment of illness on Goodenough Island. He asked people why. They were not surprised by his question and gave the unabashed answer that they valued daughters less than sons, and did less for them when they were ill. After reading so much comment by anthropologists on the strongly marked differentiation of attitudes to men and women, the frequent assertion that there are derogatory envious fearful or hostile attitudes to women to be found in cultural stereotypes, in regulations and rituals, and a marked division of labor that sometimes appears to the observers as an exploitation by men of women's labor and good nature, one might expect some effects of these attitudes and regulations to show in the health status, nutrition, and treatment of women when ill. The epidemiology of kuru shows this. Lindenbaum (1979) has analyzed the implications of the relevant Fore views on food and women's access to protein. There are differences in Gnau attitudes to men's and women's illnesses (Lewis 1975: 239–244, 297–301). The levels and nature of mortality and morbidity differ for the Huli in ways that may reflect such differences and which may also follow from the division of labor (Frankel 1986: 60–80). But we do not know enough about this and lack sufficient precise data; we should look into the question further.

MEDICAL CHANGE

Experience of change

With many different independent societies and languages, contact and colonization took time. Change has not been uniform. Contingent facts – the timing, the evidence that people had about the outside world, about Europeans and their technology, the effect of outstanding individuals – have influenced local responses. Much foreign presence in the form of buildings and personnel, roads, trucks and airplanes, belongs to the recent period and only to some of the places described in this book. An experience of particular white people and their interests is bound to have marked local implications for Papua New Guinean ideas about Europeans *(waitskin* – the Pidgin is more apt as a label for them, Australians mostly, Europeans and some others). Allen's essay here analyses the effects of European contact and rule in the Torricelli Mountains, showing how people's later responses to medical care reflect some of these experiences – the changing patterns of epidemic and disease, the medical patrols and enforced treatment, the limited effectiveness of European medicine in the 1930s, the rare visits, the attitudes of individual medical officials like the medical *tultuls,* the European medical assistants, and later the aid post orderlies.

Examples of influential individuals, by no means all white, appear in the chapters by Jenkins, Carrier and others here: they include Mickloucho Maclay who might have stepped from a story by Conrad and who now belongs to myth in certain places; Dr Braun the missionary doctor devoting most of his life to work among the people of one area; Paliau the famous Manus cult leader in the aftermath of the passage of all those American soldiers, their ships and planes and unimagined wealth of goods. We can go from such examples of striking individuals and momentous events to other people and places that were on no road, where contact led nowhere particular; perhaps taxes came, occasional government patrols, occasional visits from the mission; they talked and took names; they ordered or exhorted the people about this or that, then went away. Things did not change much; yet slowly, unplanned, a hotch potch of new things, bits and pieces, came – information, crops, tools for work, money, matches, stories of the outside world, sunglasses, scented oil, clothes, broken radios, torches and soap. These things came in, made a difference to the way of life, but how much is hard to say; some (money, axes, certain ideas), common now and no longer curious or surprising, had powerful effects.

It takes time to assimilate change. Herdt and Hyndman here describe societies whose experience of colonial change has been brief. They have been relatively suddenly exposed to modern technology in a wide range of forms; they encountered it later than many other Papua New Guineans, at a time when the development of towns, transport and government could provide more impressive evidence of it; quite soon after first meeting Europeans, local men might leave and find out about the outside world through contract labor, by visits to towns, flights by airplane.

The Sambia described by Herdt have not had long contact with Europeans, and they can compare themselves with other people in their own province or from outside it. Are these other people models to choose to imitate or to avoid? No doubt the Sambia have ideas of what progress they would like to see at home. Until the aid post came, there was little development or material change there. The aid post was evidence of progress and government interest. Their short exposure to modern things had given them hopes, new wants, and few ways to satisfy them; they have taken to using the aid post so fast because they saw it as progress, perhaps also as a way to other things as well, seeming to them almost the only way open on the spot. The government gave them that first, what else might it lead to? The Sambia provide a contrast to the Amele (described by Jenkins) or the Maisin (described by Barker) whose experience of health services linked with the work of missionaries was much longer.

Missionaries as well as government officers have been agents of change, and specifically of medical change. The accounts of various places (for example those of Barker, the Counts, Jenkins, Young) indicate the prominence of mission medicine in bringing hospitals, services and clinics to a number of areas. Evangelism was mixed up with hygiene, prayer mixed up with treatment, preacher also doctor, nun also nurse. For the people of such areas Western medicine was closely tied up with Christianity.

Even when it was not the case that the mission provided a clinic or aid post, even less a hospital, the missionaries would be likely to dress sores and offer medical advice and some treatment. Any white person in areas with little white contact might dress sores and burns, give out pills, cough medicine, even give injections; or local people assumed they could. Some knowledge of the practice of "whiteman's medicine" was naturally assumed to go with being a "whiteman". Papua New Guineans did not have such specialized division of labor as to make them expect initially that some kinds of white person might not know how to be a doctor and a nurse. It was no cause for surprise to them if a priest on patrol pulled a syringe and a half-used phial of penicillin out of his rucksack and offered to inject a sick baby. With more evidence and experience to draw on, then people might sort out the divisions of job and special responsibility and skill which we tend to take for granted; in a country like Papua New Guinea the first white people had to be jacks-of-all-trades more or less. And that was bound to make it difficult for local people to work out what was different about the patrol officer's orders for someone to have a sore treated and his orders for him to pay a fine; or distinguish the missionary's concern to stop people spitting betel juice on sores from his concern to stop them doing their puberty rituals. At first most Papua New Guineans lacked the information necessary to distinguish what were the different jobs, skills and legitimate spheres of responsibility of the various white people they encountered.

With time and with more varied experience, distinctions were established. Ideas, practice and organizational setting all played parts in this. Some of the practices and, particularly, the equipment – bandages, lint, syringes and needles, penicillin, liniment, pills – were clearly new and associated with the white people who brought them. The separate medical sphere to which they belonged was progressively made more distinct in some places when medical care became more confined to the specific places or people who would provide it, associated, that is, with clinic times, aid posts, and people whose main job obviously was to give medical care. Something initially associated with white people in general, or identified with the activities of kiap and missionary, could be differentiated. The experience of those who went to towns or centers with hospitals and surgery, the encounter with Papua New Guineans who were trained to provide medical care and to use the equipment led to changes in their views about how medical ideas and practices were to be intertwined or segregated from other new practices and ideas, or other white enterprises. The evidence and experience available to people in different areas have influenced the variations we now find in how they have assimilated Western medicine and accommodated their own ideas and practices to its intrusions. As the equipment and treatment could be put in Papua New Guinean hands, it became clear that the practice and knowledge was detachable from the white people who first provided it. When hospitals were built, the sight of complex equipment, sterilizers, operating rooms, gave more insight into the specialized complexity of Western medicine. And the "real" medicine of the white people came to be seen more generally as what went on in hospitals. That is broadly what happened, but the chapters that follow show many variations. The main things to note are the rapid changes in medicine as they saw it in some places, and that in rural and remote areas, few people were exposed to more than sporadic elements of Western medicine and even that version of it was often reduced to a bare minimum. The novelty was tied up at first with the people who brought it and the medical elements hard to differentiate from their other actions and interests. Some of the early connotations of introduced medicine have lingered on, but most have changed.

Issues of compliance and dependency

Hopes for material progress were mixed up with some interest in Western medicine, as LiPuma and others note. The questions at first were: Who were the white people? What did they want? What were their powers? What did they expect from local people, and what would they bring? In some areas the significant foreigners were missionaries because of their station, their numbers, their store and school, and their continuous presence. In other areas, government patrol officers and the police were the most important foreigners because they had power and they were the only ones who came to the village, even though their visits were short.

One must try to imagine the circumstances and the timing of events in order to get a realistic idea of what so-called Western medicine at first was in the experience of many Papuans and New Guineans. We hope that the chapters which follow will help the reader to appreciate the situations in which villagers find themselves and to see from the village perspective what it has been like to be ill.

From this perspective, there might be no apparent difference between the patrol officer (*kiap*) acting in the interests of hygiene and in the interests of law, or between the missionary acting in the interests of the body or of the soul. *Kiaps* in the past sometimes carried out health inspections, ordered treatment for yaws or sores, took absconding lepers into custody, imposed supplementary feeding for malnourished babies. Missions established clinics and hospitals, prayers went alongside treatment. *Kiaps* ordered people to dig latrines, to bury their dead, to use new sources of water, to change the position or style of houses. It was part of their task. Missionaries preached against customs, masks, dances, ritual bleeding, polygamy, sorcery; they also preached about cleanliness, diet, clothes, water and latrines. Cleanliness was next to godliness in instruction; it could easily seem to be part of godliness. How was someone who had no contact with European society to recognize the different aims and motives behind all the various exhortations and reproofs?

From the villagers' point of view, they were likely to be mixed up or conflated; they supposed there might be rewards for compliance, possibly, and punishment for disobedience; and sometimes there was. The government's motives behind measures aimed at preventing disease could be misunderstood by villagers. Languages as well as assumptions were barriers to understanding. The changes that *kiaps* or missionaries asked for were hard to make sense of in some cases unless they could be placed in the correct framework of ideas. If local people did not have the same framework in mind, they had to reinterpret the rules or instructions according to their own ideas – flies carry poison, germs are spirits, washing cleanses female pollution. The shifts may not sound great perhaps in these instances; but the significance of "poison" in English and *poisin* in Pidgin may differ considerably; ideas of female pollution make it more than a matter of washing off dirt. Their interpretations of the purpose of actions or orders depended on their assumptions about likely motives, explanations of causes and phenomena, their information and previous experience.

The activities of health workers may be baffling. For example village women may be unsure of the motives of the nurses who come to weigh their babies. The question they ask is essentially a moral one: why did the nurses come to weigh their babies and to give them injections and to tell them how to feed them? These babies were not the nurses' babies, indeed they were nothing to them, no kin. So what concern of theirs was it if the baby was fat or thin, healthy or sick? And especially, why should a nurse be able to order the child to go for supplementary feeding, even be able to report the mother to the government officer so that he would send a policeman to fetch her and the child for treatment, if the mother refused to come? It was a problem which occurred to them more sharply in the light of their own customary morality which assigns duties and ethical responsibilities to kin and neighbours in particular, not universal, terms. One's obligations to others, one's interest in them and care for them, should depend on the kind of relationship and social closeness, or distance, between people; the idea of having basic ethical duties towards other people simply because they are human beings was not grasped or else was not strong. Read's essay on the concept of the person among the Gahuku Gama illuminates this point and the idea of such distributive morality in New Guinea (1955). The puzzle for the women was what motive could plausibly account for white strangers caring about village babies so strongly. They could see that the nurses went to a lot of trouble to come; they recognized that the nurses did good for the children; they were grateful for this and touched by the evident effort put in by them; but that still left unanswered why they should bother. When the mothers did not want to follow the advice, the advice seemed like interference.

The same general problem touches other aspects of medical treatment and prevention. Certainly measures of public hygiene (for example changes in burial customs, housing, disposal of excrement and refuse) were sometimes imposed against the wishes of local populations. Others were carried out because people were told to, and they felt they had to if they wanted to please the authorities they were dealing with. Compliance with medical instructions might at times be rather similar to compliance with instructions such as orders to keep the village clean and paths maintained. The reason for doing it was that the government officers or the missionaries wanted them to, and not that they wished to, or were themselves convinced that it was good to do. Some aspects of introduced medicine were intelligible, others were meaningless to them and not explained; there were obvious problems of communication and different basic assumptions. These could not be overcome immediately. Many writers (for example, Allen, Barker, Chowning, LiPuma) draw attention to misunderstandings, twists of communication, to this patchy mixture of things: some imposed, others rejected or resented, others eagerly sought, and others neglected. Western medicine did not arrive as a whole package, but in bits and pieces.

If the span of time from first contact is fifty years or more, we need to remember how great have been the changes in treatment, its efficacy, antibiotics, numbers of trained personnel, accessibility and means and possibilities of communication and transport. People in the villages still must mostly form their opinions of different kinds of treatment from the evidence they have to hand. The list of contents of a European medical chest in the 1930s (see Allen this volume) makes us thankful we should not have to depend on that now; but in many remote and rural villages the actual situation is hardly better. In theory the aid post, if there is one nearby, is stocked with the necessary dressings and drugs; in practice it may not be. There are many reasons for this. And even when the supplies are there, much of course depends on how they are used, as Chowning makes clear in her chapter. The advantages of introduced medicine may not be obvious. A single "shot" of penicillin is not the right treatment for diarrhea, but if someone receives it from whoever is in charge, he may regard himself as having had modern treatment, and then decide it does no good. It may well be that many Papua New Guineans have made a realistic appraisal of the benefits of "Western" medicine from the way they find it practised in their home areas; it is we, the white outsiders, who are being unrealistic or blind in imagining that its benefits must be obvious, except to those with irrational beliefs or closed minds.

Why are some introductions quickly adopted? It is not a simple matter of need and efficacy. Firth (1959) pointed out the lack of work analysing people's preferences when faced with foreign introductions. Compare some of the trade items which are so attractive with some medical treatments that have so little appeal. The things introduced as measures to improve health are heterogeneous – public health controls were sometimes enforced and belonged to political experience as much as anything. To have sores or burns or wounds dressed might seem to pose less threat than swallowing unknown substances in the form of pills. Why, for instance, are injections so popular? When someone has an abscess of the jaw, why give him or her an injection in the buttock or the thigh? Lewis was asked to give the injection in the shoulder so the patient could hold her arm up in the air and make the medicine drain into her jaw. People's readiness to accept or try out new forms of treatment has as many potential sources of variation as their readiness to accept suggestions about how they should change their religious behavior or their dietary practices; or recommendations about how they should settle their disputes; or what crops to grow and how they should plant them. Suggestions aimed at improving health could involve almost any aspect of social life. Whether people were ready to discard previous practices, or change them, may often have depended on how the new practices interfered with customary arrangements. Serious illness may pose a direct threat to life and provoke people to react in special ways when they see the urgency and sense the danger.

Clearly some things were accepted readily because they were better than local remedies or more convenient – soap, liniment and cough medicine; bandages, dressings, plaster-of-Paris splints; aspirin; antimalarial drugs for some fevers; penicillin for yaws, and antibiotics for some other complaints, infections and fevers. The Gnau rarely use the old local methods for treating sores and wounds (with bark dressings, silt, termite nest powder, betel spit, juice and pith of a crushed liana); people either have their sores and wounds dressed, or cover them with a rag, or leave them exposed to be pestered by flies. What was noticeable was that the new dressings had displaced the old ones; hardly anyone seemed to use the old methods (except for sprinkling lime on a cut or sore) even though lots of people had nasty cuts and sores which, at the time, they could not (or would not bother to) get bandaged or covered. Had the people become less self-reliant than they had been before? Or had they always accepted annoyance and pain from sores and cuts as something that could hardly be escaped?

When a new method of treatment displaces an old one completely, people become dependent on the new. Bandages were not always available or accessible, yet people often wanted them, and in many cases needed them. They did not control the supply or knew how to make them, and they could not afford to buy them. As old methods are given up, people have less sense of their own self-sufficiency than they had before. The changes in some attitudes and perceived needs are not easily reversible. Antibiotics, injections and many other introductions of Western medicine are obviously outside their own control. Practical issues of distribution, distance and transport, availability, accessibility and cost may become the overriding determinants of whether someone receives the treatment he or she might like to have. Roscoe's paper draws these issues clearly to our attention. The distance and cost of getting to an aid post or a health centre or a hospital may pose difficult questions in actual situations and raise much uncertainty about what is really worth doing in the circumstances. Whether the patient can walk or must be carried and over what distance, across what rivers or steep ridges, has to be weighed against their perception of the urgency and seriousness of need, and ideas about the likely benefits of different kinds of treatment. Some of the constraints are actual physical barriers, lack of materials, cost, time and effort – not cultural constraints; but others are clearly cultural. They may depend on attitude and belief, commitments to local values and local ideas.

Access and availability are major practical problems in a country as wild and mountainous as Papua New Guinea. But they explain only part of the variation. People may not want to travel to an aid post or a health centre if it will take them among strangers whom they cannot trust, or enemies. The small scale of social units within which people feel or felt fully secure still influences some decisions about what to do and where to go when someone is sick.

The strangeness of hospitals or distant centers also deters people. Away from home, isolated, anyone might feel worried about who will support him, whether he can be sure of deciding for himself what is done, whether he can refuse treatment or get away from something he does not want done. Confidence in a new system has to be built up. In the case described here by Jenkins for the Amele, the approach of the missionary doctor and the excellent services he set up, have combined to create confidence and supplant traditional healing practices. Maddocks (1978: 28) recorded the changes in patterns of hospital use by patients from Pari, a coastal village near Port Moresby (nearly a suburb of it), in which a primary health care clinic was set up. He concludes that the increase in hospital admissions in the years of his study resulted partly from better recognition of cases needing treatment and partly from increasing confidence in the health services as a result of improved primary health care; it made people more willing to go to hospital.

Choices – passive and active

If one were to try to spell out all the indications of cause or motive for accepting or rejecting Western medicine given in the chapters of this book, it would be difficult to place them all under the head of one or two general processes, or one or two common attitudes. What might one take? Integration? Opposition? A pragmatism that is materialist and realist? Empirical curiosity? Closed conservatism? Millenarian enthusiasm? Magical outlook? Syncretic openness? Opportunism? Political pressure? Distribution of resources and access to them? Beliefs about power? Eagerness for modern things, progress and "cargo"? Differences of education and information? Shrewd assessment on the basis of limited evidence? Religious persuasion? Charismatic and forceful leaders? Innocence or ignorance?

Carrier's account of the interplay of complex influences on Ponam brings in a wide variety of these in a history of shifting events: opposition between the Catholic church and Paliau's New Way movement; the synthesis of traditional and Christian views of the relations between God, sin and sickness; the organization and effectiveness of local care; developments in education and political opportunity. Issues of illness and its explanation seem in that case thrown into high ideological relief by the bitterness of rivalry, the political and religious oppositions, the intensity and drama of some of the changes they have experienced. The attitudes of the Kove described by Chowning are quite different: Christianity has had little impact on their ideas about illness or its treatment; they have a reputation for cultural conservatism combined with a willingness to try out new remedies; they refused to have local government councils until 1977, yet some of them have travelled widely and they do a lot of trade; there is no simple correlation between education, or time spent away from Kove, and rejection of traditional beliefs. The Kaliai, like the Kove also from New Britain, use treatments that stem from their own assumptions about the causes of illness; they do this pragmatically after finding Western medicine, if it was available, to have been no help. The Counts comment on the way Kaliai hope that the health centre/Western medicine will work fast and be cheap, but if not, then they will call on their own methods to complement Western medicine. They do not seem concerned to arrive at consistent and uniform explanations. Illnesses that need their own Kaliai treatments, the cure of sorcery, may take long to work; they are uncertain of success and treatment may be costly.

It is not surprising that people grow more confident about introduced health care and more ready to trust Western medicine if in fact the quality of the services near them is good. It takes time to build this up, and time for the people involved to gain sufficient experience of what can be done. The quality and accessibility of services vary greatly, and in many places a mixture of local, traditional methods of treatment with a few bits and pieces of introduced medicine is the actual prospect for most people. These are determinants imposed from outside: material, contingent, "non-cultural" in the sense of not belonging to the culture of the people being affected. The particular response to Western medicine is shaped largely not by local culture so much as by the accident of how the people are placed: their accessibility, the timing of contact, degree of education and mission activity in their area, etc. Administrative goals were set, and they included concern for people's health. It was a responsibility that had both paternalistic and humanitarian elements.

People's perception of need depends on their past experience; their recognition of what might be done derives from local practice and local standards, unless they have opportunities to see and understand alternative ones. In most cases we read about mixtures of usage, the continuing variety of local culturally specific explanations for illness, which often bring forward social attachments and disputes as matters directly relevant to the diagnosis and treatment of the sick person. Now that people travel much more within the country and schooling has become general, expectations and standards are increasingly set by comparisons with what is going on in other parts of the country. There is more communication. Parochial or limited local views have to cope with wider horizons, and new comparisons. Sometimes this has taken the form of making distinctions between illnesses that are essentially local (*sik bilong ples*) and those that are "just diseases" (*sik nating*) or else introduced European diseases (*sik bilong ol waitskin*). The response is a complex one that derives many influences from their broader experience of rapid social change and modernization. It would be desirable to distinguish more clearly how non-medical changes interact with responses to health care changes. LiPuma states that the Maring have hopes of medicine mixed up with hopes for other material progress; they are interested not by God so much as by the prospects for a trade store and a hospital. It would be desirable to analyse more precisely how far people's interests and energies in one domain, say cash crop agriculture or town or mining experience, spill over and affect how they behave when they become ill at home; or to what extent they keep spheres of action and experience isolated from each other. The segregation of levels of remedial action in which one aspect of a medical problem is dealt with at the health centre, and another aspect of the same problem, the moral and religious one, is dealt with by ritual action at the village, suggests that levels and spheres of action are not necessarily conflated or confused. They may complement each other; they may accumulate in sequence; there may or may not be a hierarchy of resort; failure of one method may, by the elimination of possibilities, reveal another cause or the next proper course of action; or the alternatives may be opposed as when people say that Western medicine can help only Western diseases, and local medicine work only on local diseases.

In early stages of contact, sometimes epidemics of new infectious diseases occurred; village people met a few powerful white strangers with much strange equipment, wealth and material goods of many new kinds, and they got some of these items; they had to accept and try to understand rules, what it meant to be governed, the idea of law imposed by a central authority (in practice the authority represented and exercised by the local *kiap* and *polis*); and they encountered new forms of treatment. The local people had little or no control over this. Treatment, health care measures such as immunizations, hygiene rules, clinics for babies and mothers, etc., were organized, usually by white outsiders associated either with the government administration or with a Christian mission. In many cases the process and extent of change has gone forward, dependent more on outside events and outsiders' policies than on moves of opposition or support fired by local village or clan feeling. The kinds of treatment and the people who administered and controlled it were alien; insofar as they took over the management of illness, they alienated health care from the control of the local population, who became the more or less passive recipients and observers of it, rather than controllers and active participants.

Why did people accept pills and injections from strangers? How much was it because they felt they could not refuse in front of the power and authority of the strangers? Or was it curiosity? Fear? Trust? Experiment? Or because the benefits were obvious? Local people might hide or run away to avoid treatment they disliked; they might keep silent, accept the pills but throw them away in private. In time people changed how they saw the limits of white people's authority, and what they might be able to refuse or demand. The process was not just one of the introduction, diffusion and adoption of Western medicine. The recipients must not be portrayed in a passive light as the subjects or victims of administrative demands, or missionary goals, or employers' exactions. Papua New Guineans were also active in choosing what to accept, what to reject, what to try to change, and what to maintain.

Religion and medicine

Cargo cults and millenarian movements were a feature of the colonial period in Papua New Guinea – sporadic in many parts of the country, innovatory, experimental, optimistic. Some cults, for instance the Taro cult mentioned by Barker, produced new healing techniques; in others moral redemption was sought and sorcery rejected. As many used ritual and magic to cause and to treat illness, the cults allowed individual people to hope for cures for their own problems, and a magical thaumaturgical element directed at illness or sorcery might occur in many of the cults. But by comparison with African anti-witchcraft cults, spiritualist healing cults, and the profusion of new healing shrines and movements in many African countries, the Papua New Guinean cargo cults and millenarian movements do not seem to give a particularly conspicuous place to sickness or healing. Roscoe remarks on this in the Yangoru area where, despite frequent periods of millenarian activity, the movements have not been articulated with medical beliefs. There are counter examples – Paliau's New Way movement is an outstanding case. Paliau planned, as Carrier explains, a social and economic revolution, which included a break with the Catholic church and the development of a new Melanesian sect of Christianity embodying a new morality and a new theory of illness. The theory was that God caused sickness as punishment for evil thoughts. Christianity, morality, spirits of ancestors and local gods, magic and sorcery, went into the making of many cults, yet without setting the cure or prevention of illness in such sharp focus as a prominent goal. Questions of morality and of understanding sin, the social and political issues of inequality, the maintenance or change of custom, the road to wealth and goods and power, were more obviously at the heart of most movements. The disruption and distress caused by deaths from kuru among the Fore led to a series of desperate attempts to cope; among these was the movement to rid themselves of sorcery, which they believed caused the disease. It was rather like a movement of moral rearmament, with meetings (*kibungs*) so vividly described and analysed by Lindenbaum (1979), at which they tried to reforge a unity among the people by swearing to give up sorcery. The disease was the point, sorcery was their explanation, the situation was unique. In other places (for example see Barker's chapter) desire to combat sorcery seems sometimes to have provided a focus for solidarity, an identification of a threat and a need in the stress of social change; a threat of sin and evil said the missionaries, and on that they agreed.

It is surprising that illness and healing have not had a more central place in new movements. Spirits are associated with particular kinds of illness in many societies in Papua New Guinea. Sickness might sometimes serve as the trigger for organizing major ceremonial. Gnau religious beliefs and items of knowledge are pluralistic and not ordered into a smooth unitary system (Lewis 1975); the world of Gnau conceptions admits many possibilities of harm from one or other of the different principles held to be at work in it. Illness, once it has happened, requires then careful consideration of this knowledge and their beliefs to understand, if the case is serious, why it has happened and what treatment should be done. The sick person and those close to him or her must come to a decision about what they really think and believe; this gives illness a special place as revealer of unseen powers and forces that are part of everyday life but not normally given special attention. F.E. Williams (1976: 256), while recognizing the risk of an observer's personal bias or some chance event deflecting observations in a particular direction, ascribed to the Kutubu people a distinctive cultural preoccupation with bodily disease, its causes, prevention and treatment. Fortune's account of Manus religion (1963) and, as Allen reminds us, Mead's diary of the stream of events in an Arapesh village (1971) both recorded the interruption by illness of everyday life, the insistent repeated calls it made for explanation and interpretation, for reference to ideas about ghosts, spirits and ritual forces, magic and sorcery and taboos.

Certainly there are obvious resemblances and common features in the explanations of illness offered by Papua New Guinean people, despite all the cultural and linguistic diversity. Young's synopsis of Kalauna views brings out quickly and well the scatter of elements to be found in one society which is so common – the presence of intricate moral considerations in some cases, an evaluation of the state of social relationships, and the occasional depth of embedded political issues – rivalry, revenge, anger, competition. Illness may be the sanction for misconduct. And sickness may be so bad as to bring death. Almost any illness might lead to people trying to attach the blame or guilt for it on someone or some social group, but only some illnesses in practice provoke public discussion of this. Cases in other chapters (for example those described by the Counts) show how this happens both in private and in public. Moral and social considerations are acutely raised at times by illness and have had a part in moulding responses to introduced Western health care. While it is clear from some studies (for example Frankel 1986, Lewis 1975) that a relatively large proportion of ordinary sickness may be treated without particularly raising moral or social issues, some still remains that does provoke serious concern. If Western medicine is perceived by local people as paying no attention to these moral and social issues, or if it seems quite ignorant or contemptuous of them, the people find it lacking and must rely on their own resources to deal with them. They may, as some of the studies here show, turn to their own methods, while accepting some Western treatment for symptoms. But this is not a simple matter to disentangle because Christian missions have been so much involved in health care in many parts of Papua New Guinea that local people are almost bound to associate some aspects of Western health care with Christian mission action. This is especially the case in the field of Maternal and Child Health care services. In particular, for example, Young's article analyses missionary zeal in this field and the motives that may have lain behind it. Barker notes that the success of Western medicine served to reinforce the superiority and authority of the Europeans and their religion, to hasten the acceptance of new forms of thought and behavior. But overall, he notes, the provision of medical services played a very small role in strategies of evangelization and "civilization". Health measures were introduced for humanitarian reasons and did not form the strategic part of the missionaries' endeavours to alter and improve the moral and religious consciences of converts. The irony is, he writes, that Maisin today as in the past strongly associate health and sickness with matters of religion, morality and politics. But in many other places, often enough people say they have tried the whiteman's treatment and it failed; the powers at work in the illness were New Guinean ones beyond the competence of Western medicine.

Pluralism

Most writers here note the willingness of local people to use both Western medicine and their own methods of treatment. Strathern asks us to consider what it is that shows pluralism. Is it the mere presence of alternatives? Of different services? Their eclectic combination? Something about attitudes and beliefs? Or about behavior? Pluralism can refer to institutional arrangements – the multiplicity of competing interests or power groups – which may arise from functional differentiation (they do different jobs); or, through competition or conflict, they may develop specialized interests. For instance, the view that Western medicine can deal with symptoms and local medicine with causes; or one is competent to deal with European diseases, the other with New Guinean ones.

Pluralism can also refer to the replication of similar and competing organizations in the same institutional sphere because several distinct social and cultural groups coexist within the boundaries of a single polity. The processes of differentiation (involving increasing specialization of function) are different from segmentation into parallel groups and institutions. Papua New Guinea has diversity; its linguistic, social and cultural pluralism is one of its most striking attributes. Societies were small in scale: independent, contiguous, sovereign, atomistic. Colonial rule created the new political unit with boundaries, a country with a government and institutions; it contains extraordinary inherited pluralism. This is placed within a frame of Western institutions and culture. As for medical institutions, just as there is a single centralized hierarchical system of government so, roughly, there is in theory a single centralized hierarchical system of medical organization, modelled on white Western institutions, and there is also a multitude of local different Papua New Guinean forms of medicine and medical organization. Case by case we may look to see whether the Western medical system (or its local representatives) dominates and seeks to displace and suppress the local forms, or divides responsibilities and works side by side with them. That is to view it from the standpoint of official medicine. The short colonial history of the country reveals shifts of policy. The problems now are seen differently from the way they were in the paternalistic colonial phase. Questions of perceived needs, of education and information, of local participation and responsibility for choices about care, are given much more recognition than they were when Western medicine was introduced (Department of Public Health 1974, Hetzel 1978, Malcolm 1978, Radford 1980). But viewed from the standpoint of the local people, the new treatments and places for medical care were not necessarily always seen as competing with local treatments; some were too different to be seen as analogues or alternatives. Instead they were something new to add or try out. They were not seen as opposed to local methods in the way that Christian mission practice might sometimes seem to oppose them, or to oppose their local ritual practices. Conflicts of principle and/or practice were not apparent in the same way. So to many observers it has seemed that local people have integrated some things from Western medicine into their range of choices and responses to illness with little difficulty. Integration then need not imply more than adding something to a range of existing alternatives. It need not imply other effects on the preexisting system such as conflict, displacement or adjustment.

But all those effects have occurred in some places. The integration of some treatment or practice or some piece of equipment may take place without fuss, but its origins and control stay alien. The integration involved in taking over the management, production and administration of the foreign forms is a different matter. Chowning mentions an example of the problems of pills: people got them and sometimes kept them, passed them on to others, or used them, without being able to read what they were for; they might be ready to swallow them but sometimes it was in wildly inappropriate ways. Elsewhere a quick eye, innovation and experiment lie behind the worrying use of procaine penicillin powder undissolved, sprinkled direct from purloined phials onto sores; it is usually rather effective. How are they to know its risks? It is an example of adoption or integration in a more active, innovative sense. When we look in detail at current practice in villages, we can find many changes in what is done for the sick. Such changes will include both the ways in which Western medicine is actually given in primary health care in villages, and the ways in which customary local healing is now carried out. Indigenous healers have devised new methods of divination: *glasman* circulate to diagnose illness; the thermometer distinguishes God-sent illness from earthly sickness; new forms of sorcery and treatment for sorcery appear; "germs", "worms" and "dirt" and "poison" are added to the lists; theories of illness and categories of illness change.

As well as pluralism in the social and political senses which refer to institutions and organization, pluralism can refer to ideas, to ideology and culture. Pluralism as opposed to monism rejects the idea that the world is a unity: "I think the universe is all spots and bumps, without unity, without continuity, without coherence or orderliness or any of the other properties that governesses love" was how Bertrand

Russell (1931: 98) put it. An attitude of that sort should tolerate diverse views and explanations. Pluralism in philosophy contrasts most obviously with monism; but in fact discussions of medicine in Papua New Guinea are most often and obtrusively couched in a different form – that of dualism or pluralism. The contrast, and opposition, is presented as one between Western medicine and the local system whatever it is that stands in that place as the example of Papua New Guinean medicine. It is extremely easy to fall into this dualistic way of thinking; but it is misleading. The convenience of thinking in terms of simple dichotomies is always a temptation. It seems to clarify issues, but the simplification distorts them. It is misleading to speak of "system" when referring to local modes of treatment for the sick. The local forms are not usually formulated as a unified system of theory, practice and medical institutions. The local forms are not matched against Western medicine as one system against another. The view of pluralism as an ideology expressed by Chambers (1983) is based on an agnostic openness to evidence and argument. It would involve a commitment to look at other points of view; it would recognize multiple causation, multiple objectives and multiple interventions; and it would be suspicious of unicausal explanation, of single objectives, and one solution. Chambers is writing of rural development and his attitude of openness to new information, observation, and unexpected details, derives from exposure to rural reality. This need not suggest that pluralism is consciously held as an ideology by many Papua New Guineans, but the statement of agnostic openness to alternative approaches fits quite well with views that some Gnau people express to the effect that others may have different ways from them of explaining and dealing with problems of illness, and they may also be right; and really, they said, it is better to have two or more possible ways of doing something than just one.

Conversion

Conversion suggests a more radical decision to change than the mere acceptance of some new ways and a few new materials. Some moves have been conversions in the religious sense, the Huli adoption of Christianity, for example, and many instances of millenarian conversion. Such conversions entailed changes of healing practice because many of the more elaborate traditional healing practices were closely bound up with traditional religious belief and ritual. What we expect of conversion is that the new beliefs and practices will supplant the old, oust them, replace them, destroy belief in the merit or worth of the old ways of doing things. But in fact the chapters here testify to the continued life of local non-Western explanations of illness, even after local people have become Christian or have long experience of mission teaching. They do not seem to have "converted" to Western medicine if that would require them to have rejected and abandoned all their old beliefs about illness and healing practices.

It seems consistent with the pluralist attitude described above that Papua New Guineans should not feel that if they adopt some new beliefs and practices they must therefore renounce or abandon all that they had before. New methods and ideas are fitted in or adopted. The syncretism shows more as a mixture of things of mixed origins than as a new coherent synthesis. Ideas, institutional organization and techniques are different aspects of the thing we loosely speak of as a Western system of medicine. Objects and techniques, bits of the foreign technology, a needle and syringes, bottles of tablets, these can easily enter as artifacts in isolation, to be used sometimes almost in ignorance of their properties and their use in the system from which they come. You do not have to accept a particular body of knowledge or beliefs to swallow a tablet or inject someone with penicillin. All you need is the equipment. You may use it wrongly, and come to your own opinion about its value. You may adopt organizational forms without the ideas. You may open an aid post or a health clinic and people come to it; they may use the services for reasons of their own which do not necessarily match yours exactly.

In the ordinary way, people are concerned with effectiveness in medicine, with practical considerations, more than with explanatory beliefs or logic. Attention to rationality and system in the analyses of medical behavior may be overstressed. Both medicine and religion involve matters of belief and practice, but the emphasis falls differently. When medicine and religion, especially monotheistic religion, are fused or confused, the syncretism and synthesis is likely to be more coherent as a theory and practice (for example as in the ideas of Paliau's New Way movement), and less tolerant than in the syncretism or pluralism that is merely mixture.

Western medicine, for which some have suggested the label "cosmopolitan", implies that its theories about diseases and the ways to treat them are not limited in application to particular societies and cultures but have universal relevance. Like a world religion, it has a universal message, virtue for all mankind. Believers may try to justify the sweep forward of such a religion by its truth. If the religion is monotheist, they may argue that it contains the only truth, and therefore reject other beliefs and practices which do not accord with their own. Certainly those who believe in scientific medicine may also seek to justify it by its truth and virtue; yet to push it forward as the sole, exclusive truth is to adopt the attitude of monotheism rather than that of science. The idea that Western medicine, being scientific, will supplant any previous medicine may feed on the hope that truth will prevail. Some of its supporters suppose, with monotheist zeal, that the source of truth is single: the scientific method. And we may be led to think that pluralism is what is curious. On the contrary, experience shows it is the rule. Wholehearted conversion to Western medicine is the exception.

BRYANT J. ALLEN

2. INFECTION, INNOVATION AND RESIDENCE: ILLNESS AND MISFORTUNE IN THE TORRICELLI FOOTHILLS FROM 1800

INTRODUCTION

In 1981, when addressing the "burning question" of the integrated study of health and medicine in Africa, Gwyn Prins noted the "striking ... retreat from certainty" which has occurred in the study of the social history of medicine and the "introspection and doubt" which afflicts anthropological and historical studies in the same area (Prins 1981). The problems created by this confusion for the non-medically qualified, non-anthropologist geographer, who has not made a formal study of illness and misfortune are considerable. The situation is not improved by the "clashing conceptual, methodological, and philosophical perspectives characterizing present-day human geography" (Pred 1982: 157).

One way out of this confusion is offered by the structurationist argument that the form in which society is reproduced is critically influenced by the "ordinary, everyday activities, experiences and conciousness" of the members of society. Society always pre-exists its members and as such it is an "ensemble of structures, practices and conventions that individuals reproduce or transform" (Bhaskar 1979, 120). The importance of time and temporal sequencing in this process is discussed by Bourdieu (1977: 87).

Without entering into the "structuration" debate I intend to use the approach and to argue from it that present practices in relation to illness and misfortune in Papua New Guinea are the outcome of the day-to-day experiences of preceding generations of villagers. To use such an approach avoids some of the worst features of the ahistorical ethnographic present, functionalism and historical materialism (Thrift 1983).

My main task is therefore to attempt to establish a sequence of events experienced by people in a defined area and then within the same temporal and spatial frame, describe how practices relating to illness and misfortune changed. I will not attempt to speculate on what these experiences "meant" to people, beyond the conscious level, nor will I try to explain every change in practice in terms of all other events or in terms of all other changes in practice.

The area being examined is northwest Papua New Guinea, in particular the area south of the crest of the coastal mountain ranges, centered on the present day government post of Dreikikir (Fig. 2). First, the repercussions of a number of exotic infectious diseases which were introduced to this area from around 1880 on are described. Some of these diseases produced spectacular but short-lived epidemics. Others brought about longer-term changes in the existing pattern of morbidity and mortality. Whereas previously most deaths had occurred in infants, children and old

S. Frankel and G. Lewis (eds.), *A Continuing Trial of Treatment*. 35–68.
© 1989, Kluwer Academic Publishers, Dordrecht – Printed in the Netherlands.

people, now young adults became ill and died in increasing numbers.

Second, village responses to the changed pattern are described. The increase in illness and death among adults was attributed to an increase in sorcery. A radical change in personal movements, particularly among young males, resulted in the exchange of methods of sorcery and sorcery divination between widely separated groups of people, an activity which confirmed beliefs in an increase in sorcery. Nevertheless, people everywhere also immediately availed themselves of medications offered to them by foreigners, a pattern which continues to the present day.

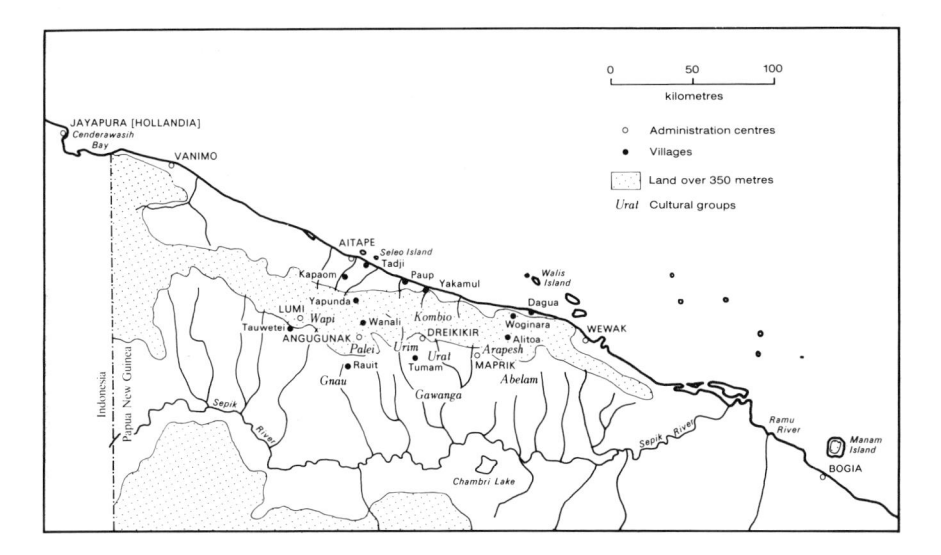

Fig. 2. The Torricelli foothills.

The third and final section of the paper looks at present day patterns of health care usage and traces them to the events experienced in the villages from 1890 to the 1950s. The basis of this section is fieldwork in five census divisions in the Dreikikir sub-province between 1971 and the present. Fifteen months were spent in the area in 1971 and 1972, followed by two months in 1978. The most recent visit was four days in 1983. The primary focus of this work was not village health, but the relationships between village agriculture and social, economic and political change.

It is obvious that great forces for change were brought to bear on New Guinea societies from the 1890s on, most of which had external origins. Above all else, I wish to show that village people were not unaware of those forces and made conscious decisions about changes in existing health care practices and the adoption of new practices, within the bounds of their knowledge. That it is important for people involved in bringing modern health services to New Guinea villagers to understand this is self-evident. It is perhaps less self-evident that villagers continue to make conscious decisions about their health care and that it is only by taking their views into account that an improvement in community health will be achieved.

THE TORRICELLI MOUNTAIN FOOTHILLS

The sequence of events begins immediately before the first direct contacts between foreigners and the foothills people and it is necessary to sketch the environmental, cultural and disease patterns of that period before proceeding to describe the events themselves. The coastal mountains of northern New Guinea run northeast to southwest in an unbroken line from the Sepik River to Cenderawasih Bay. The coast is exposed to the northeast monsoon and, except at Jayapura, lacks year round safe and protected anchorages. When foreigners arrived on the coast in the nineteenth century they found it occupied by people speaking Austronesian languages, indicative of relatively recent arrival. Villages were large, with houses built on piles and the people skilled at building canoes, fishing and making pottery. Inland however, in the mountains and among the foothills to the south of the modern coastal town of Aitape, were people speaking older, non-Austronesian languages. These were forest dwellers. In the west where rainfall is higher and seasonality less distinct, they made sago, gardened and hunted. In the east, which is drier and has a distinct dry period in the middle of the year, they cultivated tubers, yams and taro, bananas, sugar and fruit trees in swiddens cleared each year and cultivated for up to 18 months. Food production was a constant but not overbearing task. Husbands and wives shared garden work and spent much of their time together in their gardens. Houses were built on the ground, clustered close together around scarce pieces of level ground, on knolls and hilltops. Villages often comprised a series of hamlets strung along a narrow ridge, and marked by efflorescences of coconuts which rose above the surrounding forest. Men and women went completely naked, except for body decorations.

Villages of between 150 and 250 people were common. Village sites and land were occupied by fairly loose patrilineal groups and the importance of matrilineal ties was emphasized in many ways. In all but the westernmost part of this area, village men formed themselves into two ritually equal and opposed groups. These groups exchanged food and game competitively and were responsible for the initiation of each others' "sons". Exchanges and initiations normally involved surrounding villages, including "enemy" villages and men travelled to and from nearby villages to participate. So although an individual rarely travelled more than ten kilometers from his place of birth in his lifetime, the exchanges created an overlapping set of networks which connected the most distant hamlet to all other villages. Behind the ranges people lived in ignorance of the existence of the ocean but trade goods passed back and forth across the mountains from group to group.

The foothills were also inhabited by natural spirits who were responsible for the creation of the land and everything in it and for the continued reproduction of plants and animals. Some of these beings were invoked during initiation ceremonies when men ensured not only that the natural universe was reproduced, but also that social reproduction took place in a satisfactory manner. These initiations and accompanying ceremonies are now known universally in Pidgin as *tambaran,* a term also applied to the special houses and the objects which are concealed from women and uninitiated men and boys within them. The natural spirits are now known universally as *masalai.*

Masalai are capricious and dangerous and react to provocation by causing a range of illnesses. Provocation may be something as innocuous as trespassing or laughing or singing in an area known to be occupied by a *masalai.* Ancestral spirits also dwelt in the forests. They were normally supportive, or at worst benign, and ancestral and *masalai* spirits could be called upon to assist in gardening, hunting and similar enterprises.

All such magic was dangerous, however, and could cause illness if mishandled. Any items associated with the *tambaran* were dangerous and the *tambaran* spirits could be invoked to harm those who transgressed against them. Almost all misfortune, illness and death was attributable to malevolent magic directed by one person against another, usually through the medium of a specialist sorcerer. Exuviae, any small item of food, clothing or bodily excrement was picked up and stored in small bamboo containers. If the item was given to a sorcerer, or placed in an area known to be inhabited by a *masalai,* the person from whom the item had been stolen would become ill, develop an ulcer or suffer an accident. Only if the exuviae could be discovered or the person who was harboring the ill will and was indirectly causing the affliction be identified, would the symptoms abate. A range of divination techniques was employed to this end.

In the small, close-knit communities with no clearly ascribed hierarchical structure, there was much potential for rivalry, jealousy, frustration and insults, real and imagined. Sorcery was considered evil and malicious but everyone was thought capable of wanting, under certain circumstances, to cause harm to another. It was by its very nature carried out surreptitiously. Searches for the origins of an affliction among people living within a hamlet and in nearby hamlets was a commonplace activity.

LIVING CONDITIONS AND DISEASE

Conditions in the Torricelli villages were ideal for the reproduction and spread of pathogens. The ambient temperature was always warm and humidity high. People lived in close contact with the soil and their agricultural work frequently resulted in breaks in the skin, cuts and abrasions. Ridgetop villages were light and airy, but running water was far away. Waterholes, often unprotected from wild and domesticated pigs, were dug downslope. Latrines were logs upon which people squatted in low undergrowth on the edge of the village, near dwelling houses and also open to pigs. Mourning involved maintaining close contact with the decomposing body which was either put on a platform on the edge of the village or placed in a shallow open grave inside a dwelling house. Small pieces of the flesh of important people were eaten in recognition of the food the deceased had provided during his life. Mosquitoes carrying malarial and filarial parasites bred freely on tips of household refuse and coconut shells cast down the slope behind houses.

Fig. 3. Child deaths are common in the Torricelli foothills. This three-year-old died after suffering a high fever. His uncle requested a photograph be taken of him in newly purchased funeral clothes.

This is known from descriptions by old people of the villages of their childhood and from the written reports and oral accounts of officers who were responsible for bringing the area under colonial "control" in the 1920s. Less is known of the actual pattern of disease at this time. This is because village recall of the causes of deaths which occurred seventy years ago is hazy and probably emphasizes the spectacular, and early outside observers were itinerant and infrequent. Genealogies emphasize violent deaths from fighting and ambush, tree falls and injuries incurred while hunting pigs. Few deaths are attributable to recognizable diseases and among these "shortwind", some kind of respiratory problem, predominates. Deaths in childbirth are forgotten, as are infant deaths.

Colonial officers visited on average once every three years. They saw only the living and they recorded only what was directly observable: widespread frambesia among children with some secondary infections in adults, tropical ulcers and tinea. They did not observe the large numbers of infant deaths or the high maternal mortality; malaria and pneumonia they seem to have taken for granted for it is never mentioned, even in reports which deal quite extensively with the "health" of the population.

So the pattern of morbidity and mortality in the 1860s, immediately prior to colonial contact, was one of high infant and child mortality from intestinal and respiratory tract infections, tetanus and malaria.[1] Infancy survived, individuals stood a fair chance of contracting yaws in childhood and a tropical ulcer at some time in their lives, but by adolescence most had developed an adequate resistance to local infections. Women faced considerable risks in childbearing, but until old age, the only regular illness most people suffered were bouts of malaria. With increasing age the danger of pneumonia in association with malaria increased and the chances of dying from complications increased sharply. An active male had probably much the same chances of meeting a violent death skirmishing as a woman risked dying in childbearing. Any penetrating wound of the chest or abdomen was almost invariably fatal and deep muscular wounds were likely to lead to severe general infections.

The explanation of this pattern of illness and misfortune did not concentrate upon the diseases or injuries themselves, but upon the individual who had fallen ill or been injured, and his or her relationships with other people and with the supernatural. Because of this, a disease such as pneumonia could be ascribed to a number of different causes, either when suffered by different individuals or by the same individual. In general, mild illnesses or illnesses from which a person recovered fairly quickly, did not cause concern but an ongoing illness resulted in long and drawn out attempts to find its origins.[2]

These patterns of morbidity and mortality were the norm to the foothills villager. It was accepted that many infants would die and that to try and keep alive a weak, sickly or malformed infant was to condemn the child to a short and miserable life. Infants born with obvious handicaps were allowed to die and little special attention was given to an infant which became severely malnourished. The senile aged were given only minimal care and their death was seen as a blessing. The most important members of the community were married men and women in full productive life and it was their deaths which caused the greatest communal concern. Because their contribution to production and reproduction was critical to the continuance of the group, and because in the nature of things they should not often become ill or die, illness or death among them was viewed as certain covert aggression, more dangerous than a physical attack on them. The increased morbidity and death which occurred in this group during the first fifty years of colonialism brought about a greatly increased concern with the causes and prevention of illness.

THE EPIDEMIC ERA[3]

The colonization of New Guinea societies involved bringing them under "control", a process which was frequently physically violent and always psychologically traumatic (Rowley 1965: 63–89). Colonization was a time of great uncertainty, of sudden and dramatic change, of a gradual realization of a loss of independence and the recognition that extremely powerful strangers, who could arbitrarily interfere in village life, had come to take up permanent residence just beyond the horizon. But perhaps the most revolutionary change which colonialism wrought was the great increase in personal movements which occurred following the enforced cessation of inter-group fighting, the opening up of "government roads" and the establishment of the labor trade.

It can be argued from indirect evidence that a major change occurred in the pattern of morbidity and mortality from around the 1880s onwards. It began before direct colonial contact and continued until after the end of the 1942–45 war, when antibiotic drugs came into common usage. The change in pattern was caused by the introduction of a number of exotic infectious diseases which took the form of epidemics. Two, smallpox and dysentery, were highly infectious, spread rapidly and widely, had a high mortality rate, were clearly symptomatically different to existing illnesses and formed discrete and identifiable events. A third group of diseases, influenza and influenzal-pneumonia were less spectacular, had much greater variation in mortality, caused symptoms which were not too qualitatively different from those of malaria or existing strains of pneumonia, and occurred repeatedly so that it is difficult to distinguish between one epidemic and another. Two other diseases, tuberculosis and leprosy, were also probably introduced during this period. They are insidious and make their effects felt over a long period of time. I have little information about them and will not discuss them further.

Smallpox

At some time between 1880 and 1900 smallpox spread throughout much of lowland New Guinea. It is at present not possible to give an exact date. In 1890 smallpox appeared at Stephensport, south of Madang, carried there by a Malay stoker on a German ship. The New Guinea Company reported that it "first attacked the Melanesians with great severity and then spread in waves", but claim the disease did not reach Madang or New Britain (Sack and Clarke 1979). However, Parkinson reports a smallpox epidemic which he estimates killed "one quarter" of the population of Seleo Island off Aitape in 1895 (Parkinson 1900). He later wrote (1907) of how "many years ago" smallpox, which originated from Javanese laborers brought to Madang by the New Guinea Company, "spread over a large area on the coast of the mainland" and then crossed to New Britain via Rooke Island. He observes that on New Britain, "the results of disastrous epidemic, against which the natives were quite helpless, are still to be seen in districts which formerly carried a big population" (Parkinson 1907: 209). This epidemic is not recorded in the report translated and published by Sack and Clarke, nor is there any report of smallpox at Aitape. Wedgewood on Manam Island in 1932 also describes "an outbreak of what was almost certainly smallpox which occurred some thirty-five to forty years ago", that is, around 1890, of which "people still speak with awe, telling how, so great were the number of deaths, there was no time to bury the corpses properly (Wedgewood 1934: 73). Manam Islanders said the epidemic was caused by sorcery invoked by the "chief" of a village whose eldest son had died, killed, so the father believed, by local sorcery.

An inhospitable coast and a rugged mountain range caused the colonial tide to wash around the Torricelli foothills. Permanent German settlement at Aitape began in 1896 but as late as 1910 many foothills villagers and the foreigners on the coast were ignorant of each others' existence. Yet infection and death came sweeping through Urat villages as though on the wings of a bird.

> This man was angry over the death of his child [by sorcery]. His name was Bwasale. The name of his son was Morosopun. He was a fine child. So Bwasale was very angry. He went to a part of the forest called Nipkimbihi. This was his land. At Nipkimbihi he performed magic. He bled his penis. He rubbed magic "paint" over the stones there, and over his legs, his chest, his eyes and his hands. This is what he did at this masalai place, in the forest on his land.
>
> Now a parrot, a red parrot appeared and perched on the branch of tree. Bwasale spoke to this bird. He said, "when I leave here I will walk below on the ground and you must fly above through the trees". And so when he left that place the bird followed him. He walked through the forest, up the ridge and came near to the village. When he walked through the village, this bird landed on the roof of the first house. He walked, walked, walked and the bird too, came from house to house. Not one house did he miss. Up through the village, through Ngahangoro, through Ngahmbole, on, on, to the door of his own house. He put down the things he was carrying and opened the door of his house, and this bird perched on a tree beside his house, a breadfruit. This tree was called Taihumbondenge. It grew just behind where Binghoiye's house is now. Now the bird began calling, "Kolololo, Kolololo". Like that, up in the breadfruit tree, until dark. He was making them sick, in all the houses on which he had landed.
>
> Dawn the next morning. Time to get up. No. The doors remained shut. Everyone had become sick. Now, one week is too long. Just a few days was enough. Fever, high fever. Then they started to die. The adults took perhaps a week. The small children, the ones whose hands you hold and walk around; one-

two, and they went. Not everyone died at once. At first a few. They wrapped them in black-palm sheaths and took them to the streams. Some they put in the trees. This kept on, and on. It couldn't stop of its own accord. It kept going. Everyone ran away from the village. Into the small places. Into the bush.

Then he felt sorry. Bwasale, himself, went to Nipkimbihi. He made everything alright again. They had all died and gone for ever. One here, two there, three there, that was all that was left, in our village and at Ngahmbole. Those few people are the ancestors of all of us here today. *Rethuke* is a terrible thing. It could have wiped us out. But he was sorry, and went back to Nipkimbihi. Stopped the magic, and we are here in these villages today.

Worosambawi Maheyup – Tumam Village

Rethuke was like chickenpox, but chickenpox is usually a mild sickness. *Rethuke* was like fire. People burned with it. Many people became ill with it and died. If someone became ill with it, they were quickly taken out of the village to a bush house to stop other people getting it. They stayed there as long as they were sick, until they recovered or died. When people died they were buried under the water in the streams to cool the heat of this illness. If it appeared in another village, no one could go there, and no one could come back from there. This is what our fathers told us. We have not seen this sickness in our lifetime, but we still fear it. This sickness is known in all the western Urat villages by this name. Everywhere people became sick and died.

Kwaltihi Mahaiye – retired aid post superviser, and nephew of Worosambawi

Other reports of what was probably smallpox come from the Angugunak area (Marshall 1938: 63, Lewis 1975: 82) and Maprik.[4]

Dysentery

Bacillary dysentery was another early introduction into New Guinea, first being officially reported in 1888 in Astrolabe Bay. It receives annual mention in New Guinea reports from that time on with serious epidemics in New Ireland in 1899 and 1908, and Manus Island in 1912, when an estimated 1200 deaths resulted. But no documentary evidence has so far been found for dysentery at Aitape until 1932. In that year a "serious outbreak" which moved inland at least as far as Kapoam village was apparently brought under control by a quarantine on all movements inland from July until September. Dysentery appeared again at Aitape in 1935 and spread inland despite a quarantine. In Aitape it is said to have caused no deaths but a geological survey party working in the Palei area reported a 10% death rate in Yapunda village south of the range on the main inland track.[5]

The worst dysentery epidemic in the area occurred between 1943 and 1944 when villagers constructing airstrips for the Japanese at Tadji contracted a severe strain of dysentery and were ordered to return inland. They carried the disease into the area between Angugunak and Lumi from where it spread as far as Kombio and Urim villages in the east and to Tauwetei, southwest of Lumi and perhaps further, in the west (Mitchell 1978). Lewis (1977) estimates that "close to half of the population [of Rauit village] died" and he and Sturt comment on the small size of the 25–29 and 30–35-year-age cohorts in village populations in the Angugunak area (Sturt and Stanhope 1968). In Urim villages, the only area for which population figures are presently available, a 25.6% reduction in adult populations occurred between 1941 and 1945, with a corresponding 36% reduction in the number of children (Allen 1983).

The pattern of mortality in the dysentery epidemic in which more children than adults died was probably similar in the smallpox epidemic. Worosambawi's account makes specific reference to the deaths of toddlers. This was almost certainly not true in the case of repeated epidemics of influenza and influenzal-pneumonia which occurred in the period before the Pacific War.

Fig. 4. A yam exchange. Although villages are small and isolated from each other by jungle and rough foot tracks, ceremonies such as this yam exchange bring together relatively large numbers of people from a number of villages. Food is cooked and exchanged. Latrines are few. The opportunity for infectious diseases to spread is high.

Influenza

In Papua New Guinea influenza kills quietly, usually with little spectacle, and has often done its worst before it comes to the attention of health authorities. It is not possible to provide a single lifelong immunization against it. It often is a mild disease and its symptoms are sometimes indistinct and easy to confuse with other mild infections. For these reasons influenza epidemics are not remembered as discrete events in Torricelli villages.

Government reports, from both the German and Australian administrations, clearly recognize that influenza did spread inland from coastal stations, inland through "uncontrolled" areas and that the colonial medical services could do nothing to prevent it nor to assist those afflicted. The most explicit recognition of this situation is made in an Australian report of 1937:

> There is a seasonal incidence of epidemic influenza in all parts of the Territory, but the virulence varies greatly from year to year – from an epidemic of mild coryza in one season in one area to an epidemic of severe influenza, with a varying percentage of pneumonic complications in other years and in other areas. The incidence and the rapidity of spread of these local foci of influenzal infection ... and the short period between the beginning and the end of the local epidemic, render emergency treatment extremely difficult, except in villages in the proximity of medical stations.[6]

Influenza appears annually in the German reports from 1889 and is usually described as a mild disease which has not caused European deaths. But in 1891 it is noted that "losses among coloured labourers [Chinese and Malays] are considerable" and, in 1900, "many of the local natives are said to have died." After the Australian takeover in 1914, this pattern continues. In 1927, "epidemic influenzal broncho-pneumonia" is described as a "yearly scourge" in "outlying uncontrolled areas", whereas in "more settled and controlled areas the mortality is much lower." In 1931 a "very severe form" of influenza appeared and by June of the same year is reported as reaching Aitape. In Rabaul it affected an estimated 60% of villagers and had a 4% death rate, killing mainly children and old people. On the Edie Creek goldfield, where hospital facilities were available, the death rate among laborers who contracted the illness was 8.6%.[7] No details are available for Aitape, but records collected by Scragg from the Catholic Mission for the coastal villages of Paup and Yakamul show the death rate in 1931 was approximately 4.7%, compared to the 1910–1942 average of 4.2% (Scragg 1977). Mead, who arrived in Alitoa in 1932, notes that the Arapesh had "experienced some sort of an epidemic ... (probably influenza) and recognize that contagion exists in what they call "cold in the stomach"" (Mead 1947: 345 fn). Influenza again appeared in a serious form in 1939, when it was described as a "distressing fatal epidemic of Influenza-pneumonia [which] spread throughout the Territory".[8]

Measles and chickenpox, in contrast, are reported as "mildly endemic" and of "no serious significance". "Non-fatal cases" of whooping cough are also mentioned. It is not known on what sort of information this assessment was made. Even if it is generally correct in relation to adults, it is probable that these diseases increased the risk of pneumonia in children and that fluctuations in village infant and child deaths were not observed by foreigners. Epidemics of these diseases illustrate the ease with which infections could spread during this time. In June 1937 for example, German measles came from Hollandia (Jayapura) to Aitape, from where it "spread gradually through the inland villages and reached Madang in March 1938".[9] The movement of chickenpox from New Ireland to New Britain and then to Morobe in 1935 is a further example.[10]

It is at present not possible to produce population statistics to support the argument that these epidemics produced a different pattern of morbidity from that which existed previously. Village censuses were taken only about once every three years and early censuses are unreliable because many people avoided being censused for as long as possible. The reliability of the figures themselves is now an academic question however, because almost all pre-war census material was destroyed during the war and it is only from fragmentary material that the effect of some events, such as the 1943 dysentery epidemic, can be reconstructed.[11] The major piece of evidence upon which my argument is based is Scragg's 1977 article in which he shows wildly fluctuating mortality in the coastal villages of Yakamul and Paup, based on mission records. He shows similar patterns for other parts of Papua New Guinea. I believe it can be shown conclusively that diseases which appeared on the coast could and did spread inland rapidly, and therefore the inland patterns of mortality would have been disrupted in a similar manner to those on the coast. I do not argue that introduced respiratory diseases killed less children than adults but that over the long term, the number of adult illnesses and deaths increased and this was a new phenomenon which required explanation and a satisfactory response from the village community.

COLONIAL MEDICINE AND PUBLIC HEALTH

Infectious diseases were brought to Papua New Guinea and spread there as an unintended consequence of colonialism. But many of the influences of colonialism were deliberate and were intended to have a direct influence on the health and welfare of villagers. They included the enforcement of public hygiene regulations, health patrols, primary health care services delivered by specially trained village men, and Maternal and Child Health clinics. They presented villagers with their first experiences of a formal system of health care and public hygiene and must be considered, together with the exotic diseases, as formative influences on present-day responses to illness and health care.

Kiaps and liklik doktas

Most colonial officers who entered the foothills in the 1930s believed the major diseases they observed – yaws and tropical ulcers – were a result of living conditions: open latrines, the exposure of the dead, poor housing. But whether this was their opinion or not they were required by their superiors to enforce public hygiene regulations with the object of improving village health. For example, as early as 1928 the people of Museng were required to "build a cemetery and use it" and in 1933 were ordered to dig pit latrines.[12] Intermittent visiting patrols inspected the cemeteries and tried to check the number of new graves against the number of recent deaths. Bodies in open house graves or on platforms had to be removed to the cemetery by relatives, regardless of the state of decomposition, and the house burned. Latrines were also inspected for signs of recent use and the officer could order the destruction of a house if in his opinion it was too ramshackle to be inhabited. Some officers found this constant checking and badgering an unpleasant task,[13] but others carried it out zealously. When a young patrol officer died at Wanali in 1939 he was killed by the village *tultul*, who he had severely criticized before the assembled villagers for not carrying out his instruction to clean up the village. In the subsequent enquiry it was noted that numerous government patrols and survey parties had stayed in the village previously and there had never been trouble of any sort before.[14]

Patrols were occasionally accompanied by a medical assistant, a European paramedical worker, known as a *liklik dokta* and special medical patrols were also undertaken from time to time. The medical assistant inspected villagers, family by family, in order of the census. Early patrols could do little but require people with ulcers or other chronic ailments to report to the Aitape hospital, which was a more than three days walk over the ranges and through the strange coastal villages, where peoples' nakedness was made fun of and exorbitant prices were charged for food. At least one patrol officer recognized that to order people with serious ulcers to walk to Aitape "would be cruel in the extreme",[15] but other officers enforced the regulations and as a result people incapacitated with ulcers or ill with some other disease were commonly hidden from patrols. Police were often sent to search houses for people missing from censuses and suspected of being ill.

Medical tultuls

The medical patrol spent only a few hours in each village every three or four years. In an attempt to extend a more continuous medical service to villagers the German colonial administration began the medical tultul service, a precursor to the modern aid post orderly. The German *"heil tultul"* was a village man who was given very basic training and was responsible for

> the treatment of injuries and minor illnesses. He must report serious cases

immediately to the authorities. He is given a case which can be locked, containing dressings, cotton wool, bandages, soap, disinfectants and a few simple medicines such as castor oil. (Sack and Clarke 1979: 341)

Medical *tultuls* were appointed in the inland villages in the 1930s. They were commonly younger men who had spent three years on a labor contract. Their activities as health workers are never mentioned by villagers in oral accounts of this period, nor in the written reports which survive, but they are often mentioned in other contexts. They could speak Pidgin and took on a role similar to that of the *tultul*, acting as a go-between and interpreter, which often took them away from their villages for long periods and seriously reduced their usefulness to patrolling medical assistants.[16]

The only published detailed description of everyday village life in the coastal ranges during the 1930s is Mead's "stream of events" in Alitoa. Two of the leading men in Alitoa, Kule and Ombomb, had received training as medical *tultuls*, but neither appear to be carrying out their duties during the time of Mead's fieldwork there. Although Mead describes how they and the medical *tultuls* of nearby Woginara and Liwo villages are deeply involved in tracing the origins of sorcery associated with illnesses, she makes no mention of them treating villagers for minor ailments. Ombomb does treat his wife for a breast abscess but he uses a poultice of leaves from the forest (Mead 1947: 326).

The activities and effectiveness of the medical tultul service requires more investigation, but the little evidence which is available suggests that the medical *tultuls* brought very little that was new in medical practice and ideas from the colonial medical service to their villages. A military report on village health in the Sepik written in 1945 found the "use of the medical tultul seems to have been a misguided attempt to bring the blessings of European medicine to people who first need the blessing of primitive European sanitary engineering".[17]

Other extraneous events

In September 1935 a major earthquake occurred with an epicenter northwest of Aitape. Huge landslides were triggered in the mountains and foothills, and lakes were formed, some permanent. Others lasted from a few hours to a few weeks and then broke to create devastating floods. Villages were damaged over a wide area. The total number of deaths was never properly assessed but one estimate in the Wapi area was 10%.[18] Most people were killed when houses collapsed and caught fire, while some were caught on river flats by floods or buried in landslides. Aftershocks continued for some weeks.

The Urat now say they believed the earthquake occurred because a Catholic priest attacked a *masalai* dwelling in a boulder outcrop in the mountain range. A number of Urat men undertook the extremely dangerous journey over the shattered mountain range to the SVD station at Yakamul to ask the priest to stop the aftershocks. In the villages, bodies were arranged so that fluids from their decomposition dripped into the large cracks which had appeared in the ground. I cannot make any direct association between the earthquake and attitudes to health care, except to observe that its occurrence in 1935 when the repercussions of colonialism were being keenly felt can only have provided even further instability, even if the direct effect was short-lived. Another major "earthquake had occurred in 1906 and they are a well known phenomenon in this area.

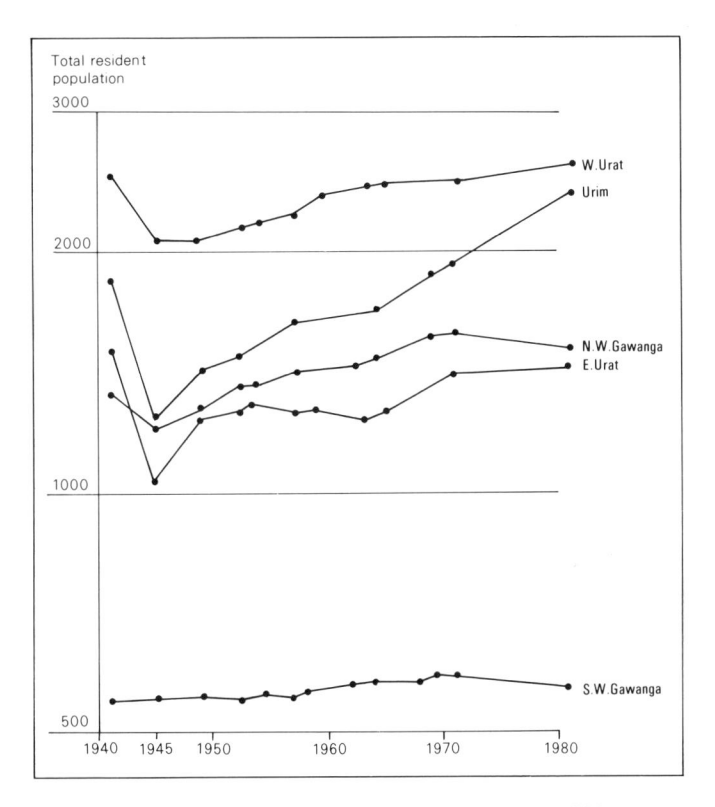

Fig. 5. Population change in five foothills census divisions, 1942–1982.

In 1942 Japanese troops landed on the New Guinea coast and forced the Australian colonial administration and the handful of foreigners there to withdraw. On the coast between Aitape and Wewak what have been called "marked disloyalty and criminal acts of violence" occurred.[19] Catechists of the Catholic Society of the Divine Word (SVD) were heavily involved. Two German worker priests and an Australian labor recruiter were murdered during this period. In 1944 Aitape was recaptured. Australian troops then forced the Japanese back to the east towards

Yangoru on both sides of the ranges. Villages in the direct path of the fighting were destroyed and people forced to take refuge for up to a year in temporary bush shelters. Inland of Aitape, the dysentery which is described above caused many deaths but, in the Dreikikir area, where the dispersion of villagers into the forest in the face of fighting probably prevented the spread of the dysentery, populations were also reduced by between 20% and 30% between 1941 and 1945. Here the adult population was reduced more than the child population. Only in the south, well away from the fighting and the dysentery, did village populations increase very slightly (Fig. 5). In the battle zone, villagers were subjected to aerial bombardment, forced labour, execution and cannibalism in addition to severe living conditions and shortage of food. When the fighting was over, many people received medical treatment from military patrols or attended the military aid post which had been set up at Yambes village to treat wounded soldiers prior to their evacuation by carriers to Aitape.[20]

Many young men were directly involved in the war as police and soldiers, or as carriers and laborers. Some were taken from Rabaul to Kokoda by the Japanese, then captured and drafted into the Australian forces. Others accompanied patrols behind Japanese lines in the Sepik. The outcome was a mixing of men from different cultural backgrounds similar to but more extensive than that which occurred at the plantations and mines, and the further exchange of ideas and practices related to illness and misfortune.

Although the Society of the Divine Word became established on the islands off Aitape in 1896, no permanent missions were set up inland of the ranges until after the Pacific War. Priests established campsites in the hills which they visited and took some youths to the coast for schooling and training as catechists. During this period the SVD did more evangelizing than education or health work. Some priests used an approach which was heavily criticized by at least one Australian officer, who blamed what he called "malevolent sorcery fears" on "declining population, disruption of the traditional social organisation, and mental confusion aggravated by two conflicting sets of religious beliefs."[21] After the war, both the SVD and the South Seas Evangelical Mission (SSEM) built bases at Dreikikir. Both missions became involved in delivering health services to villagers, but the SSEM became involved in vigorous evangelizing. Although the SVD had evangelized before the war, when the SSEM began evangelizing after the war there was a wider comprehension of Pidgin, mission staff were living permanently in the area, and the trauma of the war was fresh in peoples' minds. This made the SSEM evangelical programme particularly influential.

Senior SSEM staff working in the area in the 1970s were of the opinion that the local *masalai* and *tambaran* spirits were manipulated by the Devil. Sorcery and millenarianism were caused by the local spirits taking possession of leading individuals at the behest of the Devil, whose fundamental aim was to confuse and distress the people and prevent them from accepting Jesus as their savior. Almost all customary ceremony was also thought to be associated with the Devil. SSEM staff had received very detailed and probably exaggerated information about initiation ceremonies and sorcery killings from men who, in order to be baptized into the mission, had participated in public confessions. At these confessions it was not uncommon for people to become hysterical, go into trances and speak in an unintelligible manner, all of which was explained by the missionaries as the spirit of Jesus entering their bodies.

I have no detailed understanding of the SSEM's position on the cause of illness. A tragic incident in which an infant born to a missionary couple was seriously handicapped was viewed as a test of their faith. Nevertheless, for villagers, the corollary of the position that the Devil is the ultimate origin of sorcery is that to avoid misfortune and serious illness, one must reject all of the old beliefs and totally accept Jesus, for only in this way will individuals and perhaps their children (because children are not baptized some uncertainty exists over their position) be protected from sorcery and spirit induced illnesses. Christians must use only Western medicines and prayer and must not seek help from local curers or take part in sorcery divinations (see for example Christian Mission in Many Lands 1977: 12).

Nor can I comment with any authority on the attitudes of the Catholic mission staff towards illness. At a general level they express secular and scientific views. In the case of birth control techniques, I can only observe that I have never overheard Maternal and Child Health (MCH) nurses offering women birth control advice. Although it is unlikely that they would do so in my presence, research in the Madang area suggests that non-mission MCH nurses also give very little family planning advice (Reid 1984). I do have firsthand evidence of a local priest, who has since left the area, destroying a letter from the government health center referring a woman to the family planning clinic in Maprik.

RESPONSES

I now wish to present evidence which shows that the foothills communities responded to the changed situation in which they found themselves in three main ways: they adopted new forms of sorcery and sorcery divination to better protect themselves from what they believed was an increase in the level of sorcery activity; they resisted, as far as they were able, the imposition of public hygiene regulations and enforced hospitalization; but at the same time they enthusiastically accepted medication offered to them by foreigners outside of hospitals. I suggest that these apparently paradoxical patterns of behavior, which are not dissimilar from present-day patterns, are explicable in terms of a marked reluctance in the individual and the community to lose control over illness and misfortune.

Contagion and control

A clear distinction must be made between the short-lived, violent, easily identifiable, discrete smallpox and dysentery epidemics and the less severe but more frequent influenza epidemics. The former created a crisis which had to be met immediately and rationalized afterwards, while the latter created a long term problem which allowed a slower and more purposeful reaction.

The short-lived epidemics are important because of insights they offer into village attitudes to the control of illness and misfortune. Among the Urat, the smallpox epidemic is now said to have been caused by a villager who used the powers of a *masalai* to take revenge on the people who killed his young son with sorcery, a similar explanation to that given to Wedgewood on Manam Island, 300 kilometers away to the east (Wedgewood 1934). The Gnau say the 1943 dysentery epidemic was caused by Taklei, a local spirit responsible for epidemic disease among humans and pigs (Lewis 1977).

Urat and Gnau responses to these killing epidemics were similar. At Rauit, where people who experienced the epidemic described it to Lewis, the sickness lasted about three months. After remaining in the village for about a month, people began to disperse into forest refuges. In many cases the dead were not buried and food became short as people were too weakened to bring it from the gardens. Lewis' view on reactions to the epidemic in Rauit are important, not just because he is medically qualified and was specifically studying the knowledge of illness, but because he introduces the concept of control. He argues people based their responses on "the impotence of what they knew to control the situation" (Lewis 1977: 230).

The Rauit, Tumam and Manam accounts of these epidemics contain graphic descriptions of a loss of control; unburied dead, children dying in numbers, shortages of food and finally flight into the forest. After the event however, in the Tumam and Manam cases, control is regained by placing the cause of the epidemic with a person living right in the community. In the Rauit case, Taklei is a well known local spirit who is said by some to have a benevolent brother who protects humans by killing pigs to keep the man-killing Taklei placated. Although the Gnau appear to accept less control over the event than the Urat or Manam islanders (is this because the epidemic is relatively recent?), it is explicable in local terms, and is not a random event.

Lewis (1977: 230) also discusses the problem posed by the fact that although the Gnau have a good practical understanding of contagion, "ideas about infection have a marginal place in [their] usual understanding of illness and its causes." The Tumam story also contains clear accounts of quarantine practices. It is possible this part of the story has been added later, following experiences with other epidemics, perhaps dysentery on the Wau goldfields where quarantine measures were observed, or it is possible information about quarantine procedures spread with the disease from the German outposts from which it originated. If neither of these possibilities are true, then the only alternative is to accept that the Tumam villagers had previous experience either of smallpox or of similar epidemics. This seems unlikely, for although dispersal into isolated areas is a highly effective way to reduce the severity of an epidemic, the dispersal should occur as soon as the disease appears and not after most people have become infected. If the disease was previously known immediate dispersion would have been the expected reaction.

Knowledge of quarantine measures, however learned, logically implies a good understanding of the concept of contagion. Contagion as an explanation of mild illness is widespread and predates colonialism. The Gnau explicitly recognize it in pigs and in minor human disorders. In 1932 Aitoa residents blamed colds and mild influenza on contagion and told Mead this was the cause of an epidemic of what seems to have been distemper which killed all the village dogs. Tumam villagers blame contagion for colds and even for illnesses like dengue fever which from experience in Rabaul and Lae, they know affect large numbers of people, and rarely cause complications. But as an explanation of a disease which causes serious illness and deaths, contagion is quite inadequate. Contagion is apparently random and purposeless. But it is important that people should not die without good reason. If it is assumed illness and death strikes in a random manner, then it must also be assumed that men have no influence over the natural and supernatural world. The universe becomes chaotic and unpredictable. It is only when people lose confidence in their ability to control a disease that they panic and flee.

Innovation

Influenza and pneumonia epidemics were less spectacular than smallpox or dysentery and caused symptoms not dissimilar to existing diseases. The most noticeable change in the villages would have been an increase in morbidity and mortality among adults. The most obvious explanation was an increase in sorcery.

The 1930s was a period in which the spread, exchange and adoption of new forms of sorcery and new methods of sorcery divination were widespread. It is probable that this would have occurred in the absence of new diseases, but the coincidence of new infections with familiar symptoms and the availability of new forms of sorcery and divination combined to form a powerful and reflexive situation in which the existence of one factor confirmed the existence of the other. A greater number of young adult deaths was viewed as evidence of an increase in sorcery killings, which was confirmed by the knowledge that new forms of sorcery were being brought into the foothills. Divination techniques, old and new, relied heavily on preconceived public opinion and confirmed the fears of increased sorcery. The response among individuals and groups was to seek to acquire the new sorcery as a defense against others who already possessed it and as a means of attacking old enemies. The new methods of divination were sought to better diagnose who was causing the illness. None of this activity contradicted the generally held belief that it was humans who controlled the magic or the means of influencing supernatural beings and so the means of causing or deflecting illness and misfortune.

Sanguma sorcery began spreading into the Torricelli and Prince Alexander Ranges in the 1930s. Mead describes:

the imported magic of *sagumeh,* a form of magic which has swept the entire coast from Madang to beyond Wewak in recent years. It is popularly supposed to have come from Madang, but there is not enough evidence to state this with certainty. (Mead 1947: 202)

At Dreikikir, *sanguma* is said to have spread inland from the north during the same period, with men giving pigs and shell rings in exchange for up to two months training in the materials and techniques.

The practices were also learned by villagers during labor contracts on the Gazelle Peninsula, and in the Madang and Wau areas. Wedgewood (1934) describes a form of sorcery said to be indigenous to Manam called *nabwa* which is very similar to modern descriptions of what is known in Pidgin as *sanguma* at Dreikikir. A second form of sorcery, *dzere,* was said not to have been "practised in Manam before the advent of the white man and the introduction of the system of indentured labour, although others maintain that it was learnt from the mainland long before this" (1934: 70–71). This sorcery was spreading on Manam "since men who have gone to work in Rabaul and elsewhere have purchased the knowledge of how to make it from fellow-workers belonging to other places" (1934: 71). Of these "other places" Aitape and Rabaul are noted as the abode of "particularly powerful sorcerers". Because almost all foothills laborers were indentured in Aitape, they were known in Rabaul and Madang as "Aitapes". *Dzere* sorcery involves the collection of exuviae and the illnesses caused by it can "almost always" be distinguished from those caused by *nabwa*. Burridge describes a form of magical/physical assault very similar to descriptions of modern *sanguma* said to be indigenous to Bogia called *ranguma* (Burridge 1960: 59). So it seems probable that as Torricelli sorcery was spreading to the Madang coast and Manam via Rabaul, Madang coast sorcery was spreading to the Torricellis by the same channels.

In both places, the introduced sorcery was considered much more threatening than the old. On Manam,

> ... the course which the illness takes largely determines native diagnosis. For example, the mild attack of influenza, or a bad cold, is usually dismissed as being merely an illness. Should the attack be somewhat more severe, with pain in the back and limbs, *dzere* is usually suspected, while a really serious attack, resulting as it often does in death from pneumonia is clearly recognized as the result of *nabwa* ... it is not unusual, if a person who has been said to be suffering from *nabwa* recovers – particularly if the patient be a woman or child or elderly person – for the people to decide that the cause of the illness must after all have been *dzere,* since, had it really been *nabwa,* the patient must have died. (Wedgewood 1934: 72)

In her "stream of events" in Alitoa, Mead explains she recorded "everything which seemed significant", but admits not leaving the village for the whole of her time there. In circumstances where people spend long periods in their gardens, this has probably exaggerated the relative importance of some events. Even so the diary has rarely a day in which an argument or discussion about the cause of an illness or an accident does not take place. Mead has no way of comparing the frequency of sorcery accusations and investigations she observes to that of an earlier period and she makes no comment on the level of illness and sorcery related activity, seemingly accepting it as normal.

What is not normal for Alitoa is the almost weekly divinations in which young men, who have learned the technique during labour contracts on the coast, use real or pretended trances to discover the location of exuviae taken and hidden in the village and to answer questions about the causes of illnesses or accidents. The individuals carrying out the divinations exercise great skill in making pronouncements which fit majority opinions about an event and which are adaptable to sudden changes in opinion. Mead is quite open about her manipulation of the divinations so as to avoid village reactions which will inconvenience her fieldwork.

Resistance

The village response to enforced public hygiene regulations before the war was to resist them. People did not understand why they had to deep bury corpses and were distressed that normal mortuary practices could not be carried out. The prominent role of cemeteries in post-war millenarian movements, large and small, cannot be unrelated to the enforcement of these regulations.

The persistence with which people continued to bury their dead in houses is impressive. The last exhumation and house burning ordered by a government officer was recorded among the Urat in 1952. It seems probable that neither the enforced use of a cemetery nor the construction of deep pit latrines did much to improve village hygiene. People say that with the easily observable platforms banned, burials were increasingly made in shallow house graves. When it was known a government patrol was in the area the grave was covered with a thin layer of soil over palm spathes. Thus the policy probably brought more people into closer contact with decaying corpses and not, as was intended, fewer.

Whether or not village latrines were much used, present-day latrines are not hygienic. The dirt floors are usually soiled and wet, and the pits are a seething mass of maggots. Pit latrines in this state probably bring more people into direct contact with the faeces and bowel parasites of others than log squatting ever did and do not reduce the level of infection by flies. It is most unlikely these measures alone greatly changed the existing pattern of morbidity and mortality in the foothills villages.[22]

Acceptance

From the beginning of colonial contact however, people were more than willing to accept medical treatment from foreigners. In Alitoa in 1932, Mead wrote,

> Every native in New Guinea considers it to be one of the duties of any white man to bandage his sores. We kept a large supply of standard remedies on hand; every morning ... I had a line of people with cuts, tropical ulcers, yaws sores inflamed eyes, burns, tinea, *kuskus* [scabies], etc. and babies for cough medicine and castor oil ... They were unendingly grateful and appreciative of the dressing of wounds and sores.

But she goes on to note,

> Treating an illness was always a ticklish matter. Sorcery involved here and various native remedies, magical concoctions and emetics were likely to interfere with the cure. (1947: 240)

Geological survey teams who had the latest drugs available carried a medical chest which contained "*grilli* [tinea] ointment, petroleum jelly, lysol, sulphur powder, boracic ointment, boracic acid powder, chloride of lime, concentrated iodine, acriflavine, glaucous salts, cotton wool and lint."[23] Only sulphur powder, which was used to treat tropical ulcers was more effective than many local remedies. Mead's deprecatory remarks about "native remedies" and "magical concoctions" are unfair. When Alitoa villagers came to her seeking medical treatment she could offer only quinine and one or two popular purgatives of the time, castor oil and calomel (mercurous chloride, no longer used because of its toxicity). At almost the same time in Rabaul, a plantation manager was fined for punishing his labourers for not working hard enough by administering doses of "castor oil, quinine and epsom salts."[24]

Until the late 1930s the colonial medical service had little to offer. Villagers could not suture deep wounds and did not handle well broken bones, head injuries and obstetrical problems, but they could and did treat cuts and abrasions, ulcers, stomach upsets, headaches and skin diseases. People had a good knowledge of a wide range of herbal remedies. For example, the Urat knew how to treat tropical ulcers. The sap of a vine was used to clean out the dead flesh and the ulcer was scraped until raw. It was then packed, and repacked daily, with the shavings of a mushroom and tightly bound with leaves and vine. The treatment was long and drawn out, extremely painful in the early stages and involved the work of searching for the mushroom in the forest. This, combined with the belief that the ulcer was being caused by a *masalai* or sorcery, dissuaded most people from persevering, but some men show scars the size of a ten cent coin which they claim were ulcers treated in this manner. Similarly, a long and painful treatment for tinea was known. Despite this knowledge people eagerly sought introduced medicines. Alitoa men frequently came to Mead for a dose of purgative which they seemed to believe could protect them against some forms of sorcery. In addition, European medical chests contained convenient forms of treatment for cuts and burns, which were also decorative: white bandages on dark skins.

The general ineffectiveness of foreign medicine ceased with the introduction of novarsenabenzol injections for yaws. People literally mobbed patrols administering them. Stan Christian, a medical assistant based at Aitape in the 1930s, tells of being invited to administer yaws treatments in villages which only a month previously had scattered into the forest to avoid an administration patrol and had threatened to attack police sent to bring them in.[25] The rapidity with which the sores (known in Urat as *lesion-masalai*) healed was associated with the means of administering the treatment, by injection, and not with the drug itself. The real miracle drugs, antibiotics, which were introduced immediately after the war, were also injected into the body and served to confirm the view widely held today that no treatment is complete without a *siut*.[26]

Fig. 6. On the way to the health center. Severely ill or injured patients must be carried long distances over difficult country to reach a health center. This young man fell from a tree during forest clearing for cultivation and was bleeding from the ears and concussed. His mother meticulously recovered all the drops of blood which had fallen onto the leaf litter on the forest floor, to prevent the blood being taken by a *masalai* or a sorcerer.

PRESENT-DAY PATTERNS

Three features of present day health care have struck me during research for this paper. First is the similarity between Mead's and Wedgewood's descriptions of the handling of illness and misfortune in Alitoa and on Manam Island in the 1930s, and much of what I have observed in passing during almost twenty months residence in Tumam village between 1972 and the present. Second, most of the practices described by Mead and Wedgewood are new, whereas in Tumam in the 1970s and 1980s people speak of what they are doing as though it is customary, although most adults can still distinguish between pre- and post-colonial practices when pressed. Third, I am continually impressed at the number of people who would almost certainly have died or suffered a serious illness in the absence of two drugs, chloroquin and penicillin, and I am forced to conclude that the pattern of morbidity and mortality which existed from the early 1900s to the 1950s has now been replaced with a pattern which is more like the pre-colonial pattern, except that today many infant deaths are prevented and the lives of older people are being extended.[27] This change had become discernible in some parts of the country by 1969 (Scragg 1969). With this change, the deep concern over illness and increased sorcery which was expressed during the colonial period and which was at its peak immediately following the war, has now been considerably reduced.

The present-day pattern is one of persistent beliefs in spirit- and sorcery-induced illness; the common use of village curers who most adults consult before approaching government or mission health services; and a substantial use, especially for children, minor illnesses in adults, the immediate relief of pain and for trauma, of government or mission health services. In the latter case however, people commonly do not finish courses of treatment and strenuously avoid hospitalization wherever possible.[28]

Causes of illness and misfortune

All except very minor illnesses are thought to be due to supernatural causes, even by people who have received quite extensive basic medical training, including all APOs and many higher level staff.[29] This is not a surprising situation; rather it is to be expected (Watson 1968).

Most ordinary village men and women continue not to classify individual diseases by generic terms. Diagnosis still depends more on the recent activities of the patients and their social position than on the symptoms. Thus a young boy with a large boil on his buttock and a middle-aged man with mild pneumonia have both offended a *masalai,* the boy by shouting and throwing stones into a pool in a stream near where the family is gardening and the man by hunting near a patch of wild taro known to be frequented by the spirit.

Diagnosis and prognosis change as the disease progresses or more evidence as to the cause comes to light. An attractive young woman, married to a sickly, tinea-covered nobody, is carrying on an almost open affair with one of her husband's senior clansmen and when she develops pneumonia it is universally agreed that someone, probably her lover's wife who is childless, has arranged for a sorcerer to kill her. This theory is strengthened when the wife returns to the safety of her brothers' village. The sick woman is taken from curer to curer, all of whom confirm the diagnosis. Almost comatose, she lies surrounded by women, already wailing in mourning, who repeatedly state in loud voices that she is dying. Her lover openly weeps and her husband sits stunned and silent. I argue that if she is as good as dead then if I can arrange transport, nothing can be lost if she is taken to the health center. After some discussion this is agreed and she receives a massive dose of antibiotic and recovers. On her return to the village it is decided that the wife is innocent of causing the sorcery and she returns home, and that the woman had trespassed on a *masalai*.

In the previous case, the woman was willing to go to the hospital but was prevented by male clansmen. In other cases adults make strenuous efforts not to go to the health center. The most commonly stated reason is fear of a sorcery attack in the open wards, surrounded by strangers. Older men also dislike the authority that orderlies have over them. However, I have yet to experience an ill or injured person refuse treatment. When an older man accidently stabbed his thigh on a freshly cut bamboo and it became grossly swollen, he absolutely refused assistance to get to the health center. But he readily accepted an offer to administer a course of antibiotics to him. He remained in his house surrounded by his clansmen to protect him from attack while he was in his weakened state. He was profusely grateful upon his recovery. Another older and influential man who became ill with pneumonia refused hospitalization but was taken forcibly to the health center by a government officer. Various local curers had already prognosed death, the result of a *sanguma* attack vividly described by the patient. Although unable to walk, the patient arranged his escape from the health center and disappeared from the local area. Some weeks later he was found staying with his brother at the military barracks in Wewak, where he had been treated at the clinic and where, presumably, he felt secure from further assaults.

Maternal and child health clinics

Similar attitudes are held by many women towards MCH clinics. In the 1970s, when the MCH clinics were run by Australian Catholic layworkers, women greatly appreciated the care and concern for their well-being expressed by the nurses, but resented the authority these outsiders had over their lives. Women were anxious lest they should be forced to bring up a deformed child because the nurses insisted on seeing all newborn infants and cross-examined mothers on the circumstances of an infant's death. Threats to report infanticides to the government officer were made and the nurses often resorted to this authority to force parents to take their seriously under-nourished children to the mission health center.

Fig. 7. Child spacing. Despite two-year spacing of children as a result of restrictions on intercourse, many women are either pregnant or lactating for much of their adult life. This woman, known in the village as a good mother and an extremely hard-working person, has never lost a child. An elder son is missing from the photograph.

Immediately after Independence the clinics were taken over by Health Department nurses. Unable to get regular transport from the Papua New Guinean government officer, the nurses did not meet assembled mothers at regular clinics and women rapidly stopped waiting for them. The clinics are once more administered by the Catholic mission, but are largely conducted by Papua New Guinea nurses. Most are unmarried and youthful. Reid's description of Madang MCH clinics could apply equally well at Dreikikir (Reid 1984).

The most appreciated part of the MCH service is the ante-natal examination. Serious difficulties and deaths in childbirth are common. A breech presentation or a retained placenta throw the community into panic. Yet women remain reluctant to deliver their children at a special ward established by the MCH nurses at Dreikikir. The most commonly voiced complaint is the bossiness of the nurses, but the impracticality of waiting at the health center for labour to begin is another disincentive.

The glasman

Village curers are male, and are known by the Pidgin term of *glasman*. "Glassing" involves looking into a person's body in search of sorcery material or other objects (known in Pidgin as *doti* or "dirt") which may have been placed there by a sorcerer or a *masalai*. The practice came into the Dreikikir area after the war and became associated with a millenarian movement. Most *glasmen* are ex-sorcerers who have publicly renounced sorcery but have maintained their skills at seeking and finding sorcery materials and healing people. Older *glasmen* are often ex-servicemen or men who have travelled widely, but younger men are now taking up the profession.[30] *Glasmen* commonly make house calls, but can be consulted in their homes. A consultation consists of a careful external examination followed by a long cross-examination, which seeks to reveal any possible actions on the part of the patient which might have brought the illness upon him. The patient is asked to recall all movements and places visited during previous weeks and is asked about arguments, flirtations, thefts, sexual liaisons and any other indications of the origins of the malevolence. Treatments usually involve the removal of foreign objects from the body of the patient by sleight-of-hand or mouth. These objects are placed in a coconut shell of cold water to neutralize their power and are shown to the patient and onlookers who are invariably greatly impressed. Chewed ginger is also sprayed over the patient from the *glasman's* mouth and wiped off with special taro leaves in exaggerated flourishes which emphasize the sweeping away of the *doti* which is causing the illness. The questioning may be repeated if the illness does not improve and people often reveal matters which they had hoped to keep secret, but only after two or three sessions and a worsening of the illness.

It is not uncommon for *glasmen* to suggest to their patients that they should seek treatment at an aid post or health center. I am uncertain whether this derives from the actions of a government officer who some years ago used his magisterial powers against *glasmen* who he thought were preventing people from seeking proper treatment or whether *glasmen*, who are usually insightful and intelligent men, realize the effectiveness of drug therapy. I think the latter is more likely. *Glasmen* also frequently treat patients in the health center wards at night when the professional staff are absent, but with the cooperation of local staff.

Aid post orderlies

The attitudes of aid post orderlies (APOs) towards their work and their patients are an important influence on present-day health care usage. The most important difference between the pre-war medical *tultuls* and their post-war APO counterparts is not education or training (although the APOs have received more formal education and training), but the treatments which are available to the APOs. The standard treatment given in the aid post, penicillin, chloroquin and aspirin – known locally in Pidgin as *pul* [full] *tritmen* and which is administered almost as a matter of course without any firm diagnosis, the sprayman approach – is likely to markedly reduce the symptoms and probably effect a cure for most common illnesses in adults and children (Scragg 1968). In addition, the aid post usually has supplies of bandages and sticking plaster, burn creams and disinfectants, which are more convenient than bush remedies and more decorative.

Another important difference between the two services is that aid post orderlies are now part of a very large and unwieldy public service and have in recent years taken industrial action to gain better conditions. Medical *tultuls* gained considerable status and influence from their positions and the first generation of post-war APOs were also recruited when almost no other paid positions were open to local people in their own areas. They were highly motivated and seem to have had excellent relations with upper echelons of the health service. At this level the aid post was seen as a critical part of a campaign to improve public health. When the first APO appointed in the Dreikikir area was called "a black bastard" by an Australian medical assistant, the district medical officer, Dr John McInerney, flew in and removed the offending Australian within hours of hearing of the incident.[31] Perhaps as a result of these attitudes towards them, some of the first post-war generation of aid post orderlies seem to have viewed the position in terms of a vocation and believed they were participating in bringing about radical changes to village life. Others seem to have thought they were participating in a transfer of mystical knowledge from whites to blacks. On the other hand, many orderlies married locally and participated in the local community and were just as likely to be involved in sorcery investigations, disputes over women, pigs or land and local politics (two former APOs have become Members of Parliament and two others local government council presidents) as the medical *tultuls* of Alitoa were in 1932.

Today the position is a local employment opportunity, with lower educational requirements than clerical positions and better status than laboring. Most APOs do not view their positions as providing a service to the community and have a restricted view of their role. I have offered my personal medical kit to two retired APOs with the suggestion that they provide the simple service which I was providing in the village, of supplying aspirin and chloroquin, poultices, sticking plaster, diarrhea and cough mixtures on request. Both refused and independently used the same justification: they were no longer being paid by the government to provide that service, it was the government's responsibility to provide health care and not theirs and they would only accept the kit for their own personal use. Both these men are responsible, caring, influential villagers.

I am uncertain how to interpret these attitudes. These two men appear to lack the sense of community with which I view their village. Against my apparently romantic notions of the unitary village, based on the generally close and warm relationships people have with one another, they seem to view the village as comprising individual extended families in never ceasing competition, expressed by covert sorcery attacks on individuals. Only if they become part of an external body, the government, will they provide those who are their potential belligerents with a service which may be advantageous to them.

Changing concerns

In the early 1950s people in the Dreikikir area made several concerted attempts to radically change their social, economic and political situation. From 1952 to 1956 they planted hill rice which they thought would bring them the wealth and hence the power they saw in the hands of foreigners. When this enterprise collapsed a millenarian movement involving public hysteria, shaking, fainting, visions, marching and bowing Japanese style, spread rapidly from village to village. Since that year a number of more localized movements have appeared and disappeared until, in 1971, a regional movement known as the Peli Association spread from the Yangoru area to Dreikikir, where it was widely accepted (Hwekmarin et al. 1971, Allen 1976, May 1982). The central concerns of both movements were village autonomy and the power to maintain it against outside influences but, in the 1956 movement, sorcery, illness and death held a central position whereas in the 1971 movement, political and economic disparities between urban and rural areas was the central theme.

Many of the themes of the 1956 movement were drawn from the New Testament. They predicted the return of ancestors and the coming of an era in which sickness and death would no longer exist. A number of women were raised from the dead. The leader of the movement received the power to *"glass"* sorcery from his deceased daughter at her funeral and he and others promised to drive out sorcery and sorcerers from the community. In contrast, in 1971, self-government, the inability of village people to get access to steady cash incomes, general living conditions and a fear that Papua New Guineans from other parts of the country would rule over them as Australian officers had done, were what people were most concerned with.

In the period from 1956 to 1972, chloroquin, penicillin, sulphonamides and childhood inoculations came into common use. Morbidity and mortality were reduced to the point where they are no longer a central concern in people's lives. The death of a young adult does cause a flurry of anti-sorcery activity, divinations, public meetings and outlandish accusations, but these deaths do not now occur often enough to maintain the same level of public concern which was apparent in the early 1950s.[32]

In 1979, when public concern over sorcery was raised to the point where protest meetings were held and the local government council debated the matter, the concern was not directly related to illness or deaths. A number of youths had been taught *sanguma* techniques by a few older men so they could break and enter retail stores while invisible, and so they could kill people who tried to prevent a robbery. Police arrested the whole gang in a dawn raid and concern died down again.

CONCLUSION

The argument being advanced in this paper is that present day patterns of health service use are the outcome of the experiences of villagers during the previous 100 years. During this period patterns of morbidity and mortality changed from one in which people who survived childhood were "healthy" and suffered little major illness until their old age. Immediately preceding and following colonial contact the spread of new infectious diseases, particularly influenza and influenzal-pneumonia, increased the relative level of illness and death in mature adults. This pattern continued until the Pacific War when, in areas affected by the fighting, the adult population decreased by up to 25%. After the war the introduction of drug therapies and inoculations through rural health centers, aid posts and MCH clinics, brought about a further change in morbidity and mortality until in the 1980s the incidence of illness and death as the primary concern of village people has been replaced by economic and political concerns. Demographic evidence in support of this argument is almost non-existent but can be inferred from evidence of changed disease patterns.

Other changes which accompanied colonialism and are relevant to a study of present-day behavior were the enforcement of public hygiene regulations and compulsory hospitalization, the medical *tultul* system and the attitude of villagers to introduced drugs. Regulation and compulsion were resisted but new treatments were enthusiastically accepted.

This pattern, together with present day accounts of past epidemics and explicit statements by villagers about their objectives in initiatives in cash cropping and millenarianism, all point to an underlying concern with control. Concern with control exists at a number of levels: control over the means of social and economic advancement by outsiders; control of the reproduction of plants and animals through mediation with *masalai* and the *tambaran;* and control over the incidence and management of illness and misfortune within the village.

The future

If this argument is accepted there follow a number of related implications for future health care delivery systems.

First, health delivery systems must be shorn of as much authoritarianism as possible. In most situations in which people have to choose between receiving treatment or avoiding an outside authority, they will choose the latter, even though they know the outside authority may well be able to help them and the consequences of their actions may be a long drawn out illness. One difficulty in achieving a lessening of authoritarianism is that it is the lowest level health workers, with whom villagers have most contact, the APO, the health center orderly and the MCH nurse, who are the most overbearing and "bossy". Rural extension organizations in Africa have also found that poorly trained people placed in a hierarchical organization, when confronted with sceptical village farmers, become dictatorial and their ability to consult and communicate falls to nil (Morris 1973, Leonard 1977). In Papua New Guinea it is probable that most lower level health workers do not believe the theories of disease and misfortune upon which the health service is based. When confronted with villagers who are unwilling to acknowledge their authority, and uncertain of the basis of what they are offering, lower level health workers understandably resort to what villagers call "big-headedness", or "bossiness".

Second, health administrators and trainers must explicitly accept sorcery as a cause of illness. The persistence of a belief in sorcery and spirit-induced illnesses is striking. Sorcery is recognized in the statutes in the 1971 Sorcery Act but, even though many hospitals in Papua New Guinea allow local curers into their wards, sorcery is not acknowledged as a primary cause of disease and is discussed in teaching and training programs within the rubric of "psychological" or "village beliefs". To be more effective, health workers have to say, "Yes, this disease is caused by sorcery, and this is a treatment which may defeat the sorcery." Whatever approach is used to this problem, a more effective medical service will have to acknowledge the right of the patient to control his or her own illness and to make decisions about it which may not, in the opinion of the health worker, be in the patient's best interest. In the short term, some people, including children, may suffer but, in the long term, given the clear right to manage their own lives and with access to non-authoritarian sources of information, I have confidence that people will begin to make choices which will improve the overall health of the community.

Third, a more effective health delivery service may have to be even more decentralized than at present. Without exception in my experience, sick people are willing to accept drug therapy in conjunction with local curing in their own homes, where they feel secure and in control. It is likely to be very difficult to bring about this change. The health department is being increasingly influenced by the "inverse care law" (Radford 1980) and currently has difficulty keeping up supplies and administrating the present hierarchy of health centers and aid posts.[33] If the attitudes of the Tumam retired APOs are representative, the use of volunteer males does not seem possible. *Glasmen* are usually relatively well paid for their services however, and it may be possible for village level workers to be supplied with drugs and paid a small amount by villagers for each consultation. Whatever the difficulties, if basic treatments were available in the village or, preferably, within the home, more people would receive medication earlier and in circumstances more acceptable to them. The same observation can be applied to village midwifery services.

Fourth, the shift in concern among villagers from illness to social and economic change does not necessarily mean a decline in standards of community health. Worldwide, improvements in community health have been associated more with social and economic improvements than with advancements in medical technology.

Déjà vu?

For the student of Papua New Guinea public health, much of the foregoing will be familiar. More than fifteen years ago Watson (1968) suggested that APOs and other health workers do not accept much of their training about the causes of illnesses and Scragg (1968) argued the cost effectiveness of "properly supervised" rural health workers. More recently Radford (1980) has criticized the lack of attempts to integrate traditional medicine in the health care system and has called for "peripheral care units" based on aid posts and MCH clinics. Nor is there very much which is new for the student of therapeutic systems worldwide. The use of multiple therapies, the importance of close kinship support during illness and the degree to which illness and health care in the village are controlled by outsiders were as important as determinants of responses to diseases in seventeenth century England and in twentieth century Africa (Feierman 1979) as they are in present-day Papua New Guinea.

But the lack of change since 1968 in Papua New Guinea rural health delivery systems, and the probable deterioration in the last five years, means nothing is lost by stating the position yet again and in demonstrating that from the earliest colonial times, villagers have made conscious decisions about illness and health care. They have at no time relinquished to outsiders the control of that care and they are not likely to do so now.

NOTES

1. It is not possible to now establish without question the pre-colonial disease pattern, but it can be inferred from detailed medical studies in villages with little access to medical services. Sturt and Stanhope (1968) and Lewis (1975) are such studies.
2. See also Lewis (1975) and, for a pre-war observation Wedgewood (1934).
3. The term "epidemic era" was coined first by Scragg (1977).
4. Dan Tyson, who recently completed 12 months of fieldwork in Gweligum, an Abelam village near Maprik, reports older people distinguishing between present-day measles and a pre-contact "measles" which killed many people. The extent and demographic repercussions of the circa 1890 epidemic deserves more attention.
5. New Guinea Annual Report 1936–37. The report on deaths at Yapunda comes from correspondence between G.A.V. Stanley and J.N. Marshall of Oil Search, 25 July 1935, Stanley Papers, Box 9, University of Papua New Guinea (UPNG) Library.
6. New Guinea Annual Report 1937–38 : 55.
7. New Guinea Annual Report 1932–33.
8. New Guinea Annual Report 1938–39.
9. New Guinea Annual Report 1937–38.
10. New Guinea Annual Report 1935–36.
11. Allen (1983) uses fragmentary census material brought together from three archives and from papers in the personal possession of retired officers, to reconstruct population change between 1941 and 1945 in the Torricelli foothills.
12. Notes made by G.A.V. Stanley, from the Village Book. Stanley was sheltering from rain in the village and read through the Village Book for something to do. All village books were destroyed during the Pacific War. Stanley Papers, Diary "I", File 9, Box 7, UPNG Library.

13. Interview with John S. Milligan, South Caulfield, Melbourne, 2 December 1982.
14. "Wanali village was first visited in 1928 and since has been visited many times by patrols and by geologists engaged in the search for oil and there had been no cause to anticipate trouble." Pacific Island Monthly, 15 August 1939: 37.
15. J.K. McCarthy, Patrol Report, 1936-37, Report of a Patrol to the Wam, Muihan and Urat Areas, 8 January 1936 to 18 February 1936. Pacific Manuscripts Bureau microfilm PMB616.
16. Stan Christian was a medical asssistant in the Sepik district between 1915 and 1942. Following the war, he worked extensively on malaria in the highlands. He died in 1984. Just before his death Mr Christian talked about his Sepik experiences in an interview with Donald Denoon and myself.
17. C.N. Sinnamon, DADH HQ ANGAU, Australian Military Forces, Hygiene Inspection: Lae-Wewak-Aitape ANGAU War Diary, 7 September 1945. Document 1/10/1, Australian War Memorial Museum. It is likely this comment reflects heavily the opinions of government officers serving in the area before the war.
18. McCarthy (1963). This event has never been investigated for its impact on village life. It did cause the change in location of a large number of villages. Deaths directly due to the earthquake appear to have been relatively few, with more in the west than the east. Australians who were in the area describe the experience as the most terrifying of their lives, including wartime experiences behind Japanese lines.
19. D.M. Fienberg, Patrol Report Aitape No.4 of 1943/44, Kombio, Wam, Urat, National Archives of Papua New Guinea. Fienberg, who later as D.M. Fenbury became Secretary of the Department of the Administrator in Papua New Guinea, was a graduate of the University of Western Australia, one of the few field officers with university education during this period.
20. Government officers who had visited the area before the war wrote of the "pitiful state" of people when they re-entered the area following the defeat of the Japanese. They recommended the Australian Army's RAP at Yambes village should be kept open after light aircraft evacuation for Australian casualties became possible from Balif. Most patients treated at Yambes were not kept in a ward because of lack of food supplies. Rather they visited for one or two days *en masse* by village, when notified by ANGAU officers. See Patrol Report Aitape No. 3 of 1944-45, Urat Area, National Archives of Papua New Guinea.
21. D.M. Fienberg ibid. Fienberg wrote four foolscap typed pages subtitled "Native Disaffection and the Missions", in which he accused the German missionaries of turning villagers against the government for political reasons, interfering in traditional ceremonies and marriages, and alienating land. He provided detailed evidence of catechists leading villagers against the mission and the government and contrasted the Aitape situation with the Vanimo area, where American priests administered the mission, and where village people remained law abiding and "loyal".
22. In 1945 John Milligan wrote, "It is with "My tongue in my cheek", that I have included pit latrines as part of the installations in rebuilding villages. Pit latrines at their best are not the most efficient. Like the enforcing of medical treatment, it will have to be constantly supervised, and penal sanctions of the NAR applied, if they are to be kept in a sanitary condition. Their own methods of using streams or isolated patches of bush were, in the past, seemingly efficient, but with the higher incidence of dysentery during the Jap occupation, this becomes too dangerous – not that pit latrines are in any way perfect – but they are considered the "lesser of two evils"." Letter to HQ Northern Region from District Officer, Aitape, 1 August 1945, ANGAU War Diary, ibid.
23. Stanley Papers, Box 9 UPNG Library. Oil Search geologists prided themselves on their good health in the field and used the latest drugs available. Jack Fryer, a surveyor with the company, described to me how after a day's work he religiously had

a hot bath using germicidal soap. A folding canvas bath was carried by his party for this purpose. He suffered no tropical ulcers or other serious illness. During the war when such luxuries were impossible he became seriously ill with scrub typhus and other members of his party developed dysentery. Interview, Cairns, 22 November 1976.
24. Rabaul Times, 26 June 1933.
25. Interview, Stan Christian, Canberra 1983.
26. At Dreikikir the local government council passed a regulation banning people from demanding injections from aid posts and the health center. A short time after, the Tumam councillor fell down a steep slippery track on a dark night in pouring rain and twisted his ankle. He demanded and received an injection of antibiotic because he believed he had been pushed over by a *masalai* and that he would get an ulcer on his ankle. He did not, but he did develop a deep abscess at the site of the injection, a not uncommon occurrence.
27. Most of the area under discussion has not been sprayed as part of the Malaria Control campaign. Infants as young as two weeks become seriously ill with malaria. Some die, others become malnourished as a result of repeated attacks, but many are successfully treated with camoquin and aspirin at aid posts and the health center.
28. The main exception to this proviso is people who are receiving treatment for leprosy. They believe that unless they report regularly for their treatment, they will be forcibly removed from the village.
29. The present MP for Dreikikir-Ambunti, Aisimboro Ston, was formerly the aid post supervisor at Dreikikir. He has trained in field pathology and has a good knowledge of infection theory. His father, now dead, was a sorcerer and killed a man to convince a sceptical young son, recently trained as an APO. Mr Ston would like to see a formal scientific investigation into sorcery, not to prove that it works but to find out how it works.
30. The man who was probably the first *glasman* in the area had worked for Australian geologists as a boy and had carried for an Australian guerrilla party during the war. He had also worked on the Gazelle Peninsula. He received his power when he became hysterical at the funeral of his young daughter. After shaking violently he fell unconscious and, while unconscious, he spoke with his daughter who told him the identity of her sorcerer killer and gave him the power to "see" sorcery in people.

Haiveta (1982) describes very similar origins and behavior in relation to *"glassing"* at Vanimo. This phenomenon demands more attention.
31. From a biographical account by Binghoiye (Tomi) Retehi. Tomi had been wounded in action at Finschafen with the New Guinea Infantry Battalion and after his recovery he was trained in first-aid. After the war he received training as an APO at Wewak hospital. He walked from Wewak to Dreikikir to take up his first position. The Australian in charge of the health center had not received prior notification of his coming and after a short sharp and abusive altercation, Tomi walked back to Wewak to report he was not needed at Dreikikir.
32. Deaths which cause the greatest concern are sudden deaths of apparently fit and healthy adults and wasting diseases. The former, which exhibit symptoms of meningitis, cause intense bursts of anti-sorcery activity in which a number of villages may become involved. The latter result in repeated and increasingly desperate attempts by close relatives to find the sorcerer.
33. Problems exist at many levels. Staff who are not paid, or who have great difficulty in getting any response from headquarters over personal matters become disgruntled and inefficient. APOs who are not regularly inspected begin to spend increasing amounts of time away from their posts. Patients who must receive drug therapy regularly, such as epileptics, suffer when the supply of drugs is disrupted.

JOHN BARKER

3. WESTERN MEDICINE AND THE CONTINUITY OF BELIEF: THE MAISIN OF COLLINGWOOD BAY, ORO PROVINCE

INTRODUCTION

We know there are government and mission hospitals. You young people read and write so you know what is happening. I was told by the white priest that the mission and government hospitals give a different medicine. Our Papuan doctors do the same as those in the hospital. When people get sick they must decide whether to go to the village healer or one of the hospitals. You must go to one of these. You will either be better or you will die. You must show some trust that they will make your son, daughter or wife well.

Adelbert Sevaru, an elder in Uiaku village

An important consideration in the examination of situations of medical pluralism in Melanesia is the overall indigenous response to outside initiatives. Given the diffuse and intertwined nature of beliefs and practices concerning health, morality and religion in these societies, it is frequently the case that initiatives and responses that appear unrelated in type and time to the administrators of health programmes may have important bearings upon each other. Many studies throughout the world reveal that cultural factors influence the ways in which people perceive and deal with innovative ideas and practices introduced from the outside. The nature of the innovations themselves and their mode of introduction are no less important. Anthropologists and other scholars often overlook this latter complexity, writing of "Christianity", "capitalism", and "Western medicine" in vague terms without specifying the usually very attenuated versions of these systems of ideas and practices that are actually offered to or forced upon rural peoples in the Third World.

My present aim is to provide an analysis of Maisin medical beliefs and practices, including their use of Western medical facilities, as a single ethnographic situation. The main theme that emerges from the analysis is that up to the present time the Maisin have successfully encompassed the limited Western medical technology available to them within a framework of culturally grounded beliefs and practices. While the direct effects of the introduction of Western medicine on the Maisin's overall notions of health and sickness have probably been quite limited, the framework as a whole has been sensitive to other innovations influencing the Maisin's experience of the moral and the divine.

The analysis is divided into four parts. I first describe the specific historical circumstances in which Western style health care began and continues to be delivered in the Collingwood Bay area of Oro Province. I then examine data collected in a survey to show how the Maisin presently categorize and deal with illnesses. The third section of the analysis deals with each type of curative resort in some detail, showing how they are linked in the course of long and serious ailments into a "hierarchy of resort" (Romanucci-Ross 1977). Finally, I discuss the modality of change in the entire complex of health beliefs and practices.

MEDICAL SERVICES IN THE COLLINGWOOD BAY AREA[1]

The Maisin people live in a series of beach villages along the southern shores of Collingwood Bay in Oro Province, Papua New Guinea. One of several sociolinguistic groups located in Tufi district, they have a resident population of about 1200 with a third more living away in urban centers. Maisin were traditionally gardeners and gatherers, hunters and fishermen; for some time now they have supplemented these subsistence activities with money from sales of beautifully designed bark cloth and remittances sent home from towns by working relatives.

Captain John Moresby made the first recorded exploration of Collingwood Bay in 1873, although there may well have been earlier foreign visitors. Government officers, missionaries and coastal traders began making regular contacts with the Maisin and their neighbors in the 1890s. In 1900, the Administration of (then) British New Guinea created the Northeastern Division and erected a government station at Tufi on Cape Nelson at the northern head of Collingwood Bay. The first Resident Magistrate, the irrepressible C.A.W. Monckton (1922), put a quick and forcible end to inter-tribal raiding, killing some Maisin warriors in the process. The New Guinea Mission of the Anglican Church of Australia also stepped up its activities in the region at the turn of the century. Villagers in the largest Maisin community, Uiaku, accepted Solomon Island teachers into their midst in 1901; other Maisin villages soon followed. European missionaries supervised these "outstations" from their district headquarters at Wanigela, a village located a few kilometers north of the Maisin area. The first baptisms of Maisin villagers took place in 1911; by the beginning of the Second World War most adults had joined the Mission. Since 1962 there has been a national priest stationed in Uiaku village.

Maisin were not slow to take up such lines of economic advancement as were open to them in the colonial situation. Men routinely left their homes for varying lengths of time to work as plantation or mine laborers, as policemen and as Mission teachers. In 1942 most of the able-bodied men in the Collingwood Bay area were conscripted by the Australian wartime administration following the Japanese invasion of mainland New Guinea. After 1945 the Government and the Mission rapidly expanded educational and occupational opportunities for educated nationals. Maisin were among the first to benefit from these developments. Today many of them number among the country's national elite, working as teachers, businessmen, civil servants, priests, doctors, nurses and dentists. Collingwood Bay, however, remains an economic backwater, accessible to the outside world only by small planes and the occasional cargo ship. As in some other parts of Papua New Guinea and Oceania, the chief strategy of economic advancement open to the Maisin has been the export of labor (cf. Carrier 1981).

European missionaries and government officers began supplying some limited medical services to the Maisin from about 1900 (see Chignell 1911). From around 1910 the Mission retained the services of a European nurse at Wanigela. The Administration, on the other hand, was able only to provide intermittent medical care because of its poor finances (Gunther 1972). A Government Medical Officer visited the region on infrequent patrols. Native Medical Assistants accompanied patrol officers in the late 1930s and were apparently warmly received in the villages. In 1947 the administration opened an aid post at the eastern end of Collingwood Bay and the following year the Maisin received their own aid post at Uiaku. By 1960 there were nine aid posts in Tufi district, two of them located in Maisin villages.

Health initiatives were not limited to the provision of medical services. Patrol officers had as one of their main duties the enforcement of various regulations designed to improve village hygiene: the burial of bodies in cemeteries outside of settlements, filling in of swampy areas, destruction of diseased pigs and dogs, and regular clearing of refuse from village grounds. These regulations were enforced by the threat of internment in Tufi gaol. Whatever the overall health benefits of these measures, they appear to have done more to demonstrate the authority of the patrol officers than to teach Maisin the rudiments of European theories of sanitation.

From time to time government officers and missionaries tried to counter sorcerers and local healers. In the case of sorcerers they appear to have had the full support of Maisin communities. Maisin elders describe the sorcerers of forty years and more ago as "bad" men who were well known, respected and greatly feared. Sorcerers are described as then having a role analogous to that reported by Hau'ofa (1981) for the Mekeo. They used their power to create and to cure sicknesses as a sanction on behalf of the leaders and, more generally, in support of the indigenous morality. Maisin evidently saw the arrival of powerful Europeans as an opportunity to break the power of the sorcerers. On at least five occasions between 1904 and 1936, villagers invited visiting missionaries or officers to destroy "charms" that had been surrendered in a public place. By giving up all of their magic, Maisin apparently thought they would be able to purge sorcerers as well. On other occasions patrol officers were asked to try or arrest suspected sorcerers. It is common knowledge today that these measures along with conversion to Christianity destroyed the institution of the sorcerer as he had been known to the ancestors.

But misfortunes continue apace and so Maisin suspect that some men still resort to various forms of mystical attack. Villagers worry that not all men gave up their old "poisons" but have hidden them in their houses or passed them on with their knowledge to their sons. These "poisons" are especially worrisome because the antidotes are not generally known or have been forgotten over time. It is said that a greater number of sorcerers have turned to the use of spirit familiars which are less deadly but harder to detect than the old methods. In more recent times, the increased mobility of the young people has fired fears that novel forms of sorcery techniques purchased in towns are being imported into the villages. The conventional wisdom is that today there are fewer men practicing sorcery than fifty years ago, but the small number who do are virtually uncontrollable.

The healing techniques presently used in Maisin villages appear to have developed in the 1920s and 1930s as offshoots of the Baigona and Taro cults which made their way through the Collingwood Bay area (see Worsley 1968). Although they considered the actions of healers to be generally detrimental to the good health of the local population, government officers were willing to tolerate them so long as they did not interfere with the maintenance of "order" in the villages. The missionaries' attitudes were more ambivalent. The New Guinea Mission of the Anglican Church was a high church organization led by well-educated bishops who generally were sympathetic to what they saw as the simple values and spiritualism of the Papuan villagers and hostile to plans to "develop" Papua for the benefit of foreign capitalists. Some missionaries viewed healers as the unknowing instruments of God. They advocated introducing some form of Christian faith healing to supplement and then replace the indigenous form. This was never done. Other missionaries were far more critical of the healers, seeing their use of spirit familiars as a type of pagan "worship". These missionaries encouraged the local teachers to preach against the healers and to forbid school children from attending healing sessions. Given its limited resources and power in the villages, the Mission was not able to stop the healers. Nor did the provision of aid posts put an end to their popularity, although one of the objectives of introducing the system was, in the words of the Assistant District Officer of the time, to "stamp out" this "unhygienic" practice (Bramwell 1948).

It is possible to detect some mixed motives in the Mission's and the Government's provision of medical services and sporadic opposition to indigenous practices. The success of European medicine served to reinforce the superiority and authority of the Europeans and their religion, to hasten the acceptance of new forms of thought and behaviour, and to keep the young men healthy for working on the plantations and in the mines. But overall, the provision of medical services played a very small role in strategies of evangelization and "civilization". Health measures were introduced for humanitarian reasons and did not form a strategic part of the missionaries' endeavors to alter and improve the moral and religious consciences of converts or the government officers' ongoing work in preserving and remolding the political order. The irony is that Maisin today, as in the past, strongly associate health and sickness with matters of religion, morality and politics.

Initially, the Administration and Anglican Mission directed much of their medical effort against epidemics, many of which resulted from diseases originally introduced into New Guinea by Europeans. In 1905 the Resident Magistrate in Tufi suspended labor recruiting in the area when villages were struck by an unspecified epidemic. Labourers and coastal traders brought in venereal disease: fifty cases were detected in Maisin villages between 1906 and 1913. Influenza struck in 1923 and 1933, followed by whooping cough and dysentery in 1938. Whooping cough and dysentery broke out again in 1950, leaving thirteen people dead in Uiaku alone.[2]

The 1950s and 1960s saw a tremendous expansion in the delivery of medical services to the rural areas of Papua New Guinea. Maisin gained from this in two ways. First, European medical knowledge began to be made available to students in the community schools and, to a much greater extent, in secondary and tertiary educational institutions. A number trained as aid post orderlies, hospital orderlies, nurses, doctors and dentists.[3] Secondly, the quality and variety of health services available to the villagers improved and increased. The mission provided a district health centre at Wanigela staffed by three nurses. A weekly ante-natal clinic was established at Wanigela hospital and the nurses began making regular patrols through local villages to provide direct maternal and child health services. The administration opened its own health centre at Tufi and sponsored patrols through the region to identify and treat cases of tuberculosis, leprosy and other diseases, to carry out malaria eradication programs, and to provide some dental care. In the towns, hospitals were built or expanded and arrangements made for the transportation of people with serious ailments from the rural areas to facilities under the direct supervision of doctors.

Since the late 1970s the system has deteriorated somewhat. With the exception of increasingly irregular baby clinics, there have been no medical patrols through Maisin villages for several years. The burden of most local Western-style medical care falls squarely on the shoulders of the aid post orderlies who work with little supervision or guidance, often many kilometers from their main sources of supplies and advice.

The Maisin have eagerly accepted whatever European medical services have been offered to them. I found no evidence of resistance to Western medicine either in the past or present. Sometimes a seriously ill person is afraid of being taken away to a distant urban hospital where he may have few relatives and may die. Such anxieties are not unknown in industrialized countries. Given the fact that they know little about Western medical theories and techniques and have almost no control over its practitioners, the Maisin's trust in the introduced system of health care is quite remarkable. As we shall see in the next section, this acceptance of Western medicine has not led the Maisin to abandon their indigenous conceptions of health and sickness. Instead they handle European medicine along the lines of pre-existing categories of diseases and curative practices.

CATEGORIES AND CHOICES

If someone gets sick and the village people cannot make them better they send them to the doctors and they recover. But then when Papuans go to the hospitals and the doctors cannot make them better they must go back home so that the local healers can do it. The doctors say, "We cannot find what it is so you should go home and they will cure you there".

Stonewigg Kotena, a healer in Sinipara village

Maisin notions of the cause and treatment of illnesses conform generally to patterns reported in widely spread Melanesian societies (see Burridge 1965, Hamnett and Connell 1981, Lewis 1975, Romanucci-Ross 1977). The Maisin tend to rationalize all misfortunes primarily in terms of their supposed causes and only secondarily in terms of their characteristics. Common misfortunes include sickness, sores, accidents, attacks by wild animals, theft and crop failure. Of physical misfortunes, sickness is considered to be the most threatening, probably because it is the most common cause of death and because the tensions that arise during an instance of serious illness may touch off long-term conflicts within the community. Virtually all villagers attribute most serious ailments to attacks from sorcerers, ghosts and bush spirits. Informants told me that mystical attacks, especially the less deadly ones of ancestral ghosts, may be unprovoked but more often than not an attack is provoked by some moral wrong or slight committed by the victim or his close kin within the community. The study of the ideology of sickness and health in Maisin villages leads inevitably to matters of religion, morality and social conflict.

Towards the end of my fieldwork I undertook a survey of Uiaku and Ganjiga villagers' experience and understanding of various kinds of misfortunes. My intention was to determine the consensus on misfortunes as well as the nature and degree of variations in understanding by different groups of people. I devised a standard open-ended interview schedule in which people were asked about a wide range of misfortunes they might have suffered over the course of their lives including sickness, injuries, infections, violence and theft. The final sample comprised 55 men and women from six age groups.

Inquiries of this nature are always difficult in communities where sorcery beliefs are strong because explanations of misfortune, as Patterson (1974–75) has cogently noted, are often couched in idioms of social conflict. Several of my informants expressed a reluctance to discuss misfortunes in detail because to do so would reopen old quarrels and/or might prompt an attack from a local sorcerer. Most informants gave fairly vague explanations for misfortunes. It is difficult to determine how much of their response derived from genuine ignorance or from fear of being themselves ensorcelled. While the data collected in the survey do not allow the sort of detailed sociological assessment of sorcery accuzations advocated by Marwick (1964), they are revealing of the general structure of Maisin beliefs concerning misfortunes and of the curative options open to sufferers and their kin. As I shall show below, there is a strong consistency in the rationalizations I recorded. While I suspect that some informants held back part of their explanations for particular misfortunes, I have found no reason to believe that anyone deliberately misled me about their experiences or understandings.

The Maisin group all sicknesses, great and small, within the general category of *tatami*. A few ailments are generally referred to by more specific terms. Maisin call malarial attacks, for example, *kororo*, "coldness"; they label manifestations of mental imbalance as *kavakava*; and they identify various types of chest infections as *yaa gaga*, "breath broken". Healers make more specific identifications of diseases; but what these are and whether they form a system I cannot say as I did not investigate this topic. I was able to ascertain that few Maisin show much interest in categorizing types of sicknesses beyond noting their degree of seriousness. On the other hand, other types of physical misfortunes are more specified. The Maisin possess no word that could be accurately translated as "accident" but instead speak about various cuts, scrapes, animal bites and so forth. Sores are often described as a type of sickness, especially when they develop into ulcers. Although there would appear to be an implicit distinction between sicknesses and other bodily misfortunes, the Maisin rationalize all physical misfortunes along the same general lines. Unless indicated otherwise, therefore, the analysis given below of indigenous ideas of the cause and cure of diseases and ailments should also be extended to cuts, bruises, sores, broken bones and other non-disease complaints.

TABLE 1
Experience of ailments

			Sicknesses				Sores and accidents			
Year of birth	Sex	No.	Unknown	Casual	Spirit	Poison	Unknown	Casual	Spirit	Poison
before 1940	M	18	4	4	4	5	1	4	1	1
	F	17	3	2	7	1	1	2	1	1
1940–1960	M	10	1	1	1	–	1	3	–	–
	F	10	2	–	6	–	4	–	–	–
Totals	M	28	5	5	5	5	2	7	1	1
	F	27	5	2	13	1	5	2	1	1
		55	10	7	18	6	7	9	2	2

As I noted earlier, the Maisin generally attend more to causes than symptoms when distinguishing diseases. Table 1 summarizes the main categories of physical misfortunes and the number of respondents in the survey who at some time of their life had suffered from them. Like the Orokaiva of central Oro province, the Maisin distinguish between three types of infirmities (Williams 1930: 288ff).[4] Maisin refer to most ailments as *amai tatami* and *tamtami rati*, "just sickness" and "little sickness". Such complaints respond quickly to medical treatment of the Western or Papuan kinds or they clear up of their own accord. When pressed, some Maisin will account for these ailments in terms of cold winds, "germs", ghosts and other possible causes. Mostly they are content to see the sickness cured and do not concern themselves with its origins.

The other two categories of misfortune are radically different in that the victim and his kin must delve into the origins of the sickness if there is to be a remedy. These types of ailments are usually referred to as *vavata tatami* and *tatami beiii*, "heavy sickness" and "big sickness". Maisin further distinguish these from the casual kind by using the term *wakki tatami*, "village sickness". This term is apt because such ailments are thought usually to find their origins in breached or troubled relations within the community.[5] The actual work of causing the disease is done by a specialist – a sorcerer – who may either act on his own initiative or at the request of others.[6] (All Maisin sorcerers are said to be male; there are no female counterparts.) As sorcerers create *wakki tatami*, Western-trained practitioners are considered incapable of healing such ailments. Village healers may be more successful because they are familiar with this kind of ailment and the appropriate techniques. But if the sorcerer remains angry no one can cure his prey. It is interesting to note that when asked to recall the serious physical misfortunes of their lives, the 55 respondents reported mostly *wakki tatami* (62%).

Most sorcerers are said to make their attack on other villagers through the agency of bush spirits (*yawu*) and ancestral ghosts (*waa*). Once summoned by a sorcerer, spirits and ghosts stricken their victims by inhabiting their bodies, stealing their souls or both. Spirits may also take the form of dangerous animals such as snakes, crocodiles or wild pigs in order to attack unwary targets. Women and young children are said by Maisin to be most susceptible to attacks from spirits and ghosts because they, unlike most men, are too "weak" to fight off these invisible powers.[7] This assumption would appear to be reflected in the relatively high rate of attack by *yawu* and *waa* reported by women in Table 1.

Healers claim to be able to cure *waa-yawu* sicknesses, but to be helpless against the third and most serious class of ailment.[8] "Poison" sorcery (*wea yammei, beeta*) comes in many forms, all involving the manipulation of magical substances. Some of the techniques said to be employed by the *wea tamati*, "poison man", are familiar from the anthropological literature: the doctoring of fragments of clothes, hair and other materials belonging to the victim; the use of a long bamboo filled with *wea* to secretly poison the victim at night while he is asleep; the attacking of the victim by a group of sorcerers who remove one of his internal organs and replace it with poison (Fortune 1932, Patterson 1974–75). Sorcerers are also said to use more up to date methods, such as a doctored flashlight that bewitches anyone who comes within its gleam. Maisin consider "poisons" to be much more powerful than spirits and ghosts. This assumption may be reflected in the facts that, first, respondents reported fewer *wea* attacks than other sorts of *wakki tatami* and, second, relatively more men complained of this type of misfortune.

Returning to Table 1, we see that informants categorized their own major sicknesses, sores and injuries as of unknown origin, "casual" *(amai)*, "spirit" *(waa-yawu)*, and "poison" *(wea)*. Table 2 summarizes the curative resorts reported as being sought in each of these cases.[9] There is a clear division here between the *wakki tatami* and other categories of sickness. For the former, the respondents made use of the full range of curative options available. In the case of casual and unknown ailments they apparently recognized that a visit to the aid post or the use of some indigenous medicines had been sufficient to effect a cure.

TABLE 2
Curative choices in case histories of ailments

Type of illness	No.	Aid Post	Indigenous medicine	Priest	Healer	Meeting	Other
Unknown	19	13	3	–	–	–	4
Casual	20	12	4	–	–	–	4
Spirit	23	3	6	1	14	2	–
Poison	9	4	3	–	3	2	–
Total	71	32	16	1	17	4	8

Note: The sum of the figures in each row does not equal the number of illnesses because some respondents reported more than one curative choice.

From the evidence of this survey it appears that Western medical practices are easily contained within the indigenous framework of types of diseases and curative practices. While Maisin freely admit that Western practitioners treat many ailments more effectively than traditional healers, they classify these particular complaints as "casual" sicknesses. This is the case even when the sickness is serious enough that the patient must be hospitalized for a long period of time. Western medicine can work against *wakki tatami* in the eyes of most Maisin only after the healer has transformed it into a casual disease by removing the spiritual agent. Western medicine, therefore, is not seen as an alternative theory or explanation of sickness. Most Maisin, like the healers whose words open this section, believe that European doctors themselves recognize the limitations of Western medical care when they are confronted by *wakki tatami*.

The statistical data recorded in the misfortune survey clearly reveals a general framework of causes of sickness and curative resources. They may also reflect certain assumptions concerning the ways in which diseases strike different parts of the society. Women and children, for example, appear to be more susceptible to spirit and ghost attacks than men. The fact that it was mostly older men who reported attacks from poison sorcery agrees with the widespread assumption that *wea* is more powerful than *yawu* sorcery (and thus directed at men) and also the notion that the older methods of sorcery have been largely superseded by the malevolent use of spirit familiars.

The survey also revealed important qualitative differences between informants' knowledge of the origins of "village sicknesses". A small number of villagers were able and willing to provide very detailed rationalizations of particular illnesses. In these instances they described the social situation out of which the illness was thought to have arisen as well as the nature of the spiritual agent. Most respondents, however, were able or willing only to give categorical explanations of major sicknesses. When they explained why a sorcerer, spirit or ghost attacked, they usually told me that they acquired their information from the healer, the acknowledged expert in these matters. As in many other Melanesian societies, knowledge about local spirits in Maisin villages tends to be vague and inconsistent in details. Most people display little interest in cosmological matters (see Brunton 1980, Williams 1930).

TABLE 3
Causes given for reported deaths of adults

	No.	Casual	Sorcery	Unknown	Other
'Old people'	75	75	–	–	–
'Young people'	186	15	137	32	2
Total	261	90	137	32	2
Percent of 'young people'		8	74	17	1
Percent of total		34	52	12	1

Note: Data compiled from a sample of 66 adult respondents in Uiaku and Ganjiga who provided information on the deaths of their siblings and parents. Informants describe the 'old people' as those who are no longer able to vigorously carry out subsistence tasks. 'Young people' in this sample were adolescents and adults who were not completely dependent on other adults and still vigorous.

Finally, mention must be made of a small number of male informants, all of whom have received post-secondary education, who expressed varying degrees of scepticism concerning usual explanations of "village sickness". Only one man, a former dentist, told me that sorcery did not exist (although he suspected that actual poisonings occurred from time to time in Maisin villages). Three other men accepted the reality of sorcery, but insisted that it occurred far less frequently than most villagers believed. Three of the sceptics, all in their mid-forties were respected community leaders. I never heard them express these views in a public forum. Indeed, one of them was widely rumored to have himself been ensorcelled when he suffered a long illness in 1982 and two others were major participants in sorcery meetings that I attended. Their tempered scepticism may be indicative of the mode by which Maisin assumptions about health and illness are presently changing. I shall deal with this topic in the last section of the analysis.

The survey reveals a general agreement among the Maisin as to what it is important to know about sicknesses. It must be kept in mind, however, that the scheme I have sketched in these paragraphs is composed of post-hoc rationalizations. People are rarely certain of the cause of their sickness when they first fall ill. If the ailment comes on suddenly, sorcery will certainly be suspected and the sick person may be taken directly to a healer. But one can never be sure; even serious ailments may respond to Western medicine, thus showing it to be "just a sickness".

When ailments linger victims and their kin begin to move along a sequence of curative options in a pattern that Romanucci-Ross (1977) has described as a "hierarchy of resort". The longer an ailment lasts, the surer Maisin are that a sorcerer is at work. The success or failure of each level of curative resort helps to diminish the ambiguity of the origins of a sickness. As Table 3 shows, death usually removes the last shreds of doubt in people's minds. Almost three quarters of deaths reported to me of vigorous adults in Uiaku and Ganjiga were said to have been caused by some form of sorcery.

CURATIVE RESOURCES

My eyes are different. I can see the sickness and who caused it. Most people cannot. Most people get sick just from germs. When they get the sickness that belongs to the village, it is village people who must cure it. Others the hospital (aid post) can cure. The hospital cannot cure *wea* or *yawu*. The big hospitals (at Wanigela and in the towns) make those with germs better. It is up to the sick man and his people to try the different ways. He will go to the village healers first and, if they cannot help him, he will turn to the hospital. Or else he will come to the healers from the hospital.

Ida Nancy Sanangi, a healer in Uiaku

The aid post

The Maisin are served by two aid posts, one at Uiaku and another at Airara, about eight kilometers apart. Both are centrally located in the villages, but while the Airara building is made of prefabricated plaster board and has an iron roof with a water catchment system, the Uiaku building is composed completely of bush materials. The respective communities maintain the buildings and grounds. Improvements to schools and aid posts are funded through the Local Government Council at Tufi with money generated mostly by local taxation. Money is limited and there is much competition between villages within the Council area for projects. So people make do as best they can until their turn for improvements comes. Water at the Uiaku aid post, for example, is collected during the rainy season from sheet iron fixed to a platform behind the building or otherwise from a nearby river. It is boiled over a kerosene stove before being used.

Most weekday mornings one finds a small gathering of adults and children in and about the aid post. It is a favorite meeting place. As they wait, men usually sitting apart from the women and children, people share smokes, chew betel nut and catch up on the latest gossip. The aid post orderly (APO) usually completes his treatments within a couple of hours. If asked, he then visits people in the village too ill to come to the aid post.

The APO has a relatively unobtrusive presence in Maisin villages. He simply treats those sicknesses and injuries people bring to him in the best way he knows how. The orderlies I knew did not seek out sick people or take it upon themselves to teach villagers about Western medicine. They simply provided a service.

The Uiaku APO's greatest problem during the time of my fieldwork was in securing regular supplies of medicines. Sometimes these were available at Wanigela, fifteen kilometers to the north, but often the APO had to make his way to Tufi, more than sixty kilometers distant by sea, where he also picked up his fortnightly paycheck. The only way he could get to Tufi was by making a demanding two to three day round trip in an outrigger canoe or by chartering a dinghy at his own expense (this cost 30 Kina for the round trip in 1983). Even then there is no guarantee that all of the needed supplies will be on hand once he arrives in Tufi. Nevertheless, because medicines and dressings were quickly used up in the village, the APO had to make this trip every six weeks or so.[10]

When medical supplies are available, the APO system is an effective means of delivering basic health care to villagers. But there are some weaknesses in the system. These appear to be related to the ways in which the APO role is negotiated between orderlies and the people they serve.

Indigenous professionals, both Maisin and non-Maisin, have lived and worked among Maisin villagers for eighty years. Teachers, evangelists, priests and latterly aid post orderlies occupy a comparable niche in village society. They are specialists who receive a salary from an outside source for their services, who have more education than the bulk of the population, whose living and working quarters are provided and maintained by the villagers, and who live separately from the local people within the village on land that is not owned by any particular clan. Such professionals are in an ambiguous position in relation to the villagers. On the one hand, they are different and apart from the villagers for the reasons listed above. On the other hand, they are often like the villagers in that they come from similar backgrounds, share the same types of concerns, engage in subsistence gardens, indulge in the same cultural activities, etc. This is a situation that easily gives rise to tensions that may interfere with the work of the APO.

When the APO comes to a village as a foreigner, which has usually been the case in southern Collingwood Bay, he tends to associate mostly with the other salaried and educated specialists and with them form an enclave. Like some teachers, the APO may adopt a condescending attitude towards the villagers, considering them to be "backward", or he may simply be unhappy with unfamiliar surroundings. For their part, villagers have less hesitation in accusing an outsider of laziness and profiteering than they do any of their own. During the time of my fieldwork, the people of Airara were frequently complaining about their APO and making their way the eight kilometers up to the coast to Uiaku to go to the Maisin orderly there. The distrust that often builds up between the foreign APO and local people lends itself to a high turnover rate. In Uiaku, for example, twelve foreign orderlies worked for short periods between 1948 and 1965.

Even when the APO is a member of the community, his anomalous role gives rise to certain tensions. The present Uiaku APO, for example, was born in that village. Except for a two year period in the late 1970s he has been in Uiaku since 1965 (having first begun work elsewhere in 1960). I heard occasional complaints that the APO spent too much time fishing or in his garden and that he favored his own relatives over others when medicines were in short supply (charges, incidently, that are often levelled at any villager with public responsibilities involving access to desired goods, services and money). But the APO generally received strong support from the community. The villagers considered him dependable, especially compared to earlier orderlies.

While I sometimes heard grumbles about orderlies' "laziness" and "selfishness", I almost never heard people question their competence. When a treatment given by the APO fails to effect a cure, the sick person and his kin will usually resort to other curative techniques in the ongoing effort to find the actual cause of the sickness. Most of the tensions that develop between orderlies and local people can be traced to social relations rather than medical practice. Maisin, of course, have few resources with which they could evaluate the medical practice of the APOs.

In most cases the aid post, and to a lesser extent Wanigela hospital, serve as the first resort when people are struck by an illness. But aid post orderlies are well aware of the ineffectiveness of Western medicines against *wakki tatami*. The APO at Uiaku, for example, told me how healers had frequently produced rapid cures in patients who had not responded to his treatment. The orderly himself knew no traditional medicines, as he had been away from his village as a young man, but he accepted that they were often efficacious. In his words, the APO is an expert on "the medical side only". He cannot speak about village diseases because they lie outside of his medical training. But health workers, like anyone else in the village, can fall prey to sorcerers. A retired hospital orderly in Uiaku, for example, once confided in me that he had lost both his wife and son because of the attacks of sorcerers.

Traditional medicines

All of my informants agreed that many Western medicines are better than their own and can cure ailments that in earlier times were left untreated. I was told that many of the old medicines (*kain, bobi*) have been forgotten now that they are no longer needed. On the other hand, several traditional remedies for colds, headaches, sores, and so forth are judged by those who know them to be superior to the European equivalents. These are remembered. In a survey of 75 adults in Uiaku (out of a possible 213) I found that 58 (or 77%) knew some traditional medicines. Some individuals, especially healers of course, know many more than most people.

Knowledge of medicines is a private affair. It is passed down from parents to children, occasionally from mother's brother to sister's son and, much more rarely, from friend to friend. Most medicines are made up of the barks or leaves of selected plants found in the bush. They may be given to the sick person in the form of a hot broth to drink or bathe in, or the substances may be sprayed over the body of the patient in a bright crimson mixture consisting mostly of chewed betel nut juice. Since particular remedies for some *wakki tatami* are usually known only by the people who have the means to create that sickness, those men who possess many medicines are often suspected of being sorcerers.[11] The APO never finds himself in this position as European medicines are not considered to include "poisons".

The priest[12]

Almost all adult Maisin today are members of the Anglican Church. A national priest resides in Uiaku, serving a parish that stretches to the Milne Bay border and includes several non-Maisin villages. He is assisted by a number of teacher-evangelists, deacons, Church Councillors and Mothers' Union members in the different communities. Church workers tend to play only a minor role in the treatment of ailments. But Christianity has had a major if indirect influence on Maisin thinking about health and disease.

As participants in community life, present day clerics play a part in perpetuating some indigenous notions about health and in changing others. A priest or deacon may act as a third party in village disputes, and so mediate between parties in danger of being drawn into a sorcery feud. Some missionaries in the past spoke out against indigenous healers, seeing them as the representatives of the heathen religion, but many national priests today give cautious support. One priest told me that the healers in their work demonstrate God's power over earthly evil. Because he is seen as an intermediary between God and the people, a priest's encouragement of a healer or a healer's medicines can be a powerful support for the traditional practice of medicine.[13] Indeed, one Uiaku priest, whose father had established a reputation as a sorcerer, was well known for his own knowledge of indigenous remedies.

The priest's chief duty at a time of sickness is to offer prayer and comfort. Very few Maisin admit to praying at home alone. When sick, they or their relatives may ask the priest to come, or one of the other Church workers may report the illness to the priest who then may visit to offer a prayer and perhaps a blessing. The priests I interviewed (two worked at different times in the parish during my fieldwork) saw their duty as one of giving strength to ailing people by encouraging them to have faith in Christ and God. On the one hand, the prayer and blessing offered by the priest may give the patient the courage to withstand the illness and its ultimate cause (when it is considered a "village sickness"). One of the priests always says to those who fear sorcery, "If you trust God this poison won't hurt you." On the other hand, the priest tries to help the sick person and his relatives to accept the illness if it lingers. He tells the patient that God may have a need for him in Heaven. And if the topic of sorcery comes up, the priest may suggest that the kin of the sick person should not try to take vengeance on the sorcerer; instead they must find forgiveness in their hearts.

Village people, including Maisin church workers, take a slightly different view of the relation between prayer and healing. If one has faith in God, it is said, then one can withstand sickness. One woman told me, "God created everything, so when we ask for His help the sick people get better." I recorded seven cases in which individuals claimed to have recovered from major sicknesses after they had dreams or visions in which they saw manifestations of the Christian divine – angels, Jesus' feet, Jacob's ladder. In other instances, people told me of how God gave them the "strength" (*wenna*) to face the sorcerers who had caused their illness. To many Maisin, then, God represents a source of power accessible through one's faith. Prayer, church attendance and generosity to the Church are among the outward signs of this faith.

God provides a general type of strength to all who have faith, but He is not seen as directly intervening in the social situations that are believed to generate sicknesses. Perhaps because of this, God is rationalized as providing for general wellbeing but is not usually conceived of as a curative resort for specific ailments. The clergy regularly visit and pray for the elderly and infirm in the villages, but I knew of only a few cases in which they were specifically asked to pray for vigorous adults who had fallen ill. In these instances the kin of the sick person seem to see the clergy's intervention as an ancillary measure of precaution. Significantly, it is the healers who claim to pray regularly for strength from God. Each healer volunteered to me that before they could begin a curing session they had to pray. One healer was a member of his village's Church Council, another belonged to the Mothers' Union, and three had had visions in the past of the manifestation of God's power during which, they claimed, they had received some of their present healing abilities.

Healers

The six Maisin healers that I knew were certainly among the most remarkable people of their communities. Confident, often brash, these individuals showed little of the reluctance in discussing customary things that I experienced in my usual initial encounters with other informants. Healers are far more familiar with traditions than most of their neighbors. At the same time, healers are more concerned than most other villagers that the differences between received traditions and more recent introductions be resolved. We have already seen that healers believe they draw on God's power in their work. They regard themselves as good Christians. In their view the vocation they have taken up is on a par with that of European doctors; it is the ailments that are treated by European and Papuan curers which differ.

Healers are known as *sevaseva* and *kikiki* people.[14] The two women and four men presently practising are all elderly; only two are still capable of gardening. To my knowledge there are no younger healers practising, training or in waiting, a significant point I will return to in my discussion of change in indigenous medical beliefs in the next section. All of the healers have an extensive knowledge of Papuan medicines and must observe certain dietary restrictions in order to maintain their healing powers. Beyond these general similarities, their methods and styles struck me as both individual and eclectic. Two healers use medicines only, but others have spirit familiars (*yawu*) which they summon during curing sessions by making offerings and singing special songs. Three healers also claim to be able to leave their bodies in order to spy on sorcerers and to recover stolen souls. I heard of one instance in which a healer charged 40 Kina for her services, but most of the time healers are content to receive a small amount of money, about 2 Kina, and gifts of food and tobacco as payment.

Healers have the ability to detect the sources of ailments and to see spirits and ghosts. This allows them to select the right type of treatment and to inform the victim of the identity of his assailant and the reasons for the attack. Most of the sicknesses treated by healers are said to be caused by *yawu*, bush spirits that serve both sorcerers and healers. *Yawu* are said to have the ability to assume many guises, including that of humans. They frequently attack in the form of animals. One female healer in Ganjiga identified three *yawu* that she claimed were among the most common to attack villagers. A snake called *Nanginangi* either enters and curls up in the victim's stomach or wraps itself around their waist. A pig *yawu* called *Goreva* grasps the victim from the back in the same fashion as a single man carries a pig home from the hunt. This sickness is especially "heavy" and very painful. The eel called *Boresu* is said to be eager to have sex with females of all ages. It enters their vaginas when they are bathing and then curls up in their stomachs. The feel of its clammy skin results in coldness and fever. This spirit was often reported as responsible for sickness in little girls. The healers' familiars, which help him or her see these attackers and chase them away, are also *yawu* which may impersonate animals or humans.

Given certain clues, such as a swollen stomach or a sudden illness following an argument, a person may go at once to a healer. In most cases, however, people turn to healers only when it is apparent that the medicine from the aid post and ordinary Papuan medicines are having no effect. The sick person may be sent off to an urban hospital after seeing a healer, perhaps immediately if the ailment is very serious. To return from town still ill is considered definite proof that the ailment in question is a "village sickness". The ability of the healer to end the sickness at this point is seen by Maisin as being dependent not only on his or her talents but also on the willingness of the sorcerer to desist from appealing to his *yawu* to launch another attack or from resorting to more deadly "poisons". In serious cases the only way to stop a sorcerer is by direct confrontation or appeals from the community as a whole. Such an appeal represents a last resort before death.

Protecting the victim, confronting the sorcerer

When a person has a serious accident, falls ill or dies suddenly, most villagers will assume that there has been foul play. Relations and friends of the victim gather round his or her house during the day, while close kin and affines stay on through the night. This custom, called *gumema*, has a number of purposes depending on whether the supposed victim is living or dead. First, people gather because they wish to show their "respect" for the person. If he is alive, their talk and company cheer him up and give him the strength and desire to recover. Secondly, as the supporters talk they try to discover the possible reasons for the sorcery attack and what their best course of action might be. Finally, they provide a defensive shield around the victim. As he is already in a weakened state his enemies, as well as the sorcerer who originally caused his ailment, might try to add to it and so make the illness even "heavier".

When a victim is reasonably sure of the identity of his assailant, he or his relatives may confront or parley with the sorcerer. This is done in great secrecy. I was told that while sorcerers usually deny any knowledge of the specific causes of a disease or responsibility when they are confronted by victims, they may subsequently remove the sorcery if they feel that their target has been punished enough or that they themselves might suffer retaliation. The practice and threat of sorcery is illegal in Papua New Guinea. Maisin suspected of practising the "black art" are sometimes taken to Tufi by their angry neighbors to stand trial before a magistrate. When I was in Uiaku one man was taken to court on this charge. Such evidence as there is of the actual practice of sorcery consists mostly of veiled threats, gossip and dreams, and much of this is not admissible in court. In this instance, the man was found guilty of threatening behaviour but acquitted of the charge of practicing sorcery. There are obvious dangers in taking an alleged sorcerer to court and few Maisin are brave enough to try.[15]

Sorcerers attack in retaliation for wrongs against themselves or against the community. But sorcery attacks themselves are also wrongs which, in turn, invite "paybacks". Because of this, people in a community feel a growing sense of alarm as an illness becomes more grave, especially in the case of adolescents and young adults. As the sick person begins to slide towards death, the village leaders may call a general meeting, a *totoruga*.

The *totoruga* serves a purpose similar to that of the *gumema*. It is a statement of solidarity behind the victim and also a forum within which the causes of an ailment can be discussed and dealt with. It is an arena of last resort in which all of the differences which divide a village may be aired. The object is not so much to find the sorcerer as to resolve the internal troubles which prompted the attack in the first place. If the difficulties can be resolved, even temporarily, Maisin feel that the sorcerer will call off his attack and the sick individual can start down the road towards recovery. He may still be weak and ill, but now that the cause of the sorcery has been removed his ailment will start to respond to treatment at the aid post or the hospital.

We are now in a position to sum up the Maisin's usual response to health problems. The five choices of curative practices available in the villages fall roughly into a "hierarchy of resort". This in turn corresponds with a division of ailments into three general categories: casual, those caused by ghosts and spirits, and those resulting from "poisons". If an illness responds to medicine treatment from the aid post, Maisin assume that it is casual. When there is no response, people begin to suspect sorcery. They may then turn to healers and perhaps the priest. The *totoruga*, village meeting, is the last resort. When an individual becomes this sick, Maisin strongly suspect that poison is being used. The only way of stopping the ailment is by appealing to the sorcerer.

CHANGING PERCEPTIONS OF ILLNESS AS MISFORTUNE[16]

We say that we are Christians, but it is us. If we do bad things – steal or something else – we don't live long. People get angry with us and we die. It was the same with the heathens. Our fathers and mothers told us, "If you are good, respect people and help them, you will live to an old age."

Glassio Fisisi, Uiaku

When I was sick recently, my aunt was saying that it was sorcery. But I was concentrating on the medical side. Sometimes when someone dies I say that I don't believe in sorcery. But then my wife asks, "Why do all of these people keep dying?" If they poison you it is true. But they are not gods who can tell you to become sick!

Franklin Seri, a retired dentist in Uiaku

To many Western educated observers, the sort of medical pluralism described in the preceeding pages seems perplexing, even pernicious. A nurse I was acquainted with once complained to me that healers were fond of sending the hopelessly ill to the aid posts and hospitals to die while seeking as their own patients individuals who were on the mend after treatment by orderlies and nurses. Healers have long been accused by outsiders of exploiting the credulity of their neighbors, but my friend's point was more general than this. She felt that Maisin and others like them employed a double standard. They use medical services provided to them for free but refuse to trust the overall competence of health workers. Instead Maisin cling to their old ideas. Romanucci-Ross's study of medical pluralism on Manus Island sounds a resonant tone of puzzlement as she deals with the problem of why the islanders continue to feel a "sense of loyalty" to "native illnesses" in the face of a European technology "otherwise acknowledged as superior and invested with the highest prestige" (1977: 483). In an article comparing two instances of medical pluralism in the North Solomons Province, Hamnett and Connell (1981: 497) describe similar situations as classic cases of "culture lag": "What is apparent therefore is that behavioural change proceeds faster than cognitive change; disease aetiology and process are still conceived in traditional cognitive models yet participation in the Western medical system is commonplace." In each of these examples, the coexistence of Western and indigenous medical ideas, practices and institutions is presented as something anomalous, requiring explanation.

But from the perspective of the Maisin there is no double standard and little mystery. Few of them are aware of any contradictions between their approach to illnesses and that which is considered desirable by European specialists. This ignorance is understandable partly in terms of historical experience, namely the inability or unwillingness of the Mission and Administration to present European medicine explicitly as an alternative to the indigenous varieties. Efforts to disseminate knowledge about the intellectual underpinnings of Western medicine began only in recent years in most rural schools and, outside of high schools and higher educative institutions, are still at a rudimentary level. As Hamnett and Connell (1981: 494) cogently note for the North Solomons, the cognitive model of Western medicine remains largely invisible to most of the people who use the aid posts. In such circumstances it is hardly surprising that the challenge of European medicine to indigenous assumptions is muted.

The average Maisin villager's innocence of the contrary assumptions of Western medical practice can also be explained in terms of the ease with which he is able to fit this curative resort within an admittedly flexible framework of belief. Most Maisin see Western medical substances and practices as powerful analogues of their own medicines, useful in the fight against "casual illnesses" and in the aftermath of sorcery-related ailments. It is very possible that with improvements in health following the introduction of Western medical services the instances Maisin have identified as "village sicknesses" have declined. But there is nothing inherent in Western medical care as experienced by the Maisin that would indicate a denial of the reality of sicknesses caused by sorcery. To a remarkable extent, the Maisin have been able to encompass the curative resort of Western medicine within a larger indigenous framework of belief and practice. They have in effect "domesticated" this externally-controlled import.

Maisin today, like their ancestors, understand disease primarily in terms of quality of relationships within the moral order and the nature of the influences of divine entities, including sorcerers, on human lives. The quote that opens this section is an example of a frequently expressed attitude in Maisin villages: the view of sorcery as a semi-legitimate sanction employed to punish those who flout the conventions of the society. Behind this rationalization, revealed in the institutionalized gatherings around the sorcery victim and the crises that provoke them, lies a more complex, darker understanding of sorcery as a secret mode of conflict between those who on the surface must depend upon each other for security. Such moments suggest the danger of the community coming apart at the seams as one sorcery attack leads to another or provokes physical violence.

These themes are ancient and widespread throughout Melanesia. But in Maisin communities, as elsewhere, villagers have had to contend with new circumstances and new answers even as they have asked the old questions (cf. Zelenietz and Lindenbaum 1981). Informants uniformly insist that the sorts of "village sicknesses" people face today are very different from those of the past. In the past when a person's survival depended completely on close kin and their allies, ghost and sorcery attacks were the expected form of conflict within and between the multi-clan villages. The most powerful sorcerers were well known, feared for their ability to bring sickness and valued for their knowledge which allowed them to undo their spells. It is said that at this time misfortunes could be explained, acted upon and controlled.

The elders go on to explain that with the coming of the Europeans their ancestors learned that these forms of mystical retaliation were both wrong and unnecessary. One of the most interesting developments was the decline in importance of ancestral ghosts as a source of power. Informants told me that unlike the older "pagan ghosts", recent ghosts are Christians who are unwilling to linger around villages. At their funerals they listen to the prayers of the priest and go obediently to Paradise. The elders also tell how most of the old-style sorcerers gave up their poisons when the Maisin converted to Christianity, or let it die with them. The sorcerers who have replaced them are thought to be few in number, but much more secretive, vicious and hard to control – true criminals. The older forms of curative resort, described in the previous pages, appear to prove less and less capable of dealing with this changing threat. Maisin, however, find some comfort in Christianity as they understand it. For it is said that the good Christian man of faith will be given the strength by God to withstand the attacks of the sorcerer. The adoption of Christianity has encouraged many Maisin to see the crises of "village sicknesses" as battlegrounds between the forces of the microcosm and those more powerful ones of the macrocosm. As the Christian divinities are known to be the most powerful, the outcome is seen not so much as a contest against God and local sorcerers but as a test of the victim's faith.

There is a certain element of myth in the oral accounts I have summarised. The reader may be forgiven for suspecting that the older sorcery crises were as ambiguous to participants as those of the present. At the same time, the testimonies show that villagers are not "clinging to old ideas" but actively making sense of the implications of Government and Mission actions, Christian teachings, and the changing circumstances of their lives.

Let us inquire further into these changing circumstances. Oral testimonies and documents reveal a contact society very similar to others reported in this part of Papua (e.g., Young 1971). Maisin lived in multi-clan villages in a permanent state of tension with their neighbors. They recognized no transcendent political (or divine) authority. Outside of the narrow confines of his "security circle" of close kin and affines, to employ Peter Lawrence's useful phrase, each person joined in unstable alliances with various influential men. The colonial authorities acted in various ways to eclipse the power of these men. At the same time, the Mission and Government laid the basis for the formation of new contexts of political action by introducing and supporting local schools, churches, councils, aid posts and cooperatives.

Since the end of the Second World War, Maisin have simultaneously experienced massive out-migration, a growing dependence on money and commodities and aspirations for local economic development. They have come to some extent to recognize kin loyalties as inimical to the greater needs of the people. At the village meetings I attended, both elders and younger educated leaders enunciated an ethic that emphasized the need for and values of community solidarity. They pointed out how such divided loyalties encouraged gossiping and conflicts and in general aborted efforts to form a united work force that might improve the material conditions within the community. This contrast between the promise of community solidarity and the problems of intra-community divisions finds a remarkable resonance in the characterization of sorcery attacks as contests within the souls of participants between a saving faith in the forces of the macrocosm and the conflicts that exist in the microcosm. Indeed, informants sometimes spoke as if the conditions for economic and physical health were one and the same.

Unfortunately there are little reliable data on how Maisin conceived and responded to "village sicknesses" in the past so we cannot know the effects of these changing circumstances and understandings. The implications of the various innovations, however, are clear and consistent. While none deny the reality of "village sicknesses", all act as impediments to action. First, the common assumption that sorcerers have become more secretive suggests that it may be even futile to try to identify and stop them. Further, speculations and inquiries to find an elusive sorcerer may work against the aims of community solidarity by provoking a climate of increasing conflict. Community leaders are keenly aware of the dysfunctional aspects of sorcery fears and frequently caution those closely involved in the sickness not to "gossip" amongst themselves and only to bring an accusation forth if they have enough evidence to take the sorcerer before a magistrate. The indigenous rendition of Christianity also dissuades speculation and action in the event of a serious illness. The Christian view continues to link morality with physical well-being, but it shifts the concerns of the victim from his relation to the sorcerer to his relation with God, for it is ultimately the supreme being who decides whether a person will live or die. The injunction to forgive one's enemies also encourages an other-worldly focus during times of illness.

This brings us to the Maisin "sceptics" mentioned in the earlier discussion of the misfortune survey. I noted that these men privately criticized some aspects of sorcery beliefs but publicly acted in ways that supported the premises of the same beliefs. My impression is that they are not so much working against the given framework of assumptions as influencing from within the way that framework is applied to particular instances of sickness. One striking instance of this process occurred following the death of a little girl in the village, probably from untreated tuberculosis. Soon after the death a Maisin health officer working in Popondetta made a trip to the village concerned to tell the people that it was fruitless to try to find a sorcerer for this was not a case of "village sickness". They should not mistake tuberculosis for *wakki tatami*. Such initiatives, combined with the impediments noted above and the successes of European medical treatments, have in all probability narrowed the range of illnesses the Maisin identify and act upon as moral crises.

If this analysis is correct it indicates that while the Maisin continue to view major sicknesses within a moral and spiritual framework, they are becoming more willing to tolerate ambiguity. This may explain why there are no apparent replacements for the aging healers; the unique gift of the healers, their ability to explain an ailment in terms of present social conditions, is becoming less relevant and convincing than it once was. In my opinion the Maisin are already making close to maximal use of the limited Western medical facilities available to them, so it is difficult to see how changes in their view and approach to "village sickness" will affect this aspect of behavior. On the other hand, the historical process in which the immediate moral and spiritual context is becoming less important in the explanation of sickness as misfortune portends the day when Maisin assume the focused and amoral understanding of disease now common in industrialized societies.

CONCLUSION

The most striking theme emerging from this case study, in my opinion, is the degree to which Maisin have successfully appropriated the provision of Western medical facilities and integrated it into their general conceptions of disease. European medicine has not only added powerful options in the range of therapies available to the villagers but has also become an important factor in the diagnosis of sickness; for today ailments are identified as "village sickness" with the most certainty when the aid post orderlies, nurses and doctors are seen to fail. As in many other non-Western societies, Maisin view major illnesses as misfortunes grounded in moral and spiritual realities. They accept Western medicine as a type of technology appropriate for certain types and moments of sickness, but they are for the most part incognisant of its intellectual foundations. Whatever its effects on actual health, Western medical services have had a muted impact on Maisin ideology. Changes in the consensus regarding the etiology and appropriate response to sickness appear to have been more directly affected by larger changes in the society: conversion to Christianity, incorporation into the cash economy, extensive out-migration, to name a few.

In the analysis I have tried to identify some of the cultural and historical factors which can in part account for this type of medical pluralism. The specifics are, of course, peculiar to the Maisin people, but many of the generalizations made in this study hold true for people in other parts of Melanesia and beyond. Melanesians in general are renowned for their "pragmatism", whether this is shown in their willingness to experiment with a wide range of garden magics or to attempt to cure physical complaints with sequences of visits to the aid post, local clergy and indigenous healers. In the Collingwood Bay area, the colonial presence of poorly financed and understaffed Government and Anglican Missions, which prided themselves on a relatively tolerant philosophy of the "white man's burden", created benign conditions for the incubation of a pragmatic combining of therapy processes drawing upon both indigenous and European resources with little resulting conflict or contradiction. One of the most interesting developments has been the degree to which the Maisin have invested their vision of Christianity with implications for sickness and health. The early missionaries would certainly have been surprised, although not necessarily disapproving. The situation bears some close resemblances to that of another Anglican mission in east Africa, described recently by Terrence Ranger (1981).

I can say little about the effects of this medical synthesis on the health of the Maisin, for I did not investigate this question. Nor do I have the case material that might indicate whether Maisin, or specific sections of the Maisin population, are more likely to go first to aid posts and hospitals or to healers in the sudden advent of a serious illness (cf. Romanucci-Ross 1977). I did hear of and note some occasions when very sick villagers remained home among relatives and healers instead of going to the health centre at Wanigela (I was told that they did visit aid posts). It is possible that some deaths could have been prevented had such people been taken to Wanigela. I also knew of patients whose illnesses grew worse and who died while in the care of aid post orderlies, nurses and doctors. In many, perhaps most of these instances the decline was inevitable, but some patients may have been saved given better training, supervision, facilities and supplies. There are a great number of ambiguities that must be included in a consideration of the reasons why people faced with the crisis of a major illness or accident elect to follow one course of therapy over another, especially in places where Western medical facilities are rudimentary. No simple answers will suffice.

It should be said, however, that the present situation presents some risks to the Maisin along with the benefit of improved health. Like the community schools and churches, they have incorporated the aid posts into their social lives while being content to remain in ignorance about institutional purposes and potentials, leaving such concerns in the hands of outside experts. This innocence, on the one hand, makes the Maisin vulnerable to dangers from incompetent health workers.[17] In the long run it leaves them with little or no voice in the deployment of scarce medical resources. The analysis presented here suggests that given the secularizing trends attending the incorporation of villagers into larger economic and political systems, the rural Maisin are approaching a philosophy of disease more or less compatible with that of Western medical science. This promises greater local understanding of the aims and difficulties of rural health delivery and, in time, a fuller participation in the management of medical resources. Ironically these changes are coming at a time when the international economic crisis is forcing cut-backs in rural health care.

NOTES

The research on which this paper is based was carried out between November 1981 and August 1983 in Port Moresby, Popondetta and Collingwood Bay. Financial support was provided by the Social Sciences and Humanities Research Council of Canada. I would like to thank the staff of the Native Archives of Papua New Guinea and the Right Rev. David Hand for their assistance and permission to use the archival materials that appear in this study. To those Maisin who acted as my assistants, informants and friends, my deepest gratitude. This piece is dedicated to Sister Helen Roberts who has given almost four decades of her life to the health care of the people of Collingwood Bay.

1. This section is based upon archival materials in the Anglican Archives located in the New Guinea Collection in the Library of the University of Papua New Guinea and patrol reports deposited in the National Archives of Papua New Guinea. The materials for a more extensive historical study of health care in the Collingwood Bay area were tragically destroyed in a fire at the Wanigela health centre in 1982.
2. I unfortunately did not have access to recent health statistics for the Collingwood Bay area. I was told by health workers in the area that malaria and tuberculosis accounted today for most deaths. The *Oro Provincial Handbook* (1980) states that the province has the second highest rate of malaria parasite infestation in the country.
3. A patrol report of 1968 listed 16 of the 78 Maisin individuals either employed or in professional training to be in medically related fields (Mendaris 1969). At least four Maisin men have undergone training to be dentists and two have graduated as medical doctors, including Dr Wilfred Moi, presently Head of the Mental Health Services and the first Papuan graduate in Medicine and Surgery from the Fiji School of Medicine (Moi 1976).
4. A similar distinction between *sik nating* and *sik belong ples* is reported for the North Solomons by Hamnett and Connell (1981).
5. While my informants were usually exact about the general differences of types of illnesses, their explanations of individual cases were often full of ambiguities. Informants would often begin describing an instance of sickness as the result of an unprovoked attack by an ancestral ghost or a *yawu*. After further discussion they usually indicated the presence of a living man lurking in the background of the spiritual attack. Instances of sickness that could be traced back no further than spirits and ghosts were always relatively minor and usually involved women and children.
6. Although the distinction between the "spirit" and "poison" methods of attack is important to their etiology of disease, Maisin tend to use the terms "*yawu* men" and "*wea* men" interchangeably regardless of the nature of a particular attack. Indeed, there is little to distinguish the culteral representation of these attackers beyond the difference in methods. It is, therefore, appropriate to identify both as sorcerers.
7. For a discussion of the measures that are taken to protect unborn and newly born children from spirit and ghost attacks see Tietjen (1984).
8. As I noted earlier, healers blame this situation on historical circumstances: the revival in the use of traditional "poisons" without accompanying antidotes and the introduction of unfamiliar "poisons". But Williams (1930: 239–94) also observed in the 1920s that Orokaiva curers declared their helplessness against anything but spirits: "it remains the general rule to impute this cause [material sorcery] for the more serious complaints. Further than this, it is imputed as cause especially for those complaints which cannot be cured. Thus when a doctor has tried his methods on a patient without success he is likely to set the case down as a hopeless one of sorcery and discontinue his treatment; and, indeed, if he be astute enough, he may decide to have no truck with any case that seems too far gone. For it is generally held that sorcery sickness cannot

be cured by the ordinary methods of the healer. ... Sorcery is, in fact, the native's exegetical last card".
Orokaiva notions of the cauzation of disease, according to Williams's account, varied in one significant way from those of the Maisin; the Orokaiva apparently believed that attacking spirits operated independently of any human agents.

9. Figures given in Table 1 for each category of ailments are of the number of people in the sample who reported that complaint one or more times. Table 2 records the aggregate number of cases of the different ailments. The tables are, therefore, not directly comparable. Figures from sicknesses, sores and accidents have been combined in Table 3.

10. The aid post was often out of supplies. During these periods my wife and I provided villagers with simple treatments for colds, malaria and sores.

11. Women inherit medicines and may become healers but they are never sorcerers. A few Maisin admitted to me that it was possible for a woman to pay for a sorcerer's service, as men are often supposed to do, but they knew of no instances where this had happened. Men whose fathers were sorcerers are themselves often suspected of carrying on the craft.

12. Village Christianity was the focus of my research. The points made in this section are examined and documented in greater detail in Barker (1985).

13. The priests are not always aware that their actions are being interpreted in this way. When the priest says a prayer or blessing for an ailing healer this may be taken as approval and enhancement of the healer's art upon his recovery. Some healers interpreted the priest's blessing of the congregation during the Mass as a source for their personal curative powers. I heard of only one occasion when indigenous medicines were deliberately blessed. Clergy do offer prayers for patients in the care of healers. The priest also routinely blesses the aid post each year.

14. *Kikiki* has a wide range of meanings, including "story", "myth", "traditional custom", "clan emblem", and "origin". *Sevaseva* is a term heard throughout Tufi district in reference to healing seances, also known as *kaara* to the Maisin. *Tamatari* means "men".

15. It is usually, but not always, the village councillor (in the past the village constable) who is asked by other villagers to take the alleged sorcerer to court. I heard of only three other instances of this happening in the recent past. On each occasion the defendant was gaoled for short periods or fined. In none of the cases was the sorcerer said to have made vengeance upon his accusers following his return to the village.

16. The historical developments described in this section are discussed and documented in much greater detail in Barker (1985).

17. A small example of this is the propensity of aid post orderlies to give injections of penicillin for even the most minor complaints.

GILBERT H. HERDT

4. DOKTAS AND SHAMANS AMONG THE SAMBIA OF PAPUA NEW GUINEA[1]

INTRODUCTION

In 1975 the Central Government established small medical aid posts throughout the Sambia tribal territory. Until that time, no permanent Western medical care was available to the Sambia. Shamans were the key traditional healers. Others, such as local ritual experts, would also perform magical spells or recommend indigenous medicines and related treatments for those seeking care. The aid post in the Sambia Valley had a rocky start due to staffing and supply difficulties. By 1981, however, 97% of our respondents in a large household survey told us that they regularly used the *dokta* (the Pidgin term for physicians, medical orderlies and, more broadly, all outsiders who treat illness). Moreover, 45% said they no longer used shamans for healing. This dramatic social change must be interpreted in the light of increasing acculturation on many fronts among the Sambia, including the decline in the great prestige of traditional shamanism.

This chapter is concerned with these two interrelated trends among the Sambia. I show that changes in healing roles have made the traditional shamanic role "attenuated" (Landy 1974) but not defunct. The main changes resulted from the introduction of *doktas* and the emergent idea of "development". Shamans have been linked to "tradition" and opposed by the medical orderlies and some missionaries. Because the Sambia shaman is a "generalist" healer, this figure became, in effect, a symbolic point of opposition or support to "development". Medical anthropologists have long recognized that traditional cultures were not merely "empty vessels" (Polgar 1963) in the introduction of Western medicine. Indigenous health systems provide beliefs, rules and norms, and symbolic meanings surrounding curative practices and institutions (Kleinman 1980). However, a similar analytic approach must be taken toward the acculturative and development processes related to introduced medical practices. "Development" is not a unitary process; its regional and culture area vicissitudes differ enormously. The way in which people locally interpret "developments" and thereby reinterpret traditional practices, provides an important perspective on analyzing medical acculturation. The Sambia case is interesting in this regard because I was able to observe the introduction of the aid posts and their rapid effect six years later. In the "Discussion" I compare and contrast these points in relation to selected elements of the literature at large.

The reader must know that I will not attempt here to untangle all aspects of the complex phenomena to be discussed below. This chapter represents a partial account of an on-going study of social change among Sambia, especially regarding shamanism. In a later report elsewhere I plan to deal in more depth with these and other matters.

THE CONTEXT

Sambia are a Highlands fringe people who inhabit the extreme southeastern corner of the Eastern Highlands province. Today they number some 2400 individuals spread over a rather thinly populated periphery of the Kratke Mountains. Traditionally, Sambia were hunters and shifting horticulturalists, sweet potatoes and taro being the staples. Warfare was pervasive until the mid 1960s, when the Australian government forcibly pacified the region.

Social life is organized around residence and affiliation in small hamlets. These hamlets are built atop steep mountain ridges for defense and proximity to gardens and the forest. Hamlets number between 40 and 150 people, the size being a function of the age of the village, its location, and the process of clan fission resulting from local disputes. Hamlets are organized in an idiom of patrilineal descent and patrilocal residence. Women are often imported for marriage from neighboring hamlets. Marriage is arranged through sister-exchange or infant betrothal customary contracts between hamlets. Men, their wives and children live in "women's houses"; initiated bachelors reside in "men's clubhouses".

Hamlets are also organized into larger social units within the same narrow river valley. Propinquitous hamlet clusters, numbering two to four hamlets and usually within eyeshot of one another, engage in marriage exchange, male initiation ceremonies and mutual defense together. Sometimes, but not always, these hamlet clusters belong to the same phratry by virtue of common putative descent, geographic origin and ritual customs. This hamlet cluster I have referred to as a "confederacy" of allied groups. In larger valleys, two or three confederacies coexist and these alignments sometimes cross-cut phratry boundaries. In the Sambia River Valley for instance, two such confederacies currently organize initiation and one of these integrates hamlets of two different phratries.

The focus of this chapter is the Sambia River area, which includes eleven hamlets whose total population is about 1000. The area has no roads and, until 1983, no airstrip. Western contact with this population began in the late 1950s through reconnaissance patrols of Australian officers. Missionaries followed in the late 1960s. Steel axes and other Western goods slowly made their way into the Valley. Labor recruitment for coastal plantation workers accelerated, from the late 1960s to the mid 1970s, resulting in male absenteeism and the importation of knowledge about the cities. Pidgin, as a second language, also spread in the area; in 1975, some 10% of adult men spoke Pidgin. The mid 1970s also brought the local government council into being, an event closely linked to the medical aid post establishment described below. By 1981 – the focus of a new systematic study by the author – accumulating social changes were significantly shaping traditional culture, as discussed below.

In spite of this social change, and I do not wish to downplay it, Sambia society in 1974–1976 – the period of my initial fieldwork – remained largely tradition-oriented; in fundamental ways it still is today. Gardening remains unchanged except for the use of steel tools. Hunting continues as before, though on a reduced scale. Marriage and residence arrangements remain unaltered as well. Initiation rites continue on a wide scale, though changes have reduced the length of time and resources invested in them and their glamour. Subsequent field trips (1979, 1981, 1983) have reinforced this view (see Herdt 1981, 1983; in press).

Perhaps shamanic healing as much as anything has suffered at the hands of social change. The reasons for this will be spelled out in due course. But we must be careful to investigate both internal and external sources of the deterioration of people's faith in, and resort to, the shamans for relief of their ills. When we do so, what emerges is a history of acculturation that took its shape not only from the outside intrusion of Western practices, but from Sambian responses to these practices which led them, in turn, to revaluate and reinterpret their own resort to the shamans.

TRADITIONAL HEALING

Sambia traditionally recognized and used an extensive variety of medicines with which they treated sickness (*numboolyu*). Many forms of illness were categorized according to their perceived symptoms and, in some cases such as malarial symptomatology, their putative causes. These forms of illness had in turn conventional treatments. Treatment, however, was determined not only by symptomatology but also by diagnosis of the illness. The main diagnosticians – and healers – were shamans (*kwooluku*). Of lesser importance were ritual experts and/or magicians who held esoteric spells and provided *ad hoc* preliminary treatments for illness. Various aspects of Sambia shamanism and attitudes toward illness have been described in Herdt (1977). Here, I will summarize my previous study and amplify it with regard to the total healing process in Sambia culture.

Attitudes about illness

As a general rule, Sambia regard virtually all misfortunes as resulting from the actions or intervention of human or spiritual agents. Sambia think of these forces as superhuman but not "supernatural", because they do not categorize the world in terms of the Western "natural"/"supernatural" dichotomy. Illness is, likewise, perceived to be the result of such actions as "sorcery", "soul theft" by spirits or shamans, the inheritance of spirit familiars in family lines which leads to illness (for example tuberculosis), and the spread and infection of "epidemics" (*numbooloou*, lit. "rope of sickness") which have volition and awareness as if they were spiritual agents. Most injuries and deaths are regarded as the result of interventions of these kinds. Only rarely do people allow that injuries or illness "merely happen" without outside intervention; even then, there may be no general agreement in the community that sorcery or spirits were uninvolved.[2]

Concern with health and physical well-being is registered in many cultural domains and social arenas. Illness, sexual pollution, weakness, decay, degeneration and death are central preoccupations in the ideology and ritual, as well as in the personal experience, of Sambia life. For instance, much of male ritual lore, ingestion and avoidance taboos, incorporative and purificatory rituals revolves around the maintenance of vigour and potency. These cultural elements derive from an underlying model of "atrophy": an ethos that the body and its fluids have a "limited duration" and are gradually exhausted (Herdt 1981; in press). In this sense, then, much of Sambia ritual is concerned with teaching preventive measures for ensuring health, a point discussed below.

Local healers

Shamans are the real medical experts of traditional society. They were the main defenders of public health. Shamanic powers are categorized by Sambia into two types: the "great" shamans and the "little" shamans. The key to understanding this typology is the ability to engage in "magical flight" and to exorcise, which only the great shamans can do. This power is legitimized culturally as inherited, usually from a same-sexed parent or close patrilineal relative. "Little" shamans have weak claims to this inherited power. Historically, male shamans outnumbered female shamans by a four to one margin (a situation now changed, due to factors noted below). Shamans could divinate, exorcize, perform individual and mass healing ceremonies and practise sorcery. All of these functions were done to restore health or prevent illness, except for sorcery which was supposed to be done only for revenge or in the context of war against outside enemy groups. Shamanic skill and knowledge were enculturated and developed behaviorally over a period of many years in apprentice relation to older, more experienced shamans.

Ritual experts and magicians did minor healing for individuals who consulted them. Their medicinal knowledge was limited. They were approached, or in cases of family or close friends, they would approach patients, and perform minor healing spells. These usually involve special muds or ointments that have curative effects when magical spells are uttered over them. Special herbs, ritual leaves or other plant items were sometimes provided or advised for ingestion as well. These experts were in a class apart from the shamans; when the same practitioner was both a shaman and a ritual expert, his or her shamanic power far outweighed other attributes in the healing process.

Medicines

A wide range of items were used traditionally as medicines. Many, though not all, ailments involved treatments of ingested substances, such as leaves or flowers. Indeed, nothing is so "natural" or expected to the Sambia as a treatment prescribing the ingestion of something – an indigenous cultural view that facilitated the eventual enthusiastic response to the "medicine cabinet" approach of Western medicine. Most people have ideas about common herbs to take for such ordinary maladies as coughs or headaches. Local vegetal salt and ginger are popular items of this sort. It is usually only after one has tried these "home remedies" (with or without a magical spell, according to the knowledge of the person afflicted) and the illness persists that the patient will resort to a specialist.

Resort to healers

Specialists are consulted particularly for serious or lingering illness. According to their availability, shamans or magicians may be approached for any ailment, even the most ordinary; but their expertise is centered only on serious misfortunes. In the mid 1970s virtually every Sambia hamlet had at least one great shaman. Sometimes, such as in the instance of Nilangu village – my fieldwork site – a hamlet boasted of several great and little shamans as well as several ritual experts or magicians. Historically, the Sambia identified some fifteen great shamans in the Valley from the period of the 1940s to the present, some of whom are still living. Moreover, each of the Sambia river valleys had one or two renowned shamans whose reputations spread far and wide, such that in unusual cases of illness, or at the time of initiation rites (when shamans' curative and purificatory leadership was crucial to ritual efficacy), such shamans could be consulted or even invited to journey and perform. For such treatments they were well paid in trade items. In general, however, patients first consulted shamans in their own villages to whom they were related and in whom they could trust. Resort to healers therefore followed a chain of events that led from the persistence of illness to resort to local healers, and eventually to better known specialists in a neighboring hamlet or valley. Such resort was limited largely by politics: in times of warfare or animosity between the groups involved, patients had to rely solely upon local village specialists.

Shamans are thus more or less involved in a particular case relative to its severity and their location. They are approached to identify and then to cure an illness; so in this curative process, diagnosis comes first, followed by therapy.[3] Generally, patients had used "home remedies" and exhausted magicians' treatments before resorting to shamans. Living in the same small world as the patient, the shaman was aware of this "pre-history" of the case. This knowledge was important because the diagnostic process in shamanism often begins with the practitioner's dreams. The shaman could "speak out" and reveal his or her dreams before being approached to heal a patient. The diagnostic situation was, in this sense, a bi-directional process, with a dream, gleaned for omens, precipitating a diagnosis and/or treatment through a healing ceremony. Other events too, such as unusual happenings (sightings of animals in odd places, ritual performances, etc.) or misfortunes (deaths, fights, etc.) could also be interpreted as omens relating to the onset of an illness. Such omens usually led to divination in a healing ceremony, which would confirm the shaman's hunch about the aetiology of an illness and thus shape the diagnosis. If, however, the shaman firmly felt there was no hope for cure, the treatment process was stillborn at this point. A pronouncement would come that either the illness was incurable or death was imminent. Such a case – which led to an infant's death – is reported in Herdt (1977). This "hands off" approach, among other things, spared the shaman the shame of failure in a hopeless case and probably thwarted finger pointing and the shaman's fear of retaliation through sorcery.[4] Such instances were rare, I think, for in most situations shamans are eager to treat and further legitimate their reputations. Indeed, where one shaman takes a "hands off" approach, another may well step in and pursue treatment all the same. Diagnosis and treatment thus occur in situations with a pre-history of this sort spanning days or even weeks, as was the case with malaria and tuberculosis.

The next formal step occurred in a healing ceremony. This is done at night, usually in the shaman's or patient's hut. Cordylines and ritual leaves are procured. A song fest may initiate the proceedings. Virtually anyone can attend and small crowds are common at healing events. These elements confirm the intensely social nature of shamanic healing. Heavy tobacco smoking and betel nut are used to induce trance in the shaman. Trance provides the characteristic "X-ray" vision of the shaman, allowing him or her to see inside the patient's body for divination. Dreams or other omens are mentioned in this context, not only by the shaman but by others in the audience too. Treatment directly follows divination. In a trance state, the shaman can utilize any of several curative procedures, including exorcism. In difficult cases or when several patients assemble, and especially when a community fears epidemics, two, three or more shamans can work together in communal healing. Singing continues for some time. Later, the shaman may review the trance events in a story-like narrative that can involve fantastic episodes with ghosts or other spirits encountered in magical flight.

Repeated treatments may ensue in the following days. Shamans sometimes become involved in actually caring for or feeding the patient, when they are closely related. Patients may also continue their own home remedies or continue resorting to the magical spells and ointments of other specialists too. In this sense, Sambia used every available means to heal themselves, though the shaman's power was premier. Shamans sometimes were remunerated for their services, though they were not expected to seek compensation, or to get it, from close kin. The shaman was, after all, highly esteemed by Sambia, especially the great shaman. As a doer of good deeds – as the purveyor of a heroic complex (Herdt, in press) – praise and renown were felt to be sufficient "payment" for healing services.

There were thus two key differences separating magicians from shamans as healers. First, magicians treated on an *ad hoc* basis, usually without follow-up treatments, whereas shamans might conduct healing ceremonies several times for the same patient. Second, shamanism was a social performance, involving family and community, unlike the isolated instances of *ad hoc* spells done by magicians. These differences influenced Sambian responses to Western *doktas* in time.

HISTORY OF THE AID POST

Because the Sambia were the last contacted and pacified people of the Eastern Highlands, governmental services and particularly medical out-reach programs to them emerged late compared to other parts of Papua New Guinea (cf. Glick 1967, Schwartz 1969, Welsch 1983). Regular government patrols began in the mid 1960s. Early medical patrols treated the population on an intermittent basis, though Gajdusek (1957–1966) reports, for example, the virtual elimination of yaws through penicillin early on (cf. Lindenbaum 1979: 32).

Resident missionaries provided crucial but very limited first aid until the mid 1970s. The establishment of the local government council in 1973 recognized this situation of poor *ad hoc* Western medical care delivery. Within a year, provincial funds were allocated for construction of several medical aid posts throughout the Wonenara District, which encompasses the Sambia. By 1975, the year after I began fieldwork, construction was completed on a small two room aid post in the Sambia Valley, the first post in the Sambia territory. This post was erected on the floor of the Sambia Valley, near the mission station in the Upper Valley area, a 45 minute walk from my field site. This single aid post serviced the entire Valley until 1983, when the government established a second, same sized post in the lower Sambia Valley, two hours' walking distance south.

Subsequently, four additional aid posts have been established in Sambia population areas elsewhere beyond our Valley. They resemble in their social history and use the post I will focus on here in the Sambia Valley.

Sambia understood virtually nothing of Western culture at this time and their comprehension of Western medicine was likewise limited. Yes, government medical patrols had vaccinated and treated illness haphazardly for fifteen years and the missionaries had administered medications, bandages and the like as well. But the reasons for these procedures, their antecedents and likely consequences for health, were locally understood in only the vaguest way. A bandaged wound made sense to people, for this procedure was done traditionally. The need for its sterile conditions was not understood, however. And the concept of a prophylactic vaccination was not grasped at all (Alland 1970: 158). Early on, it seems, the generalized notion crept into social consciousness that an aid post orderly (APO) or *dokta* had special knowledge of these arcane Western ways. By the mid to late 1970s, then, *doktas* were already perceived as a major element in the treatment of illness.

Community response to the establishment of the aid post was generally enthusiastic. There were two main reasons. First, Sambia see their population as prone to illness and premature death. Perhaps this has to do with the peripherality of their society, their small population, the presence of malaria and parasitic diseases, and their ideology of atrophy; and perhaps too they feared retaliation from their neighbors against whom they warred (cf. Lindenbaum 1979). But whatever the causes, the aid post was seen as a new solution to this vulnerability.

Second, the aid post was perceived as the first concrete step by the government in the direction of local "development". (Sambia themselves do not use the term "development", but they pragmatically refer to "money" and "government" as elements in a process of opening up their territory to economic enhancement akin to the notion of "development".) These two factors are related, especially on the level of cultural ideology vis-à-vis the outside. For in both respects, Sambia perceived themselves to be unpowerful compared to the mythologized city people far away and of lesser value than them, as evidenced by the way returned Sambia coastal workers referred to their fellow villagers as *kanakas*, in the pejorative sense of an illiterate villager or country hick. Indeed, the most enthusiastic supporters of the aid post concept were these men with their outside experience. In 1975 they numbered perhaps one third of the total male population; but soon this number was to increase considerably. The support of other villagers for the post was lukewarm. Community elders and younger men were usually very supportive and contributed their labor to constructing the aid post hut. Most elderly people were indifferent and, in general, women – who lacked outside experience of any kind – were uninvolved, lacking any real knowledge of what the aid post meant.

At no time in this formulative stage, to my knowledge, was there any public or private talk that the aid post would substitute for, or even affect, indigenous healing practices. The subject simply never came up. The shamans whom I knew closely looked upon the aid post establishment with benign interest. No evidence from later fieldwork has changed this impression.

Soon, the post was supplied and staffed. Limited medical supplies were carried in over the mountains from the district office, a two day walk. An aid post orderly (APO) was assigned to staff the hut. Local government officers accompanied him first, to give a clear signal of his official status and backing and to ensure the cooperation of local *Komiti* and the *Kaunsalman* (locally elected officials in the new government council system) in providing him with a hut and garden land at local village expense. The missionaries, who have a two- way radio, promised their support as before, both in hospitality and in the use of their radio to contact the authorities for helicopter ambulance in cases of "life and death". The new orderly – the first in a long line – was a young man in his middle twenties who had a primary school education and APO training. This training consists of the rudiments of first aid, procedures for diagnosis and a good knowledge of the administration of standard medications for coughs, headaches, gastro-enteritis, malaria, etc. This APO was from a completely different ethnic group; he spoke Pidgin but had no knowledge of the Sambia language or culture.

These aid posts are conceived as the "front line" in the delivery of medical care to Papua New Guinea's predominantly rural population. Beyond the tiny posts are larger "Rural Health Centers", usually located in district capital stations or heavily populated rural areas. They can treat more serious disorders, perform minor surgery, and admit patients for limited periods. Marawaka Patrol Post has had a center of this kind since mid 1970. At the next level are the general hospitals of New Guinea's towns. The Provincial Medical Officer is located here and is responsible for the supervision and staffing of lower-level units. At the aid post, life-crisis cases are dealt with by radio contact with the provincial officer in Goroka, in conjunction with Goroka General Hospital. In theory this is the case; practically speaking, all manner of disorders are dealt with by the APO, including emergency cases of the critically ill.

Three problems have beset the Sambia aid post: (1) staffing and supply difficulties, (2) the presence and resort to shamans or local healing specialists, and (3) the popular misunderstanding and lack of use of the APO. These issues are synergistically related and, from an insider perspective, not easily separated. Analytically, however, I will discuss each problem in turn and then summarize this section of the chapter.

Inadequate staffing and supplying are the most easily described problems of the aid post. Any area as isolated as the Sambia River Valley will of course suffer from supply shortage. Until 1983, when an airstrip was opened, only transport by foot and the rare helicopter, provided supplies. No refrigerated medication or other material could be provided because of the lack of refrigeration, except when provided by the local missionary family (who have a very small kerosene-powered refrigerator). Though supplying continues to be problematic, the situation in 1983 was much better because of occasional light aircraft servicing the grass strip in the Valley. Staffing has been a chronic difficulty for the post. Perhaps half a dozen APOs have been stationed at the post between 1975 and 1981. Most of these men proved to be unable or unwilling to work in the Valley for more than a few months and again the extreme isolation was a main cause. Lacking tradestores or regular supply lines, the APOs had to rely on purchasing local produce or on people's handouts for food. Being from different ethnic groups and cut off from kin and friends, they felt lonely and socially unstimulated. Most objected to being posted in such a "bushy" area, preferring instead city life or at least a rural area accessed by the Highlands highway. Other interpersonal problems, such as adultery and irresponsibility, have forced out two of the APOs. Male APOs who brought in their wives and families have weathered the longest in the Valley. And, more recently, those Sambia trained as APOs themselves, stationed in the Valley, have proven the most successful of all. They are discussed in the next section.

Resort to shamans was another stumbling block in the early APO history, as seen from the perspective of the medical orderlies. Implementation of the aid post did not at first alter the traditional healing system of Sambia. Indigenous medicines continued to be used as ever; local specialists performed spells, and shamanic healing ceremonies remained the main resort for cure – and a crowd-pleaser as before. The APOs knew this; the more sophisticated of them tried to change the situation. They did their most to enlist the help of community leaders. The rhetoric of local *kaunsalmen* in public meetings unequivocably urged people to "help" the APO with food, firewood, etc. and to go to him with the sick. In private, though, everyone knew these same politicians used the shamans as much as anyone else. (Indeed, one notable public figure was married to a practising female shaman.) Local Seventh Day Adventist New Guinea missionaries added to the fray by becoming more vocal and denouncing the shamans as "witchdoctors" and quacks: Anti-Christ, they said. The shamans did not at first back down by changing their healing style. But the situation soured more between 1976 and 1979. One rather outspoken APO (eventually to be removed for adultery and repeated absence) publicly denounced the shamans and insinuated that "the government" would take action against them. This marked the first time the *dokta* openly opposed the shamans. It had a dire effect: it directly placed the shamans on notice that they had to defend customary healing practices; and it indirectly linked progress in development to the abandonment of shamanic healing. In this openly confrontative situation the shamans began to decline patients or refer them to the APO. Moreover, by 1981 to my surprise, there was an illicit atmosphere surrounding shamanic healing ceremonies: not quite secret, but no longer the public show and festivity of before.

Public misunderstanding of Western medicine and the APO's role has persisted until today as a basic problem in the use of the local aid post. Gradual exposure to the aid post, either directly or indirectly, has altered people's perceptions. Minor treatments for cuts, headaches, scabies, colds, burns, dysentery and such ailments had greatly increased. People – especially the elderly, women and children – still mistrusted injections. Many villagers did not understand why they had to take pills, though they did so, consistent with the traditional idea that health is strengthened through ingestion of ritual substances. Malaria, pneumonia and tuberculosis – indeed, preventive medicine in general – were no better understood by 1981 than before. However, more people, more frequently, came to the aid post for treatment of such chronic complaints: a clear change from the situation six years earlier. Complicated childbirths were treated in consultation with the APO, though to do so was to break down the enormous sex barrier against men being involved in pregnancy or present at delivery. Malnutrition and poor lactation are treated on occasion, but generally not understood at large. The APO serviced an area too large to handle for one person. People from distant villages used the post much less than people close by. The APO's absences compounded this problem, and people complained that he was never to be found. (Eventually, this difficulty was corrected.) By and large, use of the APO increased remarkably up to 1981, though misunderstanding and lack of education about the *dokta's* treatment remained widespread.

To sum up: the establishment of a local aid post in the Valley (1975) had an enthusiastic but bumpy start. Problems of staffing, opposition to traditional healers and local misunderstanding of Western medical care plagued the post for the ensuing five years. Restudy in 1979 confirmed confrontation between the APO and shamans, and the inadequate availability of the APO due to staffing problems. Nonetheless, traditional healing and the aid post seemed to be working in tandem, at least until the shamans were denounced. This event further altered the total system of resort to healers.

THE 1981 STUDY

In 1981, as part of on-going longitudinal fieldwork with Sambia, I conducted a large household survey in the Sambia Valley. With the help of a field assistant,[5] a large number ($N = 356$) of the resident adults was interviewed over a two-month period. Out of this sample, a sub-sample of adults from the Upper Valley will be highlighted here. This subsample ($N = 191$) represents better than 95% of all resident adults in the four village settlement area of the Upper Valley surrounding the original aid post.

Our method was as follows: an extensive questionnaire was administered to each adult in his or her own house. The questionnaire contained many items covering a range of questions concerning socio-economic attitudes and social change in the area. I framed these items in language and understanding to appropriately register local views and feelings. The protocol was available in English and in Neo-Melanesian Pidgin. All questionnaires were administered orally since Sambia are non-literate. We explained the general scope of the task and individually asked each respondent to participate. Wherever possible the interview was conducted in Sambia, either by me or by an interpreter assisting my field assistant.

TABLE 1
When did you last visit the aid post?

Response	Number	Frequency
1. Within the last month	42	22%
2. One month ago	56	29%
3. Two months ago	35	18%
4. Three months ago	23	12%
5. More than three months ago	29	15%
6. Never	6	3%
Totals	191	99%

The data described here come from responses to questions dealing with health issues in our interviews. Inquiries were made both on the aid post and on shamanic healing. The key interest in these questions was to understand the relative use of the aid post vis-à-vis traditional healers.

The first of our questions was directed to utilization of the aid post. We asked, "Do you visit the medical aid post?" 97% ($N = 185$) said "yes", and 3% ($N = 6$)

said "no". We then asked how frequently they visited the APO. At this time, 38% said they visited the post once a month 29% more than once a month, and 32% said they went less frequently but at least every two months.

To make these responses more concrete, we then asked respondents to pinpoint the time of their last visit to the aid post. The results are shown in Table 1.

In other words, more than half the population had used the aid post within a month of our study and 85% of all respondents said they had gone for medical care in the three months leading up to our survey.

To understand their resort to the aid post, we then asked why they had sought the *dokta* the last time they visited the post. The results show clearly that illness is the main source of APO visits. Respondents said they went because they were ill (89%), because their child was ill (9%), or because they had suffered an injury (2%). To clarify the extent to which individuals alone or families utilize the APO, we then asked: "Does your family go when you visit the aid post?" Here, 99% of all respondents said their families as a unit visited the APO.

This strong and positive response to the aid post must be seen in the context of the popularity of the then-posted orderly. In spite of the staffing and personnel difficulties associated with the past, Sambia continued to use the post in increasing numbers up to 1979. Problems remained, however. Soon after, the government wisely posted one of its most experienced APOs in the Valley, a Sambia man from a different river valley area. He moved to the post with his family and revamped the operation substantially. He was tireless in his efforts to help people. This APO's ability and desire to speak in Sambian with patients about their ills tremendously affected the users' positive feeling about the post. Soon thereafter, the month-by-month number of users dramatically increased. His likeable personality, education, and Sambian background helped greatly in giving people more confidence than they had ever had in the post. Many Sambia identify the aid post with the particular APO assigned to it, I think, just as traditionally they identified a particular shaman with the general role, as evidenced by the traditional contrast between great and minor shamans. When we asked people then if the *dokta* "helps them", people's responses to this essentially moral valuation were enormously enthusiastic, with 98% of all respondents replying "yes". The particular APO at the time of the 1981 study – who had instilled such confidence for nearly two years up to that point – was very much a factor in people's assessments.

A clear pattern of aid post use thus develops from these responses. Sambia had an extremely high use of the aid post barely six years after it was founded. They use the APO mainly because of illness, and their resort extends to their children and to the family as a whole.

Next we turned to an examination of the use of traditional healers in our household survey. My expectation was that in spite of the success of the aid post, virtually the entire population would continue to use shamans.

Our findings on this point are for me the most surprising of the study. We asked people, "Do you have *kwolyu* (healing ceremonies) performed by shamans?" Only

55% of all respondents said "yes". That 45% said they no longer use shamans struck me as a remarkable change in such a short period of time. We then repeated our previous structure of questions, in line with shamanic use. We asked when people had last actually used a shaman; the results are displayed in Table 2.

TABLE 2
When did you last visit a shaman?

Response	Number	Frequency
1. Within the last month	19	10%
2. One month ago	22	11%
3. Two months ago	24	12%
4. Three months ago	14	7%
5. More than three months ago	26	14%
6. No longer use	86	45%
Totals	191	99%

In short, only a third of the sample had used shamans in the two months prior to our study. Again, of those who still use shamans, 95% said they resorted to shamans for illness in themselves, and 4% due to a child's illness. Less than 1% used shamans to treat an injury.

It is critical to insert here an up-date on the APO's opposition to traditional healing practices. As fate would have it, the current *dokta*, so enormously popular, was as committed to the introduction of good Western medical practice as he was to the eradication of traditional healing. He was, moreover, a devoted Seventh Day Adventist who held the mission views of shamans previously noted. Though in private the APO of course acknowledged and understood the shaman's traditional role – for this *dokta* was after all a Sambian – in public he nonetheless orated and lobbied against it. His motives were, as far as I can tell, altruistic and well intentioned. There were rapid effects of his opposition. Shamans seemed to take fewer patients. They also tended to perform surreptitiously, as noted above. Though in private some shamans ignored or dismissed the APO's rhetoric, none publicly challenged his authority. Throughout this change, the magicians and ritual experts were largely by-passed. It seems that the APOs have focussed on the role – and symbol of – the shaman as a figure to be singled out in order to deal with the overall traditional healing process. My observations indicate that while less *ad hoc* healing spells are done by magicians than before the advent of the *dokta*, their users and confidence in their practices have not declined with the same rapidity as have shamanic healing practices.

Thus far we have kept the APO and shaman figures separate in our questions. Next, however, we asked all respondents to tell us if they went to see the *dokta* after visiting a shaman. Of those who did say they used shamans (i.e., 55%), fully 90% of these said that the last time they visited a shaman they went to see the APO too. The 10% who used shamans and did not resort to the APO are presumably the "hard conservative core" of those villagers who are exclusively traditional in their orientations to the healing process. My impressions, and those of the APO when I interviewed him, indicate that this minority is made up largely of the elderly.

There are two fundamental reasons why I find the drop in shamanic use so surprising. Though these were hinted earlier, their clarification here is necessary. First, the *doktas* do not discuss their healing practices with patients the way shamans do. When the APO asks for symptoms, seldom does he explain why, or what he is looking for. By contrast, the shamans usually explain their questioning of patients, often with reference to dreams or omens that indicate "causes" of the affliction. At most, APOs may refer to pragmatic effects expected of a *materia medica* approach using pills, ointments or injections, but most of this discourse is ill understood by Sambian users (cf. Welsch 1983: 45). Moreover, whereas the shaman usually follows up a treatment by a further visit, consultation or ceremony, and may reveal additional dreams or portents pertinent to the case, even the best *dokta* practitioner does not follow up in this manner, his high case load being a main reason.

But the second reason – the high ceremony and social drama surrounding traditional shamanism and absent at the aid post – is an even stronger reason for questioning why the APO has succeeded so well. The shaman was a cultural authority writ large. His status and authority pervaded religion and politics. He was a showman; pomp and drama were his tools. He performed in a social context for the patient, the family and community at large. Nothing in the *dokta*'s performance matches that drama. Moreover, the holistic approach – treating body, mind and soul as integrated parts of the overall healing problem – is so essential to the shamanic ceremony and so lacking in the *dokta*'s secular role. Indeed, the lack of explanation of the symptom collecting, diagnosis and treatment phases noted above of the APO, in marked contrast to the shaman's style, would seem to undermine the patient's confidence in the aid post. In this regard, the *dokta* had an *ad hoc* approach more in line with traditional magicians and ritual experts, though their status accords to that of the shaman. Still, it is notable that a patient often travels with his or her family to the aid post for treatment. Perhaps this and the impressive technology of the *dokta* are factors linking the past and the present in Sambia responses to the aid post.

A factor that may play a minor role here is the material cost of health services. The aid post medical services are monetarily "free" to Sambia, though many grateful patients provide food or commodities such as firewood to show their gratitude. Noted shamans traditionally could be remunerated by their patients, partly out of gratitude and partly in respect of such factors as the distance a shaman travelled or the total amount of time spent healing someone. Yet for the Sambia, no service is entirely "free", for their culture emphasizes reciprocity of exchange between persons. Thus, to use a shaman, even one who is kin, places a small obligation upon the user to reciprocate. No such generalized obligation applies to the APO, whom people know to be paid by the government for his work. In the 1981 study, 10% of those who visited shamans (or less than 6% of our total sample) said that they did "pay" a shaman for his or her services. I doubt that this is a significant factor in why others may not use the shamans for healing, but it cannot be ruled out altogether.

A more critical element in the comparative use of shamans or APOs is no doubt the local "government" opposition to shamanic healing. "Government" here is used by Sambia to refer to the Seventh Day Adventist missionaries, certain local council members and the present APO. The vigorous denunciations of the shamans over the past half dozen years have made the shamans cautious and wary. Sambia themselves regard shamanic use as "old fashioned" and traditional whereas, to reiterate, the APO represents to them "development" (i.e., "progress"). My own observations show clearly that present day shamans perform less, perhaps half as frequently as they did ten years ago. Male labor migration and absenteeism have contributed to this trend. The demographic change in the ratio of male to female shamans, which is now almost equal, is indeed a contributing factor in the decreasing resort to shamans. Young men are no longer eager to replace their elders as shamans. Yet men, at least, feel more comfortable with male shamans, of whom there are now fewer and less renowned ones. But this too is not a critical factor, I believe: it rather reflects a larger systemic acculturation widely influencing Sambia society.

When we consider the extraordinarily high number of people who say they use the APO – nearly 100% – and the surprising number who no longer use shamans (45%), what stands out next is the fact that 90% of those who see shamans also go to the aid post. They engage, that is, in multiple healing resorts, traditional and Western. Seen in this way, perhaps 5% or even less of Sambia rely exclusively on shamans for their health care. However, I must add that Sambia themselves do not much discuss in public whether to use shamans and/or the aid post. They are pragmatists. Having always been concerned in their traditional ideology with health and preservation of vitality, they are catholic in their use of many procedures to heal or prevent illness. The opposition to shamans has placed the question in a more heated political atmosphere than would otherwise have been the case. But the shamans too are pragmatic about their powers. In my experience, the Sambia shamans today see themselves as providing a complementary service to that of the APO. Indeed, Sakulambei, the noted shaman (Herdt and Stoller, in press) has told me many times he routinely refers people to the APO first. Then, and only then, if they so desire and he is willing, will he take on a patient. In this approach, therefore, the patient has the advantages of both healing systems – a "cover all bases" pragmatism that nicely fits the old Sambia concern with maximizing care of the person.

DISCUSSION

By 1981, Sambia had experienced Western medical care in some form for twenty years, though *doktas* had directly competed with traditional healers for only the last six of those years. Observations and interviews up to that time showed clearly that resort to traditional shamanism had declined dramatically. The once paramount shamans were used by less than half the population and only 10% of adults, mainly old people, exclusively used shamans. Traditional curers are today clearly attenuated in their healing activities (Landy 1974). Such is the situation that one could hardly describe the resort to both traditional and Western medical care as a *"modus vivendi"* of complementary forms of treatment (Janzen 1978: 3). The main purpose of this discussion is to consider the causes of this rapid and majority use of the Sambian medical aid posts. My discussion will be broken into four categories of analysis: changes in roles, changes in beliefs, changes in ideology, and changes in the pragmatic expectations of healing.

Role change

Traditional Sambia culture offered two normative roles to remedy illness: the shaman and the magician. The shaman was, aside from his religious and political prestige, a "generalist" healer, able to treat all sickness. By contrast the magician was a specialist, limited to the initial treatment of minor illness. We have seen that although the shamans have declined in prestige and performance, the magicians' role has not substantially altered.

Alland (1970) has argued that medical systems under the pressure of acculturative change must be seen in terms of role changes. He suggests that in rapidly acculturating societies the presence of a traditional role, analogous to that of the Western practitioner, generally facilitates change to Western medicine. Moreover, this change may occur without complementary change in the cultural content of the traditional role (Alland 1970: 159). I would argue that such a case of role change can be seen among the Sambia. Traditionally, people resorted first to home remedies, then to village magicians ("specialists") and lastly to shamans. Today, the first two phases in this process are essentially the same as in the pre-contact period. Sickness allows people the options of first using home remedies and then the magicians' herbal curatives. Only then, in the absence of cure, do they resort either to the shaman or the *dokta*. Here, the APO and shamans are treated by roughly half the adults as functional alternatives. This change has generally occurred without change in the normative content of home remedies or the magician's role. Up to this point in the healing process, then, decisions to use one or other healing mechanism are made on a "situational basis" (Foster and Anderson 1978: 248). Thereafter, other factors come into play in the process.

In resorting to either shamans or *doktas* or both, Sambia use of healers suggests that they are at an acculturative turning point. Those patients who elect exclusively to resort to *doktas* indicate that the social and ceremonial functions of traditional shamanic healing are no longer of value to them. The APO's procedures, without discussion or explanation to the patient, seem not to matter as much as his actual delivery of service. Those who resort to shamans exclusively seem to feel that the traditional social functions and familial context are still significant for their well being. For the elderly – who have believed in this process their whole lives – such "faith" may be crucial to their "cure". Here, the parallel case of the Ablon of Zaire may be telling (Alland 1970). Ablon have both medical healers and priests available to cure. But given their religious and medical interlinkages as healers, priests provide crucial socio-religious functions. Alland (1970:177–178) suggests that in such cultural contexts, missionary doctors are the most likely Western practitioners to succeed. Sambia, however, lack such figures. Among the Sambia, the large number who use both shamans and *doktas* – about half the adult population – seem to suggest that both traditional and Western roles can be used in complementary fashion to effect cure. At the present rate of change, however, one wonders how long shamanism will survive in any form.

A key cause in the acceptance of Western medicine in this regard may be the presence of curing generalists in a traditional culture. The Sambian shaman is such a generalist figure. Perhaps this generalist role serves as a symbolic stimulus to change in homogeneous cultures. Without "severe disruptions" of culture change in medical systems (Alland 1970), acculturative change in healing practices proceeds according to a complex dialectic of internal and external change, based in part on the presence of key symbolic figures – such as shamans – to support or oppose. Judging by the limited period of direct competiton between *doktas* and shamans, the shamans are not "holding their own". The Ningerum of New Guinea, by contrast, who traditionally had only healing specialists, seem to have better integrated Western and traditional curative roles (Welsch 1983). One wonders if other New Guinea cultures having generalist healing roles (cf. Glick 1967; Johannes 1980; Nelson 1971), have experienced the same acculturative sequence.

Belief changes

Opposition to shamanism by the resident *doktas* has undermined popular belief in the shamans by villagers. This reduction in faith has been facilitated by the shamans' relatively passive response to this opposition. The overall belief system regarding illness has not in itself fundamentally changed. Yet people's perceptions of healing options have been dramatically eroded by the feeling that shamans and healers are fundamentally different sorts of health providers. One could, of course, stress the bimodal persistence of those who utilize both Western and shamanic medical care. But to do so would, I believe, underrate the remarkable drop in exclusive resort to shamanic ceremony. It must be said, then, that most Sambia now express a ranking of their preferences for healing types (Woods 1977) or recognize therapeutic alternatives (Kunstadter 1976). That is, they evince a hierarchy of resort to healers in relation to their beliefs about what is the most effective form of treatment (Schwartz 1969). The sources of change in the belief system are not entirely conscious. Rather, they derive from both conscious and unconscious ideology and the perceived pragmatic effects of treatment.

Ideological changes

The old structural emphasis on ingestion of "strong" substances to enhance health or ward off illness has not changed for the Sambia. This ideology of ingestion is consistent with the *materia medica* approach of the *doktas*. I suggest that it has been a pivotal ideological factor underlying the receptance of aid post treatment. Just as acculturated Sambia have embraced the psycho-physiological effects of alcohol in fostering their ethos of strength (Herdt 1983), so they have adopted the "medicine cabinet" view of maintaining health. Moreover, the Sambia – always pragmatic – have taken notice of the material "wealth" and superior technology available to the *dokta* versus the shaman. Though the APO may not be able to comfort them spiritually as did the shaman, they are comforted by the sense that the *dokta* is in command of greater technological forces.

The ideologies of "tradition" and "development" are relevant here in an unforeseen way. We need to recognize that the seemingly "rational" choices people make in a complex acculturative situation are not thoroughly consistent. Perhaps Erasmus (1952) and Foster and Anderson (1978) are among the most vigorous advocates of the view that traditional peoples opt for Western medical treatment because they perceive the better empirical results of their Western practitioners. They argue that while traditional peoples recognize the differences between their own and Western curative procedures, they choose the latter through pragmatism. For the Sambia I suggest that the situation is not so simple. Sambia villagers do not question traditional and Western medicine in the same way. Shamans are backed by tradition, by faith and by the force and glamor of social ceremonies. *Doktas* are supported by the incipient but nonetheless powerful ideology of "development". The development model is the one which today receives regular rhetorical justification. By happenstance the shamans have been linked to opposition to "development". The shamans now symbolically represent "the old way". In this respect it doesn't matter if shamans discuss and validate their treatments with patients, while *doktas* generally do not. What matters is that the APOs have visits from government patrol officers; that they can command helicopters to arrive at will; that they can inoculate a whole village if need be; and that they provide a generalized "life-line" with an outside world constantly pressing in on the Sambia.

Some additional support of this role of ideology is provided by an analysis of Sambians who have worked outside in the towns. The most acculturated ex-migrants living in the villages are, after all, the most active opponents of traditional healing. They are the ones who have known the outside world – its pleasures and pains, its alcohol and fast food – and they offer, as "frontiersmen" who have returned home, a supposedly superior vantage point on their own culture (Herdt 1983).

Both villagers who use shamans and returned migrants who resort to *doktas* have similiar ends – health, well-being, success in life. In this respect, they merely use different means to the same ends (cf. M. Strathern 1975). But at the level of development and integration with the nation-state of Papua New Guinea, the migrants who talk of "progress" do have a fundamentally different end: "development" versus "tradition". We are all too familiar now with the anthropological complaint that tribal societies are not neutral or empty vessels for the introduction of Western medicine (for example, Kleinman 1980). Their own indigenous health systems color the process of acculturation, often in ways impossible to foresee or predict (McDermott et al. 1972). In the same sense, case studies of the Sambia and other peoples in this volume can make us more aware of the equally complex factors associated with the idea of "development" as it occurs in particular places and times.

Pragmatic changes

Social change has so far had a rather even course among the Sambia. Aside from the Australian enforced pacification of 1964, which occurred on a single afternoon, no other changes have been so sudden or far reaching. The introduction of Western medicine has occurred gradually and relatively devoid of public debate. The practical changes resulting from this history have therefore taken hold of people in a piecemeal way.

The main reality at present is that the numbers and performances of shamans are decreasing while the *dokta* is always there. The *dokta* is "free" and he provides an effortless service. As people are increasingly drawn away from traditional images of life – hunting and gardening, initiation and collective feasts – the pragmatic service image of the *dokta* better fits a people involved in road work, cash cropping and migration to the patrol station and town. The question must inevitably arise as to whether *doktas* actually do better than shamans in healing the sick. Today, many younger Sambians say "yes". Some of them still have doubts about this, however; certainly their elders feel differently. But the course of change and the shamans' response to it have not helped their cause. They were once omnipotent in spiritual matters and even in politics. That they could be reduced to such passive – some would even say "shadowy" – figures, has increased the doubts surrounding their powers and undermined even old people's faith in them. Sambia have thus reinterpreted their ideas and images of shamans as a result both of external and internal forces at work in their environment. Given another generation of change in this direction, it is not so hard to imagine that some day Sambia shamanism may be seen as a dim and antique custom recalled with amusement at the *dokta*'s door.

NOTES

1. The author gratefully acknowledges the support of the following institutions for fieldwork among the Sambia: the Australian-American Education Foundation, The Australian National University, The National Institute of Mental Health, the Department of Psychiatry at U.C.L.A., the Wenner-Gren Foundation, the Stanford Center for

the Study of Youth Development, and the Department of Anthropology, Stanford University.
2. Unfortunately, I must largely exclude from this study a description of intracultural variation in attitudes about illness and resort to treatment. In a later publication I hope to take up these matters.
3. It is difficult to know how widespread this cultural pattern of healing is, but (Welsch 1983: 40) has recently described the opposite for another New Guinea group: "Instead, Ningerum practitioners are selected because they can perform certain specialties; they are not consulted to make a diagnosis and then prescribe the appropriate therapy."
4. Sambia attribute the deaths and sickness of certain shamans, past and present, to such sorcery retaliation; thus, sorcery is a culturally constituted force with which the shaman must contend, in deciding to pursue a healing case.
5. My field assistant, Mark Janssen, greatly helped me in conducting this study, and I wish to thank him for his valuable efforts.

MICHAEL W. YOUNG

5. ILLNESS AND IDEOLOGY: ASPECTS OF HEALTH CARE ON GOODENOUGH ISLAND[1]

INTRODUCTION

The extent to which illness, disease and other bodily afflictions are socially constituted and culturally interpreted is a source of unending fascination to anthropologists. In considering aspects of medical pluralism in Goodenough Island, this chapter documents the influence of ideological factors on traditional curing and the use of modern health facilities. The core of the chapter is an examination of statistical data on in-patient and out-patient treatment at two health centers on the island. Some unexpected patterns emerge with regard to the health care bestowed on children, patterns which are highlighted by a comparison of the records from the two centers, one government and the other mission established. The peculiarities of these patterns are, I suggest, best explained by the patrilineal social ideology of villagers in the one case, and the paternalistic social ideology of the missionaries in the other.

Goodenough, one of the largest and most mountainous islands in the Massim (Milne Bay Province), is more than 300 square miles in area and more than 8000 ft. in height. At the 1979 census its population was 13,075 persons, of whom some 1400 were absent abroad. People dwell in multi-clan villages, more or less nucleated, consisting of several hundred members. Nowadays these local communities form wards of a local government council established in 1964.

Goodenough islanders are typical New Guinea horticulturalists. The staples are yams, taro, bananas, sweet potato, tapioca (manioc) and the coconut. Pigs are essential to the exchange economy, there is fishing on the coast and a limited amount of hunting in the forest. Imported European foodstuffs (particularly rice and tinned meat and fish, occasionally flour and biscuits) contribute to the diet in a minor way, mostly on festive occasions. The islanders are heavy tobacco smokers and inveterate betel nut chewers (children begin to chew areca as soon as they are able to husk the nuts, and parents do not discourage them); but men can rarely afford to purchase beer or other imported alcoholic drinks.

The main source of cash on the island is copra making, though a little cocoa is grown and the past decade has seen some experiments in cattle raising. These sources of income, however, are less significant than the thoroughly institutionalized labor migrations of young men. Since 1900, Goodenough men have shown a curious enthusiasm for regular stints of wage labor in distant mines and plantations (Young 1983a). Due partly to isolation and administrative neglect (the island still awaits its first high school), traditional culture and society on Goodenough remain vital in many essentials, though they have been modified in detail by Christian

---

S. Frankel and G. Lewis (eds.), *A Continuing Trial of Treatment*. 115–139.
© 1988, Kluwer Academic Publishers, Dordrecht – Printed in the Netherlands.

missions and the influences of migrant labor (see Macintyre and Young 1982). The festivals and competitive feasting I described in *Fighting with Food* (1971) continue to stimulate food production, and there persists in most villages a pervasive food-centered ethos. Goodenough islanders would endorse Bertolt Brecht's dictum that "at the source of everything is the belly". By modern criteria, however, nutritional standards are low and undernutrition is common among children.[2]

Nothing is known, of course, about precontact epidemiology, though one can surmise with some certainty that malaria was endemic and that yaws, tropical ulcers, tinea, worms and perhaps leprosy were common. Beginning in earnest in the 1890s, European contact brought many infectious diseases. The D'Entrecasteaux Group (of which Goodenough is one of the principal islands) suffered terribly at the turn of the century from prolonged drought, a hurricane, and several lethal epidemics.[3] These, exacerbated by poor nourishment and the initial disruptions of migrant labor, brought about a sharp decline in the population from which it took some fifty years to recover. Mission and government records indicate that some epidemic, whether of whooping cough, measles, influenza or dysentery, occurred every few years until the 1930s, though the documentation is too sparse to give much inkling of their distributions. There are a few useful figures, and I offer the following sample as merely suggestive of an epidemic's impact. In 1900, the Wesleyan missionary Bromilow reported 299 deaths from whooping cough in his circuit (AWMMS 1901: lxxxi). Such an unrounded figure indicates that he had no wish to exaggerate, though we might surmise that his circuit included only those people in the Dobu-Duau area who attended church services or were otherwise known to mission personnel. In 1900 they would have numbered about 4000, suggesting a mortality rate of about 7.5%. In 1911 dysentery caused a death toll of not less than 500 in the D'Entrecasteaux. As this epidemic also occurred at a time of famine, and since the officer who made the estimate was concerned to minimize the degree of food shortage, the figure of 500 was doubtless on the conservative side (PAR 1911-12: 112; Young 1983a: 80-1). Even so, given that the population of the D'Entrecasteaux was about 25,000 in 1911, the death toll attributed to dysentery would have been about 2%. This particular epidemic spread far and wide due to the "yearly sail about" of D'Entrecasteaux men and those of nearby islands: probably a reference to the Kula voyages between Tubetube and Duau (Normanby Island) and across to Fergusson via Dobu. Bromilow mentions 54 deaths in Ware Island that year, which could have been as high as a third of the population (AMMR 1912, Dec.4: 22). Finally I refer to a patrol report of 1957 which observed that "for many years the D'Entrecasteaux has suffered periodic outbreaks of bronchial pneumonia", and which enumerated 46 deaths in five villages (pop. 1550) of eastern Goodenough over a period of ten months. This was a year when some 42% of able-bodied men were away from the island, surely a complicating demographic factor in the ostensible poor health of a population so vulnerable to pneumonia.[4]

So much for earlier records. Despite an optimistic campaign to eradicate malaria in the 1960s, it remains pandemic. Yaws and leprosy appear to have been eradicated; tuberculosis remains prevalent. Tropical ulcers are probably as common as ever, though with the advent of clinics they are less likely to result in serious deformations. Scaly ringworm (*tinea imbricata*) is still widespread and shows some puzzling distributions, being more common in the hill villages than on the coast.[5] Thanks to traditional sanctions against sexual promiscuity Goodenough has a fairly low incidence of venereal diseases. This is in marked contrast to other parts of the Massim, particularly the notorious Trobriand Islands where syphilis still poses a serious health problem. If chastity has helped safeguard them from sexually transmitted diseases, Goodenough women nevertheless suffer other reproductive disorders and their mortality rate in childbirth must be as high as anywhere in Papua New Guinea.

TRADITIONAL CURING

It is impossible to do justice in a few pages to the indigenous curing traditions of Goodenough, though something needs to be said, however briefly, about conceptions of illness and curing practices insofar as these affect islanders' acceptance of Western medicine and modern health facilities. I shall confine my remarks to Kalauna, a hill village of 500 people in eastern Goodenough, with which I am most familiar. Among the fifty or so village communities on the island, Kalauna appears at the conservative end of a spectrum of traditionalism; indeed, in comparison with heavily-missionized Bwaidoka, the other village I know well, Kalauna is still semi-pagan. My intimate familiarity with Kalauna dates from 1966 and, notwithstanding the expansion of health services since then, I have perceived no weakening of traditional beliefs in the domain of illness and curing. Accordingly, Kalauna people appear to make highly selective use of the available services.

Goodenough people generally adopt a pragmatic attitude towards Western drugs and medical treatment. They accept a simplified germ theory of disease and the reasons for rudimentary hygiene. They know that malarial fever quickly responds to doses of *kwinini*; that headaches are eased by aspirin (commonly confused with "quinine" however) and that sores, boils, ulcers and other fleshy infections can be cured by injections of penicillin. They acknowledge that broken or mutilated limbs and lacerated bodies are more effectively treated by health center personnel than by their own curers. They know, too, that measles and influenza appear in epidemic form (though they conceive of the cause of all epidemics as a "white" wild spirit called *kwadulele*).[6] They know that pneumonia tends to "come on top" of some other illness and admit that their traditional remedies are ineffective against it. They also appreciate that a woman who suffers complications in childbirth has a better chance of survival if she can be taken to hospital (though the problem is ever one of making the decision to convey her there in time). For the rest, however, most Goodenough people remain sceptical, if not downright suspicious, in their attitude towards institutionalized modern medicine; hospitals, after all, are where people frequently die.

The most important illnesses in Kalauna, the "big sicknesses" lasting a couple of months or more, are believed to have no counterpart in Western medicine and hence no cures for them are to be found in aid post, health center or hospital. Appropriately in the light of Kalauna's food centered ethos and symbolic equation of gardens and bellies (Young 1977), the afflictions Kalauna people most fear are diseases of the belly. There is *tufo'a*, the hunger disease, which compels its victims to eat voraciously but to no effect (Young, in press (a)); there is *doke*, the skirt disease, which debilitates and finally kills a cuckolded husband by the growth of a woman's leaf skirt in his belly (Young, in press (b)); there is *daiyaya*, blood disease, which causes blood to gather and coagulate in the stomach;[7] and there are *yafuna*, witch-like spirits that invade and consume a living victim's viscera. Empirically, it is difficult to determine what might correspond to these diseases in Western medical terms. All are characterized by physical wasting and a swollen belly, though their other respective symptoms might well be more imaginary than real. With the exception of *doke*, the cuckold's disease, all are thought to be the work of sorcerers; accordingly, although greatly feared, they are curable in principle. This applies to many other Kalauna afflictions, a comparable range of which has been documented by Reo Fortune for Dobu (1963: Ch.3). As elsewhere in the Massim, a great many diseases on Goodenough are believed to be the result of inadvertent breaches of *tabu*, whether the taboos are imposed by men to safeguard their property, by ancestors to sanction their customary rules, or by spirits to protect their arbitrary domains.

There are also those diseases in Kalauna which roughly correspond to afflictions recognized by Western medicine. *Yobiyobi* is tuberculosis or other diseases of the lung (there were about ten known cases in 1980); *yahu* is jaundice or hepatitis (about six cases diagnosed in the past ten years); *tomokoyo* is a deep ulcer or abscess which attacks the bone; *motalai* are intestinal worms; *molobe* is scaly ringworm, etc. As in many systems of folk medicine, however, it is not always clear whether the name of an affliction refers to its cause or to its main symptom. For example, there is a "sleeping sickness" called *vedauna* (to make sleep); a weeping sickness, *sanibuyo*, which afflicts only women and is complementary to *kwava* or amok madness in men; a gossip sickness, *talafo'u*, which results from being maligned; a paralysis of the legs, *kasawali* (cassowary) of evidently recent introduction.

It would be necessary to discuss indigenous conceptions of physiology to understand the entire range of afflictions which Kalauna people believe their flesh is heir to, but I can only point out that in addition to the belly, the most important inner organs are thought to be the liver, the heart and, rather surprisingly, the bile sac. But this is not to neglect the importance in Kalauna thinking of skin, flesh, veins, blood and "juice" (*huyona*), the last being the "growth-stuff" that the belly extracts from food and which makes bodies sleek and healthy.

The prestige of local curers (*tokweli*: man-who-sings) and the relatively high fees they command are clear indications of the persistence of traditional medicine.

There are six or seven such specialists in Kalauna with reputations which extend beyond the village (they are sometimes called in by health center officers to supplement orthodox medical treatment). Curers are self-selected rather than hereditary (though they may get a head start by inheriting curing magic from their fathers), and no special talents such as "dreaming" or trance are required. Some curers, however, do use dreams to enhance the authority of their diagnoses. Knowledge of the correct magical incantation and the appropriate paraphernalia are all important, though a suitable bedside manner also helps. Women know a few remedies and simples and some are known for special cures, but they never gain the renown accorded to male practitioners. For a man to achieve a reputation he must show mastery of at least a dozen basic competences. These include the ability to exorcise *yafuna* and other spirits, to recover "lost" souls, to banish malicious ghosts of the recent dead, to prevent fainting, to quell pain, to cool fever, and to extract intrusive objects inserted by sorcerers. In addition to these general techniques, individual curers specialize in such things as facilitating childbirth, expelling worms, curing boils, rictus of the jaw, toothache, earache, etc.

Two important principles affect the system of disease and curing in Kalauna. The first is that social relationships, particularly in their political aspects, largely govern the diagnosis of sickness and influence the quest for a cure. The second is that curers are usually also sorcerers. For these reasons alone modern health facilities are perceived to be quite inadequate to community needs. When a person is hospitalized for a "big sickness", the cause of the sickness and hence the responsibility for it remain behind in the village. Except in those cases of illness known to be caused by alien disease (or foreign sorcerers), the search for a cure within the village is relentless and persists until the patient recovers or dies. The fact that the great majority of illnesses are believed to have their cause within the village is perhaps the principal reason why people are so reluctant to be hospitalized, despite the fact that the health center is under an hour's walk from Kalauna.

Sick people usually seclude themselves and lie comatose in their houses; if they venture out they often cover their heads with a towel or cloth. They do not wash until they have recovered ("I have washed" is conventional idiom for "I am better now"). When a curer is called in he is offered a retaining fee almost at once. This is in cash, food, or a traditional shell valuable, and more is given him when the patient recovers. The curer uses a number of techniques of diagnosis, though these rarely involve more than a cursory examination of the patient. Far more attention is given to what the patient says or is reported to have said about his own illness. The body is an icon, and the curer observes its posture and the positioning of the limbs during sleep or delirium. The patient is thought to enact the social cause of his or her sickness, to compose a "picture" of a fishtail, for example, with hands crossed over the chest, allowing the curer to pursue the possibility that the patient was ensorcelled by someone with a grievance over fish. Dreams during sickness are held to be particularly significant and, no matter how recondite the imagery, it is thought to refer directly to the patient's problem and to offer a clue to its cause. Dream images and body "pictures" then, are material for interpretation by the curer, who is able to say with some authority where the patient's disturbed social relationships lie. Until these are "straightened out" there can be no lasting cure.

Once under the treatment of a curer the patient must obey his strictures. These most importantly concern what he cannot eat. Besides a general prohibition on all "greasy" food such as pork and coconut cream, the curer proscribes the same foods he is himself denied by the protocols of his magic. There are named stages of a long sickness and food taboos appropriate to each; these too are relinquished only on the instruction of the curer. On his daily housecall the curer sits with the patient for a time observing him, learning more about his condition from those nursing him and occasionally leaning forward to massage the patient's body with charmed leaves, all the while muttering his interminable incantations. If it becomes apparent that his treatment is not working, the curer may invite a second opinion or admit his ignorance of the cause of the sickness and suggest another specialist. If diagnosis involves *talafo'u*, the gossip sickness that is often regarded as a complication, then the curer arranges a "talking out" of blame. All those in the community who think they might have spoken badly of the patient in previous months "talk out" into a piece of ginger held by the curer. They confess their anger, envy or malice, and they ask forgiveness and wish the patient's return to good health. The curer then ensures the sick person absorbs these confessions by chewing on the ginger. This is often done at the hospital bedside. If the patient remains sick, it is either because some people have failed to confess their anger or because there are still other causes to be diagnosed.

Over a period of time diagnoses may switch dramatically as the sick person continues to languish. It is not simply a matter of working through all the possibilities but of interpreting the day to day behaviour of the patient, the dreams of those close to him, and the day by day course of political events in the village. These may take erratic turns, but there is a tendency for people to seek a correspondence between them: the course of an illness is often seen to conform to the community's thinking about political events. Reciprocally, it is as if the patient sometimes makes his symptoms match expectations in reflecting those events. (In 1980 a reluctant leader, unable to cope with a crisis, suffered grotesquely swollen legs; see Young (in press (c)).

The political embeddedness of "big sickness" in Kalauna is related to the other important principle governing the system of illness and curing. Curing knowledge is but the positive aspect of disease inflicting knowledge. By definition, then, curers are also sorcerers. Their healing spells have inverse incantations. Kalauna people speak of the "back" and "front" of a spell: the "back" inflicts disease, the "front" is the antidote that removes it. This principle entails that curers are often suspected of causing the illness they are consulted to cure. Before accepting to treat a case, many curers declare that they will only do so if the patient and his kin do not blame him for having caused the sickness in the first place. Curers, then, walk a narrow line between being celebrated for their healing skills and being condemned for their sorcery. A successful curer is one who manages this conundrum, though the gratitude of his patients may often ring hollow.[8]

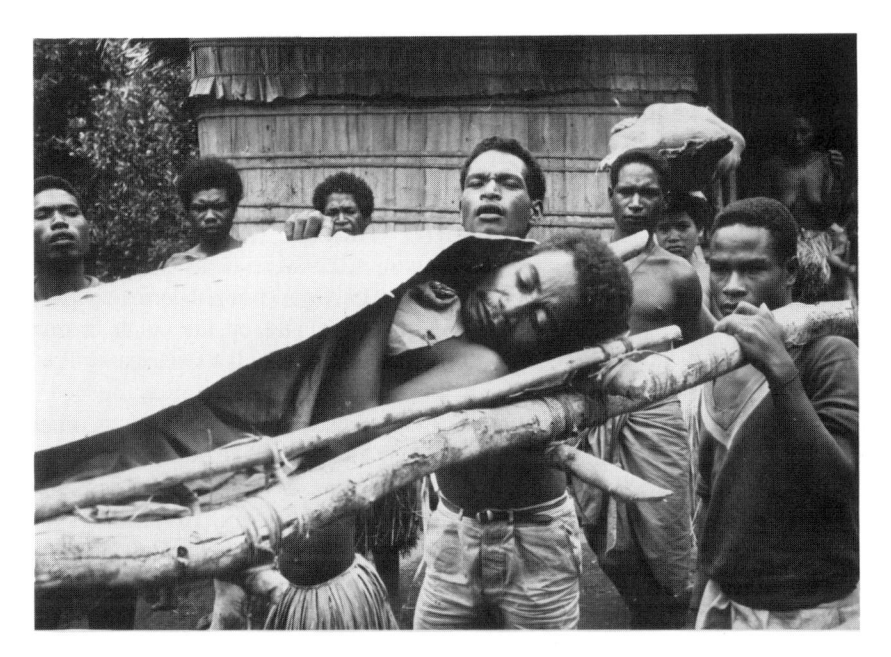

Fig. 8. Carrying a sick man to the health center, Kalauna.

Other than those few general principles I have already indicated, it is difficult to formulate the conditions under which Kalauna people have recourse to modern health facilities. Their pragmatic attitude toward Western medicine does not discount the customary fear of sorcery as the cause of most of their afflictions, while the serious "diseases of the belly", as I have said, are believed to admit of no cure by Western treatment. In some cases of "big sickness", however, the patient will be advised by traditional curers to try the health center but this is a tacit confession of failure, a way for the curer to absolve himself of further responsiblity. As far as the sick person is concerned, it is more likely to evoke despair than hope.

Few conclusions can be drawn from the statistics of hospitalization for Kalauna. During a nineteen month period (October 1978–April 1980), 32 Kalauna persons were admitted as in-patients to Bolubolu health center, representing a crude rate of about one in fifteen of the village population. As we shall see below, this is not untypical of the other villages that make up the main catchment area of the health center. Pneumonia was by far the commonest cause of hospitalization. As I have mentioned, it is believed to "come on top" of other illnesses and local curers make no claim to be able to cure it. The eleven cases of pneumonia recorded from Kalauna during the nineteen month period amounted to 34.4% of all in-patient cases from this village, a somewhat higher proportion than the 28% average of other villages (see note 4). The remaining 21 Kalauna cases of hospitalization tell us very little: malaria (2), gastric or bowel infections (3), physical injury (4),

U.R.T.I. (2), tropical ulcer (3), childbirth complication (1), anemia (3), and three undiagnosed cases. The profile of Kalauna out-patient attendance at the health center is similar to those of other villages and they will be dealt with in detail in a later section.

MODERN HEALTH FACILITIES

Until the 1950s the only modern health facilities on Goodenough were a couple of mission dispensaries; the nearest hospital was at Salamo on the south coast of Fergusson Island, which had been established by the Methodist Overseas Mission in the mid 1920s. In the mid 1950s a government hospital was opened at Mapamoiwa in southwest Fergusson, across Moresby Strait. Depending on the availability of aircraft, it was often quicker to fly emergency cases from the airstrip on Goodenough to the Trobriands (or even Port Moresby) than to beat across the strait to Mapamoiwa by launch. By the late 1950s, however, Goodenough was served by a handful of aid posts dotted around the island, and more impressively by an Infant and Maternity Welfare Hospital at Wailagi, the Methodist Mission headquarters of Bwaidoka Circuit.

Fig. 9. Patrolling nurses from Wailagi Infant and Maternity Hospital talk to Kalauna women on the importance of breast-feeding.

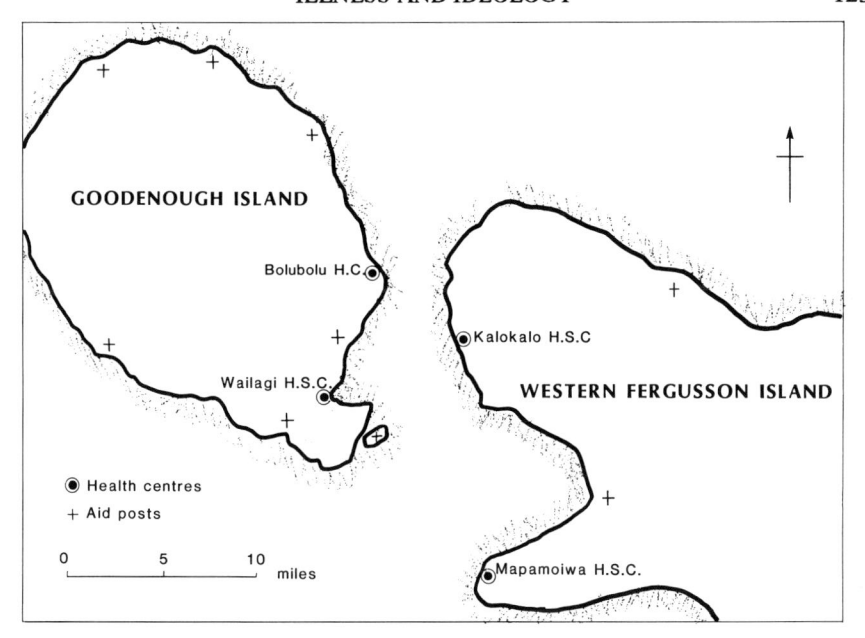

Fig. 10. Goodenough Island health facilities 1980.

In November 1961, some sixty years after the foundation of Wailagi Station, the Mission opened a refurbished and upgraded hospital and in the following year it began its operations in earnest. It was staffed by three European nursing sisters and several Papuan trainees. With remarkable energy they expanded four main areas of activity: an in-patients hospital with an average daily bed occupancy rate of 29; an out-patients clinic with an average daily attendance of 25 cases; a nursery caring for 19 children; and a patrolling infant and maternity welfare clinic which enrolled 1737 children under the age of five.

Wailagi remained the only hospital on Goodenough for over a decade. Then in 1972 the administration opened a health center at Bolubolu Patrol Post. While geographically not as central as Bolubolu (which is situated in the middle of the east coast), Wailagi has a more populous catchment area since about half the island's population dwells in the southernmost quarter. As most villages are situated within a mile or two of the coast, a more realistic expression of accessibility is given by walking distance. Thus, within four hours' walking distance of Wailagi – along 22 miles of coastline – there are almost 7000 people. Within four hours of Bolubolu there are about 5000. But it is far easier for those living beyond this range to reach Bolubolu than it is for them to reach Wailagi.

Following the reorganization of the health services after self-government and independence, Wailagi hospital was downgraded to a health sub-center and made subordinate to the health center at Bolubolu. In 1980 the latter had a staff of eleven, comprising a health extension officer (HEO), five nurses and several ancillary staff, some of whom were Goodenough islanders. Bolubolu does not conduct clinic patrols; these remain the task of Wailagi. Ideally they should be undertaken monthly to different parts of the island, but in practice (largely due to supply shortages) they occur far less frequently. Today, Wailagi is run by three mission-trained Papuan nurses and several orderlies. The last European nursing sister left in 1975.

Other health facilities on the island are seven aid posts, the distribution of which is shown in Figure 10. With one or two exceptions, the aid posts are effective in alleviating the simpler health problems of the village area they serve, and they perform an important function in referring cases to the health centers. In 1980 most aid posts were acutely handicapped by an erratic supply of drugs and dressings; indeed, supply problems are the commonest cause of complaint at all levels of the health care structure on Goodenough Island.

A brief description of the health center at Bolubolu might help the reader visualize the kind of institution this chapter deals with. Bolubolu patrol post consists of several government offices, two trade stores, a few rows of houses for government personnel, a playing field, an open space used as a market place, and a jetty or wharf. On the edge of this complex is the health center, itself comprising several buildings: staff houses, a store, a dormitory and cook house for patients' relatives, and a long, single-storey building which is the clinic-cum-hospital. Like the store and staff houses, it is made of prefabricated "fibro" walls, with louvres for windows, a smooth cement floor, and an insulated metal roof. One end of the building contains a number of small offices, a dispensary and the "reception" area where out-patients wait. Beyond this is the rest of the hospital: two rows of low beds with their heads to the walls and their feet separated by a central passageway. The single "ward" is for both sexes and mixed ages, with only flimsy partitions placed so as to form alcoves for one or more beds. From a Westerner's point of view, the hospital is shabbily constructed, badly maintained, poorly equipped, indifferently serviced and less than wholly hygienic. It tends to be hot, dusty, noisy and devoid of privacy: a doleful place full of sick people lying comatose or listlessly conversing with visitors. There are no formal visiting hours and, whether friends or relatives, visitors usually outnumber patients. Such people provide most succour and casual nursing services for the sick. They cook for them with food brought from the villages, they sit with them all day long and in the case of spouses and parents of young children, they may sleep by their beds on their own thin mats which they unroll on the concrete floor.

HEALTH CENTRE RECORDS

In the hope of gaining a better understanding of Kalauna's epidemiology I examined the health center records at Bolubolu. They proved to be singularly uninformative for this purpose, a blunt and useless tool for cross-checking "facts" I had learned in the village. The records yielded some interesting and unexpected findings, however, so much so that I was encouraged to examine Wailagi records also. These in turn threw up their own surprises. The remainder of this chapter is devoted to an analysis and some discussion of my findings; it expands slightly upon a previous publication (Young 1981).

The records of in-patient admissions and out-patient treatments at both health centers were, to put it mildly, in some disorder. I had to abandon the idea of making a detailed comparison of admissions to both hospitals, and also a plan to compare their respective out-patient records. An ambitious social epidemiology was therefore out of the question. Monthly and annual summaries of admission and discharge details were either missing or incomplete. Consequently, I found it simpler and more reliable to scrutinize and make my own counts of the figures yielded by admission books and out-patient record sheets.

The basic information recorded for each case, although minimal, was sufficient to sketch an elementary demographic profile for the people who attended the health centers, whether as in- or out-patients. The most pertinent information was in the following form: date of treatment or admission, patient's name, village, age, sex, ailment, and (if in-patient) date of discharge. Of the four key variables for each case (village, age, sex and ailment), age and ailment gave the medical staff most trouble. Estimates of actual age of in-patients were often given, but most outpatients were simply categorized as "adult" or "child". There was some agreement among the staff at Bolubolu, however, that a child became an adult about the age of fifteen. For the purpose of my own calculations I have standardized all actual ages accordingly. Diagnosis of ailment presents obvious problems, though it can be presumed that in-patients were given more carefully considered diagnoses than outpatients. For example, although "malaria" figures importantly in out-patient records (19% of all cases at Bolubolu), it is highly unlikely to have been diagnosed by blood test. Malaria is so endemic that all in- or out-patients suffering fever (whatever the cause might be) are routinely dosed with chloroquine. It is of dubious value then to maintain the distinction – which the records themselves often do – between "malaria" and "fever".

Despite the incomplete nature of the records and despite possible sources of error in them, it seemed worthwhile to scrutinize sample periods in the hope of detecting patterns in the use Goodenough Islanders made of the health care facilities available to them. I now consider each health center in turn and discuss the statistical peculiarities of their records.

Bolubolu: in-patients

Over a period of nineteen consecutive months (October 1978–April 1980) there were 508 in-patients (see Table 1). The seven commonest causes of hospitalization were pneumonia, injury (which includes fractures, burns, sprains and other traumas), bowel/gastric infections and/or diseases, tropical ulcers and infected sores, malaria, upper respiratory tract infection, and "midwifery" cases

TABLE 1
Bolubolu health center: in-patients. The ten most common diagnoses, October 1978–April 1980

		%
Pneumonia	105	(20.7)
Injury	71	(14.0)
Bowel/gastric infections	44	(8.7)
Tropical ulcer	38	(7.5)
Malaria	35	(6.9)
U.R.T.I.	32	(6.3)
Midwifery	30	(5.8)
Abscess	21	(4.1)
Anemia	16	(3.1)
Conjunctivitis	16	(3.1)
Other*	100	(19.7)
Total	508	(100)

* The next ten most common diagnoses accounted for over half the remaining cases: cellulitis (10), meningitis (9), asthma (6), arthritis (6), malnutrition (6), mental disturbance (6), heart failure (4), scabies, (4), urinary tract infection (4), spleen (4).

TABLE 2
Bolubolu health center: admission by age and sex

Men	Women	Boys	Girls	Total
132	195	106	75	508
(26%)	(38%)	(21%)	(15%)	(100%)

(confinement, retained placenta, vaginal laceration, puerperal sepsis, abortion and failed lactation). Patients classified according to age and sex were distributed as shown in Table 2.

Admissions counted by village should be (other things being equal) a function of population size and proximity to the health center. This seems generally to be the case in the present sample (see Figure 11). 42% of all patients came from five villages (including Bolubolu itself) within five or six miles of the hospital. These five "core" villages had a total population of 2583 in 1979 – about one fifth of Goodenough's – of which an average of one person in fourteen was hospitalized during this period. For the remainder of Goodenough, with another fifteen villages represented in the admissions, the average is one in 52. A disturbing statistic is the paucity of patients from the western side of the island: an average of only one in 78 persons is represented from this area. Difficulty of access is clearly the main factor for it is a two day walk to Bolubolu even for healthy adults.

An overall assessment of these in-patient figures suggests that the Bolubolu health center is functioning well enough as a centralized hospital facility, without excessive geographical bias – except, of course, that occasioned by the difficulty of access from the west coast. I should note that most of the east coast is serviced by a vehicular track and that the health center can and does call upon Station vehicles to collect patients who are unable to walk. There is also a small government boat which can be used for the same purpose, though it is at least a ten hour trip to the opposite side of the island even in the most favorable seas. It will be obvious from Figure 11 that the adjacent coast of Fergusson Island has easier access to Bolubolu than many parts of Goodenough. This fact is reflected in the admission figures for Fatavi and Kalokalo. Finally, the distribution of aid posts on Goodenough will have probably influenced (albeit in uncertain ways) the admissions figures as they relate to the more distant villages. One may surmise, for example, that the aid post orderly at Ufaufa was unusually conscientious in referring cases to Bolubolu.

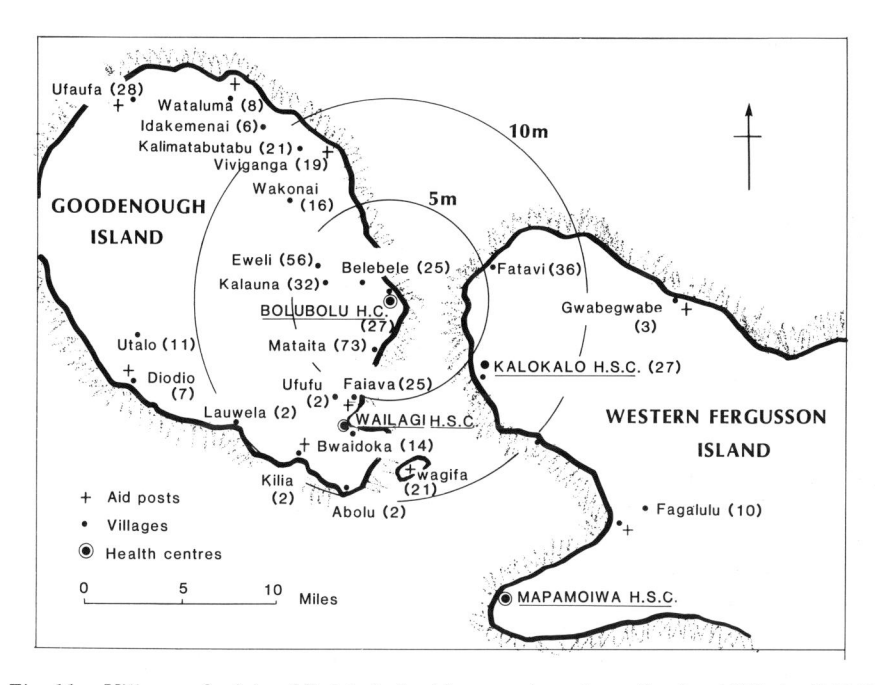

Fig. 11. Villages of origin of Bolubolu health center in-patients October 1978–April 1980 (N = 508, other = 15).

Bolubolu: out-patients

Out-patient records at Bolubolu were of two kinds: ticks on tally sheets, and more formal entries similar to those for in-patients. The former were useless for analysis indicating merely the number of people daily who had presented themselves for minor treatment. The latter recorded more "serious" cases, though it was not entirely clear to me how these were defined. From limited observation of out-patient treatment procedures, it seemed to involve one or more of the following operations: 1) the nurse or health extension officer took the patient's temperature; 2) the HEO administered drugs; 3) the patient took up more than a few moments of the HEO's time. If none of these occurred, then a tick on the daily tally sheet was the only evidence of the patient's attendance. Bearing in mind, then, that the out-patient records analyzed below are only an undetermined fraction of the total number of out-patients who presented themselves during the same period, it is reasonable to suppose that they represent the least trivial of the innumerable cases dealt with by health center staff.

Gaps in the records obliged me to use as my principal sample the four months prior to and including April 1980. There were no obvious discrepancies *between* the monthly figures I examined, and the variables showed a similar pattern for each month. I have therefore collated them in Table 3, adding the figures for another month (March 1979) which I took as an extra sample – though it was one of the few complete monthly records available for that year. With minor reservations, then, the table of out-patient cases can be taken as a fair representation of the distribution (by sex, relative age, village and health complaint) of patients who presented themselves at Bolubolu for treatment. It must be assumed that they did so voluntarily; that is, they were not referred by other medical personnel, nor "selected" by them in any way other than an evaluation of the symptoms for which the patients seek cure. This is an important point if one is to accept these figures as illustrative of villagers' perception of their own health needs. How far, on the other hand, they present a picture of the incidence of certain ailments in the villages or of epidemiological patterns on Goodenough, is entirely another question which I cannot begin to answer.

Table 3 presents distributions of ailment and village of 874 cases. The five core villages provided 92% of all cases. This is not surprising in view of the fact that Bolubolu health center serves as their nearest aid post. One might wonder, in fact, whether the reason so many patients are recorded from distant villages is that they had come to Bolubolu for other reasons than to seek medical attention. The table also shows that six categories of complaint account for 83% of the total. Malaria and "fever" together account for 57%, and influenza and cough/cold for 11%. Obviously, at the out-patient level where spot diagnosis is hasty and where the treatment for fever and upper respiratory infection is identical (consisting of doses of aspirin and chloroquine), it is likely that these four categories of illness are arbitrarily assigned in many cases. In short, there may be some justification for

TABLE 3
Bolubolu health center: out-patient diagnoses

	Bolubolu	Belebele	Mataita	Kalauna	Eweli	Other (N=28)	Total	%
Fever	85	113	48	34	34	22	336	38.4
Malaria	41	64	21	22	11	7	166	19.0
Influenza	18	10	7	2	1	1	39	4.5
Cough/cold	22	14	4	6	3	6	55	6.3
Bowel infection	7	8	6	10	11	1	43	4.9
Tropical ulcer	19	15	14	17	8	11	84	9.6
Other (N=28)	29	30	23	24	25	20	151	17.3
Total	221	254	123	115	93	68	874	100
%	25.3	29.0	14.1	13.2	10.6	7.8	100	

conflating the four complaints at the top of the table and declaring that they account for some 68% of all cases.

Turning to the distribution of out-patients according to variables of sex and age, a rather startling pattern appears. Whatever way the figures are broken down – according to major ailment, according to village or according to monthly records – the proportions of the four categories of patient (male and female adult, male and female child) remain effectively the same (Table 4).

TABLE 4
Bolubolu health center: out patients by age and sex

Men	Women	Boys	Girls	Total
119	109	417	229	874
(14%)	(12%)	(48%)	(26%)	(100%)

In other words, three quarters of all out-patients were children, and almost one half of all out-patients were boys. Boys are therefore presented nearly twice as often as girls.

When I explained this finding to the HEO in charge of Bolubolu health center he was sceptical but, after making some counts of his own and arriving at similar results, he too was puzzled. It is worth noting that his expectations (as an educated Motuan from southern Papua) were similar to my own, namely that female children would be "favored" (for that is what our health care ideology implies) no less than male children. Yet both of us could easily accept that children might be "favored" over adults in getting, as it were, more health care treatment *per capita*.

A partial explanation for the preponderance of child over adult out-patients is that children tend to suffer those complaints amenable to out-patient treatment more frequently than do adults. However, an important factor is that children, unlike adults, do not often attend the health center on their own initiative. They are usually taken there by adults, probably by their parents in most cases. Posed in its strongest form, the question then becomes: why do parents take their sons for treatment twice as often as they take their daughters? For if we accept that parental solicitude might have a lot to do with the preponderance of children in the out-patient clinic, by the same token this parental solicitude seems grossly weighted in favor of boys. Although male children are, on the whole, known to be somewhat more prone to illness and mortality than female children, there is no biological factor which could account for a ratio of two to one. The puzzle, then, is a cultural one of gender rather than a biological one of sex.

It says something about my own training as a social anthropologist, perhaps, that while I had an inkling of the best explanation for this Durkheimian social fact I resisted its implications. It seemed almost too far-fetched, a textbook fabulation to illustrate the suasive powers of culture over reason, custom over common sense. Suspecting the worst, however, I took the problem back to Kalauna and posed it to my (male) friends there. It took an effort to explain, not simply because of the conceptual difficulties of translating proportions, multiples and averages, but principally because my "problem" did not really exist for Kalauna men: it was self-evident that they favored sons over daughters, boys over girls. Ideology needs no apology, as John Lavekeluna of Kalauna indicated in his commentary:

> Our grandfathers used to call women bouncing coconuts. They do not stay with their fathers but leave them to go to some other group. Kalauna women may go to marry in Eweli, Vivigani or some other place, and their fathers will not think about them again. But men are different. They do not leave the place where they were born. They stay with their fathers and help to populate his group so that it grows big. Men are the owners of the village, its inheritors. They are like houseposts, but women are like bouncing coconuts. Men marry and look after their own villages; women marry and look after other men's villages. Again, if men die out and only women remain, who will continue the village? Who will pass on the men's names? Our sons replace us, our daughters do not. Our sons help our group to grow, our daughters help other groups to grow. This is why only men build houses, and this is why in famine-time our grandfathers sometimes squeezed the throats of their baby daughters. Today we put it this way. If a girl is sick her father will say it's of no importance. But if his son is sick he will say to his wife "Go and take him for medicine". He will take it and get better, and his father will say "Good, for he is my heir".

The author of these remarks was a man in his late thirties with four daughters and one son all of whom, I might add, were in good health. I do not think he was as indifferent to his own daughters' health as his "official" statement of agnatic ideology might suggest. But it is a classic rationale for patrilineal descent and succession, which are indeed the dominant modes on Goodenough Island. Women bounce away like coconuts; men stay and build houses. Hence, the argument goes, boys are valued over girls, their health and survival are of greater moment since they perpetuate the essential institutional forms of the community. In Goodenough thinking, men represent stability, continuity, permanence and all those values of agnation which persuade men they are the very house posts of society. In the out-patient records, then, there was a numerical expression of the value given to the principle of agnation. Alternatively, the figures might be read as a measure of ideological discrimination against girls.

Wailagi: out-patients

Out-patient records at Wailagi proved to be too incomplete for worthwhile analysis. Latterly this health sub-center has favored the anonymous tick-system (an average of 96 patients a day for one month's count) over more formal entry on record sheets. Those records of out-patients which do exist are heavily biased towards "fever" as their ailment, for a high temperature is virtually a condition of a patient's

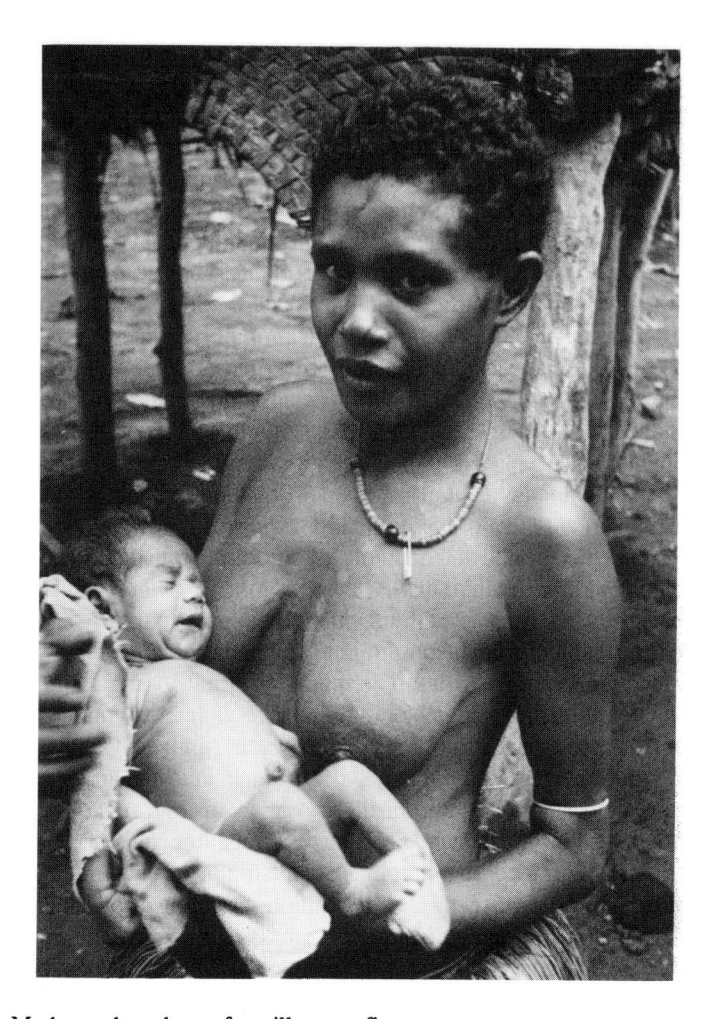

Fig. 12. Mother and newborn after village confinement.

entry into the record. Detailed comparison with Bolubolu out-patient records was therefore ruled out. A count was made of five months, however, and it yielded a similar ranking of the four patient categories as that found at Bolubolu. Boys were still favored over girls at Wailagi, but it was the women who sought more treatment for themselves.

TABLE 5
Wailagi out-patients by age and sex

Men	Women	Boys	Girls	Total
61	81	135	104	381
(16%)	(21%)	(35%)	(27%)	(100%)

Wailagi: in-patients

In-patient records date back to the official foundation of the Infant and Maternity Welfare Hospital in 1961. I selected four complete years – 1962, 1967, 1972 and 1978 – for analysis in the hope of identifying trends in hospital admissions. The most striking trend to emerge over these sixteen years was the growth and decline of the hospital *as a children's* hospital.

Admissions for the first complete year of its operation show that almost half (49%) of all patients were from Bwaidoka, the large village within which Wailagi Mission is situated. More than one-third (36%) of all admissions were Bwaidoka children. Malaria and influenza together account for 50% of all admissions (and 82% of these were children). The character of the hospital seems to have been established during this inaugural year: as catering predominantly for children, and as having a distinctly local (Bwaidokan) intake (see Figure 13, Table 6).

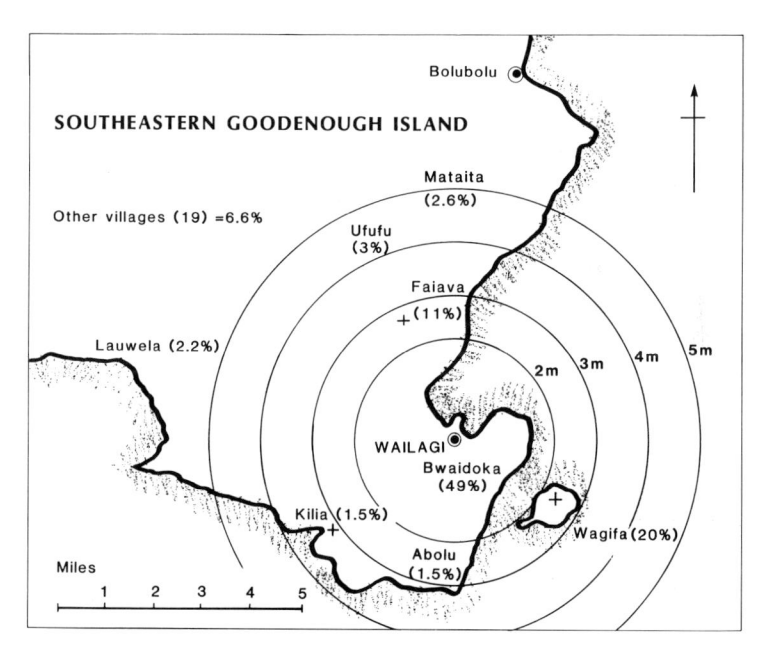

Fig. 13. Wailagi hospital in-patients 1962 (N = 715).

TABLE 6
Source of Wailagi admissions: 1962

	Men	Women	Boys	Girls	Total
Bwaidoka	29	63	129	130	351
Other villages	20	89	150	105	364
Total	49	152	279	235	715
	(7%)	(21%)	(39%)	(33%)	(100%)

Five years later this character had been fully confirmed and its tendencies exaggerated. In 1967 two thirds (67%) of all admissions were now from Bwaidoka and just under half (49%) of them were Bwaidoka children. The figure of 357 for Bwaidoka child in-patients is an astonishingly high one, for if the 1968 census figure of 430 Bwaidoka children is accurate, then three quarters of them were hospitalized during 1967 (Table 7).

TABLE 7
Source of Wailagi admissions: 1967

	Men	Women	Boys	Girls	Total
Bwaidoka	35	95	195	162	487
Other villages	14	97	68	59	238
Total	49	192	263	221	725
	(7%)	(26.5%)	(36%)	(30.5%)	(100%)

By 1972 admissions had dropped by more than a third. Bwaidokans still accounted for 60% of all admissions and 39% of them were Bwaidokan children. Malaria/fever cases were actually fewer than in previous years, but they constituted an even greater proportion (38%) of the total number of cases and Bwaidoka children admitted for malaria/fever amounted to 23% of all cases. Since there are no grounds for assuming that malaria is more prevalent in Bwaidoka than elsewhere in this part of Goodenough, it appears that admissions for this disease (or for fever generally) were highly selective in favor of Bwaidoka children. This is not to suggest that feverish children from other villages were turned away from the hospital, but that the chance of their being taken there was rather unlikely. Checking against the village census figures for 1971, it appears that about one in five Bwaidoka children were admitted to the hospital for malaria/fever, whereas only one in 65 children were admitted from the other four main villages in the area. Since for *all* diseases the rate of admission is about one in twenty, it suggests that children from villages other than Bwaidoka stood a better chance of being admitted to Wailagi if they were suffering from something other than malaria (Table 8).

TABLE 8
Source of Wailagi admissions: 1972

	Men	Women	Boys	Girls	Total
Bwaidoka	29	64	99	73	265
Other villages	26	61	47	45	179
Total	55	125	146	118	444
	(12%)	(28%)	(33%)	(27%)	(100%)

It was obvious from the figures for 1978 that there had been a severe curtailment of hospital activities. Admissions had fallen to 193, a drop of 73% in ten years. Most strikingly, children (35%) were no longer "favored" over adults (65%). Boys were doing better than girls as usual, but the latter were now getting very short shrift (10.5%). This would appear to indicate a dramatic reversal of the previous policy of "saving the children" (though it is an artefact of reading the record consecutively that the children now appear to be actually discriminated against). Bwaidoka children particularly, from being the most conspicuous category of patient (36% of 1962 cases, 49% of 1967, 39% of 1972) now represented only 26%. And this was in a year when the local bias of the hospital was more pronounced than ever (82% of all cases were Bwaidokan in 1978, Table 9).

TABLE 9
Source of Wailagi admissions: 1978

	Men	Women	Boys	Girls	Total
Bwaidoka	46	63	35	15	159
Other villages	5	11	13	5	34
Total	51	74	48	20	193
	(26.5%)	(38%)	(25%)	(10.5%)	(100%)

The contraction of the catchment area of Wailagi hospital must be considered in relation to the growth of Bolubolu health center during the 1970s, though it cannot be demonstrated that there is any clear relationship between the respective admissions of both health centers, except the occasional cases which are referred from Wailagi for treatment at Bolubolu. If the nineteen months' sample of in-patient figures from Bolubolu is anything to judge by, the number of patients from Bwaidoka and other villages in southern Goodenough (95 out of 508) scarcely begin to make up the numbers "missing" from Wailagi in 1978. So it cannot be argued that Bolubolu was in some sense taking up the slack and compensating for the reduced admissions of Wailagi.

Another expression of the trend reversal evident in 1978 is that only one in sixteen Bwiadoka children were hospitalized that year (compared to one in three in

1972, three in four in 1967). Bwaidoka adults were hospitalized at the steady rate of about 1 in 6.

In order to identify the fluctuations which my sampling had missed, and more importantly to determine the year in which admissions dropped most sharply, I counted admissions for all years between 1967 and 1977. Following a record number of admissions in 1974,[9] it proved that the steep downward trend began in 1975 (Figure 14).

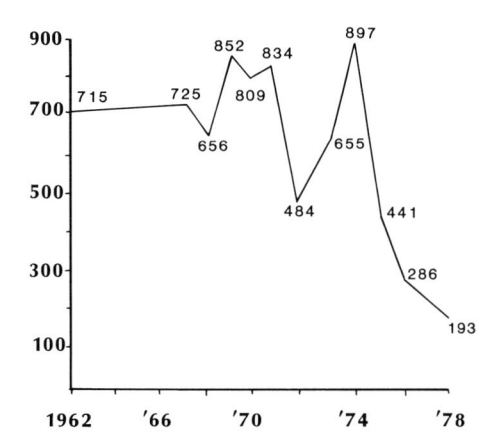

Fig. 14. Wailaga hospital/health center total admissions.

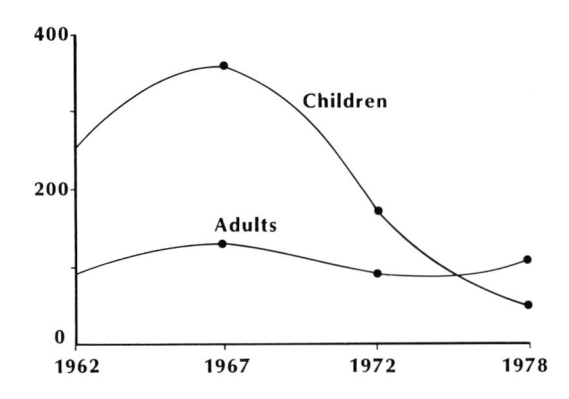

Fig. 15. Wailaga hospital/health center: Bwaidoka admissions.

A possible, though improbable, explanation for the decline in admissions is that the health of the local population improved markedly after 1974. But the second graph (Figure 15) shows how the hospital's intake of adults from Bwaidoka has remained fairly steady and does not follow the curve of total admissions. It is implausible that children's health alone, and not that of adults, could have improved so dramatically. There are some clues in the records to indicate that the decline in child admissions is due to something other than improved health. For example, the proportion of child malaria/fever cases is invariably within the range of 36–58% of all child cases for any year; other diseases have an epidemic pattern (influenza in 1962; upper respiratory tract infection in 1967; pneumonia in 1978). Gastric infections in children, however, bear a similar statistical relationship to total cases as does malaria, and for the first three sample years this category of illness remains within the range of 14–18% of Bwaidoka child cases. Only in 1978 does it drop to 8% – though to appreciate better the extent of the drop the actual figures are more telling: from 45 cases in 1962, 65 in 1967, 24 in 1972 to four in 1978. One would need other evidence than these figures to be persuaded that gastric infections in children had become so rare in Bwaidoka in 1978.

In short, the fall in child admissions cannot be explained by postulating the reduced occurrence of ailments. Whichever way the figures are viewed, it seems that admissions policy *with regard to children* is the underlying cause of the pattern. There is some confirmation for this hypothesis in the regular procedure of nursing sisters working at Wailagi in 1980. None of them were there prior to 1976 so none were aware of any deliberate policy change such that, for example, children should be discounted in favor of adults. But out-patient treatment of children nowadays seems to reflect a different assessment of their needs than the one which prevailed before 1975. Children presenting with malaria, fever, bowel

Fig. 16. Kalauna girls 'baby-minding'. The girl on the right is afflicted with *tinea imbricata*.

infections, etc. are routinely dosed with drugs, and their parents are told to bring them back next day and each subsequent day until the course is finished and the child is cured. (Such, at any rate, is the ideal procedure.) In other words, only the most serious cases, or those judged to have inadequate parental care, are admitted to hospital. What the 1978 figures probably reflect, therefore, is a shift in health care emphasis from in-patient to out-patient treatment. This would be entirely consistent with reduced or reallocated resources and a push towards greater self-sufficiency. The post-Independence years have seen not only the localization of the nursing staff at Wailagi but also an assumption of greater responsibility by Bwaidoka parents, which nullifies the paternalistic attitude of the Mission during the first twelve years of the hospital's operation.

It was missionary zeal, I contend, which hospitalized so many Bwaidoka children during the years 1962–74; zeal and a paternalistic assumption that parents could not care for their children as well as the Mission.[10] A legacy of this period is a high standard of efficiency and devotion to duty which European nurses' Papuan successors are quite unable to match – something the Bwaidoka villager unfairly grumbles about. But what strikes the anthropologist as anomalous is not the policy which hospitalizes one child in sixteen, but the policy which finds justification for hospitalizing one child in every two.

The "policy" which reduced the intake of Bwaidoka children after 1974 has not, to my knowledge, ever been committed to paper or even consciously formulated. Since it coincided with the Papuan staffing of Wailagi hospital, it might be more accurately identified as a shift in ideology, a change in the complex of beliefs and suppositions which directs action. If this is the case, then the reduced admissions figure for children is of the same order of "social fact" as the inflated admissions for children a decade earlier, and both can be viewed in the same light as the deviations from expected values which were so startling in the Bolubolu out-patient figures. We saw how villagers' ideology concerning agnation and the value of male children is reflected in health care statistics at Bolubolu. Likewise, I suggest that figures for children is of the same order of "social fact" as the inflated admissions for children a decade earlier, and both can be viewed in the same light as the deviations from expected values which were so startling in the Bolubolu out-patient figures. We saw how villagers' ideology concerning agnation and the value of male children is reflected in health care statistics at Bolubolu. Likewise, I suggest that Methodist Mission ideology, in its motivated "over valuation" of children (Young, in press (d)), is reflected in the health care statistics of Wailagi. This is not meant to denigrate the Mission's efforts in this direction; it is simply to point out that whatever takes its place must seem neglectful and inadequate by comparison.

"Child rescue", one of the principal motives of the Methodist Mission ideology (Young 1980), has certainly borne fruit in Bwaidoka over the years. It is difficult otherwise to explain the fact that the population of this community, with Wailagi at its center, has grown by an average of 2.5% per annum since 1962, while the figure for the remainder of the island is only 2%. Wailagi's lesson for Kalauna, perhaps, is that if you want your village to grow faster you do not discriminate against your daughters in the matter of health care!

NOTES

1. This chapter is based on research conducted on Goodenough Island in May–June 1980, though it incorporates observations made on earlier field trips amounting to 26 months during 1966–68, 1973 and 1977. I am grateful to the Australian National University for funding these periods of research. The second half of the chapter is an expansion of a paper published in the *Papua New Guinea Medical Journal* (Young 1981).
2. That there are problems of undernutrition on Goodenough is evident from the figure of 7% for the proportion of children (N = 1852) under 60% weight for age (NMGR 1980).
3. Whooping cough spread from Cooktown, Queensland, in November 1899. Dysentery was also reported in the Eastern Division (i.e. Massim area) that year. One of the few precise mortality figures concerns the Trobriands, where 37 deaths occurred in a period of 8 weeks in a village of 250 people (BNGAR 1899–1900: Appendix 0). The following year the famine had eased, but "whooping cough here, [i.e. Eastern Divison] as elsewhere, had made sad ravages in the population" (BNGAR 1900–01: xxxiii).
4. According to a study conducted in 1980: "nasal carriage rates of *S.pneumoniae* and *H.influenzae* observed in Kalauna Village are the highest reported for open communities anywhere in the world" (Gratten *et al.* 1981: 177). *Streptococus pneumoniae* was isolated in 16 of 25 adults (64%) and in 36 of 37 children (97%).
5. In 1967, using a census checklist of Kalauna and several knowledgeable informants, I determined that 33% of the village population was visibly infected with *tinea imbricata*.
6. Cf. Fortune (1963: 136), for a similar conception in the Dobu area. Tauwau is the mythological creator of the white race, European artefacts, and epidemics: "Any white man may be referred to as *tauwau*, a bearer of introduced diseases."
7. "Blood" disease is found in Dobu (Fortune 1963: 179-80) and Duau (Roheim 1954: 491), as well as in Molima (Ann Chowning, personal communication) and Tubetube (Martha Macintyre, personal communication).
8. See Young (1983b, Chapter 9), for a biographical account of Kalauna's most notorious curer-sorcerer of the past decade.
9. The measure of hospital size by number of "beds" does not accurately convey the capacity of a local hospital or health center, since many extra patients can be accommodated by laying mats on the floors. I do not know what the maximum capacity of either Bolubolu or Wailagi might be. If the Wailagi in-patient figure for 1974 is correct at 897, then at a conservative estimate of two days' admission per patient, an average of 37 patients a day were being accommodated that year. It is highly probable that when Wailagi was hospitalizing so many children between 1962 and 1974, it was also discharging them within a day or two.
10. There is also the cynical possibility that the Wailagi sisters were deliberately aiming to "maximize the body count" to justify requests for further funds or facilities. I have not a scrap of information to support this, however.

ANDREW STRATHERN

6. HEALTH CARE AND MEDICAL PLURALISM: CASES FROM MOUNT HAGEN

INTRODUCTION

This paper presents a discussion of some aspects of the relationship between practices and ideas of traditional medicine and those of modern introduced health care, as these are found among the Melpa-speaking people of the Mount Hagen area in the Western Highlands province of Papua New Guinea. These people, numbering today some 80,000 persons, were first contacted by Australian explorers in the early 1930s, and since 1945 they have experienced intensive processes of induced social change with the introduction of centralized government, cash cropping, and versions of the Christian religion. Their local social structure is based upon a division into tribes and clans, in which membership is nominally patrilineal, men tend to control social relations, and among men the leaders are certain forceful individuals who use resources to hand in order to establish their pre-eminence over others in a system of competitive exchanges of wealth objects, primarily pigs and valuable shells, or nowadays money. Starting with my first fieldwork as a graduate student of Cambridge University, England, in 1964–5 among these people, during which time I concentrated on the basic patterns of social structure and exchange, I have spent a number of years studying patterns of social change, continuity and responses to development, always staying with the same group, the Kawelka, with whom the first fieldwork was carried out. Methods of research have been both quantitative and qualitative, with increasing emphasis over the years on participant observation and integration with one or another of the Kawelka's constituent clan groups. I have not made exhaustive investigations on traditional medicine or introduced health care, but these are topics which are of great interest both intellectually and practically, and in this paper I try to bring to bear my general knowledge of the culture and society onto the question of "pluralism" in the people's use of medicine. It is hoped that there will be further, and more detailed, fieldwork on this theme; but in the meantime the major purposes of the paper are two:

(1) to show how traditional practices have in some instances been discarded and in other cases preserved or adapted to current conditions, and to suggest reasons for this circumstance;

(2) to indicate the value, for the healing process, of the Melpa concept of anger (*popokl*) and how this must be dealt with if a sick person is to recover. Conjunctions between Melpa ideas and concepts of psychosomatic interaction in sickness are thereby revealed and made

S. Frankel and G. Lewis (eds.), *A Continuing Trial of Treatment*. 141–154.
© 1989, Kluwer Academic Publishers, Dordrecht – Printed in the Netherlands.

available for consideration by those responsible for medical and health-related policy.

THE IMAGE OF THE HOSPITAL OVER TIME

In 1964, while I was doing my first fieldwork in the Dei Council area of Mount Hagen, I was visited one day by Dr David Kulow, from the local Lutheran mission hospital at Kotna. He complained to me that he was often unable to save the lives of patients because they were brought into hospital too late, and he attributed this to the fact that "they always have to kill the pigs first". That is, ritual sacrifices were performed prior to taking people to hospital and this meant the illness was often too advanced by the time the patient was admitted. Situations like this are scarcely likely to enhance people's belief in the efficacy of Western medicine. Indeed, there is a double negative result: patients die, and because of this the hospital comes to be known as a place where people die and this makes sick persons further resist going there. A negative evaluation of the hospital thus becomes a self-fulfilling prophecy.

Dr Kulow's observations were those of a practicing doctor and carried some truth. However, hospital authorities can be subject to misconceptions also. They tend to assume that people's traditional practices will automatically impede and frustrate acceptance of bio-medical therapy, whereas in fact this is not necessarily the case. Attitudes to medicine also change over time. In Dei Council in 1964 it was true that patients were sometimes kept at home while their kinsfolk held sacrifices. As I have mentioned, this was partly because the hospital was itself seen as a dangerous place, full of strange machines and persons whose actions could not be easily understood, but who removed blood, fluid, etc. from people in a manner rather reminiscent of the sorcerer, and did with them who knows what. But no-one, at least, had any lack of belief in the famous "injection" which they could get at hospitals and aid posts. If anything, they credited it with too many powers. There was also a general lack of awareness of the importance of timing in giving medical treatment. Twenty years later, in 1984, there was a much livelier realization of the need for speed in getting seriously sick people to hospital and much more informed discussion of hospitals in terms of their relative merits rather than resistance to the idea of taking people to hospital at all. Sacrifices are still made but do not normally interfere with the process of getting the sick into hospital. (There are exceptions, as will be detailed below.)

PLURALISM, RITUAL, AND PLANT REMEDIES

In this paper I look at a number of cases of sickness in Hagen and discuss how they reveal a situation of medical pluralism analogous to pluralism in religious, political, and economic practice.[1] I also consider ways in which the present situation of uneasy or *de facto* pluralism might be improved. The idea of a straight out replacement of traditional by introduced practices belongs to the same era as modernization theory in the economic sphere and is similarly out of date.[2] But this still leaves us with the question of what should be the relationship between the two systems. The present circumstances of pluralism result from two factors:

(1) the acceptance of introduced practices without much understanding of the reasons for, or theory behind, them;
(2) the belief that there are certain conditions which are caused by entities outside of the world view recognized by Western doctors and which, therefore, must be treated in a ritual way if the patient is to recover.

The first factor leads to people combining medical practices in an eclectic fashion with random results; the second to a positive choice to use traditional rather than introduced medicine in cases where the causes are held to be ones outside of Western purview. In addition, as an illness progresses and perhaps does not respond to one type of treatment, people are willing to switch to another type in the search for a cure. Traditional ritual, Christian prayers, and hospital treatment may all be involved in an all out effort to save a patient's life.

It is in the sphere of ritual that most questions arise regarding traditional medicine, some saying it is superstitious nonsense, others that it performs valuable therapeutic functions where there are psychosomatic aspects of illness. In such discussions it is important to explicate and differentiate the viewpoints of the participants from those of the observer or writer. The participants consider that medicine of any kind either works or it does not. In the case of Western medicine, it is thought to work because of the "strong power" of the people who invented it; in the case of their own medicine, it works because the spirit entities which cause illness are affected by the actions of ritual. Christian prayers, it is thought, may have an overriding effect on sickness because of the belief in the "miracle working power" of God. There is, however, a category of medicine in which belief is of much the same order whether it is Western or traditional remedies that are used, and that is plant medicines employed to counter minor body conditions such as skin rashes and boils or stomach pains and diarrhea. In all traditional pharmacopoeias there is a proportion of plants which do have beneficial effects of this kind, and it is commonplace to observe that important European synthetic medicines derive originally from plants used by rural peoples around the world. There were indeed numerous plants used in this way in Hagen and work on them has been done by a German scholar, H. Dosedla.[3] In 1964 I observed that when people suffered from injuries they frequently used the leaves of the *rarau* tree to cover the sore and make it dry.[4] Use of plant remedies in this way has dropped off sharply since then, with the increasing availability of medicines at aid posts and of transport into town. My points here are:

(1) plant remedies were dropped much as people gave up stone tools when steel ones became available, that is, because the new medicines were obviously more effective;

(2) this, however, has its negative aspect, because there is a corresponding loss of self-reliance in relation even to minor conditions. For example, to treat cuts people used to chew up *neng* leaves (also used to roll tobacco in for smoking) and then heat them up before strapping them onto the affected part. This probably acted as a soothing poultice and would be adequate unless the cut became infected. For toothache they would bite ginger; for joint pains they would bathe in a waterfall; for stomach pain drink sugar cane; for diarrhoea eat hibiscus leaves which are thought to be "binding". These are all useful minor practices which cost less than a bus fare into town and back to get treated with a couple of aspirins;

(3) people do not seem to buy medicines as such to keep by them as a direct replacement of their own remedies. Rather, they feel they must receive them at the hands of a medical worker or someone who "knows" about them (such as the anthropologist);

(4) even in this relatively simple sphere, then, there is plenty of room for discussion about how the use of traditional and introduced medicines may be combined in straightforward aspects of health care. "Health care" as a topic, of course, is broader than the question of medicine as such and bridges over to encompass dietary patterns, hygiene and housing standards, for example.

THE LACK OF PRIMARY HEALTH CARE

The main point I wish to make here is that health care is unbalanced. Most of the emphasis is on medicine, and there is almost no ongoing community education in health care as such. Aid post orderlies are supposed to undertake education of this kind, and in 1967 in the village I worked in at Pangia, Southern Highlands District (now Province) the aid post orderly actually did so. He inspected latrines, helped people to dig fish ponds, told them to bury their rubbish, and assisted women with advice about childbirth as well as actually delivering babies. After a number of years he was promoted to be in charge of APO training at the Pangia station health center. In Hagen I have not seen APOs doing this; more often I have known them neglect even attendance at their clinics in favor of gambling at card games, drinking beer or pursuing new wives. The gap left by their lack of attention to duty has not been filled at village level by any other agency. Only infants receive regular check ups if they live in one of the areas where nurses go round and conduct village clinics, as the Kotna mission people do in Dei Council. (The local people refer to this as *wakl kwipa roromen*, "they come to hang up, i.e. weigh, the children".) The results of this lack of attention at village level are clear: the majority of houses are still dirty and smoky, and this contributes to the high incidence of respiratory and gastrinal disorders. Latrines are an innovation which have been accepted universally, but there is never any advice given on where they should be sited or how they should be built. On the whole they are dug too shallow and their holes are uncovered giving easy access to flies, which use them as breeding grounds, as well as rats. Another area of hygiene where there is little guidance is that of water supply. Most rural areas lack any kind of supply. In mountainous parts, running streams are relatively uncontaminated, but in the flat central valley areas this is not so. Water is often in short supply and dirty. Although attempts are made to keep pigs out from water supply areas this cannot always be achieved. Further, in the area just to the north of Hagen township there is a large urban rubbish dump on which herds of pigs forage for food. The food is infected and the pigs get the *Trichinella* worm in their flesh which is then passed on to humans and causes sickness. This is a prime public health problem, but nothing at all is being done about it. In the Wahgi Valley area it seems more than likely, too, that water supplies are polluted with chemicals used in managing the numerous coffee and tea plantations established there.

On diet, the effects of contact have been variable. On the positive side protein is more readily available from tinned fish and meat and frozen poultry which can be bought in stores and this means that daily consumption of protein is much higher than it was before. Such consumption, however, also brings with it dangers. Sugar, salt and fatty foods are all very popular and may bring medical problems with them such as diabetes, blood pressure and heart attacks. Cigarettes and immoderate use of alcohol add to this negative pattern. Further, coffee gardens use up land which was previously devoted to growing mixed vegetables, so there is a dietary loss associated with this changeover. This loss could be recouped by spending money from coffee on buying greens in the market, and to a small extent this does happen, but it is very hard to estimate the net overall effect of these changes. Large amounts of money are also kept tied up in ceremonial exchanges and in purchases of pigs for these exchanges. From time to time there are also shortages of the basic crop, sweet potato, occasioned by variable wet and dry seasons and by a certain lack of attention to subsistence agriculture as a whole. Rice has then to be bought in order to make up the deficit.

In the sphere of personal hygiene, people wash more frequently than before because they almost all wear European style clothes and want to visit the town regularly. This no doubt is a good thing for their health, but sometimes the water used to wash in is itself not clean and there is little skin care beyond the act of washing itself. Bites, stings, and itches are scratched vigorously, often spreading infection; many young men, in particular, seem careless about seeing to boils and other sores on their legs. I have noted earlier that traditional remedies do exist for skin conditions. It appears that some people cannot be bothered either to get their sores bound up with bandages or to prepare traditional leaf coverings. Again, the answer lies in primary health care education.

Another sphere in which such education is badly needed is in relation to malaria. The government's programme for DDT spraying ended some years ago and malaria has come back with a vengeance. The area around Kuk, a territory of the Kawelka people, is mosquito-ridden during the wet season. A number of relatively simple measures is available to reduce the transmission of malaria, such as the use of mosquito nets, but these are not promoted or even discussed. The situation has become more serious in recent years as some of the mosquitoes now carry the dangerous falciparum type of malaria which is becoming resistant to the antimalarial drug chloroquine that is all that is available at aid posts for treatment of acute attacks or prophylaxis.

Finally, following on from the last point, a number of families have turned to the use of medicines for population control. In the past, there were strong post partum taboos in operation and these ensured a regular spacing of children at about three-year intervals, since children are not normally weaned until they are two years old or more. With social change these taboos have broken down somewhat although the ideas behind them are still current. When children are spaced too tightly, adverse comments are likely to be made on the skin condition of the older child and the married couple are said to have no shame and to be incapable of controlling their desires. The sanction of shame is sufficient to keep many couples from having children too quickly. One factor working against this is jealousy between co-wives of the same man. The wife nursing a child may feel that her husband will now neglect her and sleep with the other wife, perhaps previously put to one side - she may then entice the husband to have sexual intercourse with her before her child is properly weaned. An answer to some of these problems lies in the use of contraceptives, but it is worrying to note that at Kuk some of the Kawelka wives are receiving regular three monthly injections of the controversial contraceptive Depo-Provera which is banned in some of the metropolitan countries such as America and the United Kingdom. Depo-Provera was developed to overcome the problem of women not being likely to take daily oral contraceptive pills with sufficient regularity to guarantee success (and this problem is real). However, Depo-Provera itself carries risks for the health of its users. On the other side, therapy for the childless or infertile is left largely to traditional practices (based on a combination of vegetable substance and augury). The most common cause of sterility nowadays is blocking of the Fallopian tubes brought about by pelvic infections and subsequent scarring, notably by gonorrhea.[5] The condition can be treated in some cases, but women are often reluctant, because of shame, to seek medical advice. A sense of self-blame attaches to the attitudes here: "I did wrong, so let it stay that way, it is God's will." Here the idea is that it is wrong to try to undo what God has willed. At the same time this idea may coexist with a notion that "one day, God will give me a child". Here the idea structure is exactly in parallel with traditional ideas, which attributes fertility to the influence of senior dead kinsfolk. A father may say to a favorite but childless daughter, "When I die and go "outside", I will give you a child." The reverse may also be said: "When I die, you will have no more children, I will stop them coming to you." The dead, then, are very clearly seen as the ultimate source of children, and God is slotted in here by Christians instead of the dead. There is linguistic convergence also. Both the dead and God are described in Melpa as *pukl wuo*, "base man" or "owner". God is "owner" of course, as creator of the world and "father" of mankind. In speaking of good luck people may say *pukl wuo ti-nt Kwun murum* or *Pukl Wuo nt Kwun murum*, "an ancestor helped me" or "God helped me". In the Melpa, the sentences are exactly the same except for *ti* in the first case, which means "a".

SPIRIT ATTACK AND THE CONCEPT OF "ANGER"

The use of plant remedies, which I began to discuss above before digressing into a general survey of health care problems, was frequently combined with ritual action intended to make these remedies more effective.[6] So my earlier observation that belief in them is just like people's belief in medicines such as "aspirin" in Western societies, needs to be modified a little. There is certainly a notion that the plants have this or that direct effect, as for example when ginger is bitten into in order to relieve toothache; but it is also thought that a spell can make the process more effective still. One therefore finds there are spells for, say, diarrhea, which are spoken under their breath by ritual experts, *mon wuo*, while they also administer the *tamb mel*, that is the object, leaf, potion, etc. Where a *tamb mel* is employed, the focus of the cure is on the patient's symptoms as such, and the accompanying spell may simply announce the desired effects of the medicine. But sometimes a spell may be aimed at the imputed cause of the condition, as when a body pain is attributed to the action of "wild spirits" who shoot arrows at people as they pass by the spirits' habitual haunts. This is called *tipu kor el-nt ronom*. The spell against this is aimed at the wild spirit himself, to make him turn away and go and not harm the victim again.

The attacks of such wild spirits, *tipu romi* or *kor rakra*, are morally random, whereas sicknesses caused by dead family ghosts are deeply bound up with moral issues. A person's *min* or spirit is sometimes spoken of as hovering at the back of the head, hence the traditional rule of respect for in-laws that one should not move around behind them, in case one disturbs their *min*.[7] A person who sleeps too long and heavily while sick arouses concern on the part of watching kinsfolk in case his or her *min* should wander too far eating strange foods along with the *min* of persons already dead and so not come back to its body at all, and thus the patient will die. For this reason, sick persons are sometimes woken up and told to take a wash and walk around instead of sleeping all the time. In general, the connection between the *min* and its owner's body is seen as potentially tenuous, and a disturbance in moral relationships between people is sufficient to make angry ghosts come and seize hold of the head of a person or to give them sickness especially in the head (*kui peng*). Prayers to the ghosts particularly ask that they not send *kui peng* or, if they have already done so, that they should release (*wak rui*) the patient and thus allow him or her to be cured. In all these cases also, then, the therapy is aimed at the imputed cause of the sickness rather than simply at the symptoms of the condition itself. But where the ghosts are involved, an important element is added, that is the necessity of bringing out into the open the wrongdoing which has been committed.

Sickness may strike either the person who has done wrong or a victim of wrongdoing. In the first circumstance the wrongdoer has usually committed an offense against a kinsperson, especially one which is contrary to the rules of in-group behavior. For example, if a man commits adultery with the wife of another man inside his own sub-clan, it is felt that the sacred divinatory substance (*mi*) of the wider group to which they belong will itself strike him and he will die of the sickness unless he confesses to it.[8] Confession opens the road to curing because it enables appropriate sacrifices to be arranged and ties between people and the ghosts to be repaired. The idea of confession also acts as a bridge between traditional and introduced Christian practices. Christian prayers are said for sicknesses, but not until the patient says whether he or she is harboring any resentments, described in Tok Pisin as *bel hevi* (literally "weighing down the stomach").

The original Melpa term on which the concept of *bel hevi* is based is *Popokl*. *Popokl*, anger, is felt in the person's *noman* and this is the same "psychic organ" (as we may term it) which brings the person into communication with the ghosts. The dead, *kor kui*, and the *noman* of living persons are both unseen, spiritual entities. It is with the implications of the Melpa theory that *popokl* produces sickness in persons that we are concerned here.

The first implication is that efforts are made to forestall the likelihood that others will experience *popokl*. One source of *popokl* is inequality of treatment. Thus, when discussing whether to pick up one or two persons out of a larger number and give them a lift in my car, I have always been told, "Don't do that, either take all of them or leave all of them, because if you take only some the others will be *popokl*." A classic locus for *popokl* is the relationship between co-wives of the same man, who are proverbially jealous, *wolik*, and seek in practice to gain unequal advantages over each other while protesting verbally the need for equal treatment. Given the overall competitive character of social relations in Hagen, the ideal of equality is most often honored in the breach and *popokl* is a recurrent stereotypical emotional state. Hence the second implication that when a person becomes sick, people quickly ask if he or she is hiding some *popokl* and ask for it to be declared. If the sick person has indeed been suffering from a sense of being wronged by others, the questioning provides suitable opportunity to reveal grievances and perhaps have them removed by remedial action. Since grievances cause emotional tension, expression of them in a context of "confession" can provide a welcome release of such tension and the chance to start again on a new basis. However tenuously this process is in fact associated with the person's falling ill and getting better, there is no doubt of its beneficial effects on the social plane. Sickness among the Melpa acts as a lever for the correction of feelings between persons and for the revelation of breaches of the moral code. From the point of view of those inside the society, however, the important idea is the reverse of this: for sickness to be cured, social relationships must first be sorted out.

This theory of the underlying causes of illness need not, and does not, interfere with the use of other forms of therapeutic treatment. It is when these forms of treatment do not work very well that deeper explanations are sought. At first, there may be a simple recourse to the local aid post, or to the Mount Hagen hospital out-patient sections. If the sickness gets worse, the patient may be admitted to a hospital bed and/or sacrifices of pigs may be made at home. In the past, the *el mong* ritual was performed to determine which ghost was "holding" the sick person. This might be conducted by a specialist, *mon wuo*, or by the family head. The practitioner pushed an arrow through the walls of the house or into the floor and asked questions within a binary framework. Seizure of the arrow by a ghost indicated a "yes" answer to the question. Answers were obtained until the identity of the ghost and the type of pig required for sacrifice were both established. The sacrifice would then be held and the *mon wuo*, if involved, was paid with a part of the pork. Nowadays this ritual is not held, but there is still discussion about ghosts and attention is paid to dreams which kinsfolk have that may be interpreted in such a way as to point to the cause of a patient's sickness. To emphasize the point again, all this tends to take place concurrently with other overt efforts to secure biomedical treatment for the patient's symptoms.

It is not simply that there is a lack of trust or belief in introduced medicines. On the whole, it is acknowledged that these are powerful and treatment by qualified hospital doctors is sought after. However, it is still felt that ultimately spiritual forces determine whether a person lives or dies. This aspect of Melpa thought is reinforced by the basic presupposition of the introduced Christian religion, such that either God or the ghosts, as I have already mentioned, is/are considered to be the ultimate cause of a person's recovering from sickness or dying from it. Hence, there must be some ritual placation in order to intercede with these powerful agencies as well as an attack on the patient's symptoms with medicines. Hageners do not have the same body/mind dichotomy as is established in Western culture. Although they do distinguish between the *noman* (mind) and *king* or *kong* (body, skin), they posit a very intimate connection between them such that the state of the *noman* influences the body. A person who was thin and becomes fat is asked *Nim namba noman mat Pin nda*? "What sort of thoughts are you having?" This rather than "What sort of food have you been eating?" although this question may also be asked. And the *noman* in turn is influenced by the ghosts; it is their channel of communication with the living. The living cannot see into each other's *noman*, but the dead can see directly into the *noman* of the living and similarly they can strike them directly with sickness. Hence they must be asked in sacrifice to remove their ill will and allow the medicines applied to work. Adherents of Christianity consider that God/Jesus can nullify the power of "evil spirits" such as ghosts, so all that is necessary is to make Christian prayers. In addition, however, and unlike anything in traditional religion, they believe in God as a "miracle working God" who can effect cures that baffle doctors working with scientific, Western concepts.

SICKNESS AND WRONG-DOING: ATTITUDES TO SURGERY

Further to these observations, there is of course a range of conditions for which one or other therapeutic system is thought to be inadequate or inappropriate. So far as I am aware, no traditional cures are available for epilepsy (*goi-wai kui*), and no Western cures are available for menstrual pollution. The treatment for the latter consists of laying the patient down and then sucking out blood from various points over his back, arms, chest, face and legs, by applying short lengths of sugarcane to the skin and pulling at the blood through these. In a case I saw during 1984, two young men carried out this task, watched critically by other older men and women. They spat the blood out onto a hot drum lid. The patient, a big man, had confessed to an inappropriate sexual liaison. He was obviously very weak, and although the purificatory ritual was said to be successful he remained ill and had to be admitted to Hagen, and later Kudjip hospital with malaria and other complications. He eventually recovered. This man's case was further interesting because he sometimes "went mad", influenced by a dead kinsman who had held a grudge against him while alive, and his *peng kosa* or "brains" were now said to be rather few and might be entirely used up if he became seriously sick again. He had left his old residence near Tambul and came to live with the Kawelka at Kuk in order to avoid this baneful ghost.

One area which is surrounded strongly by beliefs and fears is that of surgery. The idea of cutting open the human body and inspecting its insides is one which at a semi-conscious level is associated with cannibalism. Cannibals are supposed to dismember and butcher their human victims and hide pieces of the meat in other people's saucepans or water containers. Frequently, after a death in which foul play is suspected, doctors at Hagen hospital perform autopsies and invite relatives of the dead person to observe these as witnesses. In one such case a wife died of a massive stroke in the middle of the night. She was a large bulky woman and complained often of severe headaches and ennui, so all the signs were there of an impending attack. However, her kinsfolk said that her husband had probably struck her and murdered her and they gathered to demand compensation. The husband's kinsmen persuaded them to let the doctors decide and, as they watched, the operating doctor made an incision and opened up her stomach and lungs. There was no sign of sickness or contusion in this area, so he proceeded to slit the skin on the skull and then saw open the skull bone itself. Then they saw clearly that one half of her brain was full of blood and the other empty and the doctor explained how this indicated a stroke.   demonstration was accepted and a fight averted. This was in 1981.

In another case, from November 1984, a woman was taking part in a game of cards at her home when she suddenly felt a stabbing pain. She gathered up her money, excused herself, and retired in high agitation. Lying down brought no relief, and she was taken to hospital. Prior to this, she had stolen K60 from a relative and additionally had taken some items home and hidden them. When accused, she denied her actions sturdily. It seems she burnt some of the evidence. The story goes that when taken to hospital she was still conscious and her relatives asked her to confess to what she had done, for otherwise the operation would kill her. The doctor himself is supposed to have said "Confess to anything you've done, if you don't when I cut you, you will die (*nim koptip kundimb*)." She is said to have admitted to only K30 of the K60 she stole. The doctor then gave her an injection and cut her. He showed her kinsmen that her stomach and insides were entirely rotted away, sewed her up again, and she was dead. The implication of the story is that "stolen money kills", especially if there is a theft of sacred property also. But the story also seems to reveal that surgery is like divination: if the person is free from wrongdoing, the surgeon's knife will not kill, but if there is wrongdoing (or "sin" in the Christian vocabulary) the person will be revealed as ripe for death.

This attitude towards surgery is predictable, given: (1) the prevalence of autopsies witnessed by kin; (2) the fact that surgery is reserved for serious cases; and (3) the likelihood that surgery will reveal in advance, incurable cancer or another serious condition in the patient. As a result, when surgery is announced, kinsfolk prepare for the patient's death.

The surgeon, then, is treated almost as a religious practitioner, because of the close empirical association between surgery and the death of patients. The general practitioner has also come to assume a status analogous to that of the traditional healer or *mon-wuo*. In Hagen town there is a very vigorous GP, who takes the somewhat unorthodox line of attempting to understand the social as well as the physical circumstances of his patients. His business is highly successful and carloads of patients even come to him from the distant Southern Highlands areas, prepared to pay his heavy fees in order to get the "strongest" medicines from him. This shows that where people trust or believe in a practitioner they will pay high amounts of money to get his services. The contrast between this attitude in the 1980s and that of the Mendi people in the 1950s is striking: then, rumor has it, people wanted the hospital staff to pay *them* for the privilege of seeing to their running sores, infected eyes, and the like.

DISCUSSION AND CONCLUSIONS

This last example leads to my conclusions. There has been a remarkable fusion (not to say confusion) of ideas in Mount Hagen. People accept the obvious benefits of introduced medicine in a quick and ready fashion, much as they accepted introduced technology. However, acceptance of a practice does not mean that the ideas behind it are fully assimilated or understood. There is a growing situation today in which many people do not fully grasp either their own culture's ideas or those of the introduced culture, and there are obvious dangers and drawbacks in this. For example, people are dependent on introduced medicine for simple remedies which they could in fact still find in their environment.[9] Yet they are not fully aware of the need to take Western medicines according to measure and to finish a course of treatment. (On 29th December 1984, a young man asked me about a bottle of Orthoxicol cough mixture I had bought for my friend Ongka. He said that his old mother had insisted on drinking half the bottle while she was ill and she had then died. He clearly thought the medicine was responsible! I offered to drink the other half and see what would happen, but the discussion was dropped.) And they may be unwilling to let surgery be carried out for serious problems, for the reasons given above. Sicknesses such as malaria and gastroenteritis can kill especially children very quickly and precautions against these sicknesses are rarely taken. I have emphasized that the whole field of primary health care is relatively neglected and underdeveloped. There is also the final problem of the future relationship between "traditional" healers and introduced medicine. On the whole, this problem appears to be solving itself, because (a) forms of treatment may be concurrent, and (b) traditional methods are used for certain specialized conditions e.g. menstrual pollution.

A valuable lynch-pin of the traditional system is the idea of stating grievances or confessing to wrongdoing. This can be a psychological aid to healing as well as to repairing damaged social relationships. On the whole modern medicine does not cater for this aspect at all, but we have seen from the example of "surgery" that people impute these functions to some medical acts of a hospital based kind. Christian prayers in the Pentecostal church movement are supplanting the traditional healer in certain respects also. There remains the residual danger, as expressed by the Lutheran Mission doctor in the 1960s, that people will kill their pigs (or say their prayers?) and only come to hospital when it is too late, but by the 1980s with greater education and more transport, this particular fear is becoming a thing of the past. Another fear however, is real, and that is that the degree of hygiene, standards of nursing care and medical treatment in the hospital itself may all themselves be declining, so that hospitalization may bring with it new dangers of infection. There is a real possibility that this fear is an accurate assessment of the situation in the hospital at Mount Hagen, and this is surely an issue to which the Western Highlands Provincial Government should turn its urgent attention. The hospital is chronically overcrowded, short of clean bedding and its toilet and shower facilities are very poor.

Remarks of this sort are based on observation and common sense. My point, however, about the importance of ideas of "anger" (*popokl*) and "confession" (*nimba not ndui*) in the indigenous therapeutic system may need to be stressed further. I would like to do this by reference to an article "The heart's worst enemy", which appeared in "The Sciences" for September/October 1984, written by Redford B. Williams Jnr.[10] In this article Williams surveys recent research on connections between the psychological syndrome known as the Type A personality and heart attacks. The classic Type A patient is "highly competitive and ambitious, speaks rapidly and interrupts others frequently, and is seized by hostility and anger with uncommon frequency" (p. 31). Of these characteristics, the one most likely to induce heart disease is that of frequently felt hostility and anger, and an important component of the "anger" is a lack of trust of others in the world (the "everyone is against me" idea). Another term Williams suggests for this component is cynicism, and he says that from experimental evidence this element is very closely linked to coronary diseases: "Cynicism, better, perhaps, than any other single word, captures the toxic element in the Type A personality" (p. 35). Now these ideas of anger, hostility, mistrust and cynicism are very close to the Melpa concept of *popokl* and its operations. Of course Melpa do not link *popokl* specifically with heart attack, but they do say that *popokl* can cause sickness, and that one way to deal with it is to confess one's feelings. Confession is a kind of sharing or expressing trust in those whom one has mistrusted, and so of reducing "cynicism". People who suffer setbacks are repeatedly advised by relatives and friends not to become *popokl* about it. Businessmen whose prosperity decline are said to become *popokl* and are liable to suffer untoward accidents causing their sudden death (a striking case in 1984 was the death of Andrew Kei, a prominent businessman. He ran his car off a bridge, into the Wahgi River and drowned). I think here that an unexpected conjunction of modern medical findings and Melpa philosophy is revealed. If so, it is clear indeed that modern medical practitioners should be educated in these aspects of Melpa thought as well as in what the biomedical schools teach them; and the Melpa, on the other hand, should be encouraged not to abandon their own conceptual schemes in favor of only partially understood introduced ones. At least, here is an area where mutual education and understanding is needed for the promotion of good health in general. The old Latin tag still has its uses: *mens sana in corpore sano*. Although this meaning is not present in the original (Juvenal Satires x, 1.356) from which the tag is derived, I would stress that the lesson to be inferred or derived from these cases among the Melpa, as from other instances of traditional medicine, is that there is indeed a subtle symbiosis between mind and body, and health practices must be in accordance with that symbiosis. The Melpa tend to give primacy to the "mind" side of the dichotomy, whereas modern biomedical practice has tended to give primacy to the "body". In fact it is on the interactions between "body" and "mind" that we should concentrate in the overall search for health.

NOTES

1. See, for example, A.J. Strathern (1984 *passim*) for discussions of pluralism in these different spheres of social action. On revivals of traditional healing in North America see Jilek (1982).
2. The World Health Organization has established a programme in Papua New Guinea for the study and recognition of traditional medical specialists, with especial reference to the work of traditional birth attendants. For another discussion of this theme see Stocklin (1984: 156–8).
3. See H. C. Dosedla (1974). Dosedla's study should be consulted for the botanical and ethno-botanical background to remarks I make here.
4. Botanical names have unfortunately at this stage not been collected. However, see above, note 3. It is also hoped that later fieldwork will remedy this defect in the data as they stand.
5. Personal communications from two General Practitioners, Dr J. Nelson in Mount Hagen and Dr. C. Marjen in Port Moresby.
6. For example, for headaches, the chewed bark of a certain forest tree might be spat onto the head; if the headache did not get better an expert would massage the head and pronounce a spell, and might follow this with blood-letting from the nose (information from Ru-Kundil 1984).

7. Compare W. Schiefenhovel's discussion of Eipo ideas (Schiefenhovel 1983). I am grateful to Prof. Schiefenhovel for discussion of the ideas in this paper and to a German reviewer for corrective comment on my use of the Latin tag with which it ends.
8. For a thorough study of the *mi* concept, see Strauss and Tischner (1962). Strauss's study remains the best and most comprehensive account of traditional religion among the Melpa.
9. For support of the viewpoint I advance here see the independent and prior observations made by Schiefenhovel (1982: 842), relating to the Eipo of Irian Jaya. The Eipo are a mountain people whose life is comparable to the traditional way of life of the Melpa.
10. R. B. Williams (1984). Heart attack from stress is, of course, a problem which is psychologically salient in American and, indeed Western society in general.

ACHSAH H. CARRIER

7. THE PLACE OF WESTERN MEDICINE IN PONAM THEORIES OF HEALTH AND ILLNESS

This paper provides a historical description of theories of health and illness on Ponam Island, Manus province. It focuses particularly on the use of Western medicine in the light of Robert Welsch's (1983) argument that Western medicine is incorporated into and interpreted in the light of indigenous theories. Ponams understood Western medicine as specific for those illnesses caused by God, in the same way that indigenous cures were specific for those caused by indigenous ancestors and spirits; therefore the choice between Western and indigenous medicine was not a choice between alternative systems, but a choice between alternative diagnoses within a single medical system. The paper also shows how preferences in diagnosis changed over time with changes in the political circumstances in Manus, particularly with the changing fortunes of the Catholic church.

INTRODUCTION

According to Robert Welsch (1982: 27) most anthropologists who study illness in developing countries have assumed that Western and indigenous health practices and beliefs exist as alternative and radically different medical systems as distinct as conventional medicine and faith healing are in the West. As a consequence of this assumption the majority of studies seek to identify the conflicts between Western and indigenous medical systems which are presumed to lead to the under use of Western medical facilities. Welsch argues, on the other hand, that such conflicts may exist largely in the minds of Western researchers. He suggests that most people from non-Western cultures do not see Western medicine as incomprehensible. Rather, they incorporate Western medicine, interpret it in the light of their indigenous knowledge, and perceive a single medical system, not a pluralistic one. In other words, people do not see these as distinct contradictory systems in the way that Western culture views conventional medicine and faith healing, but as elements in a single system in the way that Western culture views, for example, gynaecology and cardiology, as different specialties which complement each other and derive from a unifying corpus of knowledge and belief. Thus people understand Western medicine in their own terms, find it logical and sensible. Stephen Frankel, writing about the Huli, makes the same point succinctly when he says that "... a key quality of the Huli medical culture, despite its diversity, is its coherence to the individual Hulis who make use of it" (1986: 190).

Until recently, little has been written about the place of Western medicine in the indigenous medical systems of Papua New Guinea. There have been a number of anthropological studies of health and illness, but few of those carried out before the 1980s discuss Western medicine. Until that time anthropologists wrote about theories of health without attempting to describe how people understood Western medicine, even though it was both available and in use in most of the places they studied (e.g. Johannes 1976, Lewis 1975, Nelson 1971). It seems that the belief that Western and traditional medicine formed distinct systems made it possible to discuss traditional medicine without reference to Western medicine (though, interestingly, not the other way around).

Regardless of the theoretical inclinations of the discipline, such sharp segregation has long been impossible in Manus province as indicated by the fact that Lola Romanucci-Ross (1977), who studied village medicine in Manus in the 1960s, attempted to relate the interpretation of the two systems well before such an interest became general. Manus Province has long had a particularly comprehensive rural health care system. In 1979 there were two hospitals, three health centers and 57 aid posts serving a population of less than 26,000 (King and Ranck 1982: 31, 20). Ponam Island, located about four miles off the north-central coast of the province's main island of Manus, had its own aid post even though it had a resident population of only about 300. Ponam was less than an hour's boat travel away from a health center and less than four hours from a hospital.

Not only was Western medicine[2] readily available, but Ponams did (for an explanation of the use of the past tense, see note 3) not think that the principles underlying it were particularly mysterious or awesome. Since the War all Ponam children have attended primary school, many have attended secondary school, and some have pursued tertiary medical training. "Health" is a part of the basic primary curriculum and consequently most people under about forty years of age felt themselves to have a reasonable lay understanding of Western medicine. Further, because Western treatments were readily available and because Ponams saw medicine as a specialist profession, rather than something belonging to Europeans, they never looked to me for advice or medical treatment. They simply assumed that because I was not a nurse or a doctor, they would be better treated by someone who was. Predictably, Ponams' exposure to Western medical theories and facilities had not eliminated indigenous theory or practice, but it would be a distortion to discuss Ponam medicine without discussing their use and interpretation of Western medicine as well. By 1979, at least, Western medicine was not an intrusion into Ponam life, but a part of it.

Like the Ningerum and the Huli, the people of Ponam Island fused Western and indigenous medicine to form a single comprehensive theory of illness and treatment. But they created a theory very different from that of the Huli or Ningerum, a theory which started from different indigenous principles and emerged through different historical circumstances. In this paper I will describe the introduction of Western medicine to Ponam, the Western medical facilities which were available there, and the theory of illness and its causes in terms of which these were understood. In conclusion I will describe some of the important events of recent Ponam history in order to locate Ponam's medical theory and practices within their social and historical context.

THE INTRODUCTION OF WESTERN MEDICINE

It is now impossible to reconstruct accurately Ponams' pre- or even early colonial theories of illness since there has been a significant European presence there since 1900, and none of the Ponams alive during the period of my research could remember much of life before the arrival of the Catholic mission in 1916. It seems from people's descriptions of the past however, that Ponams were similar to the people of the south coast village of Pere, whose theories of illness were studied by Reo Fortune (1935) in the late 1920s, just before their conversion to Catholicism.

In Pere each household was dominated by the ghost of the head of the household's most recently deceased relative, usually a father or older brother. The dead man's skull was kept in the house as a shrine and a home for the ghost. The head of the household, his family and dependents relied on their ghost for protection from other ghosts, spirits and from all misfortune. In return the ghost required rigid adherence to strict canons of sexual morality, filial piety and economic rectitude, bringing death and disease to those who disobeyed or to their close kin and dependents. Ghostly illness could only be cured by public confession and atonement for sins, a painful and degrading process for all concerned. This theory of illness, combined with the prevalence of illness and high mortality rate, made the Pere preoccupied with sin and with detecting the sins of others, as the tension generated by illness and possible death was turned in on the family, not directed outward. Illness could also be caused by contact with totem plants and animals, by curses made by certain classes of relatives and by malevolent spirits from outside of the village, though these were of minor importance compared to the power of ancestral ghosts. Sorcery was known and possible, but it too was of relatively little importance within the village.

Pre-Christian Ponam seems to have had much in common with Pere. Totemic pollution, cursing and malevolent spirits were all possible sources of illness. Ponam heads of household also preserved the skulls or bones of the recently dead whose ghosts supervised their descendents and dependents, and many illnesses were the result of ancestral anger. However, although sexual propriety was apparently more rigid in these early days than since the War, it does not seem that Ponam ghosts were as compulsively concerned with this as those of Pere were. Ponams had a Manus-wide reputation as sorcerers at the turn of the century (Parkinson 1907) and, as Ponams now remember it, ghostly illnesses were in general less common and less important than those caused by sorcery, which was an important basis of political and economic power.

It seems likely that Ponams' first serious exposure to Western health theories occurred when they began to convert to Catholicism, following the opening of a Catholic mission station at Bundralis on the nearby Manus mainland in 1916. Unlike more evangelical churches, the Catholics seem not to have tried to eliminate all traditional beliefs, though by their teaching and by their very presence they changed these significantly. For example, the mission and the government insisted that Ponams abandon the practice of burying the dead beneath dwelling houses and later recovering the bones to use as ghostly shrines, and insisted instead that the dead should be buried in a cemetery and left there for all time. Although it may not have been intended to do so, this ruling served to weaken the power of ghosts over their descendents. As such the move seems not to have been unpopular, for although ghosts brought protection, they were also dangerous. The aspect of traditional beliefs which Ponams remember the church attacking most strongly was the practice of sorcery. When Ponam's most powerful warrior and sorcerer accepted baptism in the early 1920s he persuaded others to follow him in abandoning sorcery and Ponams held a ceremony to bury and diffuse all sorcery paraphernalia, though its evil effects continued to waft over the island even in the 1980s. Many other related techniques, especially those of divination and contact with spirits, were given up at this time as well and henceforth had to be hired or borrowed from people from mainland Manus.

Although the church seems to have significantly reduced the power of ghosts, it did not even attempt to eliminate people's belief in them. In the 1980s Ponams believed that prayers to the ancestors, and indeed all well-motivated approaches to other sorts of spirits, were perfectly compatible with good Catholicism. They did not have the idea, common among fundamentalist Christian sects in Papua New Guinea, that Christianity was incompatible with all traditional religious practices (cf. Frankel 1986: 164ff). Rather, they believed that the Catholic church and traditional religion shared the same basic moral principles, though their own ancestral ghosts were somewhat more rigid about punishing sin than was God.

Despite the presence of the mission and the colonial government, Ponams had little Western medical care until the Second World War when Manus was occupied by the American military. As many as a million soldiers passed through Manus between 1944 and 1946. Thousands of ships anchored in her harbors. Airports, hospitals, roads, electricity, and more appeared virtually overnight. When the US Navy decided to build an airstrip on Ponam, it took them only three days to move the village of 200 people to one end of the island, build a fence to separate it from the rest, level the coconut plantation, cover the island with a concrete airstrip, and build a camp for 1500 men. Ponams and 5000 other displaced Manus people, approximately a third of the district population, were totally supported by the military for nearly two years: fed, clothed, housed, provided with priests and doctors and the chance to barter their own produce for the apparently endless supply of goods which the sailors could pilfer from the Navy. The American military treated Manus people with a generosity and an apparent sense of equality which they had never known from the Australians, whose priorities as minority rulers of an under-budgeted and unprofitable colony were utterly different.

The impact of the occupation on Manus people was profound. It exposed people to wealth and technology hitherto unknown, even to the majority of men who had worked outside the district. It gave people new ideas about themselves and about their ability to master Western technology. And it gave people new ideas about the potential equality of white and black, about the potential for self government and independence, and about the potential for freedom from their own traditions which were seen by many as equally to blame with the Australians for the poverty of Manus.

Although this discontent was felt everywhere in Manus after the return to Australian civil administration and to a pre-war standard of living and style of government, it was expressed most dramatically by those, mostly from the south coast, who accepted the leadership of Paliau Molowat and joined his New Way movement (Schwartz 1962). This is probably best known as a cargo cult, an attempt to bring wealth by magical means, but it was more sophisticated than this. Paliau planned a social and economic revolution, planned to reorganize local trade and production, to overthrow traditional leadership and the economy based on affinal exchange, break the power of ghosts and ancestors and power of Australian colonial rulers. One of his many strategies for doing this was to break with the Catholic church, and all Western churches, and develop a new Melanesian sect of Christianity with a new morality and a new theory of illness. As a result, the Catholic church was one of his strongest opponents.

Margaret Mead (1968: 304-321) describes Paliau's medical theory as it was applied in Pere in 1953. Most sickness was caused by God as a punishment not for evil actions (which were a matter for the civil courts) but for evil thoughts, especially anger, which corrupts the soul and cuts one off from God. Sexual relations were no longer sinful in and of themselves, nor were they a cause of sickness, unless they led to anger and quarrelling, as they often did. The key to cure in the New Way was twofold. The new Western medicines were used in conjunction with confession, which had always been important. The sick person and his or her close kin were required to confess to all angry thoughts and bring their anger out into the open. This would free the sick person's soul to communicate with God again. Although this was the New Way's official theory of illness, another unorthodox theory competed with this, especially in explaining illness which could not be attributed to anger and which failed to respond to confession and Western medicine. These illnesses, called "diseases of the ground" were attributed to sorcery, especially sorcery brought to Manus from other parts of the country.

As I said, the New Way and Paliau's leadership of it were not accepted everywhere in Manus. Many people, especially along the north coast, feared the movement's expansionist political ambitions, and resented its opposition to the Catholic church and to traditional customs. Ponam was one of the staunchest of the anti-Paliau communities. Ponams resisted the introduction of the local Government Council (which was introduced in response to demands by Paliau and his followers), refused to elect a councillor until forced to do so in the mid 1970s, refused to destroy traditional wealth or abandon affinal exchange, and remained fiercely loyal to the Catholic church at Bundralis. Nonetheless it is clear that some of the spirit of the New Way did penetrate the island, particularly in people's attempt to regiment village life and model it on the military style they had seen during the occupation. It is difficult to say how much people were influenced by the New Way theories of illness, though the fact that Ponams' theories of the 1980s resemble those of Pere in the 1950s suggests that there was a cross-fertilization of ideas. Like Pere, Ponams associated Western medicine with illness sent by God and traditional cures with more traditional causes, which they too called "diseases of the ground" (though sorcery was only one of many possible such causes). Unlike Pere, they retained belief in the power of ghosts and made confession essential for curing ghostly illnesses, though not for curing divine ones.

In the conclusion to this paper I will return to the history of political events in post-war Manus and suggest that during the 1950s and 1960s Ponams' political opposition to Paliau drove them closer to the church and increased the salience of God as a cause of illness. During the 1970s however, the influence of the Paliau movement declined and so, apparently, did the use of Western medicine. Before I discuss this issue, I want to describe both the kinds of Western medical care which became available after the war and the theories in terms of which it and traditional medicine were interpreted.

WESTERN MEDICAL SERVICES 1950–1980

After the war, and partly in response to the New Way, the Administration and the church began to increase the level of public services in Manus. Medical services were among the first to receive attention. In 1952 two Ponam men were sent for training as an aid post orderly and a hygiene officer, as were many others from throughout the province. The aid post orderly opened the first Ponam aid post and later worked in the western islands until his retirement in the 1970s. The hygiene officer returned to work on Ponam and later took over as aid post orderly, a position he still held at the end of 1983, though his age and poor health suggested that retirement could not be far away.

In the 1950s, under the leadership of the new aid post orderly and hygiene officer and with the inspiration of the American military in mind, Ponams took a number of steps to improve community health. (Although the Administration urged these changes, they accorded so well with Ponams' concerns and beliefs of the time that they were probably justified in their modern belief that these were their own innovations.) They built toilets at the end of long bridges out over the sea as they said the military had done. They required that all pigs be kept in pens by the beach. And they passed a village ordinance declaring that as dogs were noisy, dirty and useless in an island village, it would no longer be an offense to kill another person's dog. These intentional measures, combined with such natural advantages as the good drainage from their sandy soil and an adequate supply of fresh water, meant that the basic conditions of public health were satisfactory.

Later improvements in health services included, in addition to the aid post, a mission-run health center (officially classed as a health subcenter) at Bundralis, the Lorengau provincial hospital, and regular visits from a travelling maternal and child health clinic. I will describe each of these in turn.

Having existed on Ponam for thirty years, the aid post was a fixture of Ponam life, accepted and heavily used by almost everyone. Despite this however, it did not provide the kind of service which, according to the Health Department, it should. This was largely the fault of the aid post orderly and the difficult position in which he found himself: he was a villager with a bit of medical training, but not a professional health worker. Frankel points out that the Health Department originally envisioned aid post orderlies as "villagers" who also have some medical skills, who should be supported by their appreciative clients, and who should be grateful for whatever they get from the Health Department for they also have plenty of spare time to tend to their gardens. He found that the effective aid post orderlies in Tari were not simply villagers but public servants and worked most efficiently when they were treated that way. The Ponam aid post orderly conformed to the early administration model rather than to the more efficient bureaucratic one (perhaps because he received his training in the early 1950s and had worked only in his own village ever since) and his medical practice suffered thereby. However, it would have been almost impossible for the Health Department to replace him.

The aid post orderly was an important man in the village, a clan leader and village councillor, and his salary helped to maintain these positions. Because of his status he was not subject to much control by his clients or the Health Department and was able to run his aid post more or less as he chose. He kept clinic hours irregularly and, though he usually responded to requests for help, some people were reluctant to make them except in emergencies. Furthermore, as a man of importance he was frequently away from the village for several days at a time. To complicate matters still further, his social position made it impossible for him to treat many villagers. He could not treat any of his numerous female affines without violating the etiquette of affinal avoidance, *fili'i*, and his political opponents claimed that he refused to treat them though the justice of this claim is not clear for most of them would refuse to ask for help in the first place. These factors, combined with the aid post orderly's outdated training, genuine doubts about the usefulness of Western medicine for most illnesses, and the difficulties of obtaining aid post supplies, reduced him to a supplier of bandages, chloroquine, cough medicine and usually indiscriminate penicillin injections. Ponams who wanted serious medical treatment usually bypassed the aid post altogether and went to the nearby health center instead. Though I have criticized the aid post orderly, it may be that the very presence of the health center reduced demands on him and thus led him to lower his standards. For the health center was nearby, conveniently located on the site of the local market which most Ponams attended every week or so.

The mission provided some sort of hospital facilities as early as 1952 (PR6-52/53), but apparently did not maintain them for very long. A new Bundralis health center, the one which Ponams now remember, was opened by the Catholic mission in the mid 1960s (PR13-67/68). During its first years it was run by expatriate mission nurses who, people report, were very forceful, willing to insist that people come for treatment and quick to refer patients to Lorengau hospital. Ponams apparently accepted their authority, sometimes even against their better judgement.

People often explained, for example, that they went to the health center or the hospital because the nurse "ordered" them to do so. In the 1970s however, the staff were all Papua New Guineans, and considerably less domineering than the expatriates. As I will point out later on, this has affected people's use of health center services. In 1983 the health center had male and female in-patient wards with four beds each, and a separate six-bed maternity ward. The nurses kept regular clinic hours for out-patients seven days a week and were always available for emergencies. The three wards were almost never full, so there was usually room for a patient's family to stay there as well. This was necessary because the health center provided medical care only, and patients needed kin to cook for them, do their laundry and so forth.

By and large Ponams spoke very highly of the quality of care available at the health center. The nurses, with a few usually short-lived exceptions, were seen as knowledgeable and welcoming, not merely time serving bureaucrats. Despite this, Ponams did not usually rely on the health center for the treatment of serious illness. Instead they used it as a source for treatment for injuries, children's ailments (such as colds, chicken pox and worms) and maternity care.

TABLE 1
Place of delivery for all births to a sample of 28 Ponam women

	Place of birth	Pre-health center	Post-health center	Total
Child does not survive neonatal period	Bundrails	---n.a.---	2	2
	Ponam	15	2	17
	Other	0	0	0
Sub-total		15 (16%)	4 (7%)	19 (13%)
Child survives neonatal period	Bundrails	---n.a.---	19	19
	Ponam	74	19	93
	Other	3	15	18
Sub-total		77 (84%)	53 (93%)	130 (87%)
Total		92 (100%)	57 (100%)	149 (100%)

The maternity service was considered particularly valuable. All but a few women said that they would prefer to have their babies at Bundralis and as Table 1 shows, not only have women made use of it, but it seems to have a beneficial effect on neonatal mortality. The major difficulty in doing so was the fact that they and the nurses could not predict the day of delivery, but only the month. Thus, women who wanted to deliver at the health center usually had to spend several weeks living in one of a handful of small, poorly equipped houses that Ponams had built at Bundralis, while waiting for labor to begin. First time mothers, who were anxious about their delivery and had few duties to keep them at home, could usually do this with their husbands' help. But those with large families and many obligations tried to postpone their move to the mainland until the last possible minute, and were often caught unprepared. They would not try to travel to Bundralis after labor had started unless there was an emergency, but usually visited a week or so after the birth. There were several resident Ponam women who had some sort of nurse's training and they were usually called on to help with deliveries, though everyone recognized that they did not have the same technical skills as the Bundralis nurses.

In addition to the Bundralis health center, Ponams could use the hospital at the provincial capital, Lorengau, three or four hours away by motor canoe. Hospital visits were far more difficult to manage than those to the health center because, like health center patients, those at the hospital needed the help of guardian relatives, yet there was no convenient place for these guardians to stay unless they had close kin living in town. Furthermore, Ponams complained about the standard of cleanliness and about how inefficient, slow and impersonal was the service received there. For the most part, Ponams went to Lorengau hospital only when referred by the health center, whose nurses sent only the very ill or those in need of emergency surgery. As Table 2 shows, of the eleven Ponams hospitalized with serious illnesses or for surgery between January 1979 and December 1983, only five went to the Lorengau hospital, three of these for emergency surgery. In the other six cases the patient was taken by a migrant relative to a hospital in the area where the relative worked. Often these relatives arranged for the patient to be seen by a private doctor, rather than one provided by the health service.[4]

TABLE 2
Surgery of major medical treatment received by Ponam residents, 1979–1983

Hospital	Emergency surgery	Elective surgery	Other treatment	Total
Lorengau	3	2	0	5
Other	0	3	3*	6
Total	3	5	3	11

* one patient treated at the military hospital at Lombrum.

Despite their good opinion of the Bundralis health center and the willingness of migrants to take kin to major city hospitals when they believed an illness could be cured there, many seriously ill Ponams did not receive any medical treatment at all. As Table 3 shows, of the 24 resident Ponams who died between January 1979 and December 1983, seven received Western medical treatment during the course of their last illnesses and 17 did not. None of the twelve people aged 60 or above received medical treatment and seven of the twelve under age 60 received treatment. Of the 18 who died without treatment, ten had children or siblings who could have afforded to bring them to major city hospitals for treatment and all had relatives who could have afforded to support them in Lorengau hospital or the Bundralis health center. Thus it was not simply the financial costs of treatment which held them back.

TABLE 3
Hospital treatment received during the final illness by Ponams dying 1979–1983

	Neonate	1–11mo	Age 1–29	30–59	60+	Total
Hospital treatment	2*	1	0	4	0	7
No hospital	0	0	1**	4	12***	17
Total	2	1	1	8	12	24

* Both neonates were born and died at the Bundralis health center.
** Sudden death.
**** One man had spent several months in hospital in the year preceding the year of his death.

In the 1970s the government introduced one further service, a travelling maternal and child health clinic, whose nurses visited Ponam every few months to check pregnant women and babies, and to give inoculations and family planning advice. The clinic was held at the aid post, though the aid post orderly himself was almost never there. Women were conscientious about attending the clinic: pregnant women to receive medicines; and mothers to keep their children's clinic books up to date and for them to receive injections. No mothers stayed away from the clinics entirely and most tried to attend every time. Despite the mothers' interest, the clinic did not provide the kind of service which it was intended to provide.

If the aid post suffered from a lack of bureaucratic rigor, the maternal and child health Service suffered from the reverse. The sisters were not villagers and few social constraints affected their performance. They were conscientious about time keeping, record keeping, weighing and measuring and so forth, but attended so much to these bureaucratic requirements that the children received very little clinical care. Frankel's description of the Huli clinics applies equally to Ponam: "A sister's interest in symptoms is guided far more by bureaucratic concerns than by the needs of the child ... in the main it is the cards that are treated, not the children" (1982: 45).

For the most part the sisters saw healthy children or those for whom a perfunctory dose of cough medicine was sufficient and therefore their bureaucratic attitude, which seemed at least to result in the efficient management of injection schedules, did little harm. When faced with a really sick child however, this neglect of symptoms could be very serious. For example, in the only severe case of malnutrition which I have come across, the clinic sisters steadily recorded in the clinic book the child's failure to gain weight over a period of six months until, at the age of thirteen months she was below 60% of weight for age. Her mother brought her to the clinic again at this age and, though she was obviously ill, the sisters failed to examine her or to ask her mother anything about her to elicit the fact that she was suffering from intermittent high fever and persistent diarrhea, though they entered her weight in the book and recorded a prescription of cough medicine. This kind of non-treatment was particularly serious, because Ponams saw the failure of a Western medical practitioner to diagnose and cure an illness as an indication that the illness could not be treated with Western medicine and were unlikely to seek further Western medical treatment.

In addition to these state-provided medical services, Ponams used a number of over-the-counter drugs. Aspirin, cough syrup, chloroquine, antibiotic and antiseptic ointments, liniment and similar preparations were common. People said that before the Second World War indigenous medical plants were used (sometimes by specialists) to treat many minor ailments in the same way that drugs are used now. In the 1970s and 1980s, however, only a few plants were widely used (these for treating sores and digestive complaints), and there were no specialist practitioners.

Thus Western medical care became increasingly available to Ponams from the War until the time of my fieldwork, both because the range of available services increased, and because Ponams themselves became increasingly able to pay for them. But it is by no means certain that Ponams' use of Western medicine has continued to increase as well. In fact some of the educated Ponam migrant elite, particularly those who felt a growing scepticism about traditional religious and medical beliefs, argued that during the 1970s and early 1980s the use of Western medicine decreased. They explained this as the result of people's loss of faith in the Catholic church and its medical treatments. Among islanders, not everyone felt that there had been a change in people's use of Western medicine; those who did interpreted this as the result of there having been an increase in traditionally caused illnesses and not as the result of a decrease in faith in Western cures. In the conclusion to this paper I want to come back to this point and to discuss the relation and interaction between Ponams' medical beliefs and the intellectual and political environment of those beliefs.

THE BODY AND THE POSSIBLE CAUSES OF ILLNESS

In contemporary, conventional Western medical theory disease is located in specific organs and tissues of the body and can be studied with reference to the body alone. Disease is a physiological malfunction of the body caused by pathological forces which exist within it and operate directly on it. Pathology manifests itself as illness. These physiological manifestations, symptoms, are caused by the physiological malfunctions and provide direct evidence of the physiological nature and cause of the malfunction. Only when this is known is it possible to prescribe a cure.[5] Consonant with the localization of disease in specific parts of the body and the idea that specific diseases manifest themselves in specific symptoms, Western medicine has developed an elaborate model of the body and a detailed classification of the physiological manifestations of illness. As Michael Foucault (1973) has shown, this localization of disease in specific organs of the body is relatively new in Western medicine, as is the associated emphasis on physiology and physiological symptoms.

In contrast to contemporary Western models of disease, most of the classical anthropological studies of illness in cultures other than that in which Western medicine is dominant, have focused on its moral and spiritual causes and cures. Critics and commentators (see the collection Loudon 1976b, especially Loudon 1976a:34–36; Gillies 1976: 386–89) have pointed out that these studies tend to disregard the physical or natural elements of the medical systems in question, presenting them as less natural than they really are. Recent researchers in Papua New Guinea, who have been aware of this issue, have found variations in the emphasis placed on the physical aspects of illness.

Gilbert Lewis says that the Gnau of West Sepik province did not attend to the physical manifestations of illness. "Since in their view causes were not discernible from the clinical signs, exact description or examination of these were not relevant. Cause and remedy were to be revealed by other evidence than that of the body's state" (1976: 77). Jessica Mayer's findings (1982: 257) of the Ommura in Eastern Highlands province were very similar, though she also found evidence that previously there was a greater emphasis on symptoms and symptom-specific treatments. Robert Welsch (1982) and Stephen Frankel (1986) report very different attitudes among the Ningerum and the Huli. In both of these places people were very much concerned with the physical manifestations of illness, using them as a guide to diagnosis and treatment, and people diagnosed a number of afflictions as having a primarily bodily locus. For Ponams on the other hand, most illnesses were not afflictions of the body, but afflictions of the spirit which could not be diagnosed or treated symptomatically. And while Ponams did locate the source of some illnesses in the body and attempt to cure these by treating the body, their conception of the body was no more like that of modern Western medicine than modern Western medicine's is like eighteenth century Western medicine's. To understand what physical illness was for Ponams and why so few illnesses were purely physical, it is necessary to understand something of how Ponams thought the body works.

Ponams had clear ideas about the functioning of the physical components of the body. However, they held that the interrelationship of body parts was mechanical rather than organic or physiological, as is understood to be the case in Western medicine. For example, it was physical activity that made the blood circulate, not the pumping of the heart; and it was the physical pressure of food in the bowels that kept digestion going. The body was occupied by a soul, *maluon*, which gave it life. Illness was the consequence of either the mechanical failure of the body or the removal of the soul, or parts of it, from the body. The soul could be removed by God, ghosts or spirits and in principle this fate was avoidable. Mechanical failure could be caused by injury and was inevitable in old age, the consequence of the wearing out of the body through use. This was one important reason why, as I have already described, old people often did not receive medical treatment. If their illness did not reach an acute stage, or if they did not linger long in such a stage, they were thought to be suffering from degenerative mechanical failure for which there was no remedy. The mechanical operation of the body could be upset in a number of ways. For example, breathing dust caused colds, green fruit caused diarrhea, fire burned the skin and a shock or a blow to the head could dislocate the soul. Starvation, strangulation, drowning and assault with a deadly weapon could all kill in a purely mechanical fashion.

Although in principle mechanical failure could be fatal this did not often happen. Thus people often gave me physical descriptions and mechanical explanations of illnesses which were later diagnosed as not being physical at all. For example, the intestinal troubles which hospitalized one man were explained as a mechanical complication following from his irregular eating habits. By skipping meals he left empty passages in his bowels and eventually one of these twisted itself into a knot, blocking the bowel altogether. This problem, the speaker hypothesized, could only be cured by surgery to correct the mechanical damage. The illness was eventually diagnosed as caused by ancestral anger and cured appropriately, but this does not invalidate the theory underlying the initial explanation. I think that most Ponams believed that it was always possible that a sick person was suffering from a purely mechanical failure, though it usually turned out in any particular case that the root cause was elsewhere.

Serious illness was almost always caused by soul loss rather than any mechanical failure. Soul loss could have a number of causes and could produce a wide range of physical manifestations. Therefore these manifestations, though physical, were not symptoms in the Western sense. They could not be examined to determine the source of disease, its cause and cure. A few causes would produce only a limited range of physical manifestations and when they appeared, people's first suspicion was the cause normally associated with them. However, these manifestations too were not symptoms in the Western sense, for there was no physical relationship between them, their cause and their cure. Thus, although Ponams had a model of the human body and could refer to this model in describing the nature and consequences of illness, they did not have a concept of human physiology which was comparable to that at the heart of Western medicine.

Having described something of the nature of the human body and the illnesses which Ponams believed could befall it, I now want to return to the issue raised at the beginning of this paper, the way in which Western medicine may be understood by people from other cultures. Western medical theory is constructed in such a way that it is almost impossible for it to incorporate any alternative form of medicine. The theory holds itself to be exhaustive; that is, all diseases are located in the tissues and organs of the body, can only be diagnosed by examination of the body, and can only be cured by treatments which act on the body. Further, symptoms and the diseases which cause them are, at least in principle, uniquely paired: the model does not easily accommodate qualitatively different causes for the same set of symptoms. Ponams' notions were not exhaustive in this way, and thus the existence of effective Western medicine provided no challenge to the validity of their own indigenous treatments. Instead, it was accepted as providing another type of cure for another type of sickness, albeit one which could not be distinguished symptomatically from indigenous sicknesses.

Ponams' mechanical model of the body was superficially similar to that of Western medical theory, and it would have been quite possible for Ponams to incorporate and explain Western medicine in terms of this model, as the Ningerum did. In Ningerum theory (Welsch 1982: 335, 361), Western medicine is aimed at strengthening or repairing the body and lessening pain. These physical problems may occur without cause or may be the result of attacks by sorcerers or ghosts. In the latter case a first cure is needed to remove the cause of the illness and a later one to help the body to cure itself of residual injuries. Western medicine is understood as providing treatments for these residual physical injuries. Similar divisions of labor are found elsewhere in Papua New Guinea. Michael Hamnett and John Connell report of the Evio and Siwai of North Solomons province, for example, that "Western techniques have been regarded as the means of treating symptoms, while dealing with causes remains a necessary and sometimes separate step" (1980: 64; see also Hamnett and Connell 1981).

Ponams did not interpret Western medicine in quite this way, as something which cured the physical manifestations of illness but not its causes. They did recognize that Western medical practitioners had the skill to handle many mechanical failures of the body. Particularly important in these cases were the skills of first aid, surgery and midwifery. But most medicine, especially internal medicine, did not act simply on physical, mechanical disorder. Instead it was something provided by God to cure the illnesses of the soul which He sent as a warning or punishment for sin, just as indigenous techniques cured the illnesses sent by indigenous ancestors and spirits. Thus, for the most part, Western medicine provided non-physical cures for non-physical illnesses, just as most indigenous treatments did.

I should stress that not all Ponams held the same views about illness or about Western and indigenous medical practices. Some people, particularly among the well-educated migrant elite, had rejected various aspects of the indigenous theory of disease and replaced them with popular Western theories, though as Catholics they saw God as the ultimate cause of illness and the ultimate source of medical cure. As a result, some educated Ponams had begun to see these two medical systems as being at least partially in conflict with one another. While in the remainder of this paper I describe the causes of disease which were subscribed to by most Ponam residents, it would be wrong to suggest that all Ponams believed equally in them or that people did not change their beliefs as a result of education or other types of exposure to other theories of illness. Moreover, even those who were convinced of the power of traditional causes of illness believed that their knowledge was imperfect, required testing and thought, and was subject to revision. On the whole Ponams held to a highly empirical philosophy. They were sceptical of all revealed knowledge, both that gained by divine or spiritual contacts and that revealed by other people in books or conversations, and saw personal experience and observation as the only secure basis of knowledge.

THE CAUSES OF SICKNESS

Ponams clearly distinguished physical illness from other misfortunes (cf. Lewis's discussion of this issue, 1976: 52 ff). To have something wrong with one's body was to be *miri*. Other types of misfortune might share the same cause but had other names. There was some ambivalence about the status of mental illness, *kowau*, but this was usually referred to as *miri* as well. As I have said, in principle *miri* could have purely physical causes, but serious illness was usually attributed to one of two non-physical causes: the Christian God or indigenous ancestors and spirits. Sickness caused by God was called "divine sickness', *miri paro Lapan* (literally, sickness from God), and sickness caused by ancestors or spirits was called "earthly sickness" *miri paro on* or *miri paro kol* (literally, sickness from the ground or sickness from the village).

Earthly sickness

Earthly sickness was a blanket term for illnesses caused by the ghosts or spirits which inhabited the world with human beings, who walked the streets, entered houses, owned possessions, and lived quasi-human lives. These beings had the power to injure or kill human beings by stealing the invisible human soul, *maluon*, and leaving the inanimate or weakened body to sicken and die. The body could only recover if its soul was returned and, once its soul was returned, the body would recover instantly and completely with no need for further treatment. The most important of these invisible beings were the ghosts of the recently dead, *palit*, and evil spirits, *ngam*. Spirits could act on their own evil account, or could be controlled by human beings who were sorcerers. A variety of non-fatal illnesses could also be caused by long dead human ancestors, though the mechanism of causation was not always clear in these cases.

Ghosts supervised the moral behavior of their descendents, especially their agnates, sending illness as a punishment when someone acted against agnatic interests, especially by quarrelling with other agnates. Ghosts apparently took relatively little interest in sexual misbehavior unless, as was likely, this led to disputes among kin. Often ghosts punished an innocent person, rather than a guilty one, as a way, Ponams said, of attempting to force Ponams to police their own morals: after all, if only the guilty suffered, who would care? During my first years on Ponam the vast majority of all the illnesses I learned about were inflicted by ghosts to punish quarrelling agnates. Since brothers quarrelled unceasingly (in 1979 only one pair of married resident brothers was on speaking terms) ghosts had plenty of work to do. As one old man said, "I am never sick. My wife too, and my children. Do you know why? (with a note of triumph) All of my brothers are dead!"

Ghosts were not capricious, but always responded if those whose misdeeds had called down the punishment would honestly confess to their wrongs, make atoning payments, and pray for the sufferer's soul to be returned. This process was called *njames*. If people knew exactly who had aroused the ghost's anger and could induce him or her to confess, a cure could be effected privately. If people did not know the source of the trouble it was necessary to call a prayer meeting of all of the sick person's agnates and kin closely related through female agnates, in which people confessed their grievances. These meetings were almost invariably long and arduous. Usually there were several people with grievances to be sorted out, and the more serious the grievances were, the more difficult it was to bring them out. In a prolonged illness the patient's family might hold numerous prayer meetings, most of them spent dealing with trivial confessions, while circling around the more momentous issues, ones which no one wanted to confess. Some families knew themselves to be suffering from really intractable problems which would bring sickness and death again and again but seemed almost to have given up the effort to bring cures through prayer, simply accepting the illnesses which befell them. This was particularly noticeable in two families plagued with troubles resulting from incestuous marriages.

When acting on their own, spirits were utterly capricious and unreasonable beings which killed or inflicted sickness for no good reason. They were particularly attracted to smells, such as those of food and sexual fluids, so that scrupulous washing was the first line of defense against them. But spirits could also attack anyone anywhere for no reason, possibly assuming human or animal form in order to do so. Fortunately spirits lived on the main island and visited Ponam only occasionally, so that the island itself was relatively safe. Because spirits had no moral interests they did not respond to prayer, but had to be dealt with by trickery. This could be done by a specialist who was able to communicate through dreams with lesser spirit beings who could fool the spirit into leaving the soul unguarded and then steal it back again. These specialists were potentially dangerous for they might turn their hand to sorcery instead, arranging the theft of souls instead of their recovery.

Spirits who were under the control of a human being in this way were called *ngam kowau*, "crazy spirits'. When I first went to Ponam people said that this sort of sorcery had not been used since it had been given up in the 1920s (or at least had not been used by Ponams against Ponams). Between 1980 and 1983, however, there were a number of threats of sorcery and several suspect deaths arising out of disputes about land ownership. People identified this as a re-emergence of sorcery caused by increasing population pressure and an increase in land disputes. Both of the major sorcery cases arose from quarrels between men who were neither agnates nor close cognates. A quarrel between agnates was unlikely to lead to sorcery, because ghosts would intervene before the quarrel reached that stage.

Illnesses sent by ghosts and spirits did not affect the physical body itself (even though they manifested themselves in it) and once cured left no remaining weakness or injury to be cured by other means. (This is unlike the Ningerum for whom, as I said, illnesses caused by sorcerers or spirits leave residual physical injury to be cured by Western medicine or indigenous physical treatments (Welsch 1982: 335). Thus, a Ponam who received treatment for one ghostly or spirit illness and was partially but not entirely cured, assumed that he had been suffering from two separate afflictions and therefore proceeded to seek out another cause and another treatment for the remaining one, though if it was not very severe he or she could simply decide to wait and see.

Ponams also suffered from a number of non-fatal earthly sicknesses which were not caused by ghosts or spirits. The most common of these were sent by the sufferer's matrilineage ancestors. Each Ponam belonged to a totemic matriclan and avoided all of its totems, *kowun*, on pain of suffering such degenerative afflictions as deafness, blindness, tooth decay, skin disease, and so on. He or she also had to undergo periodic life crisis rituals without which he or she would become weak, wasted, inefficient and powerless. Totemic afflictions could be cured by the prayers of senior matrilineage women and were most unlikely to be fatal. In the case of illnesses resulting from totemic pollution however the damage would be permanent if prayers were not offered within a few months of the polluting contact. These afflictions were not usually referred to as *miri*. Instead the afflicted part of the body was described as *sala'an*, bad, broken down, decrepit. The same term was used for old age.

Divine sickness

In addition to earthly sickness, Ponams could also suffer from divine sickness, sickness sent by God to punish or warn against sin. Sickness sent by God could be cured by the Western medicines which He, in His mercy, had provided. Ponams supported this assertion with both logical and empirical evidence. Logically, they pointed out that because God was not wicked or vengeful, sending illness to draw man's attention to sin but not in order to kill, He must also send medicines to cure His illnesses. Empirically, Ponams could cite a number of instances in which two people suffered from an apparently identical illness and received identical treatment, and yet one recovered while the other did not. This was interpreted as proof that although the two illnesses had identical manifestations, they had very different causes. One was sent by God and could be cured by His medicines, the other was sent by ancestors or spirits and could not. If Western medicine did not cure an illness, this was interpreted as proof that the illness was earthly, not divine.

Divine sickness could also be cured, or its medical cure assisted, by prayer, confession and the promise of reformation. Such prayers were always made privately being something between the sufferer, or those who prayed for him, and God. Generally, Ponams did not emphasize the importance of prayer and confession for curing divine illness as the Pere had done in the 1950s nor did sufferers or others take much interest in the moral dimensions of divine illness. God would always allow His medicines to cure those who prayed contritely without requiring public, or even private, investigation of the sins which brought the illness in the first place. Therefore people only began to worry about illness and probe its causes when they suspected an earthly sickness, for ghosts, ancestors and spirits were not so amenable and so forgiving as God and required more rigorous cures.

DIAGNOSIS

Because, as I have said, Ponam medical theory did not entail the idea of symptoms, it was impossible to determine the cause of an illness from its physical manifestations. Illnesses sent by ghosts, spirits, ancestors or God could not be distinguished from each other or from purely physical malfunctions by examination of the body alone. Therefore when searching for a cure a patient had either to examine his own life in search of a likely cause, and thus probable cure (did he eat green fruit, visit the mainland without washing, handle a totem fish, skip church?), or consult a diagnostic specialist. Earthly sicknesses were diagnosed by traditional specialists and divine sicknesses were diagnosed by specialists in Western medicine.

When the cause seemed obvious people usually proceeded to treat the illness directly without consulting a diagnostic specialist. This was one of the factors which could keep people from seeking Western treatment – they knew that the cause lay elsewhere. Thus, for example, one middle aged woman who died without seeking medical treatment knew that it could not help her because her husband had recently died after having been sent home as incurable from an out of province hospital. The fact that the hospital had failed to cure her husband did not lessen the faith in Western medicine which had encouraged the two of them to seek Western treatment for him in the first place, but it did convince the widow that her illness, which was related to her husband's, could not be cured there.

A number of forms of divination were used in indigenous diagnosis, but the ones most popular on Ponam were divination by reading betel leaf, *para mbrul* and divination by dreams, *mif*. There were no practising leaf readers on Ponam while I was there, though several much admired specialists lived on the nearby mainland and were consulted regularly by Ponams. Several Ponam men may have been able to divine by dreams, but most people doubted either their skills or their intentions and tended to use the mainland specialists instead. Divination by dreams was associated with power over spirits and was thus subject to abuse as sorcery. It was safer to consult people from other villages, for they were less likely than co-villagers to harbor grievances.

Divine sicknesses were diagnosed by a Western medical practitioner who examined the patient to determine whether or not he or she was *sik* (sick), and would benefit from medical treatment, or *nogat sik*, not sick, and needed to return home for treatment of an earthly sickness. The Pidgin distinction between *sik* and *nogat sik* was sometimes used in Ponam as well, with sufferers described as *miri*: suffering from divine sickness (*miri paro Lapan*), not sick (*miri pe*), or suffering from earthly sickness (*miri paro-o-ii*). The thermometer was the health worker's primary diagnostic instrument, though people said that they did not really understand how it worked. A positive reading indicated that the patient had a God sent illness and indicated what sort of illness it was (though it did not eliminate the possibility that he or she might also have been suffering from earthly sickness). A normal reading indicated that the illness was not divine. Thus a patient who felt sick but was told that he had no temperature or that he was not sick, interpreted this as a positive diagnosis of earthly sickness.

Ponams admired practitioners who could make an immediate diagnosis from the thermometer reading alone. Those who asked a lot of questions were seen to be floundering around without really knowing their business. And hedging or unclear or unenthusiastic diagnoses such as "I'm not sure, maybe we should do some tests", or "It doesn't seem too bad to me. Take these tablets and come see me again if you don't feel better", were taken to mean either that the practitioner did not know what he was talking about or that he was searching for a nice way to point out that the sickness was not sent by God.

As a result of this belief people needed positive support from health workers in order to diagnose God-sent illness. They received this kind of support from the health center when they went there with common problems (colds, sores, worms, malaria, etc) of the sort the nurses saw every day and could diagnose with confidence and success. But if the problem was recurrent, unusual or complicated and did not respond quickly to common drugs, it would almost certainly be diagnosed sooner or later as an earthly sickness. The nurses' uncertainty might itself be interpreted as evidence of an earthly sickness and the search for medical treatment abandoned. The patient might try one course of treatment but if this failed he was unlikely to return for another diagnosis, his first failure being interpreted as evidence of earthly sickness. This was a further reason why old people did not receive medical treatment in their last illnesses. Most had consulted the health center nurses or the aid post orderly off and on through their late fifties and early sixties for the variety of illnesses that routinely afflicted that age group, especially coughs, aches and pains and stomach trouble. As these illnesses continued to recur with increasing frequency through old age, the sufferers accepted that they were not sent by God and ceased to seek medical help. Finally, it was also true that the health workers with whom Ponams came into contact were all Papua New Guineans, mostly Manus, who mostly held to theories of disease very similar to Ponams' own and therefore themselves recognized that many of the illnesses they confronted were not subject to medical treatment.

Lola Romanucci-Ross, who studied medical systems in Manus during the 1950s and 1960s says (1977) that the curings she saw in Manus could be typified by a "hierarchy of resort" which was either acculturative (Western medicine is tried first with resort to traditional treatment if this fails) or counter-acculturative (traditional treatment is tried first with resort to Western treatment if this fails). Romanucci-Ross's analysis is based on a dualistic interpretation of medical theory in which there is Western medicine and indigenous medicine and people choose between them on the basis of their degree of acculturation to Western ways. I have argued, on the other hand, that Ponams had a unified theory in which Western and indigenous treatments had equal legitimacy. Individuals may have produced their own hierarchies of resort within this system but these hierarchies were idiosyncratic, the consequence of their different ability to bear the different costs of different forms of medical treatment and their assessment of the nature of the illness. Thus, the same individual might hierarchize prospective cures in one order for one illness and another order for another illness, putting Western medicine first one time and last another, all the while remaining convinced of its validity as a type of treatment.

Because Ponams held a unified medical theory which incorporated both Western and traditional cures without recognizing contradictions between them, they viewed the problem of diagnosis as a purely empirical one. In their interpretation, a sick person and his or her family would review the sufferer's symptoms and circumstances, consult specialists, try out cures and judge them on the basis of results. Those who do not accept a unified theory like this one (which is to say those who see Western medicine as empirically superior), find interpretation difficult to accept, for it poses one of the central puzzles of medical anthropology: how is it that people can reject empirically superior Western treatments in favour of less successful indigenous ones? Two common ways of explaining this absence of an overwhelming preference for Western medicine are, first, to identify social and economic factors which make Western health care difficult and second, to locate cultural factors which predispose sufferers to use traditional medicine or to avoid Western medicine.

Some research (for example Foster 1977) has suggested that people are led to avoid Western medicine by economic and bureaucratic factors such as travel time, the intimidating behaviour of health workers and the direct and hidden costs of treatment. James Young (1981: 499) calls these "extra-community factors" for they arise outside of the community in question or out of its articulation with the larger society. Health planners in Papua New Guinea seem generally to have been aware of the importance of these non-cultural barriers and to have stressed the provision of low cost, accessible, non-bureaucratic rural health services. Manus, with its dense network of aid posts and health centers, has been especially well-served in this regard. Thus extra-community factors such as these were not a major barrier to Ponams' use of Western health care. Health facilities were conveniently located; staffed predominantly by Manus people whose interaction styles were at least familiar and who were generally admired; within the budget of any family determined to use them; and required no bureaucratic expertise. (Manipulating the higher levels of the health service did require some expertise, but most Ponams either had such expertise or could turn to educated kin for help if they did not.)

Although the bureaucratic and economic costs imposed on patients by the health service were low, social and economic barriers within the community did impose significant costs on those seeking treatment for illness. Consideration of these costs did affect people's choice of treatment at least as much as their intellectual assessment of the likelihood of a cure. These barriers did not operate exclusively against Western treatments. All types of treatments had social costs. These costs were not uniform across the society but varied with the patient's age, sex, marital status, family size, personal history and so forth. For example, a young married man was likely to be able to take his wife and children to the health center and support them for a visit there but was unlikely to have the finesse to organize a series of meetings for confession and prayer, especially if he had no living parents or elder siblings to help him. An elderly person, on the other hand, was likely to be in the reverse position, able to organize the meetings but not a long stay at the health center.

Even though the health service was reasonably convenient for most people, Ponams did not make as much use of it as they could have. They used the Western health service consistently and confidently for the treatment of routine illnesses, but not for serious ones. As Table III shows, the majority of Ponams who died between 1979 and 1983 did not receive Western treatment during their last illness, but relied entirely on indigenous treatments. One important reason for this was that the health service was not particularly successful in treating serious illness. The explanation for this lay partly in the difficulties of managing health services in a distant rural province of a developing country and in the fact that the health service suffered generally from lack of supplies, bureaucratic ineptitude, under-trained and insufficiently interventionist staff. In theory, for example, the maternal and child health sisters (who saw people regularly for routine and minor illnesses) and the aid post orderly (who not only saw people but heard all of the village gossip about illness) should have been able to point out developing illnesses and urge that sufferers seek appropriate treatment. Medical staff were not interventionist in this way however, and the combination of Ponams' attitude towards and expectations of the health service with this non-interventionist approach meant that serious illnesses often went untreated or were allowed to linger until they were incurable. As I have said, Ponams believed that Western practitioners could diagnose with the thermometer alone, and therefore they did not feel obliged to discuss their illness in detail with the practitioner. Moreover, they interpreted failure to diagnose or prescribe for divine sickness as evidence of an earthly sickness, rather than as ignorance or non-recognition of sickness. Consequently the common failure of these practitioners to urge that the patient seek further treatment or see a higher level specialist (in the way that expatriate practitioners once did) meant that Western treatment was often abandoned prematurely.

Thus one important reason for Ponams' failure to take full advantage of Western medical care lay, I believe, not in their lack of faith in it, but quite the opposite: in their unreasonable expectations and their unreasonable faith in it as a cure for a specific, limited class of illnesses; in their belief that the practitioners they saw were equipped and competent to provide treatment which guaranteed rapid and infallible cures for divine illness. As a result they accepted the treatment they received, declined to look for further treatment for symptoms the health center ignored, and as a rule did not blame the health service for the deaths of patients in their care. And because they believed that many illnesses, particularly serious ones, were earthly not divine, they were quick to turn from failing Western treatments to indigenous ones.

THE CHANGING USE OF WESTERN MEDICAL SERVICES 1950-1983

I now want to return to an issue I raised earlier, the argument put forward by some Ponams that the use of Western medicine declined during the 1970s and 1980s. The educated Ponam migrants who put forward this argument suggested that this change was probably the result of people's declining faith in the Catholic church. Islanders, as a rule, denied that they lacked faith either in God or in his medicines, though they agreed that the church was less important in daily life than it had been in previous decades. I suggest that the changing position of the Catholic church and broader changes in the political environment of Manus generally have led to changes in the salience of different types of illness and types of treatment. In conclusion therefore, I want to return to a description of Manus history and to review the various changes which have taken place there over the past twenty years, and the way that these have affected both the kind of health care which Ponams receive and their attitude toward it. This history will necessarily be largely a political one for not only is the provision of Western medical care a political issue, but also Ponam medical theory has important inherently political dimensions to it.

As is generally the case where people locate the main causes of illness in the social relations of sufferers and their fellows, Ponam diagnoses were political in that they often sprang from and contributed to political tensions within the village and between it and other villages. But this is not the issue which interests me here, for Ponam medical theory was also inherently political in a much broader way. By locating the causes of illness in the Christian God and indigenous ancestors and spirits, medical theory itself was located in political debates about the proper relation between the Catholic church (and thus indirectly Europeans and European culture generally) and indigenous religion and culture, which have been crucial in Manus politics and in national politics as a whole. In addition to its importance in overtly political spheres, this debate has also influenced both the behaviour of the Catholic church (and thus Ponams' relations to it) and the quality of the health service which the church and the state provide.

The early post-war years were a time of economic growth and optimism for Ponams. People were inspired by the examples they had seen during the war and the encouragement they had received from the Americans and believed that it was possible to transform Manus in that image. This belief was encouraged by the fact that there were opportunities for Ponams to earn a living through selling trochus at unusually high prices and selling or trading off the war surplus which had been left to them when the Americans departed. The administration, under pressure from Paliau and similar movements, introduced English language schools and the aid post system and began to foster indigenous economic development by funding cooperative movements and encouraging indigenous enterprises such as tradestores and plantations. The Catholic mission, with the same aims, also opened more and better schools (including a primary school on Ponam and a high school for boys at Bundralis) and expanded their health facilities. Because of this optimism, and for other reasons I describe below, Ponams did not take part in the Paliau movement which flourished elsewhere at this time.

By the mid 1950s, Ponam's economic position had changed. The price of trochus collapsed, they ran out of war surplus and the terms of indigenous trade changed as mainlanders began to demand cash instead of fish and shell money for the garden and forest produce on which Ponams depended. Furthermore, the Paliau movement (which had heretofore been blasphemous, because it rejected both the Catholic church and many traditional customs), became directly threatening as the administration tried to induce Ponams and other north coast villagers to join in the local government council (Patrol Reports 4–56/57, 4–62/62, 5–68/69, 7–70/71). This body was founded as a result of the demands of Paliau and his followers and was seen by Ponams to be dominated by them. The Paliau movement had its center among the south coast "Manus" or Titan-speaking people who were Ponams' enemies from long before, having invaded the island twice in the late nineteenth century, and the attempt to expand the local government council to the north coast was seen in essence as another invasion. It was during this period that Ponams appear to have been most dependent on the church and most intensely Catholic. It was a period in which the church, as one of Paliau's stated enemies, stood for both tradition and commitment to the faith of their fathers (in opposition to the heretical followers of Paliau) and for future progress and development, health services, education and for employment (many Ponams worked directly for the church or as teachers in the expanding mission school system). Thus the church was a powerful institution at a time when Ponams both felt the need for powerful friends and had little access to other sources of power.

Being both driven to the Catholic church by the threat they saw in the Paliau movement and drawn to it by the opportunities it offered them, Ponams revolved around the church more than they would later on. The salience of the church at this time meant that islanders were more committed to seeing the hand of God in their illnesses (as they were to seeing the hand of God in everything), and the interventionist, expatriate-staffed health services the church offered meant that they were more likely to see their commitment ratified by the surety of diagnosis and efficacy of treatment that they received.

Beginning in the late 1960s and through the 1970s however, the Catholic church lost or gave up much of its political and economic power in Manus, particularly at Bundralis. The key factor in this was the growing impetus for self-government, then independence and the transfer of authority to Papua New Guineans. This affected Ponam in three ways, all of them weakening Ponam's reliance on the church.

First, by 1979 Paliau was no longer a threat to Ponams or the church. In achieving its aim of national independence and in failing to achieve a number of its other aims, the movement lost its political impetus and followers began to drift away. It became obvious to Ponams in the early 1970s that the local government council was not a Paliau stalking horse, and they finally accepted their enforced membership in it. With the Paliau threat removed the church ceased to be a refuge or a central focus of identity. Second, as the administration began to recognize the inevitability of independence, it opened the way for Papua New Guineans to move into white collar jobs with significantly increased wages. Because of their early access to education and their intense commitment to it, Ponams were well placed to benefit from this change, and during the 1970s those benefits began to flow back to Ponam in the form of cash remittances. This encouraged their orientation outwards, away from Bundralis, by giving them access to jobs, income and sources of influence outside of the province and hence outside the church. Finally, independence brought great changes in the church and in the services it provided. Through the 1970s the Catholic church in Papua New Guinea attempted to localize its services, to put the management of church affairs in the hands of Papua New Guineans. In large measure this meant reorganizing the mission services so that they could be managed as much as possible by Papua New Guineans without having to rely on expatriate expertise or on external funding (which expatriate missionaries often brought with them from their home churches, but which was not so readily available to Papua New Guinean church workers). Furthermore, there was also a change in emphasis from the missionary work of enticing new souls into the church to serving an existing population of Catholics: the church has become less interested in attracting rich Christians through displays of wealth than was the case in the past (Kelly 1983). These policy changes affected Ponams in a number of different ways.

As part of the effort to involve Papua New Guineans in church affairs, Ponams were encouraged to build their own village church, a project they completed in the mid 1960s, partially as an act of religious devotion. But this devotion, instead of bringing them closer to the church, served to isolate them from Bundralis by eliminating the need for the weekly trip to church. Soon afterwards the Ponam housing compound which stood on the beach near the mission began to collapse, making it difficult to stay at Bundralis for church festivals and also making life difficult for those who wished to stay at Bundralis for health center treatment. Later, Ponams were further cut off from the church when it returned the plantation that it had occupied for fifty years to the mainland traditional land owners, thus depriving Ponams of a chance to make money by working for the mission. At about the same time the church closed the Christian Brothers High School that had been at Bundralis since the early 1950s. The shabby girls vocational school which replaced it was no substitute either academically or in providing education for jobs. These moves all degraded the mission station, and thus the church itself, from a lively enticing place and a source of interest and apparent power, to a rather dreary outstation. In addition through the 1970s the mission gradually localized its personnel until by 1979 only the priest and one elderly nun were expatriate. Although Papua New Guinean church and health center workers certainly had a more intimate relation with the people they served, they were also less dominating and demanding, less insistent that people follow the church or that they come to the health center.

The decreasing threat from the Paliau movement and declining involvement with the Catholic church were accompanied by increasing tensions within the village. In 1972 Ponams launched a tax payers' revolt which led ultimately to the division of the island into competing and bitter political factions which were still unreconciled in 1979. Tensions were also heightened by population pressure, increasing land disputes and declining opportunities for employment. The internal conflicts arising from these tensions were precisely the sort that Ponams expected to lead to ancestral illness and sorcery. This heightened internal conflict, in combination with the fact that Ponams were less driven to the church and the church was less attractive to them than had been the case ten years before, seems to have produced a shift in the illnesses they expected and thus the treatments they sought.

The tensions which led to this change, tensions between church and state, Western culture and indigenous, the north coast and the south coast and so on, continued to be potent in Manus and there is no reason to believe that Ponam's position was a stable one. The most obvious evidence of the continued tension was the rebirth of the Paliau movement as the Makasol Party, which was precipitated by the Manus provincial government's attempt to introduce a new form of local government in the early 1980s. The principles of the New Way were consciously reoriented by the Makasol Party leaders to appeal to the educated Manus elite (Trompf 1983: 59-62), but continued many original themes including opposition to the ruling government and European religion and, added to these, an opposition to Western medical treatment. If the Makasol Party flourishes, Ponams may find themselves in the embrace of the Catholic church once more.

CONCLUSIONS

In this paper I have described Ponam beliefs about health and illness as forming a unified theory, by which I mean that Ponams saw Western and indigenous medical practices as complementary rather than as reflecting radically different, much less incompatible conceptions of disease and cure. This means both that indigenous medicine cannot be understood as something radically distinct from Western medicine, and that one cannot interpret individuals' choices of Western or indigenous treatment as being simply a matter of their degree of acculturation. I have also suggested that people's choices of treatments should not be analyzed in terms of medical theory alone. On Ponam, people's choice of treatment was influenced by factors well outside the purely medical realm. At the simplest level, individuals could be constrained in their choice of treatment by their personal circumstances of age, sex, family status and the like. But at a more complex level, the political (in the broadest sense of the term) environment in which people lived made certain aspects of their unified field of medical theory more prominent than others. And thus, as the political environment shifted, so did the dominant causes of disease and the dominant sources of treatment. The dominant fact of political life in Manus since the Second World War was confrontation between and attempts at reconciliation of Manus social and cultural organization and that imposed or imported from outside, and Ponams use of Western medicine should be understood as an element in their reaction to and attempts to confront this issue.

NOTES

1. The field research reported on here was conducted over 18 months in five visits to Ponam between 1978 and 1983. I would like to thank the University of London Central Research Fund and the Papua New Guinea Department of Education for their financial assistance, Manus Province and the Papua New Guinea governments for permission to do the research, and the people of Ponam Island for their patience and interest.
2. The term "Western medicine" is particularly inappropriate in this context for Ponams do not perceive that there is anything inherently Western about it other than the fact that it was first brought to Papua New Guinea by people with European ancestors. In their belief, Western medicine is God's medicine, provided by Him for all people. The fact that it emerged in the West rather than somewhere else is entirely incidental. The term "Western medicine" is conventional however, and I use it in this paper.
3. I use the past tense to describe Ponams during the period of my fieldwork between 1979 and 1983 rather than the conventional ethnographic present. I do this in order to emphasize that the events and beliefs I describe are historically situated and not timeless or changeless.
4. There are about 200 Ponam migrants. Like other Manus they are elite migrants working almost exclusively in white collar jobs and able to afford medical care for their kin (see J. Carrier 1981).
5. While there has been a growing belief in the importance of non-physiological factors (especially psychological ones) in the development and cure of disease, there is as yet no general agreement about a physiological mechanism to account for this, and consequently its impact on medical research and diagnosis seems not to have been profound, though recent concern with the doctor–patient relationship and similar aspects of medical care do reflect the awareness of these factors (see Armstrong 1983:Ch.11).

CAROL JENKINS

8. THE AMELE AND DR BRAUN: A HISTORY OF EARLY EXPERIENCE WITH WESTERN MEDICINE IN PAPUA NEW GUINEA

INTRODUCTION

The aim of this study is to document a historical example of the early days of encountering Western medicine for the Amele people of Madang province, Papua New Guinea. As an anthropological work, it attempts to reconstruct the differential impact of several facets of the contact or acculturation experience, focusing on the influence of a particular mission doctor. His name is Theodore Braun (1903-80) and he was a physician with the American Lutheran mission who spent a total of 42 years in Papua New Guinea. Although Braun became widely respected as physician and educator, he left little of his own writing.

The sources of information for this historical reconstruction are as follows:

(1)   interviews with Amele patients, co-workers and students of Dr Braun;
(2)   early medical reports for the region, German New Guinea Company reports and other published sources covering social and health conditions during the first half-century of contact;
(3)   current health conditions and demography of the Amele area, known as a result of various investigations by the Papua New Guinea Institute of Medical Research, Madang branch.

These materials are presented against a background of Amele culture and traditional medical beliefs and practices as known to the author from ethnographic studies conducted between May 1982 and August 1984.

The Amele people are an ethno-linguistic group of 6,632 people who today occupy a triangular area of about 200 square kilometers bordered on the north by the Pacific Ocean, on the east by the Gogol River and on the south/southwest by the Gum River. Their territory is situated about twelve kilometers east of Madang Town on the north coast (see Fig. 1). They are dwellers of the lowland rain forest who practice shifting bush fallow cultivation up to an altitude of 200 meters and, to a lesser extent, hunt birds and mammals, and fish in streams. In addition, approximately 10% of the adult men work for wages. They make little use of the sea, despite having within their territory a considerable stretch of coastline. Their language, one of the Gum family, Mabuso stock, is a Papuan (non-Austronesian) language (Z'graggen 1975), but the Amele are surrounded on two sides by speakers of Austronesian tongues. They have long been influenced by the maritime Austronesian cultures and genetically appear closely aligned with Austronesians

(Jantz and Jenkins, unpublished data). They possess no myth of an origin elsewhere and, from all accounts, their aboriginal culture must have been very similar to that of the nearby bush peoples described by the first European observers.

THE AMELE AT THE TIME OF EARLY CONTACT

Only 24 kilometers south of Amele territory, the Russian naturalist, Mikloucho-Maclay, arrived in 1871 and settled in at Bongu to explore the area and its peoples (Sentinella 1975). He remained for over two years and returned three times during which he travelled through the islands of Astrolabe Bay and into the hills behind the coast. His relations with the local people were apparently very good, as were his detailed observations. The examples of exotic technology, such as shotguns, glass, steel and cloth, which he brought with him and his own fearlessness convinced local residents that he was a *tibud* or ancestor spirit and therefore immortal. He introduced several new food plants (Galton 1880a), such as pineapples, pumpkins, certain types of beans and a large variety of papaya known today by the Amele as *Maklelika*. This behavior also indicated *tibud* status, as the origins of numerous foods are attributed in myth to ancestral culture heroes throughout coastal Madang. When Maclay implied that a planned inter-village war would bring about an earthquake, his words were heeded and the war called off. At one Amele village, Umuin, as well as at Bilbil and elsewhere, children were named after him. At Umuin, a child was named Makel and the name remains in use today by the Amele people. Long before white men entered the unknown territory of highland New Guinea, the name "Makarai" had reached the resident natives and even today children are given his name (Munster 1979).

Maclay's descriptions of village life and peoples' appearances take note of numerous differences between island and coastal groups (Austronesians) on the one hand, and inland hill residents (Papuans) on the other.[1] His diaries discuss trips made to the vicinity of the Gogol River and to the island of Bilbil, immediately off the Amele coast. He described inland settlements with few coconuts, A-frame ground level family houses, open-sided men's houses with raised platforms and wooden carvings of human-like figures, the raising of pigs, chickens and dogs for food, regular inter-village trade and the hard life, unkempt, dirty appearance and minimal leisure of women compared to men. Numerous feasts and privileges were reserved for men only. He noted that women had very few children and breastfed for about four years per child (Galton 1880a, 1880b, Webster 1984). He stated that the diet was nearly bereft of animal foods and observed that people habitually ate very large portions of taro, sago, sweet potatoes and bananas. Frequently he remarked on the prevalence of elephantiasis and commented on boils, large infected sores and "psoriasis" (probably *tinea imbricata*). He himself suffered numerous attacks of malaria and he noticed that the local people also had days of fever. Although people allowed him to treat badly infected wounds, they refused to take any medicine internally which he offered. External treatments were readily accepted. Further, he remarked that nasal catarrh was seen less frequently than in Europe. Before leaving what came to be called the Maclay Coast, he warned his friends that other white men would come and, unlike himself, were not to be trusted. By that time it had become clear to him that colonial interests were likely to follow his path to New Guinea's north coast (Sentinella 1975).

Shortly after Maclay left, he was indeed followed to Bongu in 1884 by Otto Finsch who, feigning purely scientific interest, had obtained detailed information from Maclay with which to aid the establishment of the German New Guinea Company. This plantation company and the German government were working in collusion to secure a large segment of New Guinea as a German colony. Unbeknownst to Great Britain, with whom Germany was engaging in verbal negotiations regarding New Guinea, the German flag was raised and the north coast renamed Kaiser Wilhelms land in 1885. Finsch travelled on to Bilbil and, seeing the fine gardens of the Bilbil people on the adjacent mainland, assumed that this land also belonged to them. However, this stretch of coastal frontage belonged to members of Amele-speaking clans. Finsch's notes were later to have serious consequences. Company representatives set about buying land from the local people with strips of cloth, knives and other trade goods, beginning at first around Bongu. By 1887 the people of Bongu were already refusing to sell any more land and were even attempting to buy back pieces already alienated.

As Amele elders describe it, life during the pre-contact and early contact eras was marked by repeated fighting among villages. Disputes concerned stolen women, pigs, sorcery and, less often, land. Most fighting took place as raids, surprise attacks in which houses were burned, pigs and men killed and women and children routed to hide in the bush. For that reason, women slept in their own houses with the young children, while the men and older boys slept together in the *yo bada* or men's house. Family size was deliberately controlled because running and hiding were too difficult with numerous children. When contraception failed, the new infant, if unwanted, was killed immediately after birth and buried under the house.

Sickness and misfortune were attributed to sorcery, repressed ill will and violation of taboo. Sorcery was widespread and men could train to become specialized killers or *emes dana*. These sorcerers learned to change into various animals, for example, dogs, hornbills or crocodiles. They could kill by object intrusion, by "poisoning" any material in contact with the victim (*eeh*) or by the special technique of breaking all the victim's bones in a severe beating without his knowledge (*emes*). The victim would suddenly sicken and die thereafter. Through divination (*do'e*) with water, cane, bamboo, betel nut or leaves, one could discover if the death had been due to sorcery and by whom. The murder could be repaid by another of the same type or by raiding, but compensation was not common. If revenge could not be levied immediately, it would wait till an appropriate time, even a generation later. Revenge could be aimed at anyone in the targeted family.

In addition to sorcery, the Amele possessed magical powers inherited through an elaborate totemic clan system. Each named patrilineal clan was associated with a territory in which were found unusual natural features, such as waterfalls, caves, large rocks or trees that possessed *hatu* or spirit guardians. If offended by trespassers, these spirits could cause sickness or injury. Only elder men of the *hatu*-owning clan could rid the victim of his affliction. Each clan also had special access to a specific animal either as charmed prey willing to be hunted or as an ally willing to destroy other people's gardens. Members of one clan could call out rats to eat the growing tubers in a garden belonging to a man of another clan. The victim could request help from members of yet another clan who possessed the magic for driving rats away. Some clans had animal familiars, for example, crocodiles, who would kill other men on command.

Powers to incite fighting, bring about peace, seduce women, cause sterility and other feats were inherited. Elders had the discretion to pass on secrets only to those sons or an occasional daughter who showed interest and ability to handle such powers. Totemic food taboos were also inherited and if not observed could lead to skin disease, birth defects or obstructed labor, a weakened state or vomiting. *Ud* is a type of fasting in which all foods consumed must be dry or roasted and no liquids drunk, a power-building sacrificial act nearly always practised by men in preparation for demanding activities.

The dead were seated in a funeral chair next to the house and allowed to rot. Relatives continued to live in the house, having to suffer the stench as part of mourning. Later the cleaned bones were buried or placed in trees. Ancestral spirits were thought to bring sickness, death and misfortune and were sometimes placated with offerings of food at the burial place. They were also implored to aid in revenge or other efforts requiring great power.

The religion of the Amele included beliefs in *dogon* or a major deity of the primary forest, *dorog* or bush spirits, and *fau' ade* or spirit people who lived in the surrounding forest and coastal land. *Tibud* were ancestral spirits returned to life. Each clan held communal rituals on its own behalf and conducted initiation ceremonies for its boys. These latter did not involve penile incision as practised by the coastal Austronesian peoples (Morauta 1974), but did involve rigorous fasting and trial by fire. Unchaste boys were submitted to trial by fire and, if guilty, would burn and have to be renewed ritually. Both earlobes and nose were punctured as a routine part of growing up. Wads of sharp grasses were used by men for nasal bloodletting as an act of purification. At the time of first menstruation, girls were secluded and later decorated with pigments and feathers for public presentation.

In 1886 the first missionary, Johann Flierl of the Neuendettelsau Mission Society, arrived at the settlement called Finschhafen. The German New Guinea Company did not at first favor the arrival of missionaries and, for his part, Flierl tried to dissociate himself from the company. He moved further up the coast, but by then the local peoples were aware of the unfair practices of the Germans and they heartily rejected Flierl. He remained, but most of the other early missionaries who soon followed either died or were sent back in poor health.

During the same years the first missionaries arrived, the Company was put under the direction of a certain Herr Kubary who, calling himself the "Lord God of

Astrolabe Bay" (Sentinella 1975: 327), ruthlessly went about the business of securing plantation lands for the Company. He went to Bilbil and "bought" from a man named Kain, a leader on the island, all the land on the mainland adjacent to Bilbil from the Gogol River to the Gum River and inland to the Hansemann Mountains. This amounted to the entire Amele territory which of course, the people of Bilbil did not own but to which they were granted usufruct rights by local Amele speaking clans.

THE AMELE UNDER GERMAN OCCUPATION

Neither the Company nor the missionaries had fruitful contact with the Amele or their neighbors for many decades. Where the first mission stations were established, both east and west of the Amele, there were no converts for sixteen years. Baptism was accepted only by a rare orphan, usually one raised by the missionary. The administration of medicine rapidly became an effective act of evangelism.

The Company's troubles centered partly on the labor supply and partly on the ravages of malaria. While a few trinkets could secure land, at least at first, nothing could secure local laborers. The Amele and their neighbours were not interested in working for wages, especially when they could obtain goods and money by selling food. When a drought caused food shortages, Company officials were pleased to offer rice to the people in exchange for labor, hoping villagers would acquire a strong liking for rice. As soon as local foods became available again, however, the labor flow ceased (Firth 1983). In the Amele language, rice was first called *ogo nag* or tiny ant eggs, which are not ordinarily considered edible.

The Amele rejected both European foods and cultural domination but sought the steel axes and other tools being introduced. When tools were stolen from a cocoa plantation at Garima (also called Marage) on the east bank of the Gogol River, a punitive expedition crossed the Gogol to the Amel-speaking side and, finding a family group not far from the river, killed them all. No attempt was made to discover the actual thieves.

The Company tried to solve its labor problem by importing Malays, Chinese and natives of the Bismarck Archipelago. By 1900 there were 2500 aliens in the country. Many of the Asian recruits were sickly opium users and the source of several epidemics, including one of smallpox which was directly traceable to them. In addition, several hundred laborers were taken from the Bismarck Archipelago where they had either experienced little malaria or had been exposed to a different variety of it. In the Astrolabe Bay area everyone, including Melanesians, succumbed to hyperendemic malaria (Sack and Clark 1979).

In 1900 Robert Koch, the well-known German bacteriologist, was sent to New Guinea for six months to investigate the malaria problem. He was able to demonstrate that more steady administration of quinine could reduce mortality and morbidity and that local people acquired immunity with age. He also noted that beriberi, hookworm and tuberculosis were common among laborers but not among villagers (Ewers 1972). Elephantiasis was present and yaws, tropical ulcers and scabies were highly prevalent in the local population. Dysentery was rare in 1880–1890 but by 1896 it was spreading rapidly (Maddocks 1973). Eventually leprosy, influenza, tuberculosis, hookworm, chicken pox, dysentery, measles and syphilis spread along the north coast of New Guinea from foci at Company plantations (Kettle 1979). When the Company headquarters shifted from Finschhafen to Fredrick Wilhelmshafen (present day Madang town) in 1891, the Amele were brought into more frequent and closer contact with the growing population of foreigners. In the following year smallpox spread into the Amele area and along the coast up to Yomba (Sack and Clark 1979).

In 1899 the German Imperial Government took over the administration of Kaiser Wilhelmshafen and began building roads and bridges. Labour was needed for these tasks as well as for house building and off-loading ships' cargoes. Police officers and armed guards were sent into villages to recruit labor. Although knives and axes were offered in exchange, few chose willingly to work. Therefore, the Germans passed an ordinance enforcing compulsory labor for one month per year without pay (Hannemann C 1949). In 1904 the inhabitants of Siar, Bilbil and Graged islands organized a revolt. They intended to kill all whites except one missionary's wife and small son. The plan was betrayed, however, by a doctor's native assistant, Nalon of Bilia, and the revolt thwarted by government rifles. Seven men from Siar and two from Graged were punished with death.

The people of Bilbil were removed from their island and placed on the mainland on land belonging to the clan of Gun of Bahor village. These Amele people were led to believe that the Bilbil people would work for the Germans on the new roads and receive food in payment. It was not expected that they would use the land for gardens and build villages there. The Germans, of course, believed the Company owned all of that section of the mainland.

Conflicts were rapidly growing over land and labor. In response the Germans attempted in 1907 to install a system of appointed native chiefs. These men, known as *luluai*, and their messenger assistants, the *tultul*, were supposed to oversee the recruitment of labor, collect the head tax of five marks per person and bring disputes before the authorities.

DEPOPULATION: DIFFERENT VIEWS

The effects on village life of the new diseases and developments were generally unrecorded, in part because few Company doctors made medical surveys of the local people. However, because it appeared that gradual depopulation was possible and this would further weaken the labor supply, the Company ordered an investigation of current health conditions and reproductive practices of the populations in their new colony. In 1919 Kultz published the results of one such investigation. He reported that abortion and infanticide were widely practised. He considered that children's growth was impaired by both inadequate breastmilk and poor supplementation (Kultz 1919).

From the Amele point of view, depopulation was a growing threat for quite different reasons. Chief among these were the loss of land, loss of male labor and the increasing frequency of epidemics of new diseases. A smallpox epidemic in the early decades of the century is remembered as especially lethal. People were unable to sleep on the traditional beds that were made from the leaf sheath of the area palm. If they did, their skin sloughed off. Instead they slept on parched banana leaves, but many people died. When during World War I Australian troops arrived they brought with them from Palestine amoebic dysentery which rapidly decimated whole villages (Rowley 1958). While some introduced diseases, such as tuberculosis, were clearly associated with the influx of foreigners, others were thought to result from the actions of traditional enemies. Raiding and other usual acts of revenge were effectively suppressed by the new government, adding to Amele frustration. Still other epidemics were attributed to the ancestral "owners of the ground" who were presumably displeased with the influx of outsiders. The people tried to appease them with *sing sings* (*duedue' ina*) or ritual musical performances.

After 1907, when control over villages had been strengthened by the *luluai* and *tultul* systems of rule, the Amele and their neighbors experienced numerous conflicts with the new government and its police. One incident remains vivid in local memory. Possibly around 1908, a fight took place between the first *luluai* of Hilu and a man of Banup, apparently over a woman. When the police, Melanesians from Finschhafen and Bougainville and quite foreign to the Amele, attempted to capture the *luluai*, he was protected by other villagers and allowed to hide in a cave. Using tactics once used in Africa, the Germans instructed their police to round up all the Amele women and children and to barricade them in a makeshift prison. Amele men were then told they could ransom their wives and children by turning in the errant *luluai*, which they did.

The conflict with state power continued. Another fight, probably in the wake of another attempted rebellion by the Bilbil people and their allies, broke out along the Amele coast where the contemporary villages of Bahor and Umuin are located. At least one man from Umuin was killed. As a consequence the Bilbil people were exiled to the Rai Coast. Years later, after the German administration gave way to the Australian, the exiles were allowed to return to the coastal land owned by the Amele who were then forced to cede it to them.

THE AMELE SOLUTION

These conflicts, epidemics and ill fortune distressed the Amele. Elders sought a solution through accommodation. They decided to obtain a missionary. At that time the Rhenish Mission Society of Germany was supplying missionaries to the new stations at Bongu and the Rai Coast. Most died rapidly from malaria only to be replaced by willing others. In 1916, Kelim, a *luluai*, and Gugulu (both of Banup),

Saig of the Su'ulu clan in Omuru and Ra of the Mahor clan gathered together a few German coins, valued items of the new trade, and, guided by Warup of Marage, went to Bongu to "buy" a missionary. For what is now thought to be about 50 toea (US 50 cents), a mission worker named Bulincourt was brought to Degir, near Banup. The Lutheran policy discouraged individual conversion, preferring instead conversion of groups or communities. This required that whole clans or villages present all their ritual paraphernalia for public burning. Four years after his arrival, Bulincourt announced seventy official converts.

By the late 1920s a new mission team, composed of Welsch and Bulincourt, was stationed among the Amele. They built schools and trained mission workers. Emphasis was placed on the abandonment of traditional supernatural beliefs and practices. They especially abhorred infanticide, abortion and traditional contraceptive practices. Families were encouraged to have many children and to send them to mission schools. They demanded an end to wife capture and to calling on ancestral and bush spirits for help.

This early encounter with Christianity took place largely in the Amele language. Welsch learned the language well enough to conduct church services, school lessons and discussions concerning theology in the local tongue. Both testaments of the Bible were translated into a written version of the Amele language (Osmers 1981). Talented converts, such as Nol and Gulal, were encouraged to compose hymns in their own language and melodies. In the earliest texts the name of God was translated as *Dogon* or Lord of the Spirits, a major deity in the traditional Amele pantheon. To this day the Amele praise the Lutherans for this effort at using their own language and attribute their current universal and relatively thorough conversion to the clear understanding it allowed.

THE NEED FOR A DOCTOR

Soon Welsch and his staff became conscious of a need for a doctor. While he and his converts prayed, Welsch wrote letters to Lutherans in several countries requesting a medical missionary. To this the Americans responded. In 1930, after spending a few years training in Germany, Austria and Australia in tropical medicine, Dr Theo Braun of Nebraska arrived. He erected a hospital at Finschhafen first and moved to the Amele area in 1932. In 1934 he joined an expedition of Lutheran missionaries trekking into the Highlands of New Guinea, as a result of which several Lutheran bases were set up near Mt. Hagen. At Suyau, the highest peak in the central Amele area where the largest mission school was located, he built the first health clinic. Accompanying him was a nurse, Hattie Engeling, who had been in New Guinea since 1924 and they were soon married. His wife learned the Amele language well and together they investigated traditional medical practices in villagers' homes. Braun had a special interest in obstetrics and made a point of observing Amele birthing practices, promising no interference unless requested (Braun 1967a).

Fig. 17. Dr Braun at Yagaum hospital, 1971.

Braun began the training of local medical assistants and their wives. Eight men were trained to diagnose and treat common diseases, and assist in surgery. Their wives were taught to nurse the sick and act as midwives. Always a prayer was offered before surgery and as an aid to healing the bedridden. These men witnessed the incredible as they saw Braun operate on the human body. Surgery had never been part of traditional medical practice, apart from bloodletting and arrow excision. The news of Braun's miracles spread far and were always viewed as acts aided by a supernatural power, the white man's God. This, of course, was the interpretation Braun himself sought to foster in the eyes of the Amele.

Although no records of that period written by either Braun or his wife have been uncovered, Amele elders remember it well. They tell of very emotional times when conversions were frequent, tearful affairs. Prior to the establishment of the first clinic, the death toll had been high. Several whole clans had been nearly wiped out, and this was believed to be due to the wrath of God. Men with knowledge of traditional magic and women who knew contraceptive spells were urged not to disclose this information to the younger generation, lest they too suffer decimation. Land was willingly donated to the Lutherans to build more schools and churches. Evangelists (*sos*) were trained and perceived as prophets. The people say they had voices like roosters, singing out to the heathens to change their ways. Cemeteries were established for each village and traditional mourning practices abandoned. Magical stones which could not be volunteered for burning were hidden by their owners so that no one could call on them for aid or power. The *lu*, or good times had begun and, though occasional inter-village fights continued to erupt, there were fewer major conflicts with government.

THE SECOND WORLD WAR YEARS

Braun's clinic at Suyau had expanded into a small hospital when the Second World War reached New Guinea in 1941. In January 1942 the residents of Suyau watched the Japanese bomb Madang Town. After receiving a warning to evacuate, the expatriates living in Madang decided on an escape route to Kainantu at the head of the Ramu River through Amele. The Brauns aided all the escapees but held on to their station as long as possible. Braun made caches of medicines and placed them in the care of five trusted *dokta bois*, Fulalec and Siming among them. These men were to continue to administer medicines to the villagers after Braun and his wife were captured when 500 Japanese took Amele on New Year's Day 1943. They were detained on Graged Island where the Brauns ran a small hospital. While on the island there were many air strikes by the American and Australian forces. Each time a bomb exploded, as many as six Japanese held on to Dr Braun and the other missionaries with the hope that they too would be protected by the God the missionaries believed in (Mennis 1974). When gardens which the prisoners were forced to plant to supply themselves with food were ready to harvest, they were moved out to Siar. After two months there, they were again moved to Manam where they joined 140 imprisoned Catholic missionaries. Again they planted gardens and again before harvesting they were taken aboard ship to be moved to Hollandia (now Jayapura) in Dutch New Guinea (Irian Jaya). This time they were placed on a warship, the Dorish Maru. As they sailed into Wewak harbor, American planes attacked the ship, on the decks of which were all the prisoners under Japanese command. Sixty persons lay dead or dying and Braun and his wife were the only medical people left to care for them. Having no equipment or medicines, Braun asked the Japanese for some. He was given a bottle of wine, a carpenter's saw and a minute amount of novocaine. With these he performed an amputation, among other procedures (Kettle 1979, Muhlenhard 1980). Of this he wrote the following:

> All in all we lost about one third of our 122 missionaries and mixed race people on board the ship. Everything was full of blood and it was horrible to see people who were still living have smoke come out of their muscles after they had been hit by phosphorous shells. We landed at Wewak and took out our dead and wounded and put them ashore. Later we were forced back on board at gun point. Then we landed at Hollandia at Hotikon beach. They put us ashore and showed us an old wood shed and said that was our new home. The Japanese were

disgusted with us because there were only about 6 or 7 people there who could work. (Mennis 1974)

One story, told by Braun to a doctor who later treated him during recovery from a coronary seizure, tells of a time when the Japanese had him at an outdoor table under interrogation. Their site was being strafed by American planes and at every attack they would all jump into a slit trench nearby. This went on several times at which point Braun decided he had had enough. The next time, come what may, he would remain at the table. The planes attacked and Braun sat still while his Japanese interrogators jumped into the trench. When they emerged to find him still sitting, they knew they had "lost face". From that time on, they too sat still while the planes continued to shell them (Riley, personal communication).

THE POST-WAR YEARS: THE FOUNDING OF YAGAUM

Eventually, the Brauns were found by the American army in the interior of New Guinea and sent back to the United States to recuperate. In May 1946 they returned to find that during the war the Japanese had taken over the clinic at Suyau for divisional headquarters. Their Amele staff had been forced to serve the Japanese Army. As a consequence of the Japanese take-over, the Allied Forces bombed and wiped out the buildings. Fulalec and others continued to administer medicine to the sick among their own people hidden in caves. The Amele people themselves had hidden in caves throughout the war, cooking by night on small fires and managing to stay alive on tiny amounts of food. Gardens were difficult to maintain as the Japanese regularly raided any that were harvestable. The Amele who lived through that period unanimously consider it an act of God that they did not come to harm despite hostilities and an acute shortage of food.

By 1949 Fulalec had converted a pre-war garage into a five room clinic at the old Suyau clinic site. He was treating yaws with intravenous injections and had sixteen patients under treatment for leprosy with drugs which were given him by the reconstructed Madang Department of Health. In addition, he had over 200 babies regularly attending special child health clinics and was giving health talks to the mothers. The Amele had become convinced that modern medicine was a blessing and when Braun returned they requested that a new hospital be built in their midst.

A site for the new hospital was found which had adequate water and was not too far from the sea and the Gum River, the only routes of access from distant places at that time. The site was negotiated for by one of Braun's trained assistants, Nagede. The land is called Yagaum after a man in the Ohuru clan who seized it in a fight years before. It is situated about twelve kilometers from Madang Town in the heart of Amele territory. When the Americans were ready to leave Papua New Guinea, they sold their 119th Field Hospital located at Buangi near Finschhafen for $10,000 to the Lutherans. It was a complete 200 bed hospital lacking nothing but an obstetrics unit. All equipment and buildings were transferred by sea, up the Gum

Fig. 18. A portion of Yagaum hospital, 1971.

River by canoe and then by road to Yagaum. A poor road was upgraded making vehicular access easier and in 1950 Yagaum opened as the nation's first major hospital. The building had taken three years to complete and was done entirely with volunteer labor.

Braun told his people that they all had five tasks: carpentry, spreading the "Good News", working at the dispensary, patrolling to distant villages and educating others. Numerous houses for staff were constructed, gardens planted with such innovations as compost and, by 1953, two more wards, classrooms and a leprosy ward were added, increasing the bed capacity to 353. Expatriate staff, such as a pharmacist, doctors and laboratory technicians also arrived. They began training Amele and other Papua New Guineans in a four year nursing course conducted in Melanesian Pidgin, not in English. The Yagaum Hospital statistics for 1956 show 3376 in-patients, 896 surgical operations and 42 leprosy patients. Yagaum continued for some time to be the only adequate major hospital in the country. In addition, it developed into a major health personnel training center. A large proportion of the nation's existing health center and hospital staff began their training under Braun's direction.

WHAT THE AMELE SAW

From the Amele point of view, Braun's behavior and the changes associated with his presence among them were phenomenal, but explicable within the context of their traditional knowledge of power. Men with special powers had always existed among the Amele. These were usually men who used their powers negatively to harm or kill others, but not necessarily so. There were men who could call on special spirits residing in stones to bring about peace as well as war. There were men who knew how to prevent pregnancy, how to aid in difficult births and to cure life-threatening conditions by reversing the negative sorcery attacking the victim. In the post-war period men such as Braun, who amazingly survived active warfare, were said to have a spirit guardian, or a *was* in Pidgin, which enabled them to become invisible when under threat. To most of those trained by Dr Braun, the mechanical procedures of injections and surgery were clearly understood, but to others these practices were as mysterious as the doings of sorcerers. The major difference was that Braun had a good spirit on his side and his intentions were always positive.

One example of the Amele interpretation of Braun's activities illustrates the point. Apparently Braun outlawed the presence of pigs and dogs at Yagaum, saying that they brought filth and disease to the hospital site. He possessed a shotgun which was presumably intended for hunting but which he also carried as he made rounds at night of the hospital grounds. If he saw a stray pig, he would shoot it, or so say several people who knew him. But the Amele living and working at Yagaum at that time tell another story. They say that he used it to shoot a *dana dorog*, or bad spirit, which would enter Yagaum at night, turning over trash cans and spreading filth. This creature had the appearance of a large dog, the size of a calf, and when shot would disappear entirely. It was actually the condensed emanations of disease released by sick people at the hospital, a fact Braun explained to them. He also was known to shoot *hud haag* or fog sickness, a little man with a big belly who walks like a drunk. He brings stuffy noses to people while they sleep. Wind like beings such as these were thought to bring many diseases. Braun's work was never done, say his admirers, as he strove to protect people from sickness both day and night.

Another example concerns Braun's special interest in obstetrics. Although he and his wife never had a child of their own, Braun delivered thousands of babies. While in the early days at Suyau he encouraged supervised deliveries only for high-risk cases, after Yagaum opened and more effective antibiotics became available, he encouraged all women to deliver in the hospital (Braun 1967b). He made that directive more palatable by allowing traditional practices to continue in the hospital setting. Women were allowed to undergo labor accompanied by their kinswomen, as was usual in the village. They could stand or walk or squat as they chose until very close to delivery. If problems arose or labor was especially prolonged, they were allowed to send for their husbands or someone else from the village who could elicit confession of silently harbored anger or guilt. He could convey these

Fig. 19. Yagaum hospital, male medical ward, 1971.

feelings to the person to whom they were directed and, in turn, elicit words or even signs, such as gifts of pig or chicken, of forgiveness. The placenta was disposed of by the hospital but the umbilical stump (*efa'an*) was buried at the base of a large bamboo clump behind the hospital, which approximates to the traditional custom.

Braun also saw the effects of decreased infant mortality leading to enlarged families and tried to introduce birth control. He performed tubal ligations and inserted older versions of cervical loops in grand multipara. One story tells of a woman with seven children to whom contraception was suggested. Her husband refused to allow it and when his wife again became pregnant, she hid from Braun in embarrassment. Finally, when ready to deliver she came to the hospital, whereupon Braun called for her husband. When he arrived, Braun lifted him off the floor by his ears, sternly ordering his compliance with tubal ligation. The man gave in immediately, telling his family later that Braun's hands were not those of an ordinary man, *"Nau mi savvy han bilong ol waitman. Em i gat pouwa olsem magnets* (Now I know the hand of the white man. It has power, like a magnet)".

To all the Amele people, Dr Braun and his wife were thought of and addressed as Papa and Mama. In discussions with Amele people who knew them, there is no trace of a feeling of social distance, despite an explicit perception of Braun as a man with extraordinary knowledge. When it became clear that he and his wife were not able to have their own children, an Amele child was given to them for adoption. Thus it appears that Braun was fitted into the role of a traditional man of knowledge, a human with very special powers. How he acquired these powers remains an area of mystery to many Amele people. While some accept the simple explanation of long years of schooling, others speculate that he went to a cemetery at night and called on the spirits of ancestors to help him.

Similar stories about Dr Braun and the special powers floating around Yagaum are legion in the Amele area. Because hospitals are a place where people die, Yagaum residents and patients report seeing many ghosts. They visit the wards and stand behind beds. They may only want to see their kin, but fear of ghosts is a cultural expectation and prayer is routinely used to drive them away. Whereas offerings were once made to the recently dead ancestors, since conversion to Christianity the Amele make offerings (*ihane*) of first fruits and money to the church.

Just as the re-interpretation of religious beliefs and practices has been easily accommodated, medical practices have also been re-interpreted to fit traditional tenets of causality. For example, women who desire an abortion may visit nurses at Yagaum who give them a red liquid (iron tonic). The women believe this red liquid will bring on bleeding if the fetus is not yet firmly implanted. As Amele women have minimal knowledge of the processes of reproduction, it is easy to see how the combination of "wishful thinking" and ignorance produces such a belief. It is, of course, possible that a nurse at some time misled a woman into thinking that this red liquid could bring about menstruation. Whatever the source, the belief is widespread.

Similar beliefs about diseases and the procedures at the hospital exist in other areas. For example, because malaria is hyperendemic in this region (Cattani et al 1986), chloroquine is regularly dispensed at the hospital. People have come to think of it as a pain killer and often take pills saved from an unfinished prescription or buy chloroquine in town to use for pain of any sort, including menstrual pain. This practice is likely to have contributed to the emergence of chloroquine-resistant malaria in the region. Although those trained by Braun and his staff recognize the true signs of pneumonia, the term "*numonia*" in Neo-Melanesian Pidgin has entered the Amele vocabulary with a different meaning. To the ordinary man, "*numonia*" is any pain in the upper rib cage, with or without cough or fever. The Pidgin term, *blut i sot* denotes anaemia but to the Amele this condition may be due to frequent finger pricking for malaria slides. This misunderstanding has led to considerable resistance to malaria survey work in the area.

While these and other misinterpretations cannot be traced directly to Dr Braun or his staff, the point to be made is that despite widespread poor understanding of the procedures and materials of western medicine, the Amele and other Papua New Guineans (Welsch 1982, Frankel 1982, 1986) have greatly benefited from its introduction. They have utilized the aid posts and health centers where accessible, in addition to maintaining some of their traditional medicinal beliefs and practices. This has been accomplished most effectively where supernatural or religious beliefs have buttressed the exposure to Western medicine. To the Amele, as in many parts of the nation, steel tools, Christianity and modern medicine arrived as a package. Attendance at church and at clinic were seen as more or less equivalent acts. Church-affiliated women's groups continue to be utilized to promulgate clinic attendance and to encourage improved personal and environmental hygiene. When the maternal and child health teams bring a clinic to the village, they must hold a short prayer service with hymns before seeing the children. The connection between God and the doctors has not been severed in the Amele area, despite greater secularization of health services elsewhere.

In 1972 the mission health authorities and government decided to change Yagaum's role in the nation. The hospital in Madang Town was upgraded, and Yagaum was demoted to a health center. At that point, the Brauns retired from service. In 1980 Theo Braun died in the United States; his wife died a few years later.

AMELE HEALTH TODAY

There are no sound statistics available on fertility, mortality or the prevalence of various diseases in the Amele area prior to this decade. Consequently trying to prove beyond doubt that Western medicine has been effective is simply impossible. There is, however, no doubt that it has been effective in the opinions of the Amele people. Everyone interviewed states unhesitatingly that maternal and infant mortality has dropped dramatically and that the average family size is larger. Similar trends are evident in many areas of the nation (ESCAP/SPC 1982).

In an attempt to obtain accurate demographic information and possibly to examine Amele claims, a reproductive history survey was conducted in 1984 on a random sample of women aged fifteen years or over in all Amele villages (N = 560). Among 100 ever-married women of 45 years or older, the average number of live births was 7.5. The average number of children dying before adulthood among the same women was 1.6. Therefore, an average of 5.9 children survived to adulthood among women whose reproductive years spanned the period of Braun's supervision at Yagaum. According to Amele men and women of the same generation, their own parents rarely had more than three living children. If we consider the general pattern among similar peoples in Papua New Guinea the picture is the same. Infant mortality rates estimated between 100 and 300 per 1000 live births among peoples with no Western medical facility were not uncommon (ESCAP/SPC 1982). Today a demographic registration system operated by the Papua New Guinea Institute of Medical Research in the Amele area and covering all 28 Amele villages, recorded 205 births in 1982 and 218 in 1983. Infant deaths numbered eleven in 1982 and eight in 1983, yielding an estimated average infant mortality rate for both years of 45 per 1000 live births. The general fertility rate for 1983 was 161 births per 1000 women.

Using the reproductive history survey data and applying Brass techniques to the records of ever-married women from ages 15 to 49 yields somewhat higher rates, i.e. a total estimated cumulative fertility of 8.4 and a total fertility rate of 7399 per thousand women. These results place current Amele fertility in the high bracket when compared with results from the World Fertility Survey (United Nations 1983). From all oral histories and the few published reports of observed fertility of the Amele and their neighbors during the period of early contact, we must assume fertility was much lower previously. This change is less likely to be due in this population to earlier age at marriage than to reduced birth spacing (Jenkins and Heywood 1985). Comparing available data on inter-birth intervals among mothers bearing children within the last fifteen years only, we find that there is a steady reduction in birth spacing by mother's age. These range from a mean of 37.4 + 19.3 months among women 45 years old or more (N = 35) at time of survey, down to 26.3 + 9.68 months among women 15–24 years old (N = 28). While this result is confounded by the fact that birth intervals usually are longer at the end of the reproductive period, in this instance it is reasonable to assume that some portion of this difference is in fact due to a recent trend toward shorter intervals. Unfortunately the data do not allow for comparison of birth interval length among women of the same ages across time due to lack of adequate recording of birth dates prior to the 1960s. Thus all pieces of evidence point in the same direction. Amele families are larger today than prior to the advent of Western medicine due to decreased infant mortality and probably to shorter birth intervals.

Among the Amele access to Western medicine has been facilitated by the establishment of excellent nearby services, a relatively rare phenomenon in rural Papua New Guinea. This has certainly contributed to a drastic loss of resort to traditional healing techniques and practitioners. In a study of treatment modes used by the villagers of Ohuru (pop. 275) during August–September 1983, only ten out of 99 illness episodes were treated traditionally and of these ten, five eventually sought treatment at Yagaum. A high proportion, some 50%, treated themselves with aspirin, chloroquine or other Western medicines. Combined with notably improved personal and environmental hygiene, utilization of modern medicine by the Amele has clearly contributed to their present improved health status. Leprosy and yaws are now only seen at Yagaum when brought in from distant non-Amele areas. The last known Amele man with elephantiasis died in 1982. Mothers now introduce foods other than breastmilk very early, often within the first month (Jenkins et al. 1984), a practice which is rarely seen among unacculturated Papua New Guineans. The prevalence of malnutrition among children under five is lower in the Amele than among comparable rural groups elsewhere in the nation (Heywood 1985). Even malaria, which is hyperendemic and continues to contribute substantially to morbidity and iron-deficiency anemia, does not take the toll of deaths that it once did (Moir 1983).

CONCLUSION

It is clear that the introduction of Western medicine in the new nation of Papua New Guinea has contributed to improved health of the local people. In this regard, Dr Braun's work is not unique. But what has been unique and, in this author's view, worth documenting is the interaction of mission-directed changes in beliefs and practices with the provision of a culturally acceptable health service. A very good statistical illustration of this is provided by another missionary doctor, John Sturt, in the Anguganak area of the West Sepik. His was a stricter sect of Christianity which prohibited betel nut chewing, smoking and many traditional practices. The people of the Anguganak area were not as easily won over to conversion and hence made less effective use of the available mission health services than did the Amele. Comparing seven "cooperative" and four "uncooperative" villages, Sturt found an infant mortality rate of 59 in the former and 177 in the latter over a ten-year period of 1962 to 1971. Thus it appears that the Amele people were very fortunate, as indeed they realize, in having been introduced to Western medicine through the hands of a sympathetic, religiously inspired doctor who cared enough to accommodate the local culture instead of ignoring it.

NOTES

1. This dichotomy is a highly simplified one, as migration, language loss and adoption and genetic intermixture have created a very complex ethnic scheme along the north coast and its hinterlands.

P. ROSCOE

9. MEDICAL PLURALISM AMONG THE YANGORU BOIKEN[1]

INTRODUCTION

Some fifty years ago, the Boiken of the Yangoru subdistrict in the East Sepik province first became aware that Europeans had different means from their own of curing the sick. In the years that followed, their growing acquaintance with this system prompted an increasing use of its novel therapies and significant modifications in traditional understandings of sickness. This chapter examines the ethnography of this medically plural situation. It begins with a brief history of Western health services in this small corner of Papua New Guinea and an outline of their main biomedical effects. Against this historical backdrop, the body of the work then attempts to identify the major influences of Western health services on traditional medicine and to trace out the implications of this interaction for contemporary health-seeking behavior. The chapter ends with a brief assessment of the sociocultural implications of Western medicine and suggests how Yangoru's health services might sensitively be expanded.

The Boiken-speaking people of the East Sepik province command one of the largest and most diverse terrains in northwest Papua New Guinea. Offshore, they are found on the islands of Walis and Tarawai and parts of Karesau, Yuo, and Muschu. On shore, their lands cut a swathe that stretches from Wewak to Dagua, rises over the Prince Alexander Mountains, and plunges deep into the rolling grasslands of the Sepik plains. Of the 28,000 people currently living in these traditional lands, about one third are to be found among the fertile southern foothills around Yangoru government station where they speak the Yangoru dialect of Boiken (Bureau of Statistics n.d. 1980; Freudenburg 1976).[2] A horticultural folk, these Yangoru Boiken base their diet on the slash and burn cultivation of yam, taro and banana, supplemented with pigs, game, bush foods, trade store goods, and a "feast and famine" dependence on sago. Their political, economic and social life is founded on patrilineages of relatively shallow depth; their ceremonial life revolves around the competitive exchange of pigs; and their magico-religious world is dominated by magical forces and peopled by culture heroes, ancestral spirits, water sprites and fiends (Roscoe 1983, Ch. 3).

The first Europeans to enter Yangoru Boiken territory were two Catholic missionaries who toured the northern villages in October 1912 (Limbrock 1912–13). Within a decade, the dense populations they found had attracted the periodic attentions of labour recruiters, but it was in the 1930s that the discovery of gold attracted regular European visits and government patrols. Shortly before the Second World War, a patrol post appeared at Yangoru, promptly to close with the invasion of the Japanese. By 1943, Imperial soldiers of the 18th Army were firmly

S. Frankel and G. Lewis (eds.), *A Continuing Trial of Treatment.* 199–215.
© 1989, Kluwer Academic Publishers, Dordrecht – Printed in the Netherlands.

ensconced in villages throughout the region, where they remained until October 1945 (Roscoe 1983: Ch. 4).

Yangoru's knowledge of Western medicines dates from these early years and the occasional doctoring administered by plantation medics, visiting missionaries (Muller 1935–36: 106) and early administrative patrols. Later, the Japanese also provided rudimentary medical care, at least until their supply lines were cut in the final months of the war. At some point, medical *tultuls* appeared, administered from the Maprik Hospital, but it is not clear if they pre- or post-dated the war. Whatever the case, there was at least one medical *tultul* in every major village by September 1949, when the administration opened the Yangoru aid post thus making them redundant. In 1952 the new post received its first European medical assistant, and in the years that followed small aid posts manned by native medical assistants expanded health care to outlying villages (YPR 2/48–49:5, YPR 5/48–49:4, YPR 5/49–50:4). For a variety of reasons, not least village politics, traditional suspicions, and the staff's limited medical knowledge, these posts met with limited success (Schofield and Parkinson 1963: 7–8). Still, the medical history of the 1950s was not without its triumphs. Yaws, for example, was virtually eliminated and patrol officers were fulsome, if a little patronizing, in their praise of the beneficial effects of aid posts on small tropical ulcers, sores, and abrasions (YPR 3/48–49:3, YPR 3/55–56: Appendix A, YPR 2/61–62:6, YPR 4/61–62:5).

The real advances in Yangoru's public health, however, came in the early 1960s with the introduction of malaria control spraying and maternal and child health services. The holoendemic nature of southern foothills' malaria had attracted a control project to Maprik in the mid 1950s. In late 1962 the project expanded its DDT spraying to Yangoru and quickly achieved large reductions in the parasite rate. Local opposition and sub-standard spraying operations later reduced the initial successes, but the parasite rate was still below 20% in the early 1970s, down from a pre-control level of 75% (Parkinson 1973, Peters 1959, 1960, Zigas and Rodrigue 1972, YPR 7/61–62:10). The second significant innovation came in July 1963, when the Catholic Mission established Yangoru's first maternal and child health clinic to serve as a base for monthly peripatetic visits to nearby villages. By 1965 the peripatetic clinic had 1200 children on its records and by 1970 had extended its itinerary to most Yangoru Boiken villages. Meanwhile, monthly attendance figures at the central clinic had grown from 40–45 in 1965 to around 100 in 1970. By 1975, when all clinic functions were transferred to the Yangoru health center, attendance had reached 200 per month (Fitzgibbon 1981).

Though patrol census data must be treated with extreme caution, figures for Yangoru leave little doubt that population rose sharply in the wake of these innovations. Prior to 1960 natural increase had averaged around 1.6% per year, but just two years after spraying and clinic visits had begun, it had risen to 2.2% to 2.4%[3] (Roscoe 1983: 130, 146–151) In Sima village, child mortality had averaged about 33% prior to 1965; in the following decade it fell to about 13% (ibid, 154).[4]

With these successes, Western medical care became a firmly established feature of the Yangoru landscape. Today it is dispensed from the fifty bed Yangoru health center, which cares for an average of 130 admissions per month, treats a constant stream of out-patients,[5] and provides a monthly maternal and child health clinic for almost all Yangoru Boiken villages. Since 1976 a family planning clinic has also operated from the center but, with only 1% to 2% of women of reproductive age using it, its impact is currently low (Roscoe 1984).

In most of the Yangoru area, the modification of traditional Boiken ethnomedicine owes more to the introduction and expansion of these health services than to any other European influence. Although Christianity and European moral codes have influenced ethnomedical beliefs and practices elsewhere in Papua New Guinea (for example, Frankel 1986, Romanucci-Ross 1977), their impact on Yangoru ethnomedicine has been slight. Beyond the immediate environs of the mission stations, Boiken and European moral and religious belief and behavior are perceived not as alternatives but as refractions of a single system, a not unreasonable assumption given a conviction that the world's inhabitants all originated on the slopes of a local mountain. Thus mission teachings are automatically identified with traditional understandings: God, Jesus, and the Holy Ghost are all said to be various culture heroes, while service and prayer, where they are comprehended at all, are viewed as magical procedures with instrumental goals. European morality – Christian or otherwise - is widely assumed to be that of the village, and where customary and moral differences between the two codes are noticed, they are usually explained as modifications ordained by lesser European culture heroes – in other words, differences which do not apply to villagers. During the periods of millenarian activity which frequently sweep this area, these differences do occasionally attract attention to village "sins" but, for most villagers, these "sins" are no more than infractions of the magical requirements for achieving the wealth and political emancipation enjoyed by Europeans. I know of no instance in which they were articulated with medical beliefs.

Just as Christianity and European morality are interpreted in traditional terms, so too is Western medicine. As elsewhere in Papua New Guinea (for example Welsch 1983), there is no conception that Western medicine forms an alternative system incompatible with its traditional counterpart. Villagers readily concede a superior European knowledge of certain types of illness, but they believe this knowledge to be an extension of traditional medicine. Thus, despite the recognized benefits of Western medical services on village health, traditional medicine continues largely unchanged.[6] Definitions and ideas of sickness and health, for example, show little evidence of latterday inspiration. Illness is still referred to as *porra*, a term covering virtually every case that a lay European would identify as illness, but including minor afflictions such as a brief aching in a limb, a fleeting spell of dizziness and, in adults, lassitude or an inability to compete successfully in the sociopolitical arena. Health and its age-specific nature is still explained in terms of the "good" blood with which one is born and the "bad" blood which accrues in adolescence and through the "unavoidable" act of intercourse. And illness is still explained in terms of *yendawing*, excessive "bad" blood, and *kilunku*, a noxious dark liquid that "covers up" good, red blood.

European-induced innovation is most apparent as extensions to ideas about the categories, causes and etiologies of illness. Many people are now acquainted with venereal disease, for example, but its etiology has been elegantly transformed into traditional terms. Women maintain it is caused by the mixing of many men's semen in the womb of a promiscuous woman, while men believe it is a consequence of semen being "wasted" in intercourse with anyone but one's wife. In another striking example of intellectualism in action, a factotum at Lae Hospital had used doctors' comments about "bugs" in patients' stomachs and his own observations of worms in their feces to weave a theory of sorcery that dovetailed remarkably with traditional etiology.

The most significant ethno-medical consequence of European contact, however, was the creation of an illness category known as *sik nating*. Literally translated this term means "trivial sickness", the triviality referring to cause rather than symptom. *Sik nating* is widely believed incapable of killing, regardless of how violent the physical symptoms it produces. By contrast *sik bilong ples* ("village sickness", i.e., sickness of traditional cause) can be fatal in the face of the mildest physical symptoms.[7] *Sik nating* was unknown in former days. Villagers attribute their first knowledge of it to conversations with Japanese soldiers during the Second World War, but its development seems to owe more to observations of Europeans and their medicines. In the village view, Europeans are known to be woefully ignorant of traditional ethno-medical agencies. Even so, they have managed to score some notable therapeutic successes over the years, although their record has been patchy – some patients died where others with similar symptoms were cured. Villagers therefore conclude that the successes must stem from the existence of a hitherto unknown type of sickness, *sik nating*,[8] which can manifest almost any type of physical symptom. Opinions are divided, however, over whether *sik nating* existed before contact. Some speculate that it was consistently misdiagnosed in ancestral times; others believe the Europeans brought with them the sicknesses they could cure.

It is against this backdrop of illness-causing agencies that decisions governing health-seeking behavior are made. These decisions can be grouped into two interrelated sets, the first concerning the amount of effort that should be invested in diagnosing and curing an illness, the second involving the diagnostic and therapeutic decisions themselves. The effort invested in diagnosis and cure is very much determined by whether it is the suffering patient or someone acting on his behalf who plays the pivotal role in deciding the issue. My data support the reasonable presumption that more effort is invested if the pivotal decision-maker is the suffering patient than if it is some non-suffering other.

In many cases, the patient is not the principal decision-maker. Infants and children who fall sick, for example, are largely dependent on their parents – in particular their mothers – for their cure, if only because they are incapable or afraid to seek help on their own. Adolescents and adult females have rather greater autonomy, but are susceptible on some occasions to pressure from parents or husbands who may have their own reasons for influencing the decision. In some cases, the indicated remedial course can only be executed by older males, who therefore become pivotal determinants in whether efforts are extended further. And no matter who the patient the more debilitating is the sickness, the more does he or she perforce rely on others to seek therapy.

In all of these cases, the effort actually expended depends very much on the patient's status. Informants readily concede that sick adults attract more concern than ailing infants, while the aged sick whose frailties have begun seriously to burden their descendents are rather less likely to be helped than a sick young adult. Sima informants gave no reason to believe sex was a factor influencing efforts at cure in these cases (cf. Young, this volume), but data from the Yangoru health center's admission records indicate there might be small differences. Cutting across all these considerations is the apparent degree of the patient's discomfort and, more particularly, the perceived severity of the threat to his or her life: the more severe the pain or threat, the more likely is diagnostic and therapeutic effort to follow.

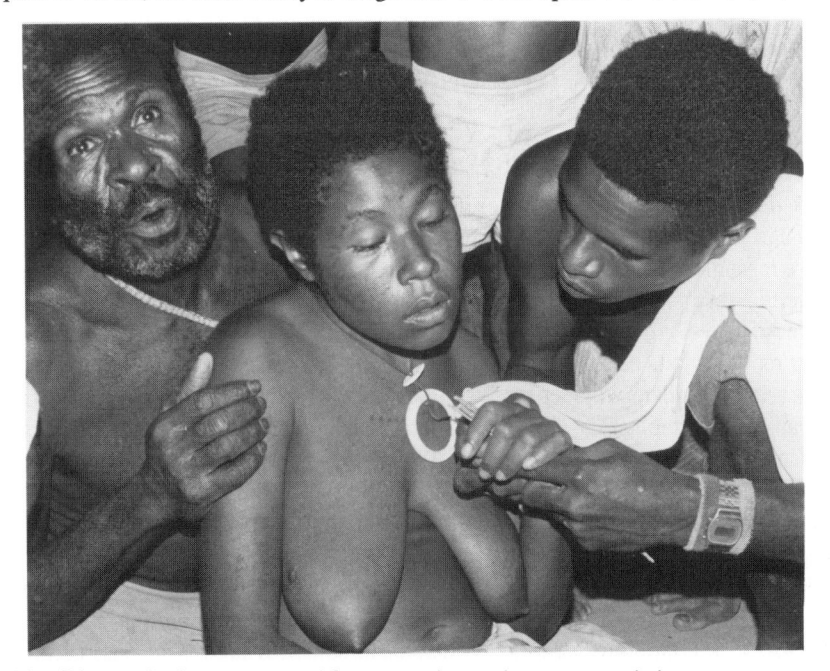

Fig. 20. Diagnostic signs are coaxed from a semi-conscious sorcery victim.

In most cases, of course, discomfort is readily apparent to the patient and is easily communicated to others, either directly or indirectly – by moans, a whining tone of voice, shivering by a fire or under a blanket at midday, and so on. The threat to a patient's life, however, is not always as obvious. Discomfort can be an indication of severity, but far more salient is evidence that the cold dark liquid, *kilunku,* has reached life-threatening proportions. If patients are incapable of standing unassisted, if their limbs or body are cold, if they complain of heart pains, if dark emissions issue from their orifices or are released during surgical undertakings, then they are in imminent danger. If they are semi-conscious, their rambling utterances can also be diagnostic because, teetering on the margins of the hyperphysical world, they are believed privy to the prognosis of their illness. Finally, there are diagnostic tests available: the fingertip can be squeezed to see if it still contains red blood, while a slow pulse will indicate that the normally vigorous heart is about to succumb.[10]

Where minor ailments are involved, people frequently seem to conclude that diagnosing a cause is not worth the effort. If quizzed about the illness, they profess ignorance or state that it is without cause: "it just came up". In such cases, the therapeutic concern is not to establish a cause but merely to alleviate discomfort and, to this end, Western medicines are believed equal or superior to the available village remedies. Aspirin, for example, is favorably compared to village means of alleviating aches and pains. Western medical attention for fractured and broken bones is now invariably sought alongside traditional treatments. European cures for *tinea imbricata* and scabies are avidly sought, and ointments and bandages are now widely preferred over the coral tree leaf for the treatment of sores. In some cases, Western remedies are popular because they are believed to have regenerative functions. Injections, for example, are viewed either as blood or as a medicine that strengthens the blood, and a minor craze for vitamin pills swept Sima village after I had described them in similar terms. The only traditional regenerative practices – the stinging nettles and penis bleeding that combat lassitude and social incompetence – are said to have been abandoned because the Western equivalents are more effective.

In more serious cases of illness, however, it becomes worthwhile to invest some effort in diagnosing the causative agent and combating it through appropriate therapy. In some cases, the assessment of severity is itself diagnostic: if the patient's life is in danger, the field of likely agents narrows to those that can be lethal. The Yangoru Boiken frequently claim sorcery to be the only cause of death besides old age but, in practice, spirits of the dead, fiends and a few of the most powerful spells to protect crops also occasionally emerge as deadly candidates.

If severity is not diagnostically conclusive, then attention turns to symptomatology, diagnostic testing and an appraisal of the patient's characteristics and recent history. It is commonly said that Melanesian societies take little note of physical signs or symptoms in diagnosing the cause of illness, the Gnau being offered as an extreme case (Hamnett and Connell 1981: 496, Lewis 1975). In fact, even the Gnau appear to have a rudimentary symptomatology (see Lewis 1975: 168–9, 254), and what is really at issue perhaps is the degree to which symptoms seem to *oblige* a diagnosis. At one end of the scale, typified by the Gnau, physical signs may enter diagnosis but are not necessary to it (ibid, p. 169). At the other end of the scale, symptoms can have the enormous determinative influence that they assume in Western diagnosis. On this scale, Yangoru Boiken symptomatology falls rather towards the Gnau pole: it lacks any great formal systematization, there are no recognized diagnostic experts, and symptoms can strongly indicate but never oblige a diagnosis. Even so, the Yangoru Boiken do make extensive use of physical signs and can readily phrase the clusters associated with different agencies. Thus, a rapid onset of illness, complaints of being hot when the patient is shivering, or complaints of being cold when the patient is seated by a roaring fire under a tropical sun, are all symptomatic of sorcery. Swollen testicles immediately indicate the work of spells that protect coconuts from theft, while swollen limbs are caused by magic to protect taro crops. Symptoms affecting the head or stomach, and fainting accompanied by a rapid pulse, are strong indicators of yam protection magic. Arthritis is said usually to be caused by spells placed on certain ritual carvings. A stylized form of entrancement that affects men and women alike is the work of magically initiated fiends from the central, Nagam, and Kubalia Boiken to the east (Roscoe 1986). Mental derangement can sometimes be caused by yam magic, but is usually the work of spirits of the dead. Conjunctivitis and the epidemics of coughing and sneezing that seasonally sweep the area are indicative of culture heroes. Thoracic pain, earache, deafness and deformity are all indications of water sprite attack. And failing eyesight, lassitude, skin disease and social incompetence are symptomatic of different sorts of bodily pollution. The patient's characteristics can, of course, influence the interpretations placed on these symptoms. An infant, for example, is susceptible to several types of magic to which adults are immune, but is incapable of the transgressions that trigger other magic. Moreover, it is not endangered by pollution, so this agency is never diagnosed in the event of lassitude or poor eyesight.

A small number of diagnostic tests can narrow the field of possible causes further. The work of fiends is diagnosed by pricking the patient's skin with dry stalks to test for a response. If a victim is in the marginal state between life and death, his or her semi-conscious mutterings and actions can help diagnose sorcery and the person responsible. If the patient *in extremis* is mute, the case can be forced by brushing his or her stomach with stinging nettles and enunciating the names of local villages. If the patient responds to a particular name, sorcery is indicated and the culprit's residence identified. The field can then be further narrowed by calling the names of the village's pig exchange moieties, the names of its clans or the names of its members.

Finally, the field of possible causes can be narrowed by grilling patients and/or their relatives about recent activities and companions. Has the patient recently dreamed of white, female water sprites or taken water from a sprite's pool? Have they stolen food from magically protected crops? Have they ventured out alone and fallen victim to fiends? Have they recently eaten with people who might have resorted to sorcery? Have they recently been "marked" by a firefly? (Ancestral spirits alert their descendents to acts of sorcery against them by directing a firefly to alight on them.) Do they have outstanding kinship obligations that might prompt an ancestral spirit to seek revenge?

One illness alone stands immune to these diagnostic probings. Although a minority of villagers exhibit a vague appreciation that fever, dizziness, and headache can be symptomatic of the *sik nating* sub-category "*sik malaria*", most are unaware of any physical symptoms, background information or tests by which *sik nating* may be positively diagnosed. It can be revealed only through resort to Western health services – patients who are cured were evidently suffering from *sik nating*.[11] For most villagers, then, the probability that an illness is *sik nating* rests on their previous experience of western medical "successes". If they have seen many patients cured by Western medicines, they will be more inclined to consider *sik nating* as a possible cause than if they have seen few. In Sima, people were unwilling to admit that *sik nating* was at all prevalent: most illnesses, they said, were *sik bilong ples*. In most cases, therefore, *sik nating* is unlikely to be the immediate diagnosis and must await the elimination, through therapeutic action, of other possibilities considered more probable.

Fig. 21. Yangoru Boiken sorcery bundless.

Set out in schematic form, the universe of Yangoru Boiken causal agents and their repertoire of diagnostic methods can appear both comprehensive and precise, fostering an impression that the diagnosis of cause is a straightforward process of deduction. In some cases, such as the entrancement caused by fiends, this may be the case. More often, though, the process is inconclusive. The main difficulty is that several different causes can produce identical or nearly identical symptoms. Sudden collapse, for example, can result from sorcery, other types of magic, or attack by ancestral spirits or fiends. A pain in the side can be caused by sorcerized yams, water sprites or sorcery. Sorcery, in fact, is said to cause the greatest diagnostic problems of any agent, because it can produce the entire range of human physical symptoms. Moreover, the sorcerer may deliberately attempt to divert diagnostic attention by making his attack emulate the symptoms of another agent. Background information can help limit these uncertainties, but they too suffer by being inconclusive. A patient may remember drinking from a sprite's pool or dreaming of a white female being, but these are only *indications*. They do not definitively point to sprites, any more than their absence rules them out. Even diagnostic tests can be deceptive and are always open to interpretation.

The Yangoru Boiken readily admit and even on occasion volunteer the uncertainties in using symptomatology, diagnostic testing and background history to identify cause; and their predicament is frequently evident in the range of possible causes advanced in actual evaluations. So how, then, do they truncate these ambiguities when faced with a sick individual, translating doubt into a diagnostic conclusion? Even in the relatively formal diagnostic system of Western medicine, this process can be unclear, leading to charges that diagnosis is as much an art as a science (for example, Blaxter 1978: 12–1, Engle and Davis 1963: 514). Yangoru Boiken exegesis on the process is even less illuminating, with comments such as: 'Alright, we think now, and we think, "Perhaps it's sorcery … or ancestral spirits;"' "I just thought of it;" or "I *know*". Close observation and questioning of practical diagnoses yields little more. Suffice it to say, the Yangoru Boiken arrive not so much at *a* diagnosis but at several, one of which is usually considered the most probable. In some cases, this plurality appears to represent a diversity of opinion among those performing the diagnosis, the most probable diagnosis being the one to which the majority subscribe. In other cases, however, it seems to reflect the ordering of salient possibilities by a single diagnostician.

Regardless of how conclusive a diagnosis may be, therapeutic action does not necessarily follow speedily from it. Nor are diagnostic conclusions the only factors determining the type of therapy sought. I have already noted that the characteristics of the patient and of the diagnostic and therapeutic executive(s), together with the discomfort and severity of the illness, influence the amount of effort invested in diagnosis and therapy. But other factors – the conclusiveness of the diagnosis, and perceptions of the costs, accessibility, and efficacy of therapy – also influence whether and how diagnostic conclusions are transformed into therapy. The less ambiguous the diagnosis, the more immediate will be the resort to therapy – if only because less time is spent in establishing cause and there is greater reason to believe that therapeutic effort will be rewarded. Even in the most ambiguous cases, however, there is some impetus to action because, as villagers point out, therapeutic failures sharpen the diagnosis. On several occasions, therapeutic action was explained thus: "We're not sure; we're just trying [this therapy]. If it doesn't work we know it's [x, y, or z]." This method of trial and error is most apparent where non-serious illnesses of ambiguous cause are involved. One elderly man, long plagued by respiratory problems, began to experience chest pains, an ailment that can be caused by several types of magic, by water sprites or sorcery. He and his family immediately suspected sorcery and a probable culprit, but his immediate resort was to anti-yam magic supplied by a lineage brother from the neighbouring hamlet. Later that day, he solicited my help: I offered aspirin and cough syrup (which he accepted) and suggested the health center (which he ignored). When no beneficial effects were apparent the next day, the yam magic diagnosis was rejected in favour of water sprite invasion. Sprite therapy was secured from a clan brother a quarter of a mile away but proved ineffective. By now, the patient and his family were convinced sorcery was at work but, since the ailment was not sufficiently serious to warrant a public examination, they contented themselves with rumor-mongering about the probable culprit.

Generally speaking, neither traditional nor Western therapies are avoided for any pain or untoward side effects they might cause. Traditional remedies, in fact, are mostly painless, the main exceptions being penis bleeding – now allegedly abandoned – and, to a lesser extent, purgatives and emetics. The only unwelcome therapeutic "side effect" ever mentioned was the ire that can be aroused by attempts to track down the perpetrators of sorcery, but since sorcery accusations are usually lodged where ill will is already present, the consequences for therapeutic resort are debatable. Western medicines are likewise largely devoid of perceived ill effects, though villagers resist gentian violet on the basis that it makes sores and cuts worse (by contrast, iodine and mercurichrome are eagerly sought). In its early years, the health center's *gratis* provision of medical care apparently deterred usage by rousing suspicions about the motives of the missionary staff, but once it became known that they were "paid" for their work these suspicions abated.[12] Nevertheless, its legacy is an attitude towards health workers that is perhaps best described as: "We do you a service by getting ill; you have a duty to help us get well."

The Abelam to the west reportedly fear hospital settings because exuviae can easily be obtained for sorcery and because spirits of the dying will have difficulty finding their way to the villages of the dead (Schofield and Parkinson 1963: 3,6). The Yangoru Boiken harbor no such fears. They know where ancestral spirits dwell and assume this knowledge transcends death. If by some mischance a spirit should become lost – if, for example, death occurs in an unfamiliar, distant town – there are procedures for returning it to its home territory. As for sorcery, the health center's "modern" status is believed to nullify the potency of any exuviae obtained on the premises.

In theory, Boiken beliefs in pollution might deter resort to the health center since adult men have no way of knowing if female staff are menstruating or whether medical instruments and blankets have been used by more polluted youngsters. Unfortunately, I omitted to make specific inquiries on these points; suffice it to say, no one ever volunteered pollution as a problem, and the "European" status of the center together with knowledge of its powerful antiseptics may prompt a belief that pollution rules are inoperable within its confines.[13]

Although traditional and Western therapies carry few perceived ill effects to deter their use, their accessibility and perceived efficacy vary considerably, which strongly influences their take up. The entrancements caused by fiends, for example, are easily and efficaciously treated since the emetics that cure them are usually to be found growing within twenty or thirty meters of any hamlet. The remedies to combat sprite attack and the more powerful crop magic are less certainly efficacious and, since they require some magical initiation, are somewhat less accessible, though there are usually one or two qualified therapists in each village. Illnesses caused by sorcery or ancestral spirits are the most difficult of all to cure, for they require that the kinship breach occasioning ancestral ire or that the disgruntled perpetrator of the sorcery is identified, an extremely time-consuming process involving trips to other hamlets or villages for announcements, more or less oblique accusations and, finally public discussion.[14] Furthermore, these efforts are frequently frustrated by deception. Innocent people may pretend responsibility if they have grievances to prosecute against victims and their families. Fraud is only suspected later, when the patient is still sick, requiring the whole process to be restarted. Not surprisingly, there is some feeling in such cases that attempts at remedy can be a lost cause. As the frustrated father of one youth gravely afflicted by sorcery declaimed: "Sorcerers hide their work. How can *we* tell who is responsible!"

These differences in accessibility and efficacy appear to weigh heavily in the Yangoru Boiken resort to therapy, as a comparison of two cases from Sima village illustrates. In both cases the patient was believed in imminent danger of death. The first involved a middle aged mother of five children. Around three o'clock one morning, a general hullabaloo summoned a small crowd of relatives and neighbors to where she sat, apparently entranced, methodically slicing taro onto her netbag. This is the classic manner of the victim of fiends, a diagnosis later corroborated by her muttered references to two men resembling me – some fiends are believed to be white. Accordingly, the immediate therapy was *worarama* grass plucked from the nearby undergrowth, an emetic that combats fiend attack. The second case involved a man of similar age who collapsed one morning, insensible to frantic whipping of his legs and bawling of his name. Talk of sorcery was everywhere. Divination supported the diagnosis but was ambiguous in pinpointing a culprit. These difficulties meant that no cure could reasonably be expected for at least several days. Thus nothing was done there and then – nothing could be done – beyond announcing the diagnosis by yodel and slit gong in the forlorn hope that the culprit would "take pity" on the patient. Meanwhile, the alarmed crowd tried the more accessible remedies against other lethal agents. The venerable Pararauwa performed magical therapy to combat his dreadful yam magic – without result. And young Hembranaka dashed into the bush to fetch emetics against fiends. Reflecting later on his actions, he said: 'I didn't know: was it fiends or was it sorcery? But I thought, "Perhaps it's fiends". So I just tried it [the fiend therapy].'

Kroeger (1983: 157) observes that in studying the acceptance of Western health services in developing countries, anthropologists tend to focus on the influences of traditional etiology and world view to the neglect of service factors such as accessibility and costs. Since the relative accessibility of traditional Yangoru therapies appears to influence their use, the same must be suspected of Western therapies. Western medical services are free in Yangoru and on this account compare favorably with traditional therapies, some of which cost K2 or more. However, as in other areas of the world (for example Garner and Giddings 1985,

Jolly and King 1966, Ram and Datta 1976, Young 1981), the distance to these services seems to moderate their take up considerably. The median distance of catchment area villages from the Yangoru health center is 4.2 miles, with a range of 0.6–16 miles, which compares poorly with traditional therapies, most of which can be found within the village. These distances pose obvious difficulties for invalids seeking the center's aid, particularly if they are the elderly or new mothers. The latter run grave risks from sorcery during their first post-natal month when the earth from their footprints can be used to kill them, their husband and the newborn in one fell swoop. Though a high risk population, they therefore seldom appear at the health center unless a vehicle takes them or a file of youngsters is on hand to erase their footprints as they walk – a risky undertaking given youngsters' notorious unreliability.

In Sima, 3.4 miles from Yangoru, distance was the most frequent explanation for a reluctance to visit the health center, and the influence of transport availability corroborated these claims. In three cases where there had been no plans to take an incapacitated patient to the health center, the sudden appearance of a truck bound for Yangoru prompted an immediate change of mind and departure. In theory, if distance is an important factor, its effects should also be apparent in attendance rates at the center. Unfortunately, these records do not include a patient's village. This information is available in admission records, but because the decisions of the admitting officer intervene between attendance at the center and admission to its wards, they leave something to be desired as an indication of attendance. Nevertheless, since Young's analysis of medical records on Goodenough suggests that the existence of a relationship between admission rates and distance is indicative of a similar relationship between attendance and distance, the Yangoru admission records deserve some consideration.

The figures for two complete years of admissions (1974 and 1980) were obtained from the health center. They yielded a correlation coefficient of -0.55 between per capita admissions and distance from the health center in a total sample of 63 villages.[15] Inspection of the scattergram revealed that two groups of villages deviated considerably further from the regression line than others – eight villages lying in the grassplains south of the East Sepik highway and a group of six contiguous villages lying in the foothills to the immediate north of Yangoru. The former group had a much higher admission rate than predicted by the regression line. As a group, they are the most distant from the health center and lie considerably off well-travelled roads. Thus they may have been admitted with less serious ailments than normal because of the difficulties of securing their return for follow up treatment. The group of villages north of the health center had a much lower admission rate than predicted, the reasons for which are less easy to fathom. Since they lie some way off well-travelled routes, they might have lower attendance rates, though other villages, similarly situated, lie much nearer the regression line. In addition, these six villages formed an ancient war confederacy opposed to those around Yangoru. Though warfare is a thing of the past, its legacy for these villages is a relatively low incidence of relatives adjacent to Yangoru. Since informants emphasize the value of nearby *wantoks* for the support of an admitted patient's relatives, the lower admission rates of this confederacy may be a product of Yangoru prehistory. In any case, if these fourteen villages are removed from the sample, the correlation coefficient rises to −0.80.

It should be apparent from the foregoing that, in greater or lesser degree, a large number of sociocultural and geographical features influence the Yangoru Boiken pursuit of therapy. The characteristics of the patient and of the person(s) directing the therapeutic effort, the patient's discomfort and the severity of the illness, all influence the effort invested in diagnosis and therapy. In most instances, diagnosis is a highly significant determinant of therapeutic action, but its conclusiveness, together with perceptions of the costs, accessibility and efficacy of the indicated therapy are also influential. For the health planner the questions of practical relevance in all this concern the Yangoru Boiken acceptance of Western health services. How do these factors affect acceptance? What are the sociocultural implications of acceptance? And how might acceptance be sensitively encouraged?

Several factors, such as perceptions of Christianity, European morality, and health service personnel and establishments, appear to have only limited influence on whether and at what point the Yangoru Boiken seek Western therapy. The beneficial effects of Western medicines incline villagers, *ceteris paribus*, towards their use *for the alleviation of symptoms*. But, as *cures*, they are believed effective only on *sik nating*, and this has several negative implications for acceptance. In cases perceived to be life-threatening, logic militates against immediate resort to Western therapy unless it is immediately to hand. The majority of the Yangoru Boiken do not believe *sik nating* is fatal, so an initial resort to Western treatment in a life-threatening case would be a foolish delay of the traditional life-saving therapies. If the illness later proves to be *sik nating*, nothing has been lost by delaying Western therapy beyond perhaps the patient's comfort. In short, Western therapy is unlikely to be considered for the acutely ill – those most urgently in need of it – at least until the more accessible therapies against lethal agents have been exhausted. In the previously mentioned case of the man in his early middle age, villagers only began to discuss the health center after all lethal causes except sorcery and its therapeutic mires had been eliminated. And the fact that the health center was even then discussed was due largely to the possibility that I could borrow a truck to transport the patient, who later died.

In cases where life is not threatened or where all but the most inaccessible therapies for lethal agents have been tried, the resort to Western therapy will largely depend on the perceived likelihood that the illness is *sik nating*, weighed against the relative accessibility of Western therapy. Thus we can expect that Western services will not even be considered until villagers have tried therapies more accessible than Western services for diagnoses considered more probable than *sik nating*. I have argued that even when a patient's life is not believed endangered, *sik nating* is unlikely to be the primary diagnosis because its emergence is at least partly dependent on the elimination of other possibilities through therapeutic action. Thus, since most traditional therapies are to be found within the village, whereas health services are a median distance of 4.2 miles away, the latter is seldom likely to be the immediate therapy, and in most cases will come some way down the "hierarchy of resort".

Two factors, though, can tip the scales in favor of Western services. The first is the status of Yangoru station – the site of the health center – as a service point that most adult villagers visit every week or two. Several case histories from Sima indicated that the ambulatory sick often combined a trip to the health center with other business related to the market, court, post office, police station, school or trade stores. In other words, the need for one or more of these services effectively increased the accessibility of Western medical help. For example, a man in his early middle age had felt a mild lassitude for several weeks and was convinced that a powerful sprite had invaded him. One day, however, he had to attend court and took the opportunity to visit the health center with his problem; unfortunately, the center was "unable" to cure him.

The second factor favoring health center use is the availability of transport. If a patient is not ambulatory, the prospects for prompt resort to the center are usually slim for they depend on the willingness of between two to four people to act as porters. In most such cases in Sima, a patient was unlikely to be carried down for medical help unless he or she was still alive and non-ambulatory after one to two weeks. The exceptions occurred when trucks happened through the village – as the cases of two young teenage girls illustrate. Each was seriously ill, apparently with malaria. In one case, the health center's truck arrived in the village for a clinic visit just a few hours following onset. With no prompting from clinic staff, the girl was brought down to the truck to be taken away and, five days later, was back in the village fully recovered. With no truck passing by during her illness period, the other girl remained seriously ill for nine days before she was finally carried down to the center, where she fortunately recovered.

Despite the factors that detrimentally influence the prompt and effective administration of Yangoru's health services, there have been significant improvements in Yangoru Boiken health. In traditional societies, though, illness is invariably integrated into social affairs, so that changes in its prevalence carry potentially significant social implications. These deserve close attention, although in the absence of an extensive analysis of Yangoru Boiken magico-religious belief and practice, only the most general assessments can here be offered. For most agencies – pollution, water sprites, ancestral heroes, for example – if anything is socially significant about the illnesses they cause, it is the fact of the illness rather than its cure. Thus only preventive medical techniques, which are not as yet widely developed in Yangoru, have conceivable implications. A reduction in the incidence of prolonged illness and premature death, by reducing the raw materials of sorcery accusation, may have some social implications, but the role of this agency in Boiken society is difficult to gauge. Still, I am inclined to believe it is primarily a tool for political advancement, in which case other types of misfortune could become substitute grist for the mills of sorcery accusation if illness and premature death begin to disappear. The most significant implications of Western medical services probably lie in their effects on afflictions attributed to ancestral spirits and protective magic. These agencies provide important sanctions on traditional kinship obligations and the rules governing theft and ritual transgression – which Western medicine might conceivably weaken by reducing fear of the illnesses they cause. The effects on kinship obligations are unlikely to be very marked. Ancestral spirits primarily cause mental derangement, an area in which Western therapy has had notably little success in Yangoru. There have been greater successes on some of the afflictions attributed to protective magic, but, at present, detrimental social effects are not discernible. If cure rates rise in the future the effects may become more pronounced, unless alternative means of enforcement evolve.

The improvement of Yangoru health appears at present, therefore, to have had limited detrimental effects on Yangoru Boiken society, and since improvements in health are among the few benefits of national development that the Yangoru Boiken will acknowledge, there is reason to conclude with a brief consideration of how they might be enhanced. As I have mentioned, the use currently made of the health center's services is largely a function of their relative accessibility, weighed against perceptions of the prevalence of *sik nating*. Greater use is therefore likely to follow from enhancing either of these factors. Since *sik nating* appears to owe its existence to village observations of Western medical successes, perceptions of its prevalence can presumably be enhanced by improving perceptions of these successes. This can be brought about both by improving the success rate amongst presenting cases and by increasing the numbers of cases presenting. Prompt and efficacious treatment is of obvious and fundamental importance to improving success rates, but the greater scope lies in increasing the number of cases presenting.

Radio announcements could well be the vital catalyst. Short, well-crafted public announcements – preferably during the popular *Toksave* programs – could emphasize the prevalence of *sik nating*, its capacity to kill, and the possibility of *positively* diagnosing it. Key symptomatological clusters could be presented as diagnostic of early stages of its sub-types: an obvious candidate is the *sik malaria* cluster that some people already vaguely accept as a positive diagnosis. The value of Western medicines in alleviating physical discomfort also deserves further advertisement. The use of the health center for confinements could almost certainly be increased by resuming the highly popular practice of outfitting the newborn with little smocks. Finally, greater attendance can be achieved by improving accessibility. More outlying aid posts could be furnished,[16] peripatetic medical personnel might be provided, and the vehicles available to the health center might usefully be expanded beyond the current single truck, which is usually unavailable for transporting the sick because of administrative and peripatetic clinic duty.

NOTES

1. The field research on which this paper is based was funded by the Emslie Horniman

Scholarship Fund, the Ford Foundation, and the University of Rochester. It was sponsored by the Department of Community Medicine at the University of Papua New Guinea. The National Archives of Papua New Guinea granted permission for publication of data from Yangoru patrol reports. The assistance of these institutions is very gratefully acknowledged. Barbara Wais Roscoe deserves especial thanks for collecting the majority of information obtained from female informants, as does Stephen Frankel for his comments on a previous draft. As always, though, my greatest debt must be to the kind people of Sima village who provided such extensive assistance and warm hospitality between 1979 and 1981.
2. 40,000 is a reasonable round figure estimate of the total number of Boiken in Papua New Guinea.
3. Thereafter, natural increase declined to about 1.6% as a rapid expansion in male urban migration temporarily separated married couples, reducing the birth rate.
4. Because of difficulties in reconstructing birth occurrences, these figures include still births and late term, spontaneous abortions.

Partly as a result of local opposition, regular maternal and child health visits were not extended to Sima until the early 1970s. However, many Sima mothers had attended the regular clinics at Kworabre village since their inception in 1963 (Fitzgibbon 1981).
5. Directed since 1968 by nursing sisters of the Yangoru Catholic Mission, the health center was fully nationalized in 1980 under a health extension officer.
6. A few changes are apparent. After the Japanese and their village assistants had regularly visited the summit of Mt Hurun without ill effect, villagers concluded that Hurun did not visit sickness on unauthorized visitors as they had previously supposed. With the demise of male initiation, there have also been changes in beliefs about pollution.

Because informants may have forgotten changes in their beliefs, there are obvious methodological perils in using oral information gathered in 1980 as evidence for a general lack of change in belief. However, Sima villagers appeared to remember changes perfectly well and were capable, for example, of tracing in detail the evolution of their ideas about Europeans, the operation of cameras, and so on.
7. A minority of villagers venture that *sik nating* may be fatal, at least to small children.
8. *Sik nating* is known to have several forms, but since most villagers believe that medical technologies are what diagnose its sub-types, they show little interest in *sik malaria*, *sik TB* etc.
9. The percentage per capita admission rates of males and females to the Yangoru health center in 1979 were:

AGE	MALES	FEMALES
<19	23.38	19.18
20–39	11.6	19.2
40–59	18.1	12.0
60–79	22.4	8.9

(Figures for females do not include admissions for birth-related events.)
10. Informants claim that testing the pulse was an ancestral tradition as well as a modern practice. There is evidence that the pulse was recognized in earlier days, but villagers' general lack of expertise in taking it, and their attempts to justify the practice by referring to Western medical procedure must cast some doubt on these assertions.
11. Villagers claim that medical personnel often diagnose an illness as *sik nating* or *sik bilong ples*. There is evidence that national health staff sometimes refer to an illness as: "Something that concerns you people up there" (i.e., of magico-religious origin). But villagers claim European workers will also diagnose *sik bilong ples*. A European nurse at the Boram hospital, who had conscientiously labored to teach herself Neo-

melanesian did, in fact, frequently employ this diagnosis. It transpired that she was using it to mean a minor ailment that had come up in a particular place in the patient's body. In other instances, though, it appears that villagers have seriously misinterpreted medical pronouncements. The actual words would be: "I don't know what your sickness is", but because villagers recognize Europeans as experts in *sik nating* and incompetents where *sik bilong ples* is concerned, they had inferred that the diagnosis must be the latter, not the former.

12. My efforts to provide a rudimentary medical service to the entire Sima population, for example, met with considerable initial resistance from members of the descent group adopting me, who argued that I should charge for my services.
13. The food at the Yangoru health center is prepared by an adult male. There is therefore no danger that food will have been contaminated by a menstruating woman.
14. Sima had as a resident one of the two or three old denizens of the southern foothills who are versed in a magic that cures sorcery by drawing the patient's exuviae out of the sorcerer's bundle. The efficacy of this practice is held in some doubt, and it was noticeable that most clients of the Sima practitioner were ambulatory patients from other villages. Sima villagers tended to the tried and trusted method of sorcery discussion and accusation to cure sorcery. Halfway through fieldwork, Sima's practitioner died without passing on her secrets.
15. Villages situated closer to the Wingei than the Yangoru health center are excluded from the sample.
16. When fieldwork ended in mid-1981, an aid post was about to open in Hambeli village.

ANN CHOWNING

10. THE DOCTOR AND THE CURER: MEDICAL THEORY AND PRACTICE IN KOVE

INTRODUCTION

Although the time covered by my visits to Kove stretches from 1966 to 1983,[1] this was not a period of major change in attitudes towards the use of traditional as opposed to foreign medical services. Most such changes had occurred much earlier. What tended to vary during this later period was the availability of certain services and consequently the use made of them. As will be seen, there has probably never been consensus about the relative worth of various diagnoses and cures and the variety of alternatives has steadily increased in recent years, leading to a complex situation which makes it difficult to predict the action taken in any particular case. At best, it is only possible to understand why the complexities exist.

Almost all of something over 4000 Kove (or Kombe) occupy a narrow stretch of the north coast of West New Britain, in the old Kombe Census Division just to the west of the Willaumez Peninsula, apart from two breakaway villages much farther west.[2] Most of the fifteen official villages in the main area are located on small offshore islands, in an effort to escape the mosquitoes of the mainland with its fringe of mangrove swamps. Over time some of these have become hopelessly overcrowded and have established additional settlements back on the mainland. With one exception, all Kove villages are on the beach or on islands and for transport they use watercraft. Even on the mainland, the streams and swamps make it impossible to travel for any great distance on foot. Canoes are particularly important to the island settlements, since most have no supply of fresh water, no firewood and no vegetable foods except coconuts and a few papayas. But apart from needing to get supplies and to work in the gardens, people like to bathe in fresh water and feel stimulated by visits to the mainland; if transport is available, most Kove spend several days a week away from the village. In addition, the pattern of ceremonial exchanges often demands that whole families stay for many months in other villages, neglecting their gardens and depending on kin for food and housing (see Chowning 1978). The Kove are famous in West New Britain for cultural conservatism, including their enthusiasm for these exchanges, but in fact much of what looks so traditional is the product of considerable change in the years since the Germans first came to Kove shortly before World War I.

The Germans had established several plantations near Kove, and some men went to work for them, but the great period for wage labor began after the Australians took over and established a government post, Talasea, on the Willaumez Peninsula. Although most Kove men worked as plantation laborers or domestic servants, a considerable number became policemen and the wives of some of these travelled

S. Frankel and G. Lewis (eds.), *A Continuing Trial of Treatment*. 217–247.
© 1989, Kluwer Academic Publishers, Dordrecht – Printed in the Netherlands.

widely through the Territory of New Guinea along with their husbands. The Kove were exposed to the customs of not only their co-workers but also to the people among whom they lived, from the Gazelle Peninsula to the Eastern Highlands. Furthermore, as pacification made travel safer, the Kove began their present careers as long-distance traders, regularly visiting and acquiring rituals from other societies, especially those to the west.

Visitors also came to Kove, notably Roman Catholic missionaries, who established a permanent mission station there in 1930 and put catechists, many of them Tolai, in several villages. Occasional government patrols came through as well, and the Kove visited Talasea as they traded with the Bakovi of the Willaumez. Patrol officers, European priests, plantation managers and the other Europeans for whom they worked, gave them some access to new types of medicine and laid the basis for the present day belief that all Europeans have a considerable amount of medical knowledge as well as possession of many medications which they only occasionally are willing to share with Papua New Guineans.

This period of freer movement around the Territory was brought to an abrupt halt by World War II. Northwest New Britain was in Japanese hands for almost two years, during which time Allied air raids forced the Kove to abandon their villages and hide in the bush, afraid to light fires in the open or to visit their gardens during daylight. The arrival of the Americans in mid-1943 was welcome not only because it brought an end to many hardships but because of generous donations of American food and medical care. To this day most Kove, including those born after the war was over, have an idealized picture of America which includes the belief that any goods of American manufacture are superior to those from other sources.[3]

During the post-war years the Kove changed their work patterns, increasingly scorning plantation labor in favor of semi-skilled jobs on ships and in fields such as carpentry. Education in the Roman Catholic schools had been minimal, but in the early 1950s a Seventh Day Adventist mission was established within Kove, at Silovuti, and in time a boarding school was attached to it. Many children insisted on going to the Seventh Day Adventist schools, even if their parents were Catholics, because the education was considered to be better. A number of the boys proceeded to the mission's high school near Rabaul. Although the new mission won some adult converts, few were able to observe all the new prohibitions, especially those on smoking and chewing betel nut; the most fervent mission adherents, and the ones most affected by mission theories about health, tend to be younger men (under forty in 1983) who had the longest mission education. For some years the wife of the pastor at Silovuti ran a clinic which was patronized even by Catholics who lived nearby. Unfortunately for the mission, it was decided that the headquarters for the Kapuluk Timber Project (see below) had to be built at Silovuti, and although the mission headquarters shifted to another part of Kove, it no longer offered medical facilities and also cut back on its educational facilities.

While a clinic was available at Silovuti, near the eastern end of Kove, the people living at the western end could go to the Roman Catholic mission station in Kaliai, just beyond their borders, which was run by European nuns. For a considerable time the priest in Kove was alone at his station, but in the early 1970s this was shifted to Sasavoru on the mainland just so it could be enlarged, with a hospital and facilities for nuns who, initially were European. They have been replaced by Papua New Guineans (two of the last three priests have also been nationals), but Sasavoru continues to offer the only hospital facilities within Kove. One of the nuns carried out the maternal and child health (MCH) programme, aiming to make a monthly visit to each village in the mission dinghy. The nun working there in 1983 wanted all babies to be born at Sasavoru, but some women had more confidence in European nuns and, if possible, preferred to go to Bitokara, the Roman Catholic mission on the Willaumez. Certainly many, though not all, women preferred to have their babies in hospital but, as far as their husbands were concerned, the problem was transportation. The canoes suitable for longer trips were likely to be tied up in the exchange system and though by the late 1970s almost every village had an outboard motor, there were constant problems of paying for its hire and for petrol, even when that was available locally.

Fig. 22. Papuan medical assistant, assisted by aid post orderly, carrying out a medical inspection.

The same difficulty of transportation applied to getting medical aid anywhere. Kove who could reach Talasea had access to medical care there. By the early 1950s a European medical assistant was assisted by men from various parts of Papua New Guinea; Talasea, sometimes with a qualified doctor in charge, remained the principal government hospital in the region until the early 1970s, when the Kimbe hospital was constructed. Kimbe was much farther away from Kove than Talasea but comparatively easy to reach once the road between Kimbe and Talasea was completed; the problem was to reach Talasea. Serious cases were sent to Nonga in Rabaul, and the many Kove working in Rabaul in recent years also made direct use of Nonga, so that its reputation spread back to the villages.

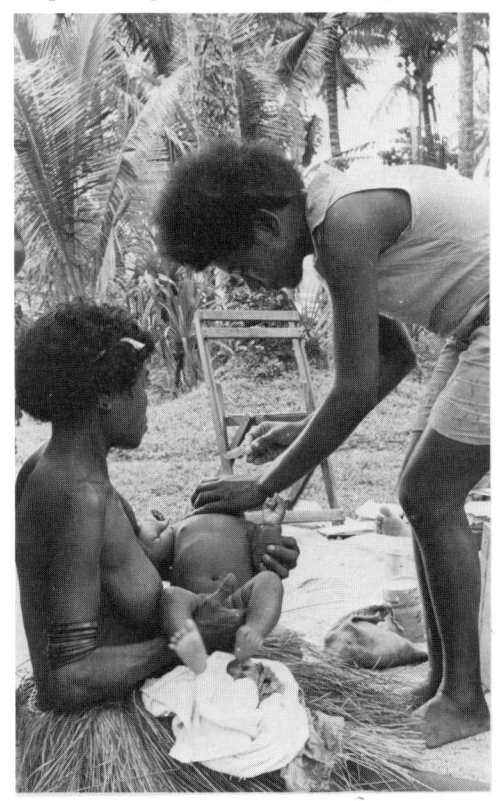

Fig. 23. Treatment administered during a maternal and child health patrol.

Meanwhile, at intervals over the years, aid posts staffed by indigenous orderlies were set up in various Kove villages and Kove orderlies were sent to other parts of New Britain. No aid posts seem to have lasted long in Kove; the few villages which have ever had aid posts report long periods after an orderly resigned or was transferred before another one would come. During the time I spent in Kove, there were never more than two aid posts functioning in the area and only in 1983 was one operating in a village in which I lived, though this was not the first one to be located there.

The final new medical influence in the area was the coming of the Kapuluk Timber Project, financed by a South Korean company. A number of Kove work at the large camp they built at Silovuti, along with people from other parts of Papua New Guinea. Some of the workers live in single barracks, while a number of families inhabit a hamlet on the edge of the site. Many other Kove regularly visit the site, called Nam Yang, to sell food to the workers and to patronize its trade store. When the official agreement was first being worked out,[4] the Kove particularly wanted medical facilities to be built on the site by the South Koreans, but as of 1983 nothing had been done. What had taken place was the purchase of "medicines" directly from South Korean workers by the Kove. Communication was greatly hampered by the failure of most South Koreans to learn Pidgin, but the Kove believed that some of their medicines were particularly effective in dealing with such problems as infertility. In addition, working at the project was thought to give the Kove additional opportunities to obtain chemical poisons with which to attack their enemies (see below).

The post-pacification emphasis on trade and travel which involves women to a much greater extent than in some Papua New Guinea societies, has meant that for many years all Kove have had some direct, and often lengthy, contact with people of different cultural backgrounds. In its effects on ideas and practice concerning medical matters, this balances their relative isolation, including their refusal until 1977 to accept local government councils,[5] and the infrequency of patrols to the area. Experience of the outside world varies greatly from one individual to another, and the variability has increased in recent years: as a number of Kove have gone on to higher education; travelled widely not only in Papua New Guinea but beyond (particularly to Australia and Japan); lived for long periods in other parts of the country; and married non-Kove, including several Australians. Although there is no simple correlation between degree of education or time spent away from Kove and the rejection of traditional beliefs, it is probably safe to say that no one retains unaltered pre-contact attitudes. Consequently, the following account of "traditional" medicine must be understood to be only partial, a reconstruction based on statements by people exposed to decades of foreign ideas and of experience, varying from individual to individual, of foreign medical practices.

TRADITIONAL MEDICINAL THEORY AND PRACTICE

Because some pertinent aspects of Kove behavior as regards health differ from those of their neighbors, a few points are worth mentioning. The traditional diet was very high in animal protein, derived mostly from shellfish collected on the reefs and in the mangrove swamps. (This supply never fails and can be obtained regardless of the weather, which often impedes net fishing by men.) All Kove expected to eat seafood every day, unless it was replaced by meat of other sorts which is even more valued: turtle or dugong, or wild or domestic pig. As elsewhere in Melanesia, domestic pork was reserved for feasts but wild pig, the only wild animal hunted or eaten with any regularity, was often caught either by individual hunters with dogs or by traps set up by garden fences. By contrast, the supply of vegetable foods, especially cultivated crops, was limited. The two starch staples were taro and sago. The villages which did not have easy access to sago stands (because it grew along streams claimed by other villages) could only obtain it by trade, but it was a highly valued food and essential when drought affected the gardens. A variety of wild fruits and nuts were also eaten, with breadfruit (sometimes planted) the one which contributed most substantially to the diet. If real famine struck, a variety of wild tubers and palms were exploited. Few green vegetables were grown or eaten; even taro leaves were rarely used.

The Kove were obsessive about bodily cleanliness, bathing in the sea daily, regardless of the weather, but complaining that skin rashes result if they did not manage to rinse off frequently in fresh water. (Rainwater caught in beached canoes was used if it was impossible to get to the mainland.) They attributed their relative freedom from *tinea imbricata* (in which they contrast notably with many of their neighbours in West New Britain) to constant bathing. They were also careful only to take drinking water from sources away from where other people bathe, because they fear illness caused by sexual pollution.

Privies did not exist, nor were faeces buried. People defecated on the beach or in shallow water just offshore, except for small children who defecated wherever they might be. Pigs also roamed freely through the villages. Human and pig faeces were cleared from the plaza, and the few waterholes that existed on the larger islands were not used if they had been fouled by pigs, but there seems to have been no idea that faeces caused disease,[6] apart from caries in children (attributed to their eating their own faeces). Children were teased for collecting and eating the tiny shellfish found along the tideline, on the grounds that these eat faeces, but adults considered them distasteful rather than dangerous. Children were allowed to play on, and with, the soil or sand of the village, and were allowed to continue eating food that had fallen onto or rested on it as long as visible dirt was brushed off.

Furthermore, there was no idea that visible insects carried disease. Mosquito and bedbug bites were much disliked, but only because of the immediate pain and effects of their bites. Flies were equally disliked, especially if they clustered on sores, but not because they were considered dangerous.

Contact with the dead was considered somewhat dangerous, in that those handling the corpse should wash carefully before eating. The idea, however, seems to be one of supernatural pollution. The dead of both sexes were buried inside men's houses (traditionally ground-based, in contrast to family houses) and later the mandible was exhumed and used in ceremonies. Other relics of the dead, particularly pieces of clothing, were worn by the bereaved or kept for months until mortuary ceremonies were made, at which time they were burned. Avoidance of the house in which someone had died was a sign of mourning and not of fear.

With perhaps a few minor exceptions such as ringworm, the traditional causes of disease and death had nothing to do with contagion. The possible causes varied somewhat with the sex, age and marital status of the victim; in addition, diagnosis partly depended on the symptoms. The death of a very young child was usually attributed to attack by spirits, either a ghost of dead kin angry with the child's parents or a spirit of non-human origin (Pidgin *masalai*) whose territory had been intruded upon by the parents. Sudden serious illness in an older child might also be blamed on a *masalai*, whereas failure to thrive was more likely to be attributed to one or both of the parents having sexual intercourse while the child was still breast-feeding (see Chowning 1985).

If, however, a child who had been doing well showed a sudden deterioration, it might be considered a changeling, a spirit child substituted for the human one when the latter cried and only the spirit came. Human carelessness alone could, of course, account for certain serious accidents or even death in children who, for example, fell off the verandah of a house or drowned. It could also produce other illnesses; for example, fever and headache in a baby might be the result of the mother's eating any of several fish which should be avoided while she was breast-feeding.

With older children, certain specific symptoms suggested that either a parent or the child itself had run afoul of a magical spell placed on someone else's property (see below). Other illnesses, especially those which either left the child disabled (as by deafness) or which killed it in a day or two, were usually if not always blamed on sorcery[7] actually aimed at parents. (Children were considered more vulnerable to sorcery than adults and, as will be seen, women than men.) Some lesser ailments had easily identifiable causes: sores on the nose, for example, were the result of eating a kind of seafood taboo to one's patrilineal descent group, and acne was simply an accompaniment of adolescence.

As with older children, serious diseases in adults, as well as their deaths from a variety of immediate causes such as "accidents" tended to be attributed to sorcery. Often the victim was thought to be chosen because of being weaker than the actual offender – a wife, a child, or an aged parent. A woman's difficulties with childbirth (delays, miscarriage) might, however, be blamed on a ghost but, if she died, sorcery would again be implicated. Essentially the afflictions of adults were distinguished according to whether or not they were seriously disabling or fatal. Those which were would, with two exceptions, be blamed on sorcery. Death in warfare or as the result of other violence might have no other cause,[8] though sometimes a man was thought to have been exceptionally weak because of too much contact with women. In a different way, this could also cause respiratory disease in a married man whose wife wanted to get rid of him. By putting vaginal secretions or menstrual blood into his food, she could slowly "poison" him and,if she was not persuaded to stop, he would die. These deaths apart, the rest were generally thought to involve some sorcery, with the single exception of a few old people who died without showing any dramatic final symptoms, simply of age. With other deaths, sorcery might be simply a contributing factor, weakening the person so that he could be finished off by ghosts or, conversely, causing one or two victims of an epidemic to die when the rest recovered.

Death in itself tended to be taken as evidence that sorcery was involved, but by that point nothing could be done but to try to ascertain who was responsible and then avenge the death. It was more important, but also more difficult, to identify sorcery as a cause of illness before death occurred. There were other possible causes – infringement of spells on property, contact with areas inhabited by *masalai*, epidemics caused by earthquakes, the efforts of ghosts to attract to them a person already weakened by some other ailment. Sorcery tended to be diagnosed if the attack was very sudden, if it seemed life-threatening and if the person or one of his close kin had offended a known sorcerer. If the disease was long drawn out, it was assumed that the sorcerer wanted to be bought off rather than to kill the victim, and it was common practice to approach a number of known sorcerers with offerings of shell money and to ask them to undo the spell. Sorcerers were often hired, and in some cases were also thought to cooperate in a single killing, so that it was necessary to pay off each one in order to effect a cure. In general, it was thought that only the person responsible for a sorcery attack could undo its effects (but see below). In contrast to many Melanesian societies, a number of Kove men found it financially and socially profitable to acquire reputations as sorcerers (see Chowning, in press), so that there was often little doubt as to whom to approach. (If one or two accepted payment and the person still died, it would be assumed that other identified sorcers had also been involved.)

Sometimes the sick person diagnosed the cause of the disease himself. Apart from knowing that he had offended a known sorcerer, he might also know that he had stolen coconuts from a man who controlled the spell that produced a certain effect, such as the kind of sore called "fish-eye". In the latter case, the offender needed to pay for the theft and apologize. Sometimes, however, a person (particularly a child) might unwittingly fall foul of such a spell, and in that case the person responsible might neutralize it on request. If it was not known who placed the particular spell, it was possible to appeal to someone else who knew the same sort of spell. Depending on his relation to the sick person, he might expect to be paid.

Revelation of the cause of illness could also come in dreams or delirium, when the soul of the sick person saw the soul of the sorcerer or a ghost and might learn more about the causes of the affliction. Sometimes the ghosts encountered were helpful ones, who explained that sorcery was not involved in an accident, or indicated how their anger could be averted. More commonly, however, specialist curers (*valuvalu*) were the ones who sent their souls in dreams to ascertain the causes of sickness and to deal with those responsible. These curers knew spells and techniques to treat a wide variety of ailments, from fits to delayed childbirth. Whether they charged a fee depended on the work involved as well as their relation to the victim. Reciting a spell over an aromatic substance (most commonly ginger or betel pepper) and spitting it onto an unconscious body required a minimum of effort, since the materials were always available. Equally undemanding were brief manipulations intended to draw sickness out of the victim's body. If the curer had to travel to another village, or had to prepare complicated concoctions, he or she was more likely to charge, and this was also true if they undertook the dangerous work of soul rescue. If sickness in a baby or young child was diagnosed as having resulted from the capture of the child's soul by a *masalai*, the curer magically sent his soul, while his body slept, into the spirit world to locate that of the child and its captor. He could then or later either bribe the *masalai* to release the soul, by offering it shell money (which he held in his hand while sleeping) or try to intimidate it by enlisting the help of the ghosts of his own kin, who "physically" attacked the *masalai* with weapons. Some curers also claimed to be able to attract the souls of sorcerers so that they could be identified, and a few actually claimed to be able to cure the effects of sorcery attacks for which they had not themselves been responsible. More generally, curers were consulted to help restore to full health those who were left thin and weak after recovery from serious illness.

It is worth noting that apart from infringement of spells placed on property, sickness brought about by magic or by spirits had little to do with moral transgressions. The ghost of a dead relative might announce in a dream that it had killed a child because it was angry about misbehavior by the child's parent, and sometimes the offense was indeed a moral one, such as adultery, but equally often the ghost was cross about not receiving a share of the bride price for a wedding that took place after the person had died. Sorcery threats were used to enforce many prohibitions, such as those that prevented a woman from showing disrespect for the rituals of the men's houses, and they also made the younger men obey their elders (see Chowning in press). Most sorcery attacks, however, were assumed to be motivated by envy or resentment rather than righteous anger. No powerful spirits or gods upheld general moral standards in Kove, or punished transgressions; only the sea creatures associated with patrilineages attacked the members who ate their representatives.

In dealing with ailments that did not threaten life the immediate, and often the only, concern was to alleviate the symptoms. For some ailments everyone knew a remedy, and there was no need to summon a specialist unless complications developed. Most people habitually carried ginger in their baskets to eat for stomach aches, and flakes of obsidian with which to make incisions along the brow line to relieve headaches. Powdered lime, used for betel chewing, could be employed to dry up bleeding wounds; alternatively, a palm frond was burned to ashes and these were applied. Stonefish abound in Kove but are considered painful rather than dangerous, and people knew how to alleviate some of the pain by incising the site of the wound ("changing the blood") and then applying crab flesh to it. Some afflictions could be dealt with simply by adjusting the diet, as by avoiding breadfruit if suffering from constipation, and salty food if one had a respiratory infection; or, conversely, eating cooked bananas (but no raw fruit) if suffering from diarrhea, and seafood or sugarcane for gastric pains.

In addition to the remedies which almost everyone seemed to know, some seem to have been specialized knowledge in a few families. If no magic was involved, the knowledgeable one apparently was willing to share his knowledge without charge, advising others to use breast milk for conjunctivitis or the juice of a particular plant for a painful wound. I do not know whether those who claimed specialized knowledge of how to reduce dislocations or resuscitate drowning victims charged for their services. The ones who did charge, if treating non-kin, were older women who specialized in gynaecological problems and ailments in young babies. The same woman[9] who prescribed contraceptives (based on charm ginger) would be summoned to deal with abdominal pains during pregnancy or delays in giving birth, all involving magical remedies; another woman who claimed to be able to produce twins (considered undesirable) in those who offended her also knew of special remedies for constipation in babies and others to promote their growth. I do not know whether any of these individuals claimed to have obtained their knowledge through contact with supernatural beings, as has happened more recently (see below).

Finally, some individuals decided on the basis of personal experience that certain foods did not agree with them, or that certain activities or places were dangerous. They did expect others to follow their example, but simply explained that fish made them feel sick, or that smoking made them dizzy.[10] It was not suggested that others should follow their example.

To the best of my knowledge, traditional curing went no further than this. Unlike the Tolai, the Kove performed no operations apart from cutting out intrusive objects. Lacking interest in the bush, they are unfamiliar with the range of both poisonous and medicinal plants that are used in other parts of New Britain. This is not to say that they took ill health or pain for granted, but that they did not feel capable of dealing with many of their afflictions except by trying to find the person responsible, if there was one, and asking him or her to stop carrying out the dangerous activity[11] or to neutralize it. The readiness with which many foreign medical practices were accepted indicates the degree of dissatisfaction with the traditional situation. (All of the beliefs and practices just described still existed in 1983.)

DISEASES IN KOVE

Before discussing changes in medical practice, it is worth mentioning what little is known about the present occurrence of specific diseases in Kove. Presumably the situation there differs little from that in most other coastal regions and, in the absence of any accurate surveys, what follows is necessarily impressionistic and incomplete with, for example, almost no data on venereal disease and little on malnutrition. The first source of data is my own observations, including comparisons with the other three societies in which I have lived. The second is statements made by medical personnel, ranging from visiting doctors to aid post orderlies, and the third is Kove reports on such matters as symptoms, the existence of epidemics, and whether certain afflictions are congenital.

The Kove were visited by medical patrols prior to World War I, the most thorough of which was Kopp's journey along the north coast of New Britain. Unfortunately he either lumps the Kove together with other societies or offers specific data only for their neighbors, so that his data do not demonstrate any local peculiarities. His impressions may nevertheless offer something of a base line for the situation from the Nakanai area to Kilenge. He noted that children and young people looked well nourished, but attributed the lack of fat in older people to inadequate nutrition. Without data on ages, he also stated that the people tended to die young. He documented the presence of yaws, scabies, two varieties of tinea, anemia (judged from the pallor of the gums), a little filariasis (but said that it is rare compared with other parts of German New Guinea), three cases of leprosy, hookworm in the region west of Kove (the only one in which he could overcome sorcery fears to get a sample of feces), and tuberculosis. Because this last disease was most common in young men, he concluded that it had been acquired through wage labor outside the area and was an introduced disease. He noted that the presence of malaria had been confirmed by an earlier expedition, and found many enlarged spleens. He assumes that other intestinal parasites were present and attributes the anemia to these. Another diagnosis was more tentative: finding numerous cases of loose teeth and bleeding gums, he suggested that the cause might be scurvy, though not ruling out other explanations. What may have been tropical ulcers ("loathsome gangrenous sores") he attributed to secondary infection of scabies, but offered no explanation of lumps under the skin, said to be common (Kopp 1913: 729–49).

When I began fieldwork in 1966, yaws had been eliminated by the government campaign of the late 1950s. My observations indicated that by comparison with Lakalai, Molima, and Kove, tinea imbricata is very rare (see above). Scabies is not uncommon, and athletes foot is said to flourish in the rainy season, "caused" by mud between the toes. Boils are very common (though no more so than in the Sengseng village I visited in 1981–2) but tropical ulcers are virtually non-existent. I saw three cases of elephantiasis of the legs. Since I contracted hepatitis while living there, it is probably safe to attribute some of the reported cases of "painful liver"[12] and jaundice ("yellow skin") to that. Conjunctivitis is also common. Complaints frequently brought to me included stomach pains, diarrhea and constipation (which is considered serious and even life-threatening by the Kove). Again by comparison with other societies, there seemed to be much deafness, as well as deformities of the external ear. Some simply developed in old age (along with difficulties with vision), and some was congenital, including two cases in siblings. Most deafness, however, was said to have resulted from serious illness in early or late childhood. That deafness is more common than elsewhere is suggested by the well-developed system of sign language, which is used largely but not exclusively to communicate with both the deaf and those with speech disorders, although some of the latter were not deaf at all and those who were seemed to be able to lip-read.

It is important to note that by contrast with many inhabitants of Papua New Guinea, the Kove do not feel that they have been afflicted by many new diseases since European contact. The smallpox epidemic of the late 1890s is part of recent history but antedated first-hand contact with Europeans. The Kove say that the later epidemic of *lepra* (leprosy and similar-looking skin diseases) which attacked the Kilenge to the west did not reach them. Neither did the dysentery epidemics that Kopp dreaded strike the Kove area. I have been in Kove during several epidemics – one reported by the nuns to be chicken pox; one (attacking mostly children) which to my eye combined symptoms of mumps and measles;[13] and at least two of respiratory disease – and although people complained, they did not feel that they were in danger, nor did anyone get seriously ill. Medically, Europeans are seen as a source of new remedies and not of new ailments.

The early years of contact may in fact have brought with them new diseases unbeknownst to the Kove, but they also brought some overall improvements in their situation as regards general health. The prohibition of warfare did not wholly prevent violent encounters between armed groups, which still occur from time to time, but it did eliminate the sort of raid in which an entire village would be attacked. Presumably the general shift to offshore islands also greatly reduced exposure to malaria, though in time the advantage would have been reduced because of lengthy visits outside Kove. The introduction of new crops also improved nutrition; specifically, the relatively drought-resistant starch staples (manioc, sweet potato and Xanthosoma) almost eliminated the frequent drastic food shortages of the past. The shift has not been wholly advantageous; over the years, especially after the taro blight of the 1960s, gardeners have increasingly relied on manioc, though many people dislike it as a steady diet. Rice is very popular (and because of its use on plantations is considered a European staple), but the local tradestores do not have a steady supply, nor is money always available to buy it. For the rural Kove, trade store foods are still luxuries.

A major change in diet resulted from the compulsory planting of coconuts prior to World War II. Intended by the government as a source of cash income, they have been more important as food and drink. Once coconuts were few and largely reserved for feasts; now people drink the milk and eat the flesh, raw or cooked, daily. Introduced fruits such as pineapple and papaya, while much liked, are eaten more sporadically, and such new vegetable crops as tomatoes, onions, and stringbeans are grown by only a few people. There has been some improvement in village water supplies with the construction of tanks by a few individuals but, except when rainfall is heavy, the owners restrict access to the water. Most people still get most of their water from the mainland. If it is too stormy to travel, they drink coconut milk instead.

New fishing equipment and techniques, ranging from hook and line to, more recently, home-made spear guns used with goggles, has reduced dependence on hand nets and spears, enabling boys and old men to get fish without waiting for large groups to assemble to use seines. On the whole, apart from the period when bottle feeding of babies was favored by some (in emulation of "European" behavior, on the assumption that it benefited the child), nutrition has probably improved in recent years except for the Seventh Day Adventists (see below). The situation is likely to deteriorate, however, as it already has for Kove living in towns. Kove generally believe that all European foods are not only tastier and more pleasant to eat than their own, but nutritionally superior. They point out the large size of European children and the superior health of Europeans of all ages as evidence. Having an erroneous idea of the actual composition of a European diet (which is assumed to contain no fruit or vegetables), they think that a two-year-old is better fed on dry biscuits and very sweet milkless tea than on village foods (see Chowning 1985).

As has been noted, the influence of Seventh Day Adventist teachings has only affected some of the Kove, and a number of them are reputed or known to ignore some of the taboos. For the observant, the prohibition on pork, all shellfish and many other seafoods such as shark, stingray, and turtle reduces available protein to bony fish. When the weather makes fishing for these impossible, those who cannot buy tinned fish or meat from a trade store may have no animal protein in their diets for lengthy periods. (Those at boarding school at least eat a wide variety of vegetables, but do not plant these when they return to the village.) Of course, this disadvantage is somewhat balanced by the other prohibitions – on tea and coffee, alcohol, tobacco and betel nut. Reports from converts indicate that the attitude towards pork is the most strongly entrenched; they are taught that all pork is infested with disease. The Kove hardly needed to be instructed in bathing by missionaries, but the use of soap was new and so, probably, was hot water. (So is the insistence on clean nails, still observed by only a few.) As regards both body and clothes, soap is certainly not used every day, since most bathing and rinsing of clothes is still done in salt water. When fresh water is used, soap is considered desirable, but not everyone can afford it (and for those who do, the water once used for bathing and washing clothes is often muddy and full of soap scum).

CHANGES FOLLOWING CONTACT

Of all the changes produced in the colonial period that affected theory or practice relating to disease and death, the least significant was Christianity. Both Roman Catholic and Seventh Day Adventist missionaries regard the Kove in general as notably resistant to their teachings, and my observations confirm their impressions. Doubtless there are exceptions, but the behavior of even those who represent themselves as pillars of the church usually indicates only partial acceptance of that church's doctrines. By contrast with other societies with an equivalent length of exposure to missionaries (such as Lakalai and Molima), the Kove rarely attribute ailments to God, and even more rarely employ prayer for curative purposes. One man did tell me of averting what he thought might be a serious illness (heralded by an odd pain in his temple) by reciting numerous prayers, but his action was exceptional.

When the anger of God is suggested as the cause of misfortune, the usual reason is violation of a holy day. I have heard this offered as the cause of the death of a man who fell from a tree while gathering nuts on a Catholic holy day; of the death in childbirth of a woman who worked daily rather than observing the rest day of either mission; and of an old man getting lost in the bush, "because he went hunting at Christmas" (actually two days after it.) The mother and sister of a boy paralyzed by a fall from a tree, themselves members of different churches, suggested that the reason was that the boy had changed his church affiliation several times. That such offences might be punished so severely indicates much about what the churches stress. I have never heard a Kove suggest that God punishes theft or adultery, though one man, on the basis of a vision when he had "died", concluded that sorcerers were condemned to a miserable after-life and said that he had abandoned sorcery for that reason.

The one moral offence it seems to be widely agreed that God would punish is infanticide. In the traditional society, this was not an offense (though impregnating an unmarried girl was) and infanticide, not so construed, still is practiced if a child is born badly deformed and so "not human". From all accounts, illegitimate births have greatly increased in recent years as a result of the loosening of sexual standards (partly because of the colonial laws licensing intercourse between the unmarried and partly because of emulation of "European" ways). Such births are still deplored, however, and it is not uncommon for the woman or her kin to try to kill the baby. When one succeeded in 1983, the reaction of both men and women to the news was, "God will punish her" (along with the government). I also heard two different women ascribe the reproductive history of one woman, who had had many children die shortly after birth, to God's punishment because her husband had killed his sister's illegitimate baby (but see below). They gave the same reason for the handicaps of some of the sister's children (two deaf, two cross-eyed); she had allowed her brother to kill the child. Both of them had also been gaoled, so again God's punishment was additional. Essentially this is regarded as similar to the punishment inflicted by ghosts. Nothing can be done to mitigate either kind, though God may voluntarily decide that someone has suffered enough, as when He allowed the last two children born to the first woman to live. In traditional Kove belief, there were no spiritual beings other than ghosts that punished moral offenses, and even ghosts rarely did so. For most people, the possibility that God is involved simply affords an explanation for baffling cases. For example, the paralyzed boy was too young to be a likely candidate for sorcery and his father was long dead. Retaining their traditional belief that such disasters cannot be accidental, the boy's kin proposed this explanation.[14]

Over the years, the importance of traditional sorcery is thought to have diminished somewhat, as the old men die without having taught their spells to their sons. The reason seems to be patterns of migrant labor rather than as in some other societies, obedience to mission pressures to eliminate sorcery. (Nevertheless, sons of well-known sorcerers are often assumed to have learned the techniques, and are likely to be among the suspects when someone becomes seriously ill). Going away to work did, however, give Kove men many opportunities to learn new ways of harming their fellows. In particular, they are often supposed to have bought new forms of magic from various people in East New Britain who have a reputation for possessing powerful sorcery. From time to time, rumors that a new technique or magical substance has been acquired spread throughout Kove and even reach government officers.[15] Some of these introduced forms are greatly feared, not only because they may be thought to act very rapidly (being called "one-day") but because no one may know the counter-spells. As with traditional sorcery, the threat of using these is often used by men trying to collect debts.

In addition, the Kove have long had a reputation for using chemicals acquired from European sources as direct non-magical poisons. Traditionally, no chemical poisons were used for killing others, though swallowing Derris (cultivated as a fish poison) was and is a common way of committing suicide. But long before my first visit to Kove, I heard that they were given to killing by putting battery acid in a victim's food. I doubted that this was done or, if done, that it was successful, because Kove food is so bland that it seemed unlikely that much acid could be ingested without detection. Nor did the Kove themselves mention this particular poison. Over the years I have heard many accusations within Kove of the use of chemical poisons, acquired by workmen of various sorts, being used to kill. It is also reported that various chemicals have been found hidden in houses or buried outside them, and these have been cited as evidence in murder cases. With the recent great increase in the consumption of alcohol, beer is assumed to be the usual vehicle; if a man collapses and dies soon after a drinking bout, deliberate poisoning is suspected. In the cases I have heard discussed, the motives are envy (for example, of one man's financial and social success as a carver) or revenge (for a heavy blow struck during a quarrel, or as payback for sorcery performed by the victim). Men do not advertise their possession of these substances except to close kin who wish to use them, as they do with magical spells, and so their social use is more limited.

The new forms of sorcery and the chemicals are both used for the same reasons that motivated the use of traditional sorcery, but I have not heard it suggested that anyone uses other than traditional techniques to uphold such norms as respect for the men's house and for rituals. Indeed, such respect is reported to be declining as the old men die. Power is gradually shifting to the younger men, and now much of it is based on new knowledge.[16] Because even chemical poison, with no magic involved, is called by the same term in both Kove and Pidgin as sorcery, in discussions of threats or killings it is not always clear that new methods are thought to have been used, but obviously present day Kove feel as vulnerable to surreptitious attack by their fellows as in the past. If foreign magical techniques are suspected, and if the sorcery does not kill rapidly, the victim may then seek the aid of a foreign curer (see below).

Foreign chemicals are also used, or tried, for suicide (for example DDT, which is handled carelessly by the spray teams and is easy to obtain). Some experts claim to know methods of saving would be suicides which differ according to the poison taken, but I have never heard of success. Certain substances are simply thought to be poisonous; for example, one man asked me to hide his wife's soap powder when she was threatening suicide (possibly they had confused its effects with that of bleach). On the other hand, foreign substances may be thought to have a variety of benefits. As I have described elsewhere (Chowning 1982a) Kove think that drinking alcohol fattens babies but is a contraceptive for women. In 1983 women discussed with me the rumor that abortions could be produced by swallowing tea leaves or tobacco. The substance most widely believed to be medicinal, if used externally, is kerosene. It is considered to be an antiseptic, and is routinely applied to wounds, including the incisions made in the foreskin and earlobes of children. Other Papua New Guineans share this idea about kerosene, and I suspect that the Kove learned it on plantations.

Some people, however, have individual theories about foreign substances that are their own conclusions. One man, for example, advocated constant bathing in hot water to counteract poisoning caused by eating shellfish contaminated by the "red tide"; he blamed several deaths of children on their parents' laziness in heating the water. Others suggested that bathing in hot water would alleviate the symptoms caused by an imported form of sorcery which produced temporary insanity. Bathing in hot water is not traditional, and presumably these ideas are an expansion on mission teachings about its use. Again, although washing with soap is often tried as a remedy for skin rashes, a female curer who used soap suppositories on a sick baby was following her own inspiration. (She claimed to have received special medical knowledge while being possessed by the ghost of her dead husband.)

In at least one case, the idea of lancing infections with a miniature bow and arrow was brought back from the Eastern Highlands by policemen who had been stationed there. More frequently, individuals have gone directly to foreign curers for remedies. Sometimes doing so has been inevitable, because the person fell sick when away from home and could not be cured by other means. To an increasing degree, however, foreigners living in or near Kove acquire reputations as curers and are called upon frequently, even when long trips are necessary. They are especially useful for dealing with foreign sorcery, but may also tackle seemingly hopeless cases of other sorts. One Kove man who fell sick after hopelessly offending the man thought to be the most powerful local sorcerer knew that he had no chance of obtaining mercy from him, and tried a Tolai curer who, by using non-Kove techniques which made him vomit up the poisoned substance, cured him. (The Kove repaid him by helping him buy his wife). Often these foreign curers imposed special taboos that the person has to follow for the rest of his life, and so add to Kove theories about the treatment of disease.

With all of these new treatments, the underlying attitudes seem to be two. The first, obviously, is the success of the treatment. Lacking confidence in their ability to deal successfully with all of their afflictions and sharing, with other Papua New Guineans I know, a willingness to experiment with new techniques so long as these do not involve great effort, danger, or expense, they were willing to try new cures. If these succeeded, they would be adopted. Second, but perhaps more important was a general willingness to try anything if conventional methods failed. When someone was desperately sick, volunteers might come forward to try still another remedy or, hearing of a curer elsewhere who had a high reputation, the family of the sufferer might visit or summon him. In short, the reactions are wholly similar to those found within Western contexts, except that a wider choice of treatments might be available to the average person. Only in a few cases did I hear of someone's deciding that he had been sorcerized, refusing treatment and dying in a short time. (One was a man who suddenly found himself unable to straighten his back when he went fishing shortly after a major quarrel with a renowned sorcerer; he assumed that only sorcery could explain his condition). As will be seen, the actions taken do not necessarily conform to a unified theory of cause and possible cure. A person afflicted with what is in theory an incurable ailment does not necessarily cease to seek remedies for that reason. In any case, a major result of change is that there now exist many alternative explanations of particular ailments and deaths. The case of the woman who lost so many children was ascribed to several causes other than the wrath of God; the woman herself suggested that she and her husband were too closely related, an idea that I suspect came from foreign medical personnel. The increased recognition that diagnosis and treatment may be incorrect of course makes it possible for individuals to retain confidence in their own theories.

PRACTITIONERS OF WESTERN MEDICINE

Since the days immediately preceding World War I, the Kove had interacted with specialists in Western medicine. The sole survivor of an attack by one Kove village on the men of another, caught on a fishing expedition, was saved when a German government ship took him to hospital. Over the years, the Kove have sometimes been visited by medical patrols but more often, and to an increasing degree, visit these specialists themselves. My knowledge of the actual attitudes of the foreign specialists is very limited, derived only from what I have seen on a few occasions; from Kove reports, which are not always trustworthy; and from various conversations with one foreign aid post orderly stationed in Kove. There may nevertheless be some useful conclusions to be drawn.

The Kove themselves tend to distinguish professionals according to whether they are European or indigenous, and further according to their particular place of origin. Rarely do they have much idea of differences in expertise; the Pidgin terms *dokta* and *sista* encompass a wide range. Sometimes additional information, or lack of it, may affect the perception of certain individuals. The fact that a European medical assistant stationed at Talasea had an affair with his cook's wife seems to have reduced the respect to which his presumably superior knowledge might otherwise have entitled him. By contrast, a husband and wife pair of doctors later stationed at Talasea were highly esteemed as Americans but, because their Pidgin was poor, the Kove never learned that they were vegetarians whose ideas about diet even the local Adventists would have found unacceptable. It is pertinent to note here that the Kove consider themselves naturally superior to all other human beings (with, for some, the exception of Americans) but think that at present the knowledge held by Europeans is superior to their own. They tend to assume that few Papua New Guineans have reached a European standard of learning, but are willing and indeed happy to acknowledge that such people exist. A doctor from Bougainville who was stationed at Talasea for a period was spoken of with much respect. On the whole, however (and also in fields apart from medicine), the older and less-educated Kove consider a Papua New Guinean usually to be less competent than a European in the same field. Only the better-educated young men tend to express a different view, and they only to a limited degree. For those ailments thought to be definitely or possibly curable by European medicine, there is consequently an ideal hierarchy of resort, though logistically choice tends to be available only in certain cases.

From the point of view of outsiders, the cultural conservatism of the Kove and their reputations for disapproved behavior (for example, as people who do not garden but simply exploit their foreign affines) keeps others from sharing their high opinion of themselves. Some of the impatience with which they are treated by outsiders seems to reflect simple disdain for people considered inferior and some of it, probably, the common arrogance of experts dealing with those who do not know what is best for them. Some of it, however, shows ignorance of local conditions (as does the belief that the Kove do not garden) and insensitivity to cultural differences, coupled with reluctance to learn these things. Misunderstanding does, however, operate in both directions. The Kove have their own ideas about the motives and behavior of these specialists, and not necessarily accurate ones.

In considering what I have heard or seen, it might seem useful to distinguish all indigenous personnel from Europeans, on the assumption that the former, for example, might be likely to share some beliefs with the Kove, as in the power of sorcerers, while the latter probably do not. I have no data that would justify distinguishing European and Papua New Guinea nuns or other medical personnel apart from the aid post orderlies. I have consequently treated only the APOs as a distinct category. My impression of the others is based only on what I saw during patrols to Kove villages.

The first patrol, which included the American doctors (with poor Pidgin), had the primary aim of vaccinating everyone against smallpox. At the time, 1966, it was feared that the disease might spread from Indonesia; something was said of the dangers of the disease, but nothing of the possible consequences of the vaccination. In fact many people became ill with fever and swollen glands, and a few stated that they intended to avoid medical patrols in the future. The patrol also offended by asking the villagers to open their mouths while they were lined up in public; showing the inside of your mouth is a breach of the strongest affinal taboo in Kove, and the order caused much embarrassment.

The next three patrols involved Papua New Guinea personnel, and had the aim of inoculating the children against childhood diseases. At no point did I hear anyone attempt to explain what they were doing, and why; they simply complained that many people were away, even though they sometimes arrived without warning at times when the village was likely to be fairly deserted. The lack of understanding of their task was shown when one Kove said that, in view of the bad weather, his village did not intend to obey the summons of the team to go to another village for injections, because it was the "paid work" of the team to visit each village. Given the aloofness of many of the medical personnel, it is not surprising that the Kove expressed reluctance to ask for the contraceptive advice that many of them wanted.

When indigenous but non-Kove nuns started making the patrols, they tended to be equally impatient with the local people and with their failure to be in the village when the patrols arrived. In 1972, a sister had to be persuaded by the *tultul* to give any injection (of triple antigen) because so few children were around, although she came too early in the afternoon for people to have returned from the gardens. She also refused to examine a pregnant woman who complained of pains in her belly on the grounds that her husband should have taken her to the mission station. The sister who came twice during my stay in 1983 was also short-tempered, although she divided her complaints between the councillor, who had not told them that she was coming (by this time, impending visits were supposed to be announced over the radio); the aid post orderly, for being away during one of her visits (see below); and the people themselves, for asking her to treat ailments that they should have taken to the orderly, who was back during her second visit. After scolding, however, she did pass people who wanted injections or sores and coughs treated on to her assistant, who dealt with these matters. The sister confined herself to weighing the babies and younger children; asking the parents if the children were sick, and specifically if they had sores or coughs; taking a quick look at those said to be sick, including poking the spleen in some cases; and examining in privacy the pregnant women who presented themselves. She did have a list of the children, most of whom had cards issued by the mission which were checked against her book. On both occasions she announced on the basis of the weights, that a child was in difficulty. Possibly because she said they were sick (*sik–bun–nating*), the kin indignantly denied that anything was wrong, although the small size and slow development of one of the children occasioned much comment in the village. (It was reported that another sister had blamed the condition of this and another tiny child on the mothers' excessive smoking during pregnancy. Both women continued to smoke.) The other child, though a little smaller than his identical twin, did seem healthy, and the sister herself said nothing when she weighed him again less than a month later.

On the other hand, when the mother of several children consulted the sister because she was worried about the floppy legs and inability to stand of her youngest, the sister just said "He's still young; let's wait and see." The child's appearance (flat face, small slanting eyes, protruding tongue – Down's syndrome?) was so abnormal that it was often commented upon, some women asking at once if he was mentally deficient, and yet the sister seemed to notice nothing wrong.

Some pregnant women who were present at the time of the patrol were also given brief examinations in private, though not all presented themselves. Women were scolded if they did not give birth at the Catholic mission; they have to pay extra for the children's medical history cards if the child is born in the village. (The aid post orderly, however, does not object to village deliveries unless there is reason to suspect trouble, such as malpresentation, in which case he also urges the husband to get his wife to the mission.)

In addition to the patrols, the sisters are said recently to have taken around slides or films illustrating certain health hazards, from smoking to the use of a rusty razor blade to cut the umbilical cord. Very curious ideas about physiology, such as a brain blackened by smoke, have resulted from these shows, but some people report having been impressed by them.

Clearly reports on the behavior of Western practitioners are not always trustworthy. In particular, it is often asserted that any disease that could not be diagnosed or treated was said by the doctor to be the result of sorcery ("something of the village") or even of a *masalai* attack. Some Kove know that Europeans (who have argued with them) do not all believe in sorcery, but most think that they not only believe in it but may even practise it. Even if another diagnosis was given to the sufferer, the public at large often state that sorcery was said to be the cause. I was told this as regards the death of the daughter of an APO, though her father said that the cause had been diagnosed in Sydney as an inoperable brain tumor. In effect, saying that nothing can be done and sending a sufferer home is likely to be taken as evidence that sorcery is involved and that traditional cures should be sought. If, however, there was no traditional cure, as with paralysis, difficulties with sight, or persistent pain, then the reaction may be different. Even if the immediate cause is considered to be something like sorcery or a *masalai* attack, the sufferer or his family may continue to hope that some European will be able to effect a cure. I was frequently asked to procure American medicine to remedy the increasing blindness of one old man. The mother of a paraplegic told me that only pressure from her other children kept her from trying to take the boy to Port Moresby, after she had been told at Kimbe hospital that nothing more could be done. An old woman with painful legs also talked of trying Port Moresby (where her grandson was working), since none of the injections that she had been given over the years had alleviated the pain.

Mixed with this hope, if not trust, concerning possible Western cures, are occasional tales of the incompetence of their practitioners. A story that provoked much hilarity in 1983 dealt with the purported rescue by a woman of her still living husband from the "morgue" at Nonga; she claimed to have scolded the staff, and been admired for her behavior, as she revived her husband and took him away. On the other hand, the failure of people to follow the advice of doctors does not necessarily imply any lack of faith in it but the simple difficulty of obeying instructions to stop smoking or for a sufferer from stomach ulcers to avoid work and worry. Why some people will not take medicine prescribed for them is less clear, since the ones I asked gave no explanation.

What some doctors undoubtedly do is to prescribe medicines for future use or for the use of others, apparently oblivious of the fact that they will go to people who cannot read the instructions. One man boasted to me of his private "medicine box", saying that he preferred to go to a "private doctor" to get better medicines and instructions than are available at clinics. At the same time, he complained that many such doctors do not speak Pidgin well. (Misunderstanding may account for his telling me that on a doctor's advice he and his wife had switched from tea to coffee to cure anemia – "no blood"). I once came along as he was about to administer a strong laxative to a dying man; although he checked the instructions with me and said that he preferred to do so before passing out the medicines or taking them himself, I am sure that he usually takes a chance. Most others who have such medicines, usually bought over the counter, make no attempt to check on the purpose of the medicine or the dosage before using them. One young man said that he had recently "persuaded" a female pharmacist to sell him something that he had successfully used for producing abortions in the village. His older brother, when their father was diagnosed at the mission hospital as having tuberculosis, flew back to Kove from Port Moresby with an array of medicines, some prescription and some not, which he gave his father with the explanation that they would be superior to the mission medicines because they were from America (and had cost him a great deal of money). In fact, apart from one of the prescription drugs which I did not recognize, the only article with an American label was Benadryl Cough Expectorant. This man, one of those with an unexplained reluctance to take medicine, was said by his wife not to have used any of them, but he did pass on some of the Codral tablets to his older brother, who because of his thinness and cough was also thought to have "TB".

I should add that as in other parts of Papua New Guinea, the most popular Western medicine is *"prokain"*, a phial of procaine penicillin intended for injections, which many people have and claim to have received from aid posts or orderlies. It is used for skin and eye infections (and seems to work well).

Apart from the use of Western medicines, however procured, many Kove fear hospitalization and operations. Specifically, they are afraid that they will die. Some are afraid to stay even in the nearby mission hospital, much less in more distant ones. Overheard conversations suggest that what some individuals fear are the ghosts of the recently dead; not only are patients accommodated where others have died, but the wards are not lighted at night, and ghosts walk in the dark. Ghosts are considered a danger to adults only if they are already sick.

This point apart, the common fear of hospitals, operations and, for a few individuals, injections, seems to differ in no way from similar fears expressed by Westerners. Some fairly young and relatively well-educated people are reluctant to undergo or to let their children undergo even minor operations, such as to repair a hernia. Others may be persuaded by the success of a major operation on a kinsman to submit to a similar one. Differing reactions on the part of individuals will be examined further below.

As a final comment on attitudes towards Westerners and their medicines, it is worth noting that the colonial experience, including contact with missionaries, has left many Kove convinced that Westerners regularly lie to them or, at best, conceal part of the truth. The cargo cult of course is based on this assumption, and I am frequently accused of lying when I refuse to confirm its teachings (for example, that Americans, and perhaps all Europeans, return to life three days after death). I was also called a liar when I said that I could not procure powerful American medicines for the use of the Kove. Scepticism about medical advice from Westerners has a complex base, including observed discrimination (such as the strongly disliked spraying of houses with DDT, which they know does not happen to European houses) and the assumption that if they were receiving fully Western care, they might be as large, healthy and long-lived as Europeans. (The problem of sorcery would still remain, however).

AID POST ORDERLIES

Rather than generalize, I shall discuss them in terms of the one mentioned above, the Bakovi married to a Kove woman. My knowledge of such orderlies elsewhere, particularly in Molima, and my conversations with former Kove orderlies, suggest that he is in his general attitude typical of those of his age (perhaps mid-forties), village background and degree of training. This man has spent much of his professional life at Talasea, his own language area, but has also been stationed in two Kove villages, the second his wife's, Nukakau.

With the re-establishment of an aid post, the relations between it and the mission station have become complex. (At least one other aid post has been staffed for much of the time that the mission hospital has operated, but I had no opportunity to observe it). In contrast to some other aid posts I have seen, the aid post at Kukakau had no refrigeration, so certain drugs were available only at the mission. Neither did the aid post have any elaborate equipment; to receive an enema or have a bone set, it was necessary to go elsewhere. It also contained only the most makeshift accommodation for the sick and their families. At the same time, the orderly considered himself more knowledgeable than the present sister, saying they are only trained in "welfare" and often have to send patients back to him for expert care. He also resented it if he was not consulted before a patient was taken to the mission. The situation in 1983 was complicated by his frequent absences; although he insisted that each trip involved official business, such as trying to get a dinghy for the aid post, everyone was well aware that much time was spent on family matters. Even when in residence, he might be in his garden on a nearby island, accessible in a real emergency, but not for minor matters. He was also reluctant to work on weekends or to treat people who in theory, because of the location of their villages, should have been attending the other aid post in Kove (during the periods that it was manned). Finally, he sometimes refused to intervene in serious emergencies if people did not summon him at once and if they continued to try traditional cures in his presence rather than standing back to give him immediate access to the patient. He said that the provincial government had told him to act that way, and so justified his failure to give injections to two women suffering post-partum hemorrhage, both of whom died (see below).

As regards some diseases, the orderly believes in causes that have no element of the supernatural, and some of these causes differ from those recognized by lay members of the community. At the same time, his medical knowledge is much more limited, not to say erroneous, than he realizes. He is a Roman Catholic and prays before such endeavours as cutting into an abscess but, like most Christians in Papua New Guinea, he also believes in sorcery, omens and ghosts. He is uncertain as to whether diseases caused by sorcery can be cured by Western medicine alone, but he is always willing to try. He attributes much of his success in dealing with sorcerers to information from his father's ghost and, according to reports from others, he occasionally practices soul rescue and uses spells in curing. Apart from his use of spells, the data that follow come from what he has said in my hearing.

He is particularly concerned with persuading the Kove that children get sick because of poor diet. The sisters have made the same point concerning one family in which some of the children are thin and have swollen hands; they told the father to garden more and fish less, and the mother to serve more meals including coconut soup rather than only baking food on the fire. The mother is reported to have replied that they felt cheerful and did not quarrel when they ate so much fish, and the family seems not to have changed its diet. The orderly also failed to influence one of his Kove sisters-in-law, married to a man from elsewhere and living in Kimbe town. He attributed the extreme thinness of her children (who struck me as very unlike their sturdy cousins from Kove) to their diet of foods from stores rather than the market, including meals consisting of soft drinks and Twisties, but she simply replied that the children reject the vegetables she sometimes prepares for them. (A very few Kove advocate a varied diet and also deplore excessive reliance on food from trade stores, but the reason for the latter attitude is usually financial.)

On some other matters, especially where his ideas either fit theirs or do not contradict them, the statements of the orderly are acceptable even if they are not acted upon. Like the Kove, he thinks that bad smells are dangerous, so no one argues when he tells them to keep the village cleaner because the smell of animal excrement rises to the brain and causes sickness. If an illness is not attributed to sorcery, the Kove may also accept his explanation of it, especially if his cures work. For example, one man is said to have had an operation two years ago for a peptic ulcer, and was told to avoid work for a long while but, having no children, felt that he had to return to work to provide for his old age. When symptoms of stomach distress recurred, including bloating and pain, he disregarded kin who wanted him to consult a curer and went to the aid post. The orderly thought that the symptoms indicated recurrence of the ulcer but that the immediate problem, diagnosed as faeces "like stones", could be relieved by an enema, so he sent the patient to the Catholic mission to have that done, with reported success. In explaining the victim's condition (and that of another Kove with a similar ulcer, whom he claimed to have cured by himself "because he recognized the illness and knew what to do"), he said that worry produced an internal infection which produced pus which produced germs, leading finally to the ulcer. His accounts of the movements of a retained afterbirth, including its rising above the navel and pressing on the victim's lungs, indicates an equally shaky knowledge of anatomy, but no one is in a position to disagree.

Aspects of the case involving the retained afterbirth, which was also one of those referred to above in which the woman bled to death, indicate his shifting attitudes and behavior, as well as those of other villagers. Everyone agreed that the woman had been warned by medical personnel – presumably the nuns at the mission, but sometimes said to be "doctors" – not to bear more children after one difficult birth which had required forceps and a subsequent transfusion. Her previous six children had been born in hospital, one dying immediately after birth. Only one child was a girl, and her husband was very eager for another daughter. The woman herself said that she wanted no more children, and took the charmed ginger that is supposed to produce sterility, administered by the village specialist. She claimed, however, that the magic was undone when her husband surreptitiously fed her a kind of fish that has that effect. The orderly said that he had tried to explain the wife's condition to her husband and gave him contraceptives, but the husband threw them away. The orderly added that he thought that additional troubles resulted from the wife's having taken the ginger (saying that this always caused difficulty with subsequent pregnancies) and from the husband's recently having had syphilis, though he claimed to have cured the disease. If the woman got pregnant again, she should have visited the Catholic mission regularly for medication, especially that intended to strengthen her blood, said to have been finished by her previous pregnancies.

Once pregnant, the woman did not make a point of visiting the mission, though (contrary to later rumor) I saw her consult the sister when she was in the village at the time of a patrol. She was put on a canoe to go to the mission when labor began ahead of schedule, but was brought back when the baby was born en route. When she failed to deliver the afterbirth, village women tried to help and it was at this point that the orderly held aloof to some extent, though he (and his wife) both examined the woman and advised her to lie flat and not try to expel the afterbirth until she got back to the mission again. He blamed the hemorrhage on her disregarding his advice. In the time that followed, the canoe started for the mission again; returned because the woman felt that she was dying and wanted to see her other children again; hesitated first while the husband considered seeking a curer on another Kove island and second while funds for petrol for the outboard motor were sought; and waited at the mission, after an unsuccessful transfusion, until the mission dinghy returned, so that she could be taken to Talasea. Her closest kin accompanied her on the rest of the journey, but she died on the beach of the Catholic mission at Bitokara.

During the wait for news and the discussions of the following days, on which four seances were held to determine the cause of death from the dead woman's ghost, the orderly's opinions changed constantly. Even while he condemned people from crowding around and preventing him from taking such actions as fastening a bandage to impede hemorrhage, the orderly talked with disquiet of the behavior of the afterbirth, slipping around "as if trying to escape" when he tried to put pressure on her belly. On hearing that the attempted transfusion only made her hands and arms swell, he announced that this was a sign of sorcery, but later suggested that perhaps the sister had been frightened by her condition and had missed the vein. He also said that if the priest managed to get an ambulance to Bitokara so that she reached Kimbe hospital quickly, and if an operation was successful then no sorcery was involved but, if the operation failed, then sorcery was involved. When she did die, however, he reverted to talking of natural causes, arguing in terms of her gynaecological problems with the councillor, who had been convinced of sorcery by the results of a seance. He also used the case, along with others, as supporting his need for his own dinghy, saying that if he had had it he would have taken her off to hospital regardless of what her kin said.

Similar shifts of opinion typified his interpretation of other cases. He described a recent one in which a woman was left in very bad shape, including paralyzed legs, after a difficult birth at the mission. Her kin insisted on taking her home to seek a Tolai curer living nearby, but also stopped at the aid post, where he gave her an injection of vitamin C. Her recovery after she saw the curer was so swift and dramatic that the APO concluded that only sorcery, countered by magical means, could account for the sequence of events, though he had not suspected it earlier. On the other hand, he ascribed a recent bad abscess on his father-in-law's hip to sorcery, but the cure wholly to the Western style medical treatment that he administered.

THE COMPLEX OF PRESENT ATTITUDES

The varied influences from outside Kove, the changes within the society, and the differing experiences of individuals have produced a situation in which it is almost impossible to generalize about present day Kove attitudes towards the causes and possible cures of various ailments. It was probably always true that personal experience helped convince a person of the claims made about, for example, sorcery, but now, with travel and work abroad and other sorts of interaction with foreigners, few people have the same experiences. Obviously some medications are ineffective, and so are some operations; it is not surprising that no one expresses complete confidence in Western medicine, any more than anyone thinks that traditional medicine can always succeed. Most people believed a woman who said that she had been rendered sterile by a drink given her by an Australian woman who then left the country without giving her an antidote; her failure to conceive despite several marriages and affairs supported her claim, especially since she was eager to have a child, and her explanation fitted general assumptions (which long antedated the development of the pill) that European women with their small families knew simple methods for preventing pregnancy. When, however, a few people announced that tooth decay in children was caused by sugar rather than faeces, they had simply accepted the teaching of the nuns because of having been impressed by their knowledge of medical matters in treating a specific illness. Similarly, the better educated young men talked knowledgeably of the transmission of hookworm, and a few tried to keep flies and cockroaches off their food; they accepted what they had been taught in school. Others in the village saw no reason to believe their explanations, however; if they voted to exclude pigs from the village, it was either because they were Seventh Day Adventists or because they subscribed to the much more widely accepted theory that bad smells alone cause illness. Even the educated do not seem to have absorbed more general Western theories about contagion; children are allowed to play freely with pus-laden cotton wool and discarded dressings, and the sick are almost never isolated. The only exception I noted was that children were warned not to eat discarded food handled by a man thought to have "TB" who was actually spitting blood.

As well as possible new causes, new labels for disease have also been widely accepted "TB", *sik malaria, lepra* (leprosy and similar looking skin diseases:), "polio". The entities so labelled need not correspond precisely to Western categories; "TB" can be any chronic respiratory disease and, in men, it is still likely to be attributed to deliberate malice by a wife (see Chowning, in press). Even today almost no one thinks that mosquitoes carry disease; attacks of malaria may be attributed wholly to exposure to cold air or to mental distress (for being slapped) on the part of a small child. "Polio" is used to designate any crippling other than that resulting from an accident; I have heard it used to explain the condition of a victim of cerebral palsy and of boys suffering transient leg pains that kept them out of school for two days. The significant point is that diseases so labelled are thought to be treatable by Western medicine, whereas other ailments with the same symptoms may not be.

The dangers of alcohol are subject to debate and, apart from the Seventh Day Adventists, it tends to be the older men who feel unwell or suffer from liver pains after drinking who decide to avoid liquor (see Chowning 1982a). At the same time that new causes are admitted, some of the older ones are losing their force. A number of people claim to have eaten their taboo fish, though a firstborn, most likely to be afflicted, usually still avoids it. Doubts are expressed as to whether earthquakes cause epidemics. Although everyone still gives lip service to the idea that babies do not get sick if both parents not only abstain from sexual intercourse but observe certain food taboos, men in particular seem to be getting increasingly careless. It may be, however, that the resulting illnesses are no longer taken so seriously; one grandfather said that with the availability of Western medicine, there was no need to worry about ailments that could be cured so easily.

Probably everyone still believes in sorcery, and almost everyone in harmful ghosts, though to Seventh-Day Adventists these are manifestations of the devil. Many think that *masalai* are no longer so powerful. Some very young men believe in the power of foreign types of magic that their elders have never heard of. There is, on the whole, no simple correlation between age and degree of education and willingness to employ either Western or traditional techniques of cure. Everyone seems willing to accept Western medicines which have no drastic side effects for ailments that had no traditional cure, such as coughs, constipation, skin infections and muscular pain (liniment is often requested), and also will seek them if traditional remedies fail to end a headache or stomach ache. As was noted, many people fear injections and two women blamed the permanent crippling of their children on injections in the buttocks received in babyhood. A woman who was the daughter of one Kove APO and recently married to a former one told me that she considered it dangerous to take medicine unless she was actually sick; that is, she would have avoided the medicines normally administered to pregnant women by the nuns. Those who have been cured by Western medicine or operation urge others to follow their example, while many others express scepticism and cite successful cures by renowned Kove or other Papua New Guinea specialists, or simply say that operations kill. Often, it must be remembered, it is not the victim who makes the choice, but those who can arrange transport, pay for medical services, and look after a person who is being treated away from home. As with the case of the woman who died in childbirth (herself one of the strongest believers in Western medicine), such considerations may be as important in determining the outcome of a particular situation as any general preferences.

CONTEMPORARY TREATMENT OF DISEASE

Patients frequently reject medical treatment offered them; children in particular may be more successful in evading than in obtaining treatment. They often refuse to swallow pills or even to approach strangers, and mothers in particular may not force a screaming, struggling child to accept treatment. In addition, where the problem is not considered dangerous, many Kove ignore children's ailments even when they would seek treatment for an equivalent problem in themselves.

While not precisely callous, the Kove are not much moved by the suffering of others; my attempts to comfort a child in pain were regarded as amusing. Sometimes help is sought wholly on the grounds that a child's crying is keeping others awake, but many parents took no action about badly infected sores, conjunctivitis or rashes, all considered curable by injection. Expense was not necessarily a factor; prior to the establishment of the aid post I frequently found that in walking through the village in the afternoon I was hailed by people wanting me to treat sores on a child who had not made the short trip to my house during the preceding hours. As long as he is mobile, however, an older child or adult will seek immediate relief on his own behalf. There is no tradition of stoicism by either sex, adults openly weeping or groaning with pain and complaining of being kept awake all night by it. Neither do people hide or deny sickness (with the single exception, in at least one case, of a woman embarrassed by a genital infection). On the contrary, sickness is often suspected of being offered as an excuse for inaction when the real motive may be laziness or fear.

Assuming that a person is well enough to seek aid or to ask others to obtain it, the action taken, if any, varies considerably with the individual. The availability of a remedy is naturally a prime consideration, and the first thing (or person) to hand will be tried first. If it is ineffective, an alternative may be sought. In emergencies, often two or more remedies are used simultaneously or in rapid succession, without waiting to see if one of them succeeds. The reason is not that the remedies have different functions (compare Welsch 1983:49), but that it might be dangerous to delay and nothing is lost by using the whole arsenal. Traditional curers do not seem to resent having other experts called in, and it is common for people to volunteer advice and services in cases involving, for example, loss of consciousness or difficulty in breathing.

If several remedies fail, the next step depends not only on ease of travel to seek outside aid, whether from another village or from a professional with Western training, but on personal evaluation of the situation and of the available options. Romanucci-Ross, discussing the "hierarchy of resort of curative practices" in

Manus, says "Depending on the degree of acculturation, choice of healer and/or cure would begin with usage of either native or Western medical categories" (1983: 5). As I indicated, what matters in Kove is not so much where one begins but what is done later. Older people may have much more confidence in Western medicine than do their juniors. In a recent case, a little boy was crippled after a fall that injured his knee. The parents, suspecting sorcery, wanted to take him to a traditional curer, but grandparents of the mother intervened and transported him to an aid post, from which he was sent to Kimbe hospital and cured, after an operation and physiotherapy. When a middle aged man diagnosed at the mission as having tuberculosis left the hospital without waiting for the prescribed injections, his action was condemned by several contemporaries and elders, one of the latter saying "We should think of our bodies and attend to the doctors when they diagnose a disease they can treat." Among the critics was his wife, herself a traditional curer specializing in female problems. She also criticized her husband's failure to take the medicines he was given, saying that she had been cured of an earlier sickness by the mission personnel. Furthermore, after the death from post-partum hemorrhage described above, this woman insisted that the problem was purely physiological and had nothing to do with sorcery or God's wrath, as others suggested. The victim should have heeded the advice of Europeans and doctors.

Even if the patient is willing to go to hospital, the problem is getting there. Many prefer to have their babies within reach of pain-killers and skilled aid if anything goes wrong, but husbands may be reluctant to take them. If a child gets sick, parents frequently talk of a visit to the hospital without doing more; the physical effort involved, or the expense of buying petrol and hiring a motor, often outweigh the perceived advantages of the trip. If travelling in that direction for other reasons people often stop off at the mission station or aid post to get medication. Bad accidents are an exception; when a man cut the tendons of his wrist while gardening, and when another man was gored by a wild pig, they were taken to foreign experts as quickly as possible. Aid is also sought for any condition that seems to threaten life, for which, as with these wounds, no satisfactory local remedy exists; an example is a child with a fishbone stuck in her throat which prevented her eating. Frequently, however, people fail to realize how dangerous a particular condition is.

CONCLUSIONS

Over the years since Europeans first came to the area, the Kove have learned to recognize new syndromes and to employ new medicines, including ones of "Western" origin that are not usually part of Western practice. They have not, however, abandoned traditional attitudes. Change has been lessened by geographical factors and the history of medical services in the region – the latter few, poorly supplied, irregularly staffed and hard to reach. At the same time, Kove patterns of travel have exposed them to better services than those available locally; everyone has visited towns. Most individuals have received a range of medical treatments, ranging from those of the village to those of the clinic or hospital, and sometimes for exactly the same condition. If no great physical effort or expense is involved, anyone will seek treatment for certain afflictions. If the standard treatment (injections, hospitalization) is unappealing to one person, he may reject available treatment which another Kove would seek. In addition, of course, there still exists much disagreement within Kove about the probable causes of certain ailments, and their handling varies accordingly. Where real uncertainty exists, any treatment may be tried in any sequence or combination, and the same thing may happen if the disease seems very serious and the first attempts at cure are unsuccessful. I found no indication of the "loyalty to native diseases" that Romanucci-Ross (1977: 487) reported for Manus. Although the Kove are notably and self-consciously conservative in many respects, they dislike pain and sickness and dread early death, and wish to evade them by any means available. Their high opinion of most aspects of their own culture does not, as the popularity of the cargo cult shows, extend to these areas. For that matter, they are aware at one level that much of the "traditional" culture developed after pacification, and their conservatism is focused on retention of the old but not on rejection of the new. So long as the new does not displace what is valued, it is welcome. The willingness to try new remedies, especially if they are offered by people considered more knowledgeable than the Kove, is one indication of this willingness to experiment.

Sometimes no alternatives are visualized; a single standard treatment is known and the choice is between that and no action, though the possibility that a new cure has recently been found is often discussed and rumors circulate that the Americans particularly can now perform some medical miracles. There still may be reasons for evading the standard treatment, such as the difficulty of travel or fear of the hospital. Today, however, the norm is to visualize several possible remedies (often reflecting uncertainty about diagnosis) and to follow both the advice of others and one's own inclinations. Very rarely did I hear of absolute refusal to try a certain cure on ideological grounds, such as that because a disease was caused by sorcery, only a sorcerer could cure it. Furthermore, it has become increasingly rare to tie cause and cure together in this way. An unfortunate consequence of the recent attitude is belief that injections can cure anything, but a benefit is the willingness of a person thought to be sorcerized to seek help from a specialist in Western medicine. It is now common to hear people talk of someone with an internal disease caused by sorcery who was cured or survived for years after an operation reinforced, in one case I know, by constant prayer. The fact that sorcery is still believed to be the cause reflects a combination of factors, from the attitudes and knowledge of the medical personnel encountered along the way to the entrenched Kove conviction that their own people constantly practice sorcery against each other. They are now capable of asking the ghost at a seance if the victim died of natural causes, but the majority will expect the answer to be that a human being was responsible.

While the Kove openly boast of being sorcerers, this attitude will not change.

The willingness to try alternative treatments will probably increase so long as these are not too expensive. It would also be useful if the health professionals they most often encounter took the time to explain matters to them in terms that were intelligible as well as accurate; far too much impatience is shown at present, and the Kove react badly to being scolded or patronized. On the other hand, they too can be rude, assuming that it is the "paid job" of any mission or government employee to help them on demand, regardless of personal inconvenience. They consequently strike outsiders as ungrateful and uncooperative, and it will take some time for the Kove to appreciate what in fact is being done for them by others.

In contrast to what colleagues working in other parts of the country have found, my experience in Kove, and elsewhere, has been that the members do not have much confidence in their own systems of therapy and are usually delighted to be offered alternatives, so long as the people dispensing them live nearby and are willing to deal with them as equals. Use of the health services will probably never be ideal, given certain peculiarities of local conditions and attitudes, but improvement is possible. After better medical training for the specialists, combined with continued attempts to impress on the local people the dangers of certain[17] of their present ideas and practices, the most useful innovation might well be an attempt to impress on the specialists the need to understand the cultural background of the people they are endeavoring to help and, as far as possible, to work within it and with the people, rather than dealing with them as ignorant and recalcitrant outsiders.

NOTES

1. In the course of fieldwork I have lived in three different villages, Kapo (1966), Somalani (1968, 1968), and Nukakau (between 1971 and 1983) for a total of 18 months. My research was supported by the Australian National University (1966–69), the University of Papua New Guinea (1971–3, 1975–6), and Victoria University of Wellington (1983). In 1978 I spent three weeks in Kove on behalf of the Papua New Guinea Department of Environment and Conservation.
2. Because of their very different history of contact, these two villages have been excluded from the discussion.
3. A cargo cult started at the end of the war was ostensibly inspired by contact between a Kove and an American army officer. Many Kove still adhere to its teaching, which stresses the ties between Kove and the USA, and the endowment of Americans (by the Kove culture hero) with much special knowledge.
4. My task for the Department of Environment and Conservation was to ascertain Kove desires as regards their relations with the South Koreans.
5. Apart from the disruption caused by World War II, there was also a period of virtually total neglect when the Kove refused to accept local government councils.
6. I do not know whether contemporary belief that the smell of feces can produce disease is a traditional one.
7. By sorcery I mean malevolent magic intended to make a specific individual sick or kill him. I exclude protective spells placed on property and also "poisoning" by female secretions, which involves no use of magical spells. All Kove sorcerers are men.

8. In one case, however, it was suggested that sorcery must have been involved when a woman died from a purportedly light blow to her neck. This was not the case when heavy blows or spears were used.
9. A few men also performed contraceptive magic, but it tended to be a female specialty.
10. Tobacco was introduced into Kove in German times; some Kove claim that they smoked a wild plant before that.
11. If a child was endangered by nursing from a pregnant woman, it could sometimes be saved by being weaned at once. The milk of a pregnant woman was considered more dangerous than that of a woman having intercourse occasionally (see Chowning 1985).
12. Like many other Melanesians, the Kove attribute a variety of ailments to disturbances of the liver, and are vague abouts its location (judging from the position of scars for reputed operations on the liver). It is not safe to assume that the term really designates that organ.
13. It was characterized by red eyes, cough, rash, fever, and in most cases, extremely swollen glands in the neck. This was not reported to be its first occurrence.
14. It may well be that non-kin blamed sorcery directed against the mother, who had detractors and who was burdened with the care of the boy, but I did not ask other people about the case.
15. These officers have sometimes asked me to investigate such rumors for them.
16. Much "traditional" sorcery was also acquired from outside Kove, but in the days before wider travel, usually from nearby societies. Foreign sorcerers were also hired.
17. An example of the failure of present attempts to educate is that of a councillor who had attended high school and then worked for many years as a pest exterminator for Flick who told me that government attempts to make the Kove build and use privies had been part of their "colonial enslavement, of which they were now free".

DAVID C. HYNDMAN

11. GENDER IN THE DIET AND HEALTH OF THE WOPKAIMIN

INTRODUCTION

The Wopkaimin are one of several Mountain Ok peoples (Fig. 24) located in the center of New Guinea. They live in a small-scale society of around 700 with common territory of around 1000 square kilometers divided into five parishes (Fig. 25). Their subsistence ecology is based on kinship and customary rights and obligations. Ancestral territory of the Mountain Ok peoples is of great antiquity and is maintained by strong cultural ties. Until the transnational Ok Tedi mining project started full-scale construction on Wopkaimin land in 1981 they exercised the only effective control over their ecosystem through their possession of a sophisticated and detailed understanding of local biota and environments and through their time proven, ecologically and culturally adapted management of resources. They lived with rain forest through knowledge and techniques accumulated over as much as 15,000 years (Swadling 1984) of practical *in situ* testing and experimentation. By encoding gender roles, ethnoscience not only socially adjusted each sex to food-getting but also ecologically adjusted the population to their environment over time.

Status between the sexes in Wopkaimin, and other Mountain Ok societies (Barth 1975, Poole 1981, 1984), is unequal because of exclusive male participation in ritual life. Recent ethnographic focus on inequality in the Highlands (M. Strathern 1980, A. Strathern 1982) has not explored the long-term impact sexual inequality may have for a population's health and well-being. This medical anthropological study of the Wopkaimin people provides the first in-depth analysis of gender relations in the diet and health of a pre-contact Highland fringe population in Papua New Guinea.

Data presented in the paper are primarily based on human ecological research with the Wopkaimin people over the period of 1974–5. From the beginning I coordinated multidisciplinary fieldwork in Wopkaimin communities, primarily in the Kam Basin (Fig. 25). My studies have benefited from the cooperation of Wopkaimin colleagues as well as those of zoologists, botanists and medical specialists. The following medical-clinical data deserves special mention. The 1975 director of the Papua New Guinea Institute of Medical Research (IMR), Dr R. Hornabrook, accepted my invitation to conduct a medical survey among the Wopkaimin. Hornabrook lead the research team in October 1975, but unfortunately I was unable to be present at the time. The IMR team took anthropometric readings, made physical examinations, collected blood samples for typing and hemoglobin analysis, collected hair samples and fingerprints and conducted serum analysis for yaws, syphilis and viral biochemical parameters. The work sheets were removed

S. Frankel and G. Lewis (eds.), *A Continuing Trial of Treatment*. 249–275.
© 1989, Kluwer Academic Publishers, Dordrecht – Printed in the Netherlands.

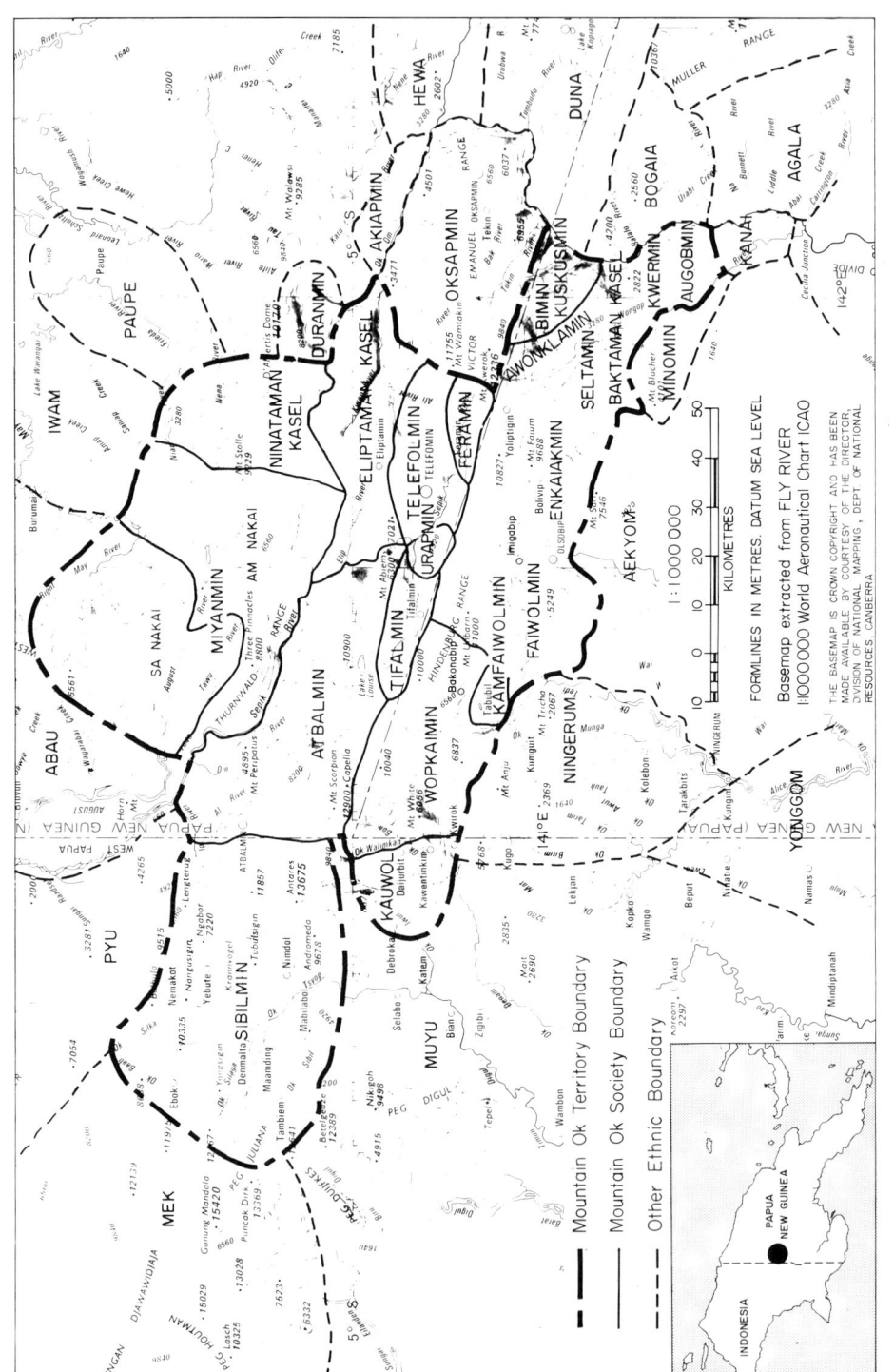

Fig. 24. Mountain Ok peoples of Central New Guinea.

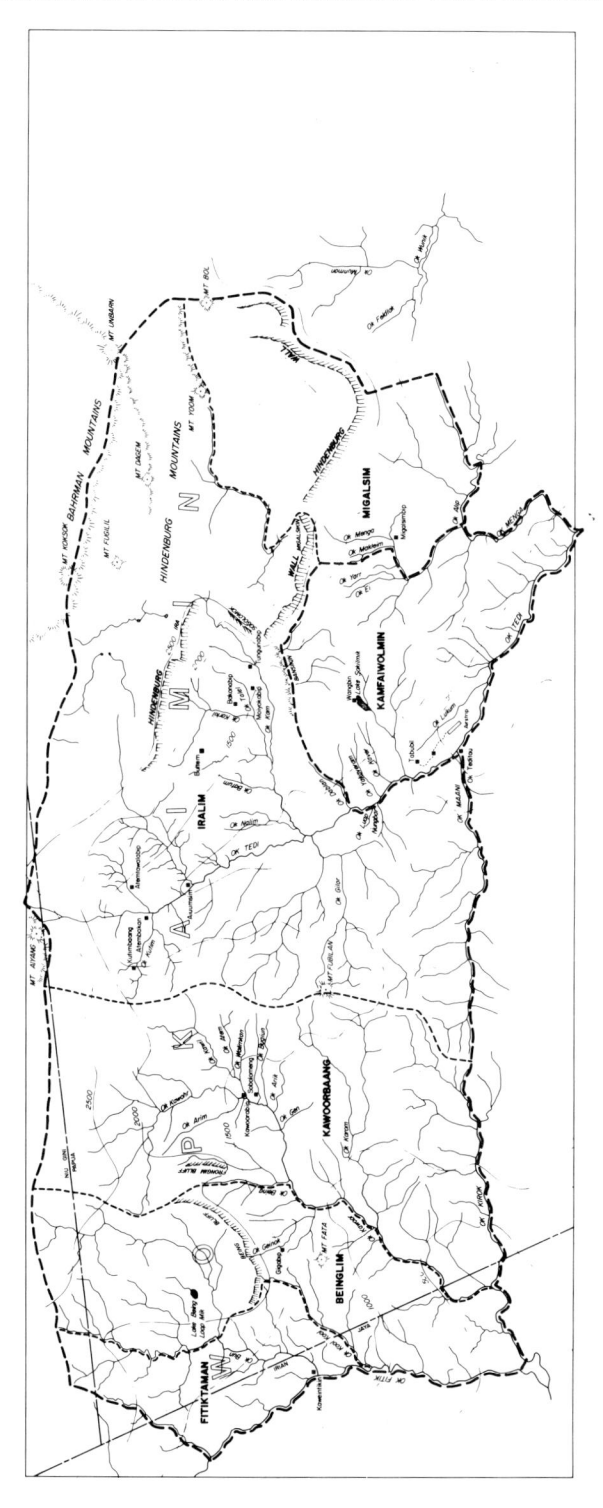

Fig. 25. Wopkaimin parishes.

from IMR and no analyses are available. My statistical analysis of the anthropometric and hematological data is only possible because of the generosity of Professor John Lourie, a co-investigator into changing patterns of Wopkaimin human ecology, who kindly provided me with raw data he located nearly a decade after the original survey.

Fig. 26. Bakonabip hamlet men's house and *amokam* cult house surrounded in sacred *Cordelyne* shrub.

SIZE AND FORM OF THE WOPKAIMIN POPULATION

There has not been another government patrol to make an appearance in each of the five Wopkaimin parishes since the Australian colonial administration patrol of May–June 1975, that led up to independence. The parish populations (Fig. 27) making up the 1975 census total of 694 (Fig. 28) include 108 Kaweintikin, 111 Kavorbang, 124 Beinglim, 239 Iralim and 112 Migalsim. Government services have been drastically curtailed in remote regions and Wopkaimin villages are not visited by Papua New Guinea government officers. Historically there has been a lack of success in fully censoring Wopkaimin. While figures from colonial administration census patrols should not be accepted as precise population data, the two decades of sporadic census taking provide the basis for some useful generalizations. Of the 694 Wopkaimin shown in Fig. 27, twelve men were laborers at Tabubil (Ransley 1975) and 39 boys were students at the Tabubil primary school

(Bird 1972: 38). A reasonably accurate estimate of the size of the Wopkaimin population in 1975 is approximately 700 +/- 25.

AGE GROUP

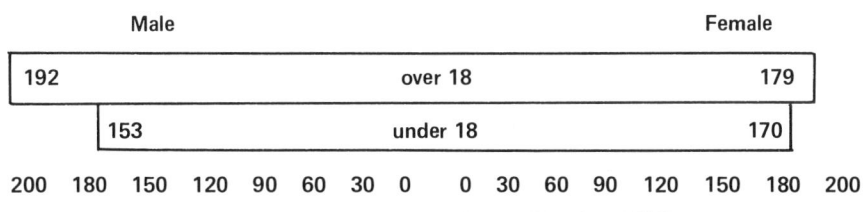

Male		Female
192	over 18	179
153	under 18	170

200 180 150 120 90 60 30 0   0 30 60 90 120 150 180 200

Fig. 27. Wopkaimin population by age and sex (source Ransley, 1975).

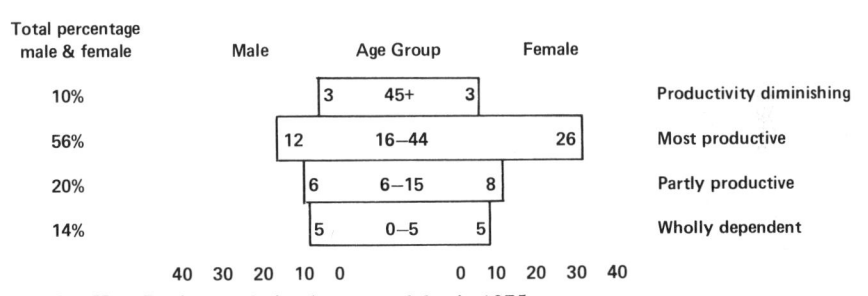

Total percentage male & female	Male	Age Group	Female	
10%	3	45+	3	Productivity diminishing
56%	12	16–44	26	Most productive
20%	6	6–15	8	Partly productive
14%	5	0–5	5	Wholly dependent

40 30 20 10 0   0 10 20 30 40

Fig. 28. Kam Basin population by age and dex in 1975.

Figure 27 shows that adults in the Wopkaimin population outnumber children. The upper, adult tier of the population pyramid is wider because it contains 53% of the population. Initial field trips among the Wopkaimin from 1974–75 were with the Kam Basin residents of Iralim parish. The age–sex structure for the population residing in the Kam Basin in 1975 is shown in Fig. 28. Ages were calculated in reference to eventful years such as 1953 when the patrol officers and policemen were killed in Telefomin, 1957 when the first patrol officer came to the Kam Basin and 1969 when Kennecott prospectors first arrived. Like the larger Wopkaimin population, the Kam Basin population has an older age composition.

The amount and degree of subsistence production is roughly correlated to age–sex groups. In subsistence systems such as that practised by the Wopkaimin the objective of production is for a subsistence fund, a maintenance fund and a ceremonial fund (see Wolf 1966). Only the young are wholly dependent in the Wopkaimin subsistence system; everyone else is productive according to his ability and social responsibilities (Hyndman, in press a). During fieldwork in the Kam Basin, 66% of the resident population regularly contributed to subsistence production (Fig. 28).

As to the physical type of Melanesian peoples, Chowning (1977: 4–5) has written:

The people of Melanesia are usually taken to constitute a separate physical type or local race, which is often assumed to have two or three main divisions: Melanesian, Papuan, and, for some writers, Negrito ... This combination of dark skin and frizzy hair, otherwise characteristic of sub-Saharan Africa, has also led the inhabitants of Melanesia to be called Oceanic Negroes ... It remains to discuss the validity of the division into the subtypes labelled "Papuan" and "Melanesian" ... Confusion has been caused by the use of the same terms to designate linguistic groups, which do not coincide with the physical types assigned to their speakers, and also by the use of the same terms for geographical and political divisions, which coincide with neither. But the real argument against continuing to use these terms is that they are meaningless as applied to the local populations. Melanesians simply cannot be separated into two or three physical types.

The Wopkaimin are one of numerous regional populations inhabiting New Guinea, all of which are considered to belong to the Melanesian physical type (Chowning 1982b).

There is great diversity in skin color among the Wopkaimin from yellowish brown to very dark brown. Their hair is woolly and dark brown in color. Men can and often do wear full beards and many have copious body hair. Nose shape varies from quite wide to hooked. Variations in height, skin color and facial features as found among the Wopkaimin are duplicated among other regional populations of Papua New Guinea (Clarke 1971: 21). As to the probable causes of these variations, Chowning (1977: 9) summarizes that "undoubtedly movement of populations have contributed something to the physical diversity of Melanesians but local evolution, including both adaptation and genetic drift, has probably been just as influential".

TABLE 1
1975 survey of Wopkaimin parishes by age-sex groups (source: IMR)

	Beinglim		Kavorbang		Migalsim		Iralim		
Ages	M	F	M	F	M	F	M	F	Total
1–2	1	1	0	1	1	1	4	2	11
2–4	2	2	1	1	0	0	6	4	16
5–9	2	2	3	2	4	4	2	6	25
10–14	1	3	0	3	1	6	1	4	19
15–19	1	6	1	1	1	4	3	4	21
20–24	2	8	1	1	3	6	6	15	42
25–40	3	8	5	5	6	4	14	10	55
40+	3	3	2	1	2	1	2	3	17
Totals	15	33	13	15	18	26	38	48	206

Observed frequencies — Parishes

TABLE 2
Heights and weights of Wopkaimin adults in 1975 (source: IMR survey)

	25–40 age group	
	Male	Female
Weight average (kg)	48.3	44.4
Height average (mm)	1535	1487

Table 1 shows the age–sex groups for each parish population sampled during the 1975 IMR Wopkaimin survey. Weights and heights of Wopkaimin adults taken during the survey are presented in Table 2. The Wopkaimin are small people. The average adult male weighs 48.3 kg and is 1533 mm tall, whereas an adult female is less heavy and shorter, averaging only 44.3 kg in weight and 1486 mm in height. In general Wopkaimin men are lean and muscular. Wopkaimin women range from delicate to sturdy and always have protruding abdomens. Adults have remarkable endurance. However, there is considerable physical variation between the sexes.

Taking into account that they have a territory of over 1000 km^2, the Wopkaimin, with less than one person per km^2, have one of the lowest population densities of any Mountain Ok group. The remainder of this paper demonstrates how the Wopkaimin population is stabilized at a very low population density in their location on the southern face of the Star and Hindenburg Mountains because of the synergistic relationship between gender, diet and health.

GENDER AND DIET

The set of cultural rules, conventions and determinants encoded in the Wopkaimin ethnoscience system transforms information about the environment into practices which affect ecological relations (Hyndman, in press (b)). They possess a folk model of the environment as well as for behaviour directed towards the environment (Hyndman 1984). The factors limiting accessibility of food in the biotically diverse ecosystem are shown in Fig. 30 which illustrates the Wopkaimin ethnoclassification of food. There is a wide range of potential food resources but access to them is limited by space, time and cultural availability. Food is limited spatially because resources are not distributed equally in the major biotopes occuring in the ecosystem (Hyndman 1982). Time limits on accessibility involve temporal scheduling of various subsistence activities (Hyndman, in press (a)). Food ethnoclassifications (Fig. 30) limit the cultural availability of resources by defining what is considered to be food, by classifying food into a scale of preferences, by influencing the intensity and frequency of which species will be hunted, collected and cultivated and by assigning consumption rules (Hyndman 1984).

Fig. 29. Wopkaimin cult house leader prepares to work in his taro garden.

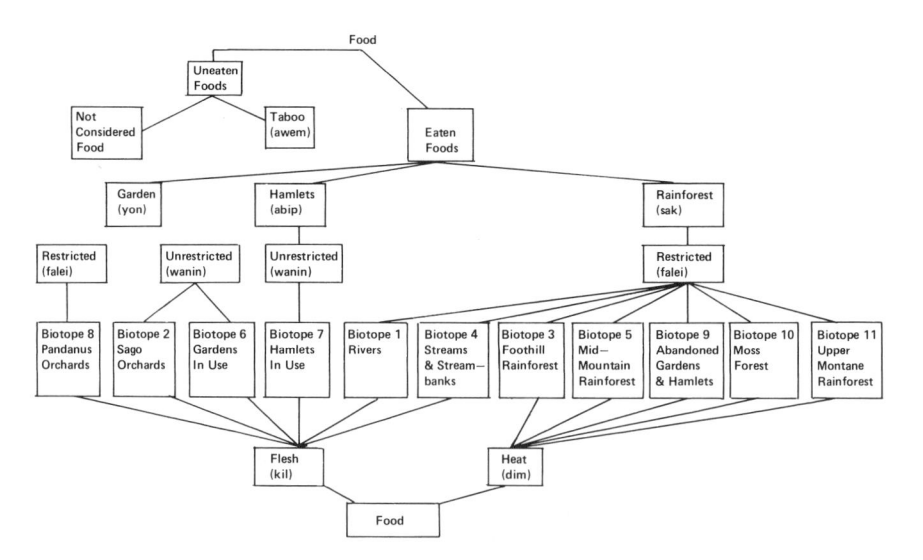

Fig. 30. Wopkaimin food ethnoclassifications.

TABLE 3
Wopkaimin ethnoclassifications of major game animals

Food no.	Taxonomic identification	Biotope no.	English taxon	Wopkaimin taxon	Wopkaimin food category dim (meat)	kil (flesh)	Wopkaimin status restriction Children	Women	Men
1.	*Aprotelos bulmerae*	11	flying fox	*sikkam*	×		+	+	−
2.	*Casuarius bennettii*	5,11	cassowary	*kubomeno*	×		−	−	+
3.	*Casuarius unappeniiculatus*	3,5	cassowary	*bia*	×		−	−	+
4.	*Dendrolagus sp.*	9,10,11	tree kangaroo	*nuk*	×		+	−	+
5.	*Dobsonia moluccensis*	10,11	bat	*sikkam*	×		+	+	−
6.	*Echymipera clara*	3	bandicoot	*nuk*	×		+	+	+
7.	*Echymipera kaluba*	5	bandicoot	*nuk*	×		+	+	+
8.	*Hyomys goliath*	3,5,9	giant rat	*nuk*	×		+	−	−
9.	*Mallomys rothschildii*	3,5,9,10,11	giant rat	*nuk*	×		+	+	−
10.	*Peroryctes longicuada*	5,10	bandicoot	*nuk*	×		+	−	+
11.	*Phalanger atrimaculatus*	3	cuscus	*nuk*	×		+	−	+
12.	*Phalanger carmelitae*	10,11	cuscus	*nuk*	×		+	−	+
13.	*Phalanger gymnotis*	3,5,9,10,11	cuscus	*nuk*	×		−	−	+
14.	*Phalanger interpositus*	5,9	cuscus	*nuk*	×		+	−	+
15.	*Phalanger orientalis*	3	cuscus	*nuk*	×		+	−	+
16.	*Phalanger vestitus*	3,5,9,10	cuscus	*nuk*	×		+	−	+
17.	*Pseudocheirus corinnae*	9,10	ringtail	*nuk*	×		+	−	+
18.	*Pseudocheirus cupreus*	5,9,10,11	ringtail	*nuk*	×		+	−	+
19.	*Rattus ruber*	7	rat	*nuk*	×		+	−	−
20.	*Sus scrofa papuensis*	3,5	pig	*samin*	×		−	−	+
21.	*Tategalla fuscirostris*	3	bird	*awon*	×		+	+	−
22.	*Thylogale bruijni*	3	wallaby	*nuk*	×		+	−	+

TABLE 4
Nutrient requirements for the Wopkaimin

Age category	Sex	Calories low value	Calories high value	Protein g low value	Protein g high value	Fat g low value	Fat g high value	Vitamin A I.U. low value	Vitamin A I.U. high value	Vitamin B₁ Thiamine mg low value	Vitamin B₁ Thiamine mg high value	Vitamin B₂ Riboflavin mg low value	Vitamin B₂ Riboflavin mg high value	Niacin mg equiv. low value	Niacin mg equiv. high value	Vitamin C Ascorbic Acid low value	Vitamin C Ascorbic Acid high value	Calcium mg low value	Calcium mg high value	Iron mg low value	Iron mg high value
20+	m	2000	2400	33	38	48	84	2500	4000	1.0	1.4	1.0	1.3	16.0	19.0	25	40	400	600	10	14
20+	f	1700	1900	25	30	40	72	2500	4000	0.8	1.1	0.8	1.0	12.0	15.0	25	40	400	600	10	14
15–19	m	2100	2300	30	35	50	88	2500	4000	1.0	1.4	1.1	1.4	16.0	20.0	25	40	500	600	12	16
15–19	f	1700	1900	27	32	40	72	2500	4000	0.8	1.1	1.0	1.2	12.0	15.0	25	40	500	600	10	14
10–14	m	1750	1900	27.5	32.5	42	74	2200	3500	0.9	1.2	0.9	1.2	12.0	16.0	25	40	600	800	10	12
10–14	f	1750	1900	20.5	25.5	42	74	2200–3500		0.8	1.0	0.7	0.9	12.0	15.0	25	40	600	700	10	12
5–9	mf	1600	1700	21.6	26.6	38	74	1500	3000	0.5	0.7	0.6	0.8	8.0	12.0	20	30	500	700	8	10
0–4	mf	900	1200	13.5	18.5	22	38	1000	2500	0.3	0.5	0.4	0.6	6.0	8.0	15	25	500	700	6	8

TABLE 5
Nutrient percentages provided by plant and animal foods during diet study

	Calories	Protein	Fat	Calcium	Iron	Vitamin A	Vitamin B₁ Thiamine	Vitamin B₂ Riboflavin	Niacin	Vitamin C Ascorbic acid
Percentage from plant foods	78	53	05	97	90	99+	67	66	68	100
Percentage from animal foods	22	47	95	03	10	–	33	34	32	–

TABLE 6
Percentage of times age-sex groups receive more or less than fifty percent of required nutrients

Age	Sex	Calories %	Protein %	Fat %	Vitamins Vit A %	Vit B$_1$ %	Vit B$_2$ %	Niacin %	Vit C %	Minerals Calcium %	Iron %
20+	m	40	49	22	64	74	43	45	87	64	85
20+	f	32	57	4	64	72	45	43	87	57	83
15–19	m	32	51	6	64	66	30	36	87	51	83
15–19	f	34	53	6	64	74	38	49	87	51	83
10–14	m	36	53	6	64	70	36	49	87	43	83
10–14	f	36	60	6	64	74	49	49	87	43	83
5–9	m f	36	60	6	76	83	60	72	87	51	83
0–4	m f	68	72	9	83	80	72	83	87	51	83

TABLE 7
Diet study nutritional returns from wild animals

Food name	Edible amt H$_2$O	Fat Protein	Cals Carbo	Calc mg Iron mg	Phos Potas	Vit A Vit B$_1$ mg	Vit B$_2$ mg Niacin mg	Vit C mg Fibre G	Ash
Large Game (hunting)									
casuarius spp.	22.90 15.60	2290.0 5267.0	40075.0 .0	3435.0 343.5	40075.0 000.0	.00 34.35	229.00 1374.00	.0 .0	229.0
Sus scrofa papuensis	21.80 9.80	9810.0 2616.0	98100.0 .0	1526.0 348.8	000.0 000.0	.00 109.00	30.50 632.20	.0 .0	183.1
Small Game (hunting)									
Dactylonax palpator	0.16 0.11	9.6 30.4	200.0 .0	16.0 4.0	288.0 000.0	.00 0.57	.40 8.00	.0 .0	1.6
Dobsonia Moluccensis	5.30 3.90	318.0 1007.0	6625.0 .0	530.0 132.5	9540.0 000.0	.00 393.30	13.30 265.00	.0 .0	58.3
Gymnophaps albertsii	1.50 0.90	150.0 375.0	300.0 .0	0.0 0.0	000.0 000.0	.00 .00	.00 61.50	.0 .0	.0
Eudromicia caidata	0.48 0.35	28.8 91.2	600.0 .0	48.0 12.0	864.0 000.0	.00 3.20	1.20 24.00	.0 .0	5.3
Mallomys rothschildi	1.44 1.05	84.0 266.0	1750.0 .0	140.0 35.0	2520.0 000.0	.00 1.96	3.50 70.00	.0 .0	15.4
Melomys rubex	0.05 0.03	0.9 11.3	54.0 .0	18.5 0.0	146.5 000.0	.00 .00	.00 .00	.0 .0	.7
Melipotes fumigatus	0.75 0.44	75.0 187.5	1500.0 .0	0.0 0.0	000.0 000.0	.00 .00	.00 30.80	.0 .0	.0
Myzomela rosenbergii	0.15 0.08	15.0 37.5	300.0 .0	0.0 0.0	000.0 000.0	.00 .00	.00 6.15	.0 .0	.0
Neophascogale lorentzi	0.16 0.12	9.6 30.4	200.0 .0	16.0 4.0	288.0 000.0	.00 0.36	.40 8.00	.0 .0	1.76
Opopsitta diophthalma	0.23 0.13	23.0 57.5	460.0 .0	0.0 0.0	000.0 000.0	.00 .00	.00 9.43	.0 .0	.0
Melidectes rufocrissalis	0.23 0.13	23.0 57.5	460.0 .0	0.0 0.0	000.0 000.0	.00 .00	.00 9.43	.0 .0	.0

Peroryctes longicuada	0.60	36.0	750.0	60.0	1080.0	.00	1.50	.0	
	0.45	114.0	.0	15.0	000.0	0.84	30.00	.0	6.6
Pseudocheirus corinnae	0.80	48.0	1000.0	80.0	1440.0	.00	2.00	.0	
	0.60	152.0	.0	20.0	000.0	1.12	40.00	.0	8.8
Pseudocheirus cupreus	11.60	696.0	14500.0	1160.0	20880.0	.00	29.00	.0	
	8.50	2204.0	.0	290.0	000.0	16.20	580.00	.0	127.6
Phalanger atrimaculatus	4.30	258.0	5375.0	430.0	7740.0	.00	10.80	.0	
	3.20	817.0	.0	107.05	000.0	6.00	215.00	.0	47.3
Phalanger carmelitae	4.60	276.0	5750.0	460.0	8280.0	.00	11.50	.0	
	3.30	874.0	.0	115.0	000.0	6.40	230.00	.0	50.6
Phalanger gymnotis	3.30	198.0	4125.0	330.0	5940.0	.00	8.30	.0	
	2.40	627.0	.0	82.5	000.0	4.60	165.00	.0	36.3
Phanlanger interpositus	3.70	222.0	4625.0	370.0	6660.0	.00	9.30	.0	
	2.70	703.0	.0	92.5	000.0	5.20	185.00	.0	40.7
Phalanger vestitus	9.00	540.0	11250.0	900.0	16200.0	.00	22.50	.0	
	6.60	1710.0	.0	225.0	000.0	12.60	450.00	.0	99.0
Small Game (fishing)									
Neosilurus eguuinus	5.00	140.0	4800.0	10000.0	11250.0	.00	10.00	.0	
	3.70	850.0	.0	65.0	000.0	2.50	95.00	.0	135.0
Oxyeleotris fimbriatus	1.50	42.0	1410.0	3000.0	3175.0	.00	3.00	.0	
	1.20	255.0	.0	19.5	000.0	0.75	28.50	.0	22.5
Small Vertebrates (collecting)									
A. Snakes	0.04	0.8	34.0	0.0	000.0	.00	.00	.0	
	0.02	7.2	.2	0.0	000.0	.00	.00	.02	2.8
B. Frogs	4.90	58.8	3822.0	784.0	35525.0	.00	5.90	.0	
	3.80	808.5	.0	88.2	000.0	1.50	245.00	.0	245.0
C. Lizards	0.34	3.7	380.8	85.0	867.0	119.00	.70	.0	
	0.4	82.3	.0	11.9	000.0	.20	23.80	.0	5.8
Totals	104.83	15355.1	211175.8	23388.5	172958.5	119.00	392.80	.0	
	69.35	21943.3	.2	2011.9	000.0	600.70	4785.80	.02	1323.2

TABLE 8
1975 age-sex group dietary patterns

Age	Sex	Calories P*	Calories A*	Calories total	Protein P*	Protein A*	Protein total	Fat g P*	Fat g A*	Fat g total	Vit A I.U. P*	Vit A I.U. A*	Vit A I.U. total	Vit B$_1$ mg P*	Vit B$_1$ mg A*	Vit B$_1$ mg total	Vit B$_2$ mg P*	Vit B$_2$ mg A*	Vit B$_2$ mg total	Niacin mg equiv. P*	Niacin mg equiv. A*	Niacin mg equiv. total	Vit C mg P*	Vit C mg A*	Vit C mg total	Calcium mg P*	Calcium mg A*	Calcium mg total	Iron mg P*	Iron mg A*	Iron mg total
20+	m	1600	717	2317	26	52	78	2.7	60	62.7	7079		7079	1.45	.67	2.12	.67	.57	1.24	13.7	4.2	17.9	184		184	763	37	800	27	3.6	30.6
20+	f	1600	195	1795	26	9	35	2.7	17	19.7	7079		7079	1.45	.17	1.62	.67	.07	.74	13.7	2.1	15.8	184		184	763	13	776	27	.99	27.99
15–19	m	1600	231	1831	26	15	41	2.7	18	20.7	7079		7079	1.45	.20	1.65	.67	.07	.74	13.7	2.9	16.6	184		184	763	15	778	27	1.3	28.3
15–19	f	1600	231	1831	26	15	41	2.7	18	20.7	7079		7079	1.45	.20	1.65	.67	.07	.74	13.7	2.9	16.6	184		184	763	15	778	27	1.3	28.3
10–14	m	1600	231	1831	26	15	41	2.7	18	20.7	7079		7079	1.45	.20	1.65	.67	.07	.74	13.7	2.9	16.6	184		184	763	15	778	27	1.3	28.3
10–14	f	1600	231	1831	26	15	41	2.7	18	20.7	7079		7079	1.45	.20	1.65	.67	.07	.74	13.7	2.9	16.6	184		184	763	15	778	27	1.3	28.3
5–9	m f	1600	231	1831	26	15	41	2.7	18	20.7	7079		7079	1.45	.20	1.65	.67	.07	.74	13.7	2.9	16.6	184		184	763	15	778	27	1.3	28.3
0–4	m f	1600	231	1831	26	15	41	2.7	18	20.7	7079		7079	1.45	.20	1.65	.67	.07	.74	13.7	2.9	16.6	184		184	763	15	778	27	1.3	28.3

P* Plant foods
A* Animal foods

Taboo (*awem*) explicitly forbids potential foodstuffs to everyone regardless of age–sex category. Food preferences classify foods as possessing a quality which, in essence, is predominantly flesh (*kil*) or meat (*dim*). All plants that are eaten are classified as having flesh, whereas all animals that are eaten are divided between those that possess the quality of meat such as cassowaries, pigs and marsupials and those that only possess the quality of flesh such as fish, frogs, snakes and lizards. All foods are either restricted (*falei*) or unrestricted (*wanin*). Indexing gender by the avoidance of certain foods is a common pattern among the Mountain Ok (Barth 1975:165). Of the 168 principal Wopkaimin foods, 64 are restricted to initiated men in their adult ritual status, 19 to women of childbearing age and eight to children. Among the 91 restricted foods 87 are animals. Animals are an overriding concern and nearly the entire range of local fauna is restricted.

Avoidances based on gender are pre-eminent in the distinctions made between meat- and flesh-bearing animals. As men acquire adulthood and ritual status they stop eating the flesh-bearing animals of females and childhood. Table 3 shows that the 22 major game animals classified as possessing meat carry a heavy load of status, age and sex avoidances. Gender is such a fundamental distinction in the allocation of these animals that less than 30% of the largest, most regularly esteemed and hunted game are allowed to women of childbearing age.

Children have special growth requirements because they weigh less than adults and therefore need more protein per unit of body weight, and women have special nutritional requirements because of pregnancy and lactation. When establishing the baseline diet of an indigenous, subsistence oriented people like the Wopkaimin, it is crucial to examine nutrient returns from the perspective of food allocation. Nutrients which can appear just adequate on a per capita basis may be limiting for certain age groups in the population, such as children and women, due to cultural patterns of distribution. Woodham (1968: 53) indicates that there is considerable evidence in New Guinea that men and women are well-developed physiologically and able to work hard on "a total daily intake of no more than 30 g of regular protein [but that] children and pregnant women [do] suffer from protein deficiency" (but see also Oomen 1971). Gender patterns food restrictions in such a way as to create systematic undernutrition among adult Wopkaimin women.

Although Wopkaimin hamlets are the relevant food-getting unit and food returns are in good balance on an average per capita per day basis (Hyndman, in press (a)), it does not necessarily follow that the nutrient requirements of all segments of the population are equally satisfied by food returns. Each age–sex group of the Kam Basin population was scrutinized during a three month diet study conducted from June–August 1975. Methods used in the diet study are provided in detail elsewhere (Hyndman in press a); here the analysis of consumption patterns reveals that allocating food on the basis of gender inequality, rather than nutritional equality, produces long-term effects on the health and well-being of the Wopkaimin population, especially the women. Diet systems of other indigenous peoples regulate allocation of foods that is not nutritionally in the best interest of certain age–sex groups in the population (see Dornstreich 1973: 394; Nietschmann

Fig. 31. Birds carry few dietary restrictions and this dove (*Gymnophaps albertisii*) was eaten by the young boy after his father shot it in an abandoned garden.

1973: 214). The amount and frequency of food consumption for different age–sex groups of the Wopkaimin population reflects adjustments to food procurement and distribution patterns as well as to cultural conditioning of appetites and digestive habits. Eating is a complex cultural, social and physiological arrangement which is an expression of the interrelationships among food accessibility, acquisition and adequacy.

The values chosen for nutritional requirements strongly influence any conclusions reached about the interrelationship between diet and health among the Wopkaimin. I have used figures that are comparable with the allowances set by human ecologists for other Highland fringe populations. There is approximately a 4-kg difference in weight between adult Wopkaimin (Table 2) and Gadio Enga men (Dornstreich 1973: 54). Allowances for Wopkaimin nutritional requirements (Table 4) are based on a Gadio Enga baseline (Dornstreich 1973: 430) with minor calorie, protein and fat adjustments. FAO/WHO (1973: 34) calorie allowances are adjusted lower than Gadio standards. Townsend, Liao and Konlande (1973: 95) suggest a basal requirement for adult Sanio-Hiowe males of only 1200 calories. Rajalakshmi and Ramakrishnan (1969:169) calculate that one tropical Indian population with similar activity patterns and weights similar to the Wopkaimin requires less energy than indicated for the Gadio. Considering these recent findings, I have adjusted Gadio caloric requirements to the lower figures shown in Table 4. The FAO/WHO (1973: 70) low value requirements for adults are five grams lower than Dornstreich's allowance for the Gadio. Because FAO/WHO (1973: 87) has reduced the theoretically safe level of protein intake, I have adjusted Gadio protein requirements down to those shown in Table 4. The remaining nutritional requirements presented in Table 4 are based on Gadio values except for fats which are recalculated as a percentage of the adjusted caloric requirements.

McArthur (1977: 107) suggests that accepting recommended standards as a baseline for measuring nutritional status is wrong because: (1) requirements are based on assumptions that make no allowances for children up to the age of puberty, and the bulky nature of vegetable diets in the Highland fringe prevents small children from eating quantities necessary for supplying calories and proteins specified for their age group; (2) FAO/WHO (1973) caloric scales are derived from healthy people and do not reflect a proper understanding of the relationship between various nutrients and health; (3) caloric requirements are average figures that only refer to groups and not to individuals; and (4) FAO/WHO (1973) protein scales are not average figures like calories, but are instead safe levels of intake intended to exceed the actual physiological need of all but a small minority of people. McArthur's (1977: 125–26) inescapable conclusion is that scales of requirements for measuring adequacy of diets must only be used in conjunction with clinical and biochemical examinations. Bearing in mind McArthur's admonition, I organized cooperation among the Kam Basin residents for the IMR survey of October 1975 in order to produce an integrated clinical, nutritional and ethnographic understanding of the Wopkaimin diet.

Nutritional requirements are impossible to prescribe without taking into account the cultural and ecological situation of a population. There are always certain biological and environmental circumstances outside of culture and human control. There are other demographic and ecological factors that are interrelated to culture and partially under human control. Anthropological enquiry establishes the patterns of group and individual decision-making that culturally adapt a human population to their ecosystem, such as food allocation, patterns of activity and medical treatment (Dornstreich 1973: 382). The literature on the wide range of factors affecting nutritional requirements of the remote indigenous peoples inhabiting the Highland fringe is voluminous and often contradictory. The high and low figures in

Table 4 are certainly not precise, but they are in accord with recommended allowances as they pertain to Highland fringe population conditions and should be satisfactory to support the generalizations to follow.

Table 5 shows the percentage of different nutrients supplied by plant and animal foods during the diet study. The greater the percentage a particular nutrient is derived from animal foods, the less equitably it is supplied to all age–sex groups of the Wopkaimin population. Dornstreich (1973: 395) has noted a similar relationship between animal foods and nutrient allocation among the Gadio Enga. Over 50% of fat is supplied by animal foods. Protein is just under 50% supplied by animal foods, and vitamins B1, B2 and niacin are each approximately one third supplied by animal foods.

Table 6 shows the percentage of times, at the conclusion of the diet study, that each age–sex group received over 50% of required nutrients. Fats, which are 95% supplied by animal foods, for most of the time did not meet the necessary requirement of any age–sex group of the Wopkaimin population. Indeed, all age–sex groups except adult males, are over 90% of the time inadequately supplied with dietary fat. Proteins are 47% supplied by animal foods (Hyndman, in press (a)) and are satisfactory in the diet just marginally more than half of the time for all age–sex groups, with the interesting exception of adult men who only acquired high value protein requirements on 49% of occasions during the diet study. Vitamin B1, which is 33% supplied by animal foods, satisfied the minimal requirement values most of the time. Vitamin B2, 34% supplied by animal foods, and niacin, 32% supplied by animal foods, only reach low levels in the diets of all those over nine years of age.

The nutrients predominantly supplied by plant foods in the diet include calories, calcium and vitamins A and C. In general, these four nutrients are adequately supplied in the diet, with the significant exception of calories. Table 6 shows that calories in the diet fail to satisfy low requirement values approximately two thirds of the time during the diet study. Calcium is adequate with only a small safety margin, particularly for the 10–14 age group.

When a particular nutrient falls below the low requirement allowance over 50% of the time, the nutrient is probably limiting or certainly adequate with only a small safety margin. From Table 6, it can be seen that the four nutrients that are stress points in the Wopkaimin diet, especially during periods of food shortage, are calories, fats, vitamin B2 and niacin. The limiting nutrients in the dietary of the Highland fringe Gadio Enga are calories, protein, fat and vitamin B2 (Dornstreich 1973: 396).

Each limited nutrient is differently patterned in the Wopkaimin diet. Calories averaged out to adequately meet requirements. The pattern of limitation is a regular oscillation back and forth between a deficit and a surplus of calories. Average caloric consumption obscures the fact that daily food intake is variable in timing and amounts. Meal times are irregular, but the main meal of the day is in the late afternoon, usually around 1700 hours. Hunger is an accepted condition and smoking is common. Hunters say that smoking dulls hunger and better enables them to travel light and fast. The highest daily per person plant food energy intake is 5451 calories; the lowest is ten calories. Per person daily energy intake from animals ranges from 5269 calories to two calories. Hunger tolerance combined with such a large capacity for eating could be a physiological and cultural buffering mechanism that counteracts inconsistencies in food procurement and availability (see Nietschmann 1973: 215). Fluctuating caloric intake between periods of food abundance and food shortage is also a feature of the dietary pattern of the Highland fringe Gadio (Dornstreich 1973: 397).

Fat and vitamins B2 and niacin are correlated with the supply of animal food in the Wopkaimin diet. Without doubt, fat is the least well supplied nutrient in the diet. As with calories and protein, the intake of fat, vitamin B2 and niacin greatly fluctuate from day to day. Some amount of animal food is expected to be regularly available in the hamlet. If not, the low animal food intake is not tolerated for more than about a week before movement of the hamlet takes place to alleviate the shortage through hunting, fishing or collecting.

Wopkaimin food ethnoclassifications (Fig. 30) operate to systematically favor the allocation of animals to adult men over other age–sex groups in the population. Comparing the regular supply, by New Guinea standards, of game animal returns during the diet study (Table 7) with Table 3 showing their appropriate consumption classification indicates that animals are 5.5 times as frequently available to adult men as to adult women and 3.6 times as frequently available to adult men as to children. Fats come predominantly from animals, but since the greater percentage of vitamins B2 and niacin are supplied by plant foods, they are more equitably consumed than fats by each age–sex group of the population.

Table 8 shows how the encoded and observed system of food ethnoclassifications among the Wopkaimin has produced a quantitatively and qualitatively superior diet for adult men compared to other age–sex groups of the population. The most pervasive taboos of the Wopkaimin and Baktamanmin concern eating, especially animal foods (Barth 1975: 164). These are specific taboos (see Basso 1973) that fall upon persons of particular social categories defined in terms of sex and relative age. Food ethnoclassifications have important nutritional consequences because they do not allow the equitable consumption of animal foods.

Barth (1975: 165–166) alludes to the gender basis of Baktamanmin (Figure 24) food taboos and how they revolve around social distinctions drawn on the basis of age–sex groups but incorrectly assumes that the system of food ethno-classification does not monopolize privilege for men:

> Clearly we are not dealing with a system for the monopolization of privilege; men are subject to far more dietary restrictions than women and children. Senior men do enjoy the exclusive right to eat wild pig, cassowary and honey (this latter is a weak taboo occasionally broken by the women), but this is almost balanced by the prohibitions against many marsupials, reptiles and invertebrates. Men in the prime of life carry the greatest load of prohibitions, children the smallest.

Table 8 illustrates how men are nutritionally the most privileged age–sex group. Small game animals, reptiles and invertebrates are denied to adult males and they outnumber adult male foods. They are fairly regularly consumed, but they are nutritionally less significant animal foods compared to the feral pigs and cassowaries which are exclusively for adult male consumption. Furthermore, many large game mammals are denied to women, especially those who are pregnant or lactating (Table 3). Table 8 demonstrates that the consequence of food ethnoclassifications is to make the daily diet of men in their prime of life nutritionally superior to that of women and children. Gender relations specifically operate in a very real way to monopolize privilege for adult men.

Human ecological and nutritional fieldwork from the Highlands (Venkatachalam 1962: 11, Hipsley and Kirk 1965: 8, Sorenson and Gajdusek 1969: 304–07) and from the Highland fringe (Rappaport 1968: 79–80, Townsend 1969: 61,69, Clarke 1971: 24–25; Dornstreich 1973: 403–412) indicate that some age–sex groups in other New Guinea populations are better nourished than others. Clines of decreasing adult female stature are also reported in several parts of the Highlands and Highland fringe. Although North Simbu has no such cline (Harvey and Heywood 1983: 67–8), there is declining female stature from east to west in South Simbu that parallels the distinction between Pawaian and Dairibi language speakers (Hide 1984: 187). Stature declines from east to west in Enga (Freedman and MacIntosh 1965: 299–300) and from northeast to southwest in the eastern Highlands (Littlewood 1972: 38–41). Buchbinder and Clark (1971: 124–125) indicate that stature among the Highland fringe Maring declines from east to west. In the Eastern Highlands in all cases of inequitable food allocation, it is women and children which require special scrutiny. It is not just that women and children eat different types of food from men; the game animals appearing in Table 7 after being socially allocated according to their ethnoclassification status result in the quantitative variation in nutrient intake between age–sex groups presented in Table 8.

As a population, and as individuals, the Wopkaimin are nutritionally affected by the social allocation of foodstuffs, by the pattern of food-getting behaviour, by the dividing and sharing of food and by age–sex specific food taboos. The pattern of food-getting behaviour is a crucial factor of nutrient allocation. Size and amount are important variables in the regulation of access to highly valued animal foods. Size is fundamental to the distinction between feral pigs, cassowaries and large game mammals which possess meat (*dim*) and fish, reptiles and invertebrates which only possess flesh (*kil*). Different food-getting behaviour (Hyndman 1984) is appropriate in acquiring animals having meat and animals having flesh; men hunt meat-yielding animals, while women and children fish for and collect flesh-yielding animals.

Children of the Wopkaimin and other Highland fringe peoples regularly collect small animals as food (Rappaport 1968: 78, Clarke 1971: 92, Dornstreich 1973: 405, Barth 1975: 41). Since most of these small animals are channelled to children, they are easily underestimated in diet studies. Women eat fish, reptiles and invertebrates only when they are available in amounts exceeding about 500 g; otherwise these small animals are given to the children. Table 7 lists all small animals that entered Bakonabip hamlet or other shelters during the diet study, but not those eaten elsewhere in the Kam Basin. Among the Wopkaimin animal size and amount affects the allocation of nutrients. Collected animals are regularly consumed away from the hamlets, which definitely creates a nutritional pay-off for settlement shifts and mobility (see Dornstreich 1973: 406-7).

Sago working near Ulatem shelter during the diet study was an occasion when the diet of women and children was marginally superior to that of their Bakonabip hamlet diet. In four days, 57 kg of sago, 7.2 kg of *Athyrium*, 1.5 kg of *Oxyeleotris fimbriatus*, 1.6 kg of frogs and 0.5 kg of larvae were consumed at Ulatem. The average daily intake of 3722 calories was 50% higher than normal; all other nutrients were just marginally under normal intake. Sago boosted caloric intake, but since it contains few other nutrients, all of the small animals consumed did not adequately compensate to boost per day nutrient intake above normal.

After the first four days of sago working, several women and children shifted from Ulatem to hunt and fish. Two brothers, their sister and their families moved for four days to Tambik shelter. They harvested *Xanthosoma*, *aibika* and *Sechum edule* fruits and leaves from an abandoned garden. With gathered wild yam and *Athyrium*, their average daily plant food intake was 1202 calories. Hunting, fishing and collecting returns were extraordinarily high. Bag weight returns from hunting included one cassowary (17 kg), many birds (2.9 kg) and a *Phalanger rufoniger* (5.5 kg); fishing returns included *Neosilirus equinus* (6.2 kg) and *Oxyeleotris fimbriatus* (0.6 kg); collecting returns included 140 g of frogs.

Daily animal food intake for women and children averaged 320 calories; the intake for men averaged 2080 calories. Women and children averaged a daily intake of 76.6 g of protein and 18 g of fat per day; the daily average for men was 325.8 g of protein and 118.5 g of fat per day. By leaving Ulatem the women and children traded off a superabundance of calories for a protein intake 47% higher than normal. Because of food ethnoclassifications the intake levels for the men averaged 30% higher for calories, 76% higher for proteins and 48% higher for fats. Clearly, food ethnoclassifications overwhelmingly favor adult men. However, the Ulatem and Tambik portions of the diet survey reveal that if women and children are merely mobile and present for food-getting away from their residential hamlets, it raises their calorific and protein intake levels above normal, but not proportionately as high as for men.

In terms of food distribution, only large returns of animals exceeding 2 kg are associated with the decorum of public sharing. Animal food shares for women and children are typically small animals and less desirable cuts of meat. Food distribution reinforces the age-specific dietary pattern of small animals for children, a pattern widespread among Highland fringe peoples (see Bulmer 1967, Dornstreich 1973: 409, Barth 1975). Everyone present, regardless of age–sex group, receives some portion of any large return of animal food as a general rule. In actual practice the combined effects of mobility, private eating, animal sacrifice in the cult system and food ethnoclassifications operate to allocate animal foods inequitably. To the extent the Wopkaimin do not obey their own taboos, the negative nutritional consequences of their taboos are diminished. However, during the diet study there was no distinction among the Wopkaimin between norms (taboo) and behaviour (eating) because they rigidly observed their food ethnoclassifications. Maring food taboos operate to the advantage of women and children (Rappaport 1968: 80, Thomas 1976), Gadio Enga food taboos favor men over women and children in animal food intake, but Dornstreich (1973: 410) found it too difficult to gauge the extent to which food taboos were followed. Table 8 shows that for every nutrient responsive to animal food intake, which only excludes vitamins A and C, the intake is greater for men than any other age–sex group, which is the behavioral result among the Wopkaimin of observing their food ethnoclassifications.

The diet of Wopkaimin women and children is nutritionally inferior to the diet of adult men. Adult men receive adequate calories, proteins, fats, vitamins and minerals; their diet actually exceeds high value requirements for six out of ten nutrients (Table 8). The diet of women and children is inadequate in comparison with that of men and they are actually nutritionally deficient in fats and vitamin B2. Moreover, women have only a marginally adequate calorie intake.

The impact of gender on nutrient allocation is for women and children to receive more of those foods that supply calories and less that supply fats and vitamin B2. In other words, men eat more meat than do women and children. The pattern of Wopkaimin food-getting behaviour is for men to perform arduous, irregular activities, while women perform the monotonous and constant activities (Hyndman, in press (a)). The serious implication is that women require, but only marginally receive, regularly adequate nutritional returns to sustain their constant levels of energy expenditure. Table 4 indicates that nutritional requirements for women equal or exceed the levels necessary for children; yet Table 8 shows that women have to sustain themselves on lower amounts of every nutrient than the normal intake of men and children. The outcome of food-getting behaviour, gender and food ethnoclassifications is a system that channels not only more collected animal food to children than to women but also more hunted animal food to men than to women.

GENDER AND HEALTH

The North Fly Clinico-Epidemiological Pilot Study (NFCEPS) has released two health assessments of the Wopkaimin population. The NFCEPS (1979a) among the Wopkaimin was carried out from 5 October 1978 to 13 October 1978 by Dr B. Pilecki, WHO Consultant in Leprosy and Tuberculosis, and by Dr R. Ashford, Senior Lecturer in Parasitology, University of Papua New Guinea. They examined 51 self-selected Wopkaimin, Faiwolmin and Ningerum residing in the prospecting camp at Tabubil as well as the entire population of 53 residing in the Beinglim parish hamlet of Atemkit. Their summarized health assessment is as follows

(NFCEPS 1979a: 8):

1. The pattern of disease in the Star Mountains differed appreciably from that in the Fly River valley. 16 persons (30%) at Atemkit and 16 (31%) at Tabubil were found to have hepatomegaly, while 33 of the villagers (62%) and 21 (41%) of the self-selected sample at the mining camp had enlarged spleens. The mean grade of liver enlargement at Atemkit was 1.3 and at Tabubil 1.25; mean splenomegaly at Atemkit was 2.4 and at Tabubil 2.1. Seven cases of clinical malaria, not substantiated by examination of the slides were seen in either place.
2. Though lymphadenopathy was not found to be an important sign, 13 of 104 daytime slides revealed the presence of *W. bancrofti*, and in 94 further slides taken during an evening cinema performance at Tabubil filaraemia was detected in 19. Since the majority of these people had not lived outside the Star Mountains, this appears effectively to establish the presence of filariasis in an area where it has hitherto been thought not to occur.
3. Skin diseases were not common in this area. Only one rash and one boil were seen in Atemkit, and two rashes, two leg ulcers and one case of scabies in Tabubil.
4. Dental caries was not noted to occur, but there was one case of pyorrhea in Atemkit.
5. Chronic respiratory disease is not common in the mountains. Of the 50 people who complained of respiratory symptoms, only three were found to have signs: one bronchitic and one possible pulmonary tuberculous case in Atemkit, and one asthmatic in Tabubil. One left-sided cardiac failure was detected in Atemkit, and one breast tumor, one abdominal mass, possibly amoebic, and one case of deafness in Tabubil. There was no clinical evidence of malnutrition, and the people of Atemkit appeared to be successful hunters and well provided with protein foods. What was particularly striking in this area was the absence of elderly people: there appeared to be no one older than the mid forties.

Dr T. Taufa, lecturer in Community Medicine, University of Papua New Guinea, carried out the NFCEPS (1979b) in the Faiwolmin villages of Olsobip and Golgobip and the Enkaiakmin (Figure 24) village of Bolivip. Helminthological investigations reported in the NFCEPS (1979b) indicate that filariasis, *W. bancrofti*, is absent in the Wopkaimin population living in Atemkit, although it is found among the Ningerum residing in Tabubil. Intestinal protozoa *Ascaris* and *Trichuris* are also very rare among the Wopkaimin and other Ok speaking peoples. Hookworm, probably *Necator americanus*, infects all of the Lowland and Mountain Ok populations in the pilot study sample. 84% of the Atemkit residents are infected with hookworm, the highest reported rate of intestinal helminth infection of any Ok speaking population.

The 1975 IMR Wopkaimin survey and the NFCEPS (1979a, 1979b) establish a baseline health assessment for the population. *In vitro* tests confirm the existence of chloroquine-resistant *Plasmodium falciparum* malaria. The major health abnormality among the Wopkaimin and other Ok speakers is malaria. Endemicity of malaria is derived from considering the prevalence and degree of splenomegaly. In the Ningerum foothills splenomegaly ranges from 51% to 89%; the mean grade of liver enlargement in Hackett's classification ranges from 1.4 to 2.0. From the Ningerum foothills into Wopkaimin territory splenomegaly drops slightly to 62% with a mean Hackett grade of 2.4 in the low altitude (500 m) hamlet of Atemkit. Among the mixed Ok speaking population residing at Tabubil (700 m), splenomegaly drops to 41% with a mean Hackett grade of 2.1. Malaria is hyperendemic in the lower elevational ranges of Wopkaimin territory; with increasing altitude malaria drops to holoendemicity and ranges from 3% to 9% in the higher altitude hamlets (1500 m) of Golgobip and Bolivip.

Figure 32 summarizes the statistical differences between females and males for anthropometric and hematological data collected during the 1975 IMR Wopkaimin survey. Hackett grades taken during the 1975 IMR survey follow the typical trend (Figure 32) of no significant male–female differences until adulthood. Although *t* jumps from 0.55 for the 15–19 age group to 1.41 for the 20–24 age group, it is just statistically below 5% significance. Throughout adulthood women have more enlarged spleens than men. The IMR Hackett grade means for adult men and women are 0.71 for men and 1.36 for women in the 20–24 age group, 1.08 for men and 1.13 for women in the 25–40 age group, and 0.57 for men and 0.14 for women in the over-40 age group.

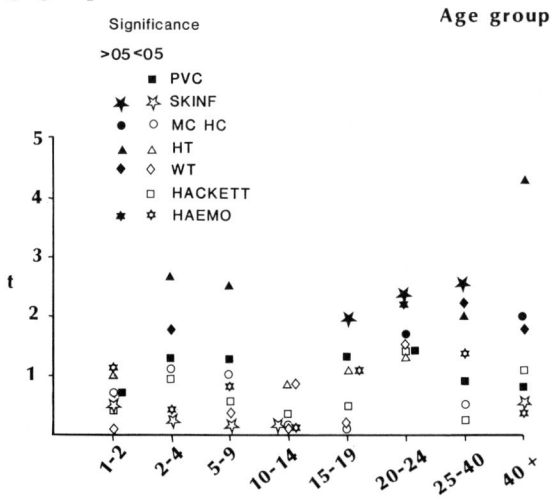

Fig. 32. Summary of differences between females and males for anthropometric and hematological data collected during the 1975 IMR survey.

Hepatomegaly is strongly associated with the high prevalence of splenomegaly and the NFCEPs (1979a, 1979b) indicate the disease is present among 31% of the Atemkit residents. Repeated bouts of malaria and other factors are involved in the pathogenesis of hepatomegaly. The work of Buchbinder (1973) and Venkatachalam (1962) indicate that protein deficiency is an important factor contributing to the pathogenesis of hepatomegaly. Wopkaimin subsistence ecology (Hyndman 1982, 1984, in press (a)) is intimately associated with the population undergoing repeated bouts of malaria when they temporarily shift settlements to altitudes under 1000 m to hunt, fish, and process sago, succumb to malaria attacks and return to higher altititude hamlets around 1500 m to escape the zone of hyperendemic malaria. Protein energy undernutrition among adult women is intimately associated with gender relations and food ethnoclassifications.

Mean hemoglobin levels are significantly lower than values set by the World Health Organization (WHO). Standards recognized by the WHO for populations without a high incidence of parasite load or nutritional problems range from 13–17 (g/100 ml) for adult men but only range from 12–15 (g/100 ml) for adult women to account for menstruation and child-birth. Hemoglobin levels (Fig. 32) are one of the most significantly different health parameters between men and women. The mean for men in the 20–24 age group is 11.93 and for women it is 10.73. In the 25–40 age group the male mean is 11.74 and the female means is 11.13. For the over forty age group the male mean is 11.46 and the female mean is 11.09. Women in the 20–24 age group exhibit the most significantly different hemoglobin levels from men because of the combined effects of hookworm, menstruation, ovulation and food ethno-classifications depriving them of adequate protein and energy at the very time they are most required, during childbirth and lactation. Wopkaimin women and men are anemic because of hookworm and malaria but women are more acutely anemic because gender affects their diet so as to deprive them of adequate protein, iron and folic acid intake (Table 8).

Packed Cell Volume (PCV) and Mean Corpuscular Hemoglobin Concentration (MCHC) further substantiate the high incidence of anemia. Both of these health parameters follow the typical trend (Fig. 32) where significant male–female differences peak in the 20–24 age group and start levelling off in the older age groups. t test results for PCV and MCHC in the 20–24 age group are respectively 1.46 and 1.71, with women being statistically different for MCHC. MCHC is the amount of hemoglobin per red blood cell. Even where malaria is hyper- and holoendemic, hemoglobin is often normal and is only lower when there is the additional problem of nutritional anemia. MCHC is consistently lower for adult women than men in all except the over-40 age group; the male–female comparison in the 20–24 age groups is 30.39 to 31.67, in the 25–40 age group it is 30.45 to 30.71 and in the over-40 age group it is 30.89 to 29.57. PCV is normally 45–50%. All adults fall below 40% PCV volume which is the cut off point indicative of anemia. Adult women have consistently lower PCV volumes than adult men; for the 20–24 age group they are 35.3% compared to 37.4%, for the 25–40 age group they are 36.2% compared to 37.8% and for the over-40 age group they are 35.9% compared to 38.1%.

Summarizing the Australian colonial administration census information on the Wopkaimin population reveals a significant decline since contact. According to Parker (1972) the Wopkaimin numbered 632 in 1969, 631 in 1970, 609 in 1972. They were back up to 622 by 1973 (Philip 1973). This population history does not include the Fitiktaman first censused by Ransley (1975). Subtracting the Kaweintikin parish population, the 1975 population declined by approximately 7% since contact, probably due to an outbreak of influenza and dysentery (Eggleton 1968). Buchbinder (1977) reports a similar post-contact population decline among the Maring, a Highland fringe population of the Bismarck mountains.

The Wopkaimin do not have a strong resistance against disease and this problem is related to the absence of many people older than their mid forties (NFCEPS 1979a). Nutritional stunting occurs in the over forty age group as manifested in declining weight, height and skinfold with increasing age. Not only is nutritional stunting indicated in the patterns of weight, height and skinfold but, in addition, each parameter is statistically different between women and men (Fig. 32). Stature and weight in adults, as previously mentioned, is 1535 mm. and 48.3 kg for men and 1487 mm. and 44.7 kg for women. For the over forty age group male stature actually increases to 1565 mm. with a modest weight drop to 47.3 kg, – whereas women significantly decline to 1457 mm. and 41.0 kg Skinfold, mean triceps thickness, measures subcutaneous fat in the body, which in Papua New Guinea is normally low. Fat is a limiting nutrient in the Wopkaimin diet (Table 6). Although skinfold measures are higher for adult women than for adult men, the decline with advancing age among women is much more dramatic. Mean triceps skinfold in the 20–24 age group is 4.7 for men and 7.0 for women, in the 25–40 age group it increases to 4.8 for men while plummeting to 4.6 for women. Height, weight and skinfold all indicate that nutritional stunting is most significant with advancing age for women. Even though adults outnumber children, the Wopkaimin are a young population and women die sooner than men.

CONCLUSION

The interrelationship of gender and diet creates a negative feedback nutritional problem among the Wopkaimin, widespread in New Guinea (Hipsley and Kirk 1965: 8), whereby continuous energy demand and quantitatively marginal nourishment produces women who experience gradually deteriorating energy storage status as they grow older. Statistical interpretation of the anthropometric and hematological data collected during the 1975 IMR Wopkaimin survey substantiates that the Wopkaimin system of diet and health produces adult women who are in significantly poorer health than are adult men.

Adult women show a statistically significant difference from adult men for nearly every anthropometric and hematological variable (Fig. 32). Other than height and weight in the 2–4 and 5–9 age groups, males and females do not significantly differ in health parameters until the onset of adulthood. Likewise, the full impact of gender and food ethnoclassifications on dietary differences between the sexes first occurs at the onset of adulthood. Elaborate male initiation sequences begin in adolescence and do not terminate until men are in the 20–24 age group (Barth 1975, Poole 1982). During the decade that young men completely alter their gender and ritual status through staged initiations (Poole 1981), they also gradually acquire the dietary changes necessary to attaining their superior adult nutritional status.

The Wopkaimin successfully limit their population size through the process of women's gradually deteriorating energy storage and health status. Gender and food ethnoclassifications systematically channel animal food away from women. Their lowered nutrient intake produces protein energy undernutrition, anemia, advancing age, nutritional stunting and earlier death. Wopkaimin ethnoscience is based on ancestral knowledge and techniques accumulated over 15,000 years (Swadling 1984) of practical *in situ* testing and experimentation (Hyndman in press b). Ethnoscience encodes gender roles by assigning appropriate quest and consumption behaviour to men and women (Hyndman 1984) and functions to ecologically and socially adjust the population to the environment. Ethnoscience has guided varying mixtures of ecologically-integrated sustained-yield subsistence activities that have had minimal impact over time on resources but substantial impact over time on diet, health, morbidity and mortality between the sexes.

DAVID R. COUNTS AND DOROTHY AYERS COUNTS

12. COMPLEMENTARITY IN MEDICAL TREATMENT IN A WEST NEW BRITAIN SOCIETY

The Lusi are an Austronesian-speaking, horticultural people living in the Kaliai area of the northwest coast of West New Britain province in Papua New Guinea. Kaliai was contacted and pacified around the turn of this century by German colonial representatives. Despite the fact that small parcels of land were alienated in the early 1900s for a mission station and for a private plantation, the peoples of the northwest coast of New Britain have remained, until very recently, among the most isolated of coastal-dwelling societies anywhere in Papua New Guinea. There is still, in 1984, no government administered office closer than 100 kilometers by sea from the central part of the Kaliai coast. The land bought by the Roman Catholic mission was not occupied by a priest or by sisters until after World War II, and while Iboki Plantation has been in nearly continuous operation from German times until today, its effect on the local population has been small except as an occasional source of casual employment, as the location of a tradestore or, more rarely, as a market for local garden produce.

Access to medical care from professionally trained persons came to the Kaliai region only after 1952 when a clinic staffed by a triple certificate nursing sister was opened in connection with the Kaliai Roman Catholic mission. Now known as the Kaliai health center, the clinic has passed into the control of the Health Department of the government of Papua New Guinea, and continues to provide the only professional Western medical care available for at least 80 kilometers in any direction.

In this essay we examine the way in which the people of Kaliai perceive the opportunities for medical therapy that are available to them. Those opportunities clearly include the care offered by the nursing staff of the Kaliai health center and may occasionally include care from more distant medical centres, such as the one at Cape Gloucester, 80 kilometers to the west or the general hospital located in Kimbe, the provincial capital, 160 kilometers to the east. The medical treatment available to the Kaliai also includes that offered by indigenous healers or curers who proceed from different assumptions and operate by different methods than do the personnel practicing at aid post, regional health centre and hospital.

Because these alternatives are available, when a Lusi experiences injury or illness she/he must make a decision about the level or kind of treatment to seek. This decision is made, as are those that follow through the course of the illness, on the basis of notions about the nature of illness and disease, the causes of such health problems and the efficacy of the available treatment. Such notions arise from Lusi culture and it is on that culture, with particular attention to the domain of illness and its treatment, that we focus in this essay.

S. Frankel and G. Lewis (eds.), *A Continuing Trial of Treatment*. 277–294.
© 1989, Kluwer Academic Publishers, Dordrecht – Printed in the Netherlands.

The research on which this essay is based has taken place during four periods of residence in the Kaliai area beginning in 1966 when we resided in Kandoka village, the largest of the five coastal villages of Lusi speakers, for a period of eleven months. We returned to Kandoka in 1971, in 1975–76, and in 1981.[1] During our nearly thirty months of residence there, what began as fairly standard graduate field research in anthropology has become a long-term study of a people's accommodation to increasingly rapid change. None of the research projects that took us to live among the Lusi has been directly concerned with their ideas of health and illness, but the general circumstances and particular events of our residence there have made us intensely aware of the problems that threaten their health and of their attempts to deal with illness, injury and death.

In part, our awareness of Lusi concern with illness and injury arose because we have actively conducted research into the domains of aging and death (D.R. Counts 1976–77, Counts and Counts 1983–84, D. A. Counts 1980, 1983, 1984b). This research has led to considerable discussion with consultants about the nature of the infirmity that comes with age and about the kind of illness and injury that leads to death. The data that we have collected may also be ascribed in part to the fact that among the most dramatic events occurring during our residence in Kaliai have been those occasioned by someone falling victim to serious illness, suffering traumatic injury, or dying. In all these kinds of occurrences we have, because the Lusi spend a lot of their time discussing it, become aware of the cause and course of illnesses as the villagers conceive them to be. Finally, though neither of us has medical training, our friends in the village regularly come to us for first aid, and often seek our help in much more serious cases.

The nature of our training and, therefore, of our data clearly do not let us speak with authority of the clash between Western medical conceptions of illness and those held by the Kaliai. They do, however, permit us to discuss the Lusi's views of illness and what they regard as the respective merits and failures of the systems of therapy available to them.

Since 1966, Kandoka village has experienced a modest growth in population, and the shape of the village has changed to accommodate the creation of new households and the loss, through death, of others. One small group of kinsmen has moved away to start a new community but, in general, the physical setting of the village has not altered much in nearly two decades. There have, however, been other dramatic changes, for the outside world has literally come closer to Kandoka. Administrative appointment of village headmen (*luluai*) has been replaced with local self-government by council; political administration by Australia of New Guinea as a United Nations Trust has been replaced by independence for the state of Papua New Guinea; western New Britain was separated from eastern New Britain first as a district and subsequently as a province; finally, the new provincial government has been situated in a town, Kimbe, which came into existence in the 1970s as part of a major development scheme centred on the production and processing of palm oil.

These developments, giving the Lusi increased access to cash and the ready availability of local transport to move people and goods to the town, have combined to reduce the isolation of Kaliai. One aspect of reduced isolation is greater access to Western medical care. Before about 1975, care for serious illnesses or situations requiring surgical treatment was available only from the hospitals located in the extreme eastern part of New Britain, at Rabaul and Kokopo. This was a difficult journey from Kaliai and one that few made because of lack of transport and the time and distance involved. By 1981 hospital care for the seriously ill was no more than a few hours away on a canoe powered by one of the numerous outboard engines to be found in every coastal Kaliai village.

While reduced distance and greater availability of locally controlled transport have improved access to Western medical treatment for the Kaliai during the last fifteen years, the cost of using these facilities has risen marginally by the imposition of small fees for the services offered. These fees – of ten toea[2] for pain-relief tablets and fifty toea for an injection of penicillin for example – were originally instituted in the early 1970s when what had been a mission and hence supported by contributions from abroad, became a parish and expected to provide its own support. The increased availability of cash from the sale of copra has meant that the fees have not been a serious deterrent to use of the health facilities, but villagers sometimes grumble and delay going to the clinic because each visit requires the outlay of still relatively scarce money.

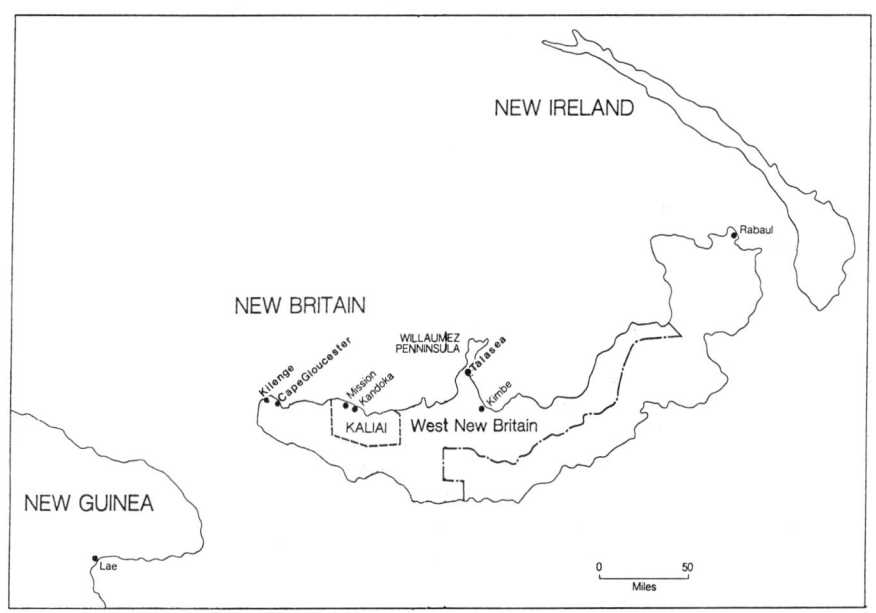

Fig. 33. Map of West New Britain.

Kaliai health center is located on the grounds of the Roman Catholic mission station near the village of Taveliai in the central coast of the Kaliai census subdivision of the Gloucester District of West New Britain Province (see Fig. 33).

It is now a government staffed and supported health centre and the personnel are all nationals of Papua New Guinea. Despite the departure of the last expatriate nursing sister (a nun) about a decade ago, the ties of the Kaliai health center to the Catholic mission remain close. The centre serves the entire area of the Kaliai census subdivision, supplemented by two aid posts in the interior of the 2000 square kilometer area. The aid posts, staffed by medical orderlies and offering only extended first aid, are located inland on the Vanu and the Aria rivers, the major drainage systems of the region. Serious cases are referred by the aid posts to the central health centre where there is a registered nurse in charge. From there, in turn, difficult cases may be referred to the district centre at Gloucester or to the general hospital at Kimbe. All referrals and patient transfers must be made by sea, as no roads currently link Kaliai to any other part of the province. Kandoka is located on the coast, some ten kilometers east of the Kaliai health center, and it is there that Kandokans routinely go for care when they are injured or ill. The distance separating the coastal villages from the Kaliai health center is not a major problem limiting access except in the worst times of the year during the northwest monsoon season. At such times even poling a shallow draught outrigger canoe may be an arduous and daunting task and may be an occasion for delay in going to the clinic.

Reasonably ready access to Western medical care has not caused the villagers to give up their indigenous system of treatment of serious illness and injury. On the contrary, they often rely on their own system of treatment in addition to, or instead of, the care offered by the Kaliai health center personnel. One aspect of traditional Lusi therapy has, however, fallen into disuse. For first aid treatment of minor wounds and sores, they are now completely dependent on the services of the clinic. Our oldest consultants have identified for us a number of leaves, plant saps, barks and other sources of potions that were applied as medicines and bandages to cuts, abrasions and the like. But among the coastal Kaliai few people use these any longer and younger people are only vaguely aware of their existence. What remains of the indigenous treatment of illness and injury is almost entirely restricted to conditions that the Lusi regard as life-threatening.

It is questionable whether the non-Western therapy that the Lusi use can appropriately be called "traditional". It is traditional in the sense that it proceeds from assumptions about the causes of disease and the efficacy of treatment that are part of Lusi culture. This does not necessarily mean that the specifics of treatment that may be applied in a particular case are the same treatments that might have been applied in a similar case fifty or one hundred years ago. Since pacification and the imposition of colonial government, the people of Kaliai, in spite of their isolation, have been exposed to ideas about the etiology and treatment of illness from many sources. From the beginning of this century, they were recruited to work as plantation laborers throughout Papua New Guinea. Today they travel widely, frequently visiting the town of Kimbe, and they have people from other social and linguistic groups living in their villages. Given the assumptions and beliefs about illness that we detail below, each foreigner with whom a Lusi comes into contact is a potential source of illness and of treatment for illness. This situation is unlikely to be a new one, for the people of Kaliai have long been engaged in the overseas trading network that links northwest New Britain to the northeast New Guinea mainland (see Harding 1967). Also, Lusi readily borrow the cultural equipment of others. This is no less true of the methods of curing than it is of the songs, dances, masks and numerous other things that they use as their own but that derive from others. The point is that it would be unwise to infer that there is something exclusively Kaliai in the medical pluralism that they currently use in their treatment of serious illness.

Lewis has observed that the Gnau draw a major distinction between the illness or injury of a *part* of a person's body and the illness of a person expressed as a general condition (1975: 130–132). This broad division of conditions requiring therapeutic attention works for the Lusi with only a slight modification. By illness we mean any condition that causes general discomfort or pain but that has no clearly perceptible surface manifestations. This condition normally causes a Lusi to use the term *rivalinga*, "illness", "sickness", or to say *ngarivali*, "I am ill". Conditions that are clearly localized, or that have an obvious surface manifestation, will almost always be described with reference either to the condition of the affected part, for example *ravagu iaiai* "my head hurts", *ahegu aia voto* "my leg has a sore", or to the nature of the injury, as in *aketi limagu* "I've cut my hand".

These two categories of conditions requiring medical treatment are not clear cut taxonomic classes, and there is no cover term in the Lusi language to include all of the conditions that are minor, localized or superficial and that would stand in opposition to the statement, *ngarivali* "I'm sick". A minor condition may, indeed, become an "illness" if it does not disappear or heal in the expected time. Despite the lack of elegance of these categories, they are important because of the implications underlying a Lusi's statement that she/he has an "illness". A person who says "I'm sick!" is, of course, calling attention to the fact that she/he is suffering from general discomfort that requires treatment. She/he intends that the statement be taken to mean that the condition is so serious that should the course of the illness not be altered and healing obtained, death may well follow. Finally, the person intends that it should be understood that something serious may be wrong, not only with his body but with his social relationships as well.

When we assert that a Lusi's statement "I am ill" contains the implication that his social relationships may be unwell, we are stating a corollary of the underlying assumption that most illnesses do not just happen. The causes of illnesses that lead to death are to be found not in nature, but in society. There are, to be sure, illnesses that may be caused by natural occurrences, and all of the conditions that Lusi consider minor are initially assumed not to have a social cause. However, any minor condition that either fails to respond to treatment or that worsens in spite of treatment, will probably come to be perceived as life-threatening and as having its origin in society rather than in nature. Bad social relations that can give rise to

TABLE 1
Categories of health problems and their causes

Human action	'Ghosts'	'Spirits'	'New' illnesses	Minor problems	Sexual contamination
Fevers	Infant fevers	Filariasis	Malaria	Sores	Infant colic
Bloody diarrhea		Fever in adults	Leprosy	Colds	Bloody sputum
Hemorrhoids			Pneumonia	Conjunctivitis	Tuberculosis
Malaria					Any severe respiratory illness
Serious infection					
Yaws					
Suicidal depression					
Lassitude					
'Wild' behavior					
Childbirth difficulty					
Stillbirth					
Persistent pain					
Persistent swelling					
Mental retardation					
Blindness					

illness are not restricted to those that obtain between living human beings. The social relations that may require repair before the body can be made well may exist between ghosts and their living relatives as well as between living persons.

Illness of the very young is frequently attributed to the activity of ghosts, while the illness and death of the extremely aged is likely to be thought merely the working of the natural order. On the other hand, almost all serious illnesses of mature persons stem from bad relationships existing among the living and may be attributed to the practice of sorcery or to the contamination of the body by sexual fluids, especially menstrual blood.

To a limited degree, it is possible for the Lusi to ascertain the cause of a particular condition from its expression in symptoms. We choose the term "condition" in the foregoing statement because the Lusi think of some states which in Western medicine are considered to be illnesses, as being of the same nature as physical deformities. They are unfortunate conditions arising from the actions of particular agents, but they lack the implication for social relationships that inhere in the notion of "illness". A good illustration of this is the attitude toward the disfiguring effects of filariasis. Filariasis is common on the northwest coast of New Britain, and the enlargement of the extremities associated with this disease affects a number of people in the villages of Kaliai. Our consultants have offered two explanations for the condition. The first, most commonly expressed view, is that the swelling is the result of the sufferer having violated the territory of a type of *masalai*, bush spirit, who has retaliated by causing the disfigurement. A contrary view is offered by those who note that the enlarged extremities are often seen in several members of one particular family, while they are totally absent from another. These consultants argue that the condition is clearly an inherited one. The point is that in neither case do people regard the condition as an illness and no one attempts to relieve it. Filariasis is, from this perspective, not a disease to be avoided or cured; rather, like a deformed limb, it is a condition to be endured.

At the same time, some states that a Western medical practitioner might not regard as similar sorts of illnesses are classified together and accorded similar treatment by the Lusi because their causes are perceived to be the same. For example, extended periods of lassitude and inertia that cause a person to fail to meet his ceremonial obligations or to repay his debts of shell currency are considered to be *rivalinga*, illnesses, because the sudden onset of an inability to meet one's obligations stems from sorcery. A rival has ensorcelled the victim. In Table 1 the categories of conditions that afflict people are arranged according to the causes commonly suspected in such cases. The list of afflictions is not exhaustive, but it gives an idea of the possible causes of complaints requiring attention and indicates the kinds of conditions that are attributed to different causes. One implication of the list of causes that appears in Table 1 is that "human action" is the most important source of health problems that are thought to require medical attention. While this is an accurate assessment of Lusi thinking, the situation is more complex than we can indicate in the Table. For example, there is a major distinction to be made between human action that is diffuse in its intent to cause illness or injury and that which is specific in intent. Diffuse human action refers to those acts that may cause injury or illness (1) where the particular victim was not chosen by the agent, though the effect was intended for anyone who came into contact with the disease causing substance or situation, or (2) where the effect of the human action was inadvertent, where the victim was, in effect, an accidental victim. The first category includes such action as placing magical devices to protect one's property – gardens, isolated houses, trees, etc. Such devices are marked by a clear sign warning the public at large that the device is in place and that the property should be avoided. Anyone injured as the result of contact with such a device has, in the opinion of most Lusi, only himself to blame. The second category is best illustrated by the use of a protective device by a sorcerer who is afraid of his rivals. A sorcerer who is likely to be in the presence of other sorcerers will prudently protect himself with a device called a *kisinga*, protective spell. He signals the existence of the protective spell by wearing an armband in which special crotons are placed. Although intended to be purely protective, the power of the spell is so formidable that anyone coming near or touching the device may be made ill. For children, who are particularly vulnerable, the effect may be serious illness or death. By specific human action we have reference to sorcery in which, through the use of magical rituals and spells, the sorcerer *intends* to harm his victim. All of the human actions that cause illness or injury are united by their use of spells, incantations and/or other magical devices in order to manifest their effects. In Table 1 the category "sexual contamination", although caused by the action of a human agent, is thought by Lusi to be more akin to the effect of a chemical poison than to the action of a sorcerer or a magician. Menstrual blood, widely regarded as a contaminant in Papua New Guinea societies (Frankel 1980, Lindenbaum 1979, Herdt 1981, Brown 1978), may be given to a man by his wife with the *intent* of making him fall ill. However, the careless contamination of her own (or someone else's) food by a menstruating woman is thought to have precisely the same effect. Similarly, semen which can contaminate the milk of a nursing mother and cause colic in her infant, requires no spell to do its work. The baby's consequent illness results in the indictment of the careless mother and not of the man whose semen caused the child to be ill (see D.A. Counts 1984a for further discussion of this point).

Another complexity that is not delineated in Table 1 arises from the fact that there are some conditions for which our consultants give contradictory explanations. We noted one such contradiction above in the case of filariasis. Some others are even more problematic. The health problems that we have listed in the column under the heading of "new illnesses" have been grouped together by some of our most reliable consultants under the Kaliai term *pura aiaoa*, the mouth of God or white person's mouth. These conditions, it is said, were unknown in northwest New Britain before the coming of the Germans and the Australians. The consultants who make this assertion and who link the appearance of leprosy, malaria and pneumonia to the arrival of the white-skinned foreigners, say that they are reporting the beliefs of their forefathers in denying the appearance of these problems before first contact. At the same time, these informants are able to give us names for these diseases in the Lusi language. The fact that these health problems have Lusi names strikes us as *prima facie* evidence that they are conditions of some long standing. Furthermore, at least in the case of malaria, a series of recurring attacks of increasing severity is likely to lead the sufferer to conclude that the source of his illness is sorcery and to seek a remedy in the repair of social relations rather than from the Kaliai health center.

This extended discussion of the Table showing health problems and their causes is intended to underscore the lack of consistency and uniformity among Lusi with regard to knowledge of illness. Largely, the explanation that is given for any condition will depend on the circumstances of the particular case. The most general rule that can be stated with regard to Lusi judgements about illness is that any condition that responds to Western medicine is likely (1) to be just an illness, i.e. not to have its origin in the practice of sorcery, and (2) to be thought a *sik bilong ol waitskin*, white person's disease, one brought with the Europeans when they came. The corollary of this rule is that any condition that does not respond to the efforts of practitioners of Western medicine will be asserted to have a local cause and to be susceptible only to traditional types of cures.

In order to illustrate the foregoing observations about Lusi understanding of conditions needing medical attention, we present below a series of vignettes drawn from a combination of field observation and consultant's recollection. Each is a real situation, not a composite, though the names of those involved have been changed.

Oneleg

The garden cleared by Michael and Melissa was not bearing well because it was shaded by a large tree that was occupied by a *masalai*; Michael was afraid to cut the tree and anger the spirit. He was, therefore, especially interested when the Catholic priest sprinkled holy water on a similarly occupied piece of land, rendering it safe for clearing and gardening. When the people who used this exorcised land suffered no ill effects, Michael decided that he could safely cut the bush spirit's tree and open up his garden to the full sunlight. A few months after Michael cut the tree, Melissa gave birth to a son who was deformed: one leg ended at the knee with a vestigal foot; the other foot was webbed at the toes. The angry bush spirit had entered Melissa's womb and had cut the leg of her child in revenge for Michael's cutting its tree. Melissa quickly buried the child alive, but he was found by other villagers who took him to the mission. The priest returned the infant to his parents with the exhortation that they must care for him as they would for any other child. When we first met Oneleg in 1966 he was a boy of about twelve years who ran with the aid of a stick and who participated in games with the other children. In 1981 he gardened with his parents, played soccer with the other young men, worked alongside his cohorts and was expected eventually to marry. No special provisions were made by the villagers for Oneleg as he grew up, but neither was there any opprobrium attached to his condition. His nickname, Oneleg, is an observation of fact, not ridicule, and he answers to it with good humor. Villagers agree that Michael and Melissa should have been more respectful of the bush spirit and maintain that Oneleg's condition reaffirms the potency of the spirits of the forest.

Fig. 34. Oneleg, victim of an angry bush spirit.

Christy and the kisinga

Christy is a woman in her late twenties. When we first arrived in Kandoka village in 1966 she was a child of about six or seven years. She appeared to be, and was regarded by the villagers as being, profoundly retarded. Though she could walk and her physical development appeared normal for a child of her age, she could not speak intelligibly and could not be trusted by her parents to wear clothing, behavior that is expected of all village children older than about five or six years. Christy was frequently the butt of jokes played by other children and often cried as though she were a much younger child for things that were denied her. When we inquired about her condition, the nursing sister at the mission said that Christy had been a victim of cerebral meningitis at about age two. This illness had left her in her severely retarded condition. The account of the illness given by the villagers is initially consistent with the nurse's report. According to them, Christy accompanied her parents to a ceremony where she fell ill and remained in a coma for three days and nights. Here the two explanations diverge, for the villagers say that the ceremony was also attended by Bou, a well-known sorcerer. Fearing other sorcerers who would also likely be present, Bou wore a protective spell, a *kisinga*. Bou's *kisinga* was prepared with a small hole in the wrapped leaves of his armband so that any sorcery directed at him would be caught in the hole and rendered harmless. Unfortunately, Christy's parents carelessly allowed her to come too close to Bou and her spirit was caught in the *kisinga*. Some time elapsed before her parents realized what had made the child ill, and by the time they had appealed to Bou to open his *kisinga* and release her spirit, the damage had been done. Our consultants suggest that had her spirit been released earlier, Christy would not have been damaged and, had her parents not appealed to Bou to open his device, she would shortly have died.

Paul

In late 1966 Paul and his wife were returning from the mission by canoe when they were caught by a sudden storm. Going ashore, they sought shelter under a small house isolated near the pig pens of a fellow villager. When the storm passed they resumed their journey. Soon Paul caught a fish and, while landing it, was finned in his left thumb.

Paul thought little of the injury until it began to become swollen and painful a few days after the incident. At that point he came to us for first-aid treatment and we cleaned and bandaged the wound. The infection continued though, and became severely painful, so Paul went to the mission clinic where the puncture was cleaned and newly bandaged and he was administered a penicillin injection by the nurse. Nothing seemed to bring any relief, and the swelling and pain worsened. Paul could not get to a higher level of Western medicine because it was the rainy season and there was no transport moving from the northwest coast to either Talasea or Rabaul where the nearest hospitals were located. He soon concluded that he was a victim not merely of an infection that would have responded to the penicillin but of the action of a protective magic spell placed to warn off intruders from the house under which he and his wife had sheltered from the storm. He was aware of the charm placed there, he said, but sceptical of its power to harm him and besides, he was not breaking into the house but only seeking cover from the rain. Nevertheless, Paul and the villagers with whom he discussed the problem now agreed that the *iha aimata*, fish eye magical lock was the only viable explanation for the severe infection that was spreading to affect his entire arm. Paul went to Loa, the elderly woman who had placed the spell on her property, and requested a *luanga*, cure, so that the infection could heal. Agreeing that the charm she had placed was the fish eye, Loa tried a curing spell. Shortly thereafter, Paul went to Cape Gloucester for his installation as the first local Government Councillor from the ward that included Kandoka. When Paul reached Cape Gloucester, his still swollen and now foul-smelling left hand was diagnosed as gangrenous by the medical assistant and he was sent by air to Rabaul hospital where his thumb was amputated. Throughout the course of this incident, no culpability was attached to Loa. Though there was unanimity of opinion on the part of the villagers that her "lock" had caused the infection, Loa had left a clear warning that her property was protected by a fish-eye magical spell, and she had done what she could to undo the damage. Instead, Paul was the object of considerable ridicule for having ignored the power of the "lock" in the first place, and for having delayed in seeking Loa's cure in the second.

Nathan

Early one morning in 1971 a neighbor came to tell us that Nathan was dying and wished to tell us goodbye. We hurried to find him lying under a canvas shelter just outside his sister's cooking house (a sure sign that he expected death to be imminent), surrounded by his grieving relatives. The day before the left side of his face had begun to swell painfully. He had gone to the Kaliai health center where the nurse had given him a penicillin shot. The medication had not helped; he was running a temperature, his face was badly swollen, and he was in considerable pain. He and his kin were convinced that he had been ensorcelled and that he was dying. We urged him to return to the clinic but he refused, reasoning that because the illness had not responded to earlier therapy it was due to sorcery and not susceptible to Western medical treatment. Finally, after a few minutes of discussion, Dorothy got our *Merck Manual* and read to Nathan and his assembled relatives the section on peritonsillar abscess, arguing that if a description of the illness were found in an American medical book it was a sickness known to whites and not one caused by sorcery. Nathan had not slept during the night, so we gave him two codeine tablets and a tetracycline. He was to sleep for an hour or so and, when he awoke, we would take him to the clinic for treatment. While he rested, the abscess ruptured spontaneously and began to drain. We, and our pills, were credited with predicting the time of his recovery and with his cure. There was no further discussion of sorcery.

Bertha

Bertha was an old woman of about eighty years who was dying of tuberculosis in

1981. Years earlier her husband, Lawrence, had died of the same disease which he had contracted, according to his sons, as a result of *mail*, menstrual blood poisoning. When he was in early middle age, Lawrence had an adulterous affair with a young woman from another village. The woman wanted to marry Lawrence and, even though he paid compensation to her family, her desire turned to rage and she somehow managed to contaminate something he ingested – food, water, tobacco or a bit of betel mixture – with her menstrual blood. During his long illness, Bertha cared for Lawrence, wiping his mouth, bringing him food and water, and eating and drinking from the same containers he used. Shortly after his death, she also began suffering the symptoms of tuberculosis. Her sons denied that she was sick as a result of her carelessness with her own menstrual effluvia, although this is usually considered to be the source of respiratory disease in women. Instead, they argued that she had contracted the illness as a result of her close association with her husband. Her sickness seemed to be a matter of quiet pride for her sons who considered it to be evidence of her loving concern for Lawrence and absolute proof that she was in no way responsible, either through malice or hygienic negligence, for his death.

Tina and the ghosts

When we arrived in Kandoka in 1981, Tina was an infant of about six months, healthy and developing well. Conversations with Mary, her mother, about her apparent health in contrast to other colicky babies led to insight into the possibility of the contamination of mother's milk by semen, and the dangers that such contamination entail for the children (see D.A. Counts (1984a) for discussion of this point). Tina's mother, concerned about the well-being of her baby, never permitted anyone else to serve as wet-nurse, even though carrying the infant to the gardens was often inconvenient. A month or so after our arrival, Tina fell ill with a high fever and became listless and unresponsive. Her sickness was a matter of great concern to her parents but, because of bad weather, they did not take her to the Kaliai Health center. Rather, they brought her to us to see if we could help. We thought Tina's high fever was probably symptomatic of malaria, so we gave Mary sufficient infant camoquin and acetaminophen to reduce the fever and urged her to take Tina to the clinic as quickly as possible. The next day the fever continued unabated and Mary, convinced that because our medicine did no good something else must be at issue, went to Cookie for help. Cookie is an elderly woman with a long standing reputation for traditional medical knowledge. She prepared ginger and passed it around Tina's body and then gave it to Leo, a man in a neighboring village who was known to be on good terms with the spirit of ginger. Leo's dream while he slept on the ginger provided both the explanation and the treatment for Tina's illness. Once, when Mary had left the baby unattended in the house while a fire was burning, her dead maternal grandfather had seen Tina and had been sorry for the child left in the smoky house. A small child's spirit is only weakly attached to its body, and Tina's grandfather had taken hers so that she would not suffer in the smoke. While Tina's spirit was with her grandfather, her father's brother, only recently dead and very lonely, had decided that Tina should stay with him and had refused to let the grandfather send her spirit back to her body. Tina's body, therefore, had begun to sicken and, should her parents not be able to convince Tina's father's brother to release her spirit or somehow draw it back to her, she would surely die. When Cookie received this message she knew how to proceed. She prepared the baby, singing over her while brushing downward along her body with the leaves of the *molmolo* croton. The ritual pulled Tina's spirit away from her uncle and back to her body. She soon recovered.

The death of Bruno

In 1967, while returning from a canoe trip to Kilenge with his father, twelve-year-old Bruno became lethargic and complained of a sore throat. The next day we were called to look at the boy and found him lying on a mat, the inside of his mouth and throat covered with running, ulcerated sores. His back was arched, his head was thrown back, and he appeared to have a high temperature and to be in great pain. We thought we could do nothing for the boy, so his parents took him to Kaliai health center about four o'clock in the afternoon. He was dead at dawn the next morning.

Fig. 35. Bruno's ghost was called from his grave to identify the sorcerer who killed him.

The people who accompanied Bruno to the clinic were critical of the nurse's diagnosis and treatment. She reportedly told Bruno's father that the child was ill with malaria – a diagnostic that no one was willing to accept – and she bathed him in cool water in an attempt to lower his temperature which had reached 106 degrees. Because the nurse's diagnosis violated local knowledge of the symptoms of malaria, and because her treatment seemed to be both bizarre and ineffective, the villagers concluded that Bruno had been a victim of sorcery. For the next two weeks the identity of the sorcerer was a primary topic of conversation. The question finally culminated in a ritual of divination in which the ghost of the dead child was asked to identify the person who had brought him his poison [For details of the ritual see Counts and Counts (1974: 135–141). Similar rituals are reported by Valentine (1965: 174) and by Mitchell (1978: 153–155).] During the course of the divination, the ghost suggested that Bruno had somehow been ensorcelled by his father – a suggestion that was generally rejected – and the divination did not satisfactorily resolve the question of the sorcerer's identity. In 1981 the attitude of our consultants towards Bruno's father had changed. Now the man is suspected of practising sorcery and, people explained, in 1967 Bruno's ghost had accurately pointed to his father as being the source of the poison that killed him. People thought that during the canoe trip the child had touched, or perhaps consumed, some ensorcelled item in his father's handbasket and, even though the poison was not intended for him, being a vulnerable child he succumbed to the power in his father's magic paraphernalia. The possibility that Bruno died of some Western illness has never been seriously considered. Instead, it is now generally believed, Bruno was his father's first victim.

In the foregoing vignettes we have tried to present a variety of cases that permit us to illustrate and examine the relationship between Western medicine and traditional Lusi practice. First, we will state briefly what we think are the propositions that can be derived from this examination and, second, we will discuss the reasons why we believe each of these propositions to have validity in today's Lusi society.

(1) There are two complementary medical systems available to the Lusi. The term "medical system" includes norms accounting for the recognition, etiology, significance, and treatment of illness and injury.

(2) Both of the available medical systems are complete and each is capable of yielding satisfactory results.

(3) The Lusi choose which system to use, decide when to change systems, or perhaps choose to activate neither system according to the perceived etiology of the problem in each particular case. While such decisions may take symptomatic complaints into account, symptoms often are only a minor factor in the choice.

(4) In the event that the causes of a condition are not immediately apparent, Lusi will seek treatment from Western medicine first.

DISCUSSION

Traditional medicine and Western medicine are neither in conflict nor in competition with one another, and the use of one system does not preclude the subsequent use of the other. Rather, the Lusi view these two systems as being in complementary distribution. Inasmuch as a set of symptoms may be appropriately explained by either system, the decision as to which is the correct assignment can be known only on the basis of the efficacy of treatment. Therefore, in the case of Nathan, when relief was obtained as a result of finding a description of the illness and the prescribed medication in a book of Western medicine, everyone agreed that Nathan had been suffering from a white person's disease. The discussion of sorcery that had preceded his cure was dropped, Nathan lost his conviction that he was dying and he made a full recovery. In a reverse instance, the inability of Western medicine to alter the course of Bruno's illness and avert his death led his survivors to reject the explanation given by the nurse and to assume that his illness was caused by sorcery. Although it was too late to treat Bruno, they could try to ascertain the identity of the responsible party and attempt to make sure that he did not kill again. A further point to be noted here is that the two medical systems consistently ask different questions concerning illnesses. Lusi understand and accept that Western medicine asks which disease is making a person ill and proceeds to treatment through the examination of the illness itself. Traditional practice, in contrast, asks who or what is causing this person to be ill and proceeds by identifying the culpable party and trying to alter his/its behavior.

In addition to being complementary with one another, each medical system is valid and complete. As far as the Lusi are concerned, both systems work as they should and provide satisfactory results if people diagnose the problem correctly and follow through on the proper course of action. Neither failure nor success in any particular case causes either system's validity to be called into question. In general, people respond to failure by assuming that the wrong system has been applied. If there is time, then the alternate system will be activated. It appears, however, that if both systems have been tried and the patient dies then Lusi will always revert to the traditional system to explain the death.

The response to success is generally simple: if a treatment works, then the Lusi look no further for an explanation. However, a success or even a series of successes by one system will not cause the alternative system to be questioned. For instance, should another person fall ill as Nathan did, the same process of system trial would likely be followed again. The cure of Nathan's illness by Western medicine did not place that *kind* of illness firmly in the category of "new" illness or white person's disease. Rather, it established that Nathan's particular problem was a white person's illness. The possibility that a sorcerer could cause a victim to suffer in the same way has not been called into question.

Finally, we think it is important to elaborate on the way in which Lusi proceed when they recognize a condition that requires treatment. We noted above that they may not regard as an illness a condition that is so defined by Western medical practitioners, and if the condition – filariasis for example – is not an illness, then it has no cure although there may be prescribed ways of attempting to prevent its recurrence. One should avoid the swamps where bush spirits that cause the disfigurement are known to reside. Similarly, since the birth of Oneleg, no one has been foolish enough to cut down the tree of a bush spirit in order to remove shade from a garden plot.

For those conditions that are illnesses and can, therefore, be cured by the appropriate treatment, Lusi will usually choose to go to the Kaliai health center first. They do not seek Western medicine because of a general feeling that such treatment is more efficacious although, as we noted in the early sections of this essay, first aid has virtually replaced traditional cures for non-problematic conditions such as simple sores, minor wounds and seasonal eye infections. For more serious conditions, though, people seek Western medical care first. Their choice is, we think, based on the fact that Western medical care is considered to be accessible, fast and inexpensive. Accessibility refers not to the proximity of a village to a clinic or aid post, but to the fact that the persons who are capable of practising Western medicine are clearly and unambiguously designated. Note that nearly anyone who is perceived of as having a white person's living standard and who has medications available falls into this category: a plantation manager, a nurse, a priest, or a visiting anthropologist.

The fact that Lusi consider Western medicine to be fast in curing illness is less a vote of confidence in the system than a problem for it. It is a problem because, in those circumstances when a clinical treatment does not produce relatively dramatic and immediate effects that convince the victim that she/he has chosen correctly by coming to the clinic, the person may terminate the Western treatment in favour of a traditional one. It is clearly a logical choice for a Lusi given the premises from which she/he operates, but it has been for decades a source of frustration for the agents of Western medicine practicing in the area. Dramatic remission of illness is not required of the traditional system, as everyone is in a sense "well-educated" in it and understands that just as it takes a long time for a sorcerer to perform his work, it may take a long while for it to be undone.

As to the low price of Western medical care when compared to the potential cost of acquiring the services of a traditional curer, the treatment offered by a Western medical practitioner is both inexpensive and simple to obtain. If one pays the Kaliai Health center a small fee and obtains a cure, then that is the end of it. If the Kaliai health center treatment fails and a person must seek out the sorcerer who has been hired by his enemies, then all bets are off. The sorcerer will delay agreeing to try his *luanga*, cure, in order to throw suspicion away from himself; his first several attempts will fail because he has, after all, been paid to make the victim suffer; he will charge for each attempt and the more difficult and complicated his cure, the higher his fee will rise. A person will, therefore, first seek Western medical treatment in the hope that it will work because the alternative is expensive, slow-acting, difficult and complicated. It is complicated because any illness that is caused by a sorcerer suggests that both the victim's body and his social relationships are in trouble. Anything that will respond to Western medicine is merely a sickness of the body. Conditions that do not respond are much more dangerous and complex. Illnesses of the body, those that respond to Western medicine, do not kill. In Kaliai people may die benignly, but they do so of old age. The death of active people is not a matter of illness that will submit to the ministrations of a nurse or doctor. Small wonder, then, that Lusi hope that Western medicine will work for only then can a person who is ill cease to worry that he is being killed.

NOTES

1. Our research was funded by predoctoral research grants from the United States National Science Foundation and by Southern Illinois University in 1966–67; by the Canada Council, Wenner Gren Foundation Grant 2809, and the University of Waterloo in 1971; and by the Social Science and Humanities Research Council of Canada and sabbatical leaves from McMaster University and the University of Waterloo in 1975–76 and 1981.
2. One hundred toea make a kina. One kina was equivalent to one Australian dollar in 1975.

EDWARD LIPUMA

13. MODERNITY AND MEDICINE AMONG THE MARING

INTRODUCTION[1]

The Maring first encountered the West in the early 1950s when Anglican missionaries, seeking to spread the Word of God, opened outposts at Koinambe and Simbai. But Maring were little interested in the Gospel per se, rather they sought God's power as invested in trade store and hospital. From the outset, the advent of medical care was inseparable from more global social transformation.

The confluence of medicines in the Maring region embodies three issues. First, the character of cultural transformation, how medical practices have evolved from initial contact to the present. This encompasses questions of change in the cultural perception of illness, the evaluation of healing, the goals of treatment, and the terms of integration. These questions have a wider implication because the transfer of medical control from shaman to Western health personnel is a transformation in the structure of power. Maring concepts and examples of the extraordinary person who attains the normalcy of health through the supra-normal use of magic and spells take us to the center of their images of power and potency, and the ordinary practices whose meaning and value anchor the social world.

Understanding transformation requires an analysis of the interplay between the objective structure of medicine and the cognitive and motivating structures which drive behavior. My perspective is that not only does advance of Western medicine restructure Maring attitudes and dispositions towards the use and usefulness of medicine, but that indigenous attitudes and dispositions, as embedded in practice, inflect the nature of biomedicine in the Maring region. It is thus essential to ask both how the advent of Western health care is reshaping ethnomedicine (i.e. people's behavior, sensitivity, and practices), and how this determinate appearance of Western medicine under the auspices of the Anglican mission is inseparable from – because mutually determined by – ethnomedicine.

Second, medicine in the context of contact raises the issue of the relationship between social epistemology – the categories by which the world is known – and the body of individuals. Thus the study of pluralism is a commentary on the cultural status of body and mind and the relationship between individual experience and the cultural order. The technical and ritual practice of healing mediates this relationship.

Finally, there is the issue of the meaning and function of ritual/medical practices. How can analysis interpret or account for the determinate shape of illness and cure, the symbolic and pragmatic functions which accrue to them, and the effectiveness of healing rituals? These are all concerns which have appeared in the New Guinea literature, not least with respect to Maring. With this in mind, I argue that under-

S. Frankel and G. Lewis (eds.), *A Continuing Trial of Treatment*. 295–310.
© 1989, Kluwer Academic Publishers, Dordrecht – Printed in the Netherlands.

standing medical practices is not a question of recovering their psychological or physiological functions but of restoring their practical necessity. Analysis must come to terms with the significance and functions that people, immersed in a determinate society, confer on determinate medical practices and experiences, given the conceptual schemes which structure their vision of health and illness.

Briefly, these three issues or themes are brought together in the following argument. Maring make a cultural distinction between social and natural cycles. This leads to a distinction between socially and naturally induced illnesses. When Western medicine appeared, it was slowly incorporated into the natural cycle, people coming to believe that biomedicine works well for natural illnesses and for the physical dimension of illness in general, while ethnomedicine resolves socially induced problems. Since the late 1960s, certain segments of the Maring population have more readily accepted treatment at the aid posts and local hospitals, and have become increasingly adept and confident in managing Western medicine. This use and acceptance of Western medicine is being played out against the cultural opposition of tradition and modernity. The result is that its integration is an instrument of social differentiation and a key stake in the struggle for social power and control. The growing influence of biomedicine in local thought and experience is expressed in the fact that illnesses are increasingly being classified as natural and thus amenable to Western treatment, as opposed to social and thus in the province of ethnomedicine.

SOCIETY AND HEALTH

Patterns of health and the establishment of Western medicine are intertwined with local geography and politics. Maring reside in steep, rugged, heavily forested terrain straddling the slopes of the Bismarck Mountain range. Land ownership follows the contours of the mountainous environs, territorial units cultivating vertically banded strips that reach from the valley floor to the mountain crest. The society is organized into more than twenty clan clusters (for example Tsembaga, Kauwatyi) whose constituent clans are aligned through a history of intermarriage, common residence and exchange.[2]

Until pacification in the mid 1950s, the growth and decline of clan clusters was tied to the relationship between the politics of war and incidence of disease. Lowman (1980) illustrates that too much success as well as too little could force a clan cluster into decline. Repeated victory in war would escalate the influx of affines and refugees, causing environmental degradation and a drop in community health; repeated losses made it difficult for a group to attract wives and forced them to seek the protection of nucleated settlements, leaving them more vulnerable to parasitic infection (Lowman 1980: 16–17). The wars waged in the mid 1950s left a bitter taste for losers and winners alike: the losers suffered many casualties while pacification denied winners the spoils of victory. Conflicts are restaged nowadays in the political arena of the local government council and in economic competition for modern goods and services.

Lowman (1980: 198) suggests that because the Maring exploit the transition zone from lowland to highland habitat, they are exposed to a greater variety of diseases than people living in one habitat or another. Most pathologies found in the Maring region are water related, the absence of strict sanitation and water management promoting their transmission. However, one of the biggest changes in the past five years has been in people's attention to sanitation. There have, for instance, been recent court cases in which people have been fined for defecating too close to settlements and for not building latrines.

Some of the most common diseases are respiratory infections, influenza, measles, conjunctivitis, hepatitis, various forms of worms, and malaria. Lowman (1980: 210–238) notes that immunity to malaria seems marginal and that its prevalence has increased with contact. A clear sign that Western medicine is leading to better health is the robust population growth of the past decade (LiPuma 1985a). This is causing problems of its own with respect to land tenure and dispute settlement.

SOCIAL AND NATURAL CYCLES

Maring society rests on opposition and complementarity of natural and social cycles – the first centering around fertility and gardens and women, the latter around warfare and ancestors, exchanges and alliances (Rappaport 1968). These two cycles are reflected in an implicit distinction between social and natural types of illness.

Concepts of cause of social illness and misfortune revolve around generative schemes for the construction of the cosmos and human activity within it. It is the cultural application of the generative schemes which imbue order and disorder, well-being and affliction, with practical meaning. Maring culture expresses a fundamental opposition between the realm of society, the locus of social and symbolic organization, and that of nature, perceived as wild (see Fig. 36). The Maring are mountain horticulturalists whose settlements are located in the middle altitudes between the bush of high and low ground. Spatial arrangements, the rituals of war and peace, as well as most ordinary activity, articulate a continuum from social life at the center of the settlement to wildness at the periphery. Between the two extremes are gardens and sacred groves, the first associated with women and fertility and the latter with men and spiritual power. These generative schemes can be applied to the social order as well as the cosmos.[3]

The logic embodied in the generative schemes shapes concepts of social body, health and illness, and gives substance to cause and modes of healing. The categories are simultaneously opposed yet complementary, mutually threatening yet interdependent (cf. Wagner 1972). Thus, the cooperation of affines in the making of exchanges and alliances, the joining of sexes in intercourse and gardening, the interplay of the social and wild in horticulture and warfare, are essential for social reproduction.

The disorderly or anti-social commingling of these elements leads to illness, misfortune and pollution. They are connected because generative schemes always apply to action and embodied knowledge: eating with enemy clansmen or sexual congress at the wrong time or place. Disorder in the Maring universe is not so much a conceptual break, although the most reflective informants can think the conceptual schism, but disorder in social action, improper uses of the social body.

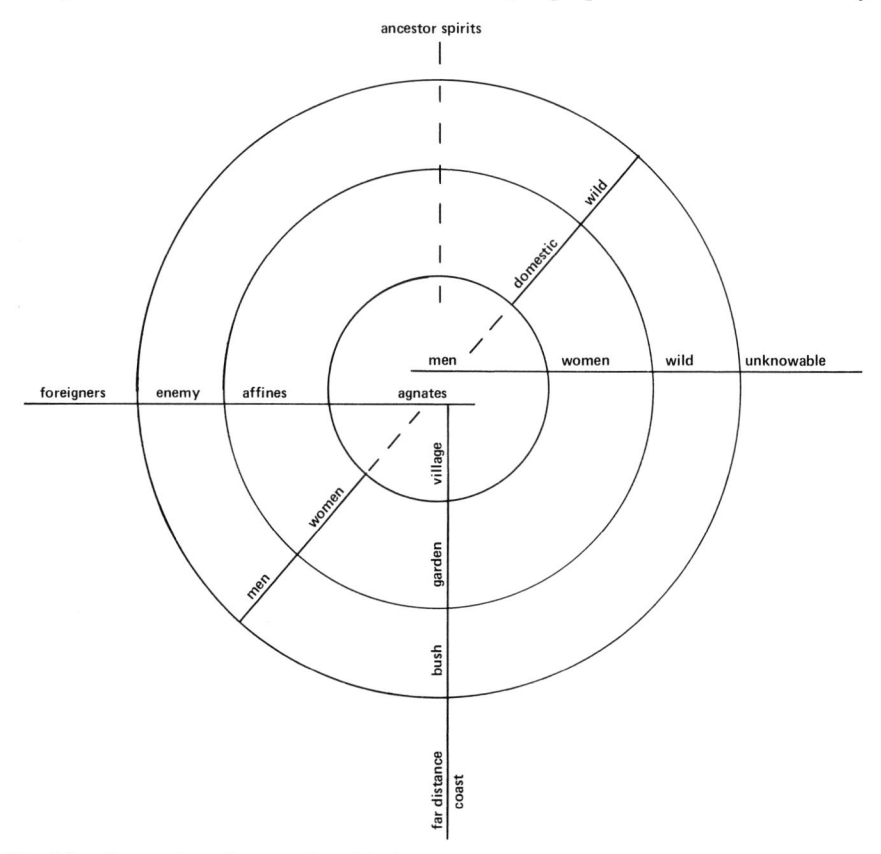

Fig. 36. Generative schemes of the Maring cosmology.

Hence, each set of symbolic relations, each generative scheme, can be used practically as an etiology. Behavior that bridges the social customs set down by the ancestors (for example failure to share pork with clansmen) invites their retribution. Rivalry and bad blood among affines surfaces as sorcery (especially within a clan cluster). A disruption of proper relations between men and women results in pollution and ancestral wrath. The maintenance of improper conduct with enemy clans (for example eating forbidden food) also leads to pollution. And finally, confusion of social and natural domains (for example making a garden in the bush) can provoke the attack of wild spirits which lurk outside the dominions of man. I should add that Maring do not determine the causes of illness by acts of cosmogony; rather the generative schemes at their disposal continually refer them back to cosmological values.

Place maintains a critical position in Maring cosmology and social geography. The clan lands literally embody the substance and history of clansmen. The cycle of social reproduction links food, land, procreation and death with the formation of agnatic identity (LiPuma 1985b). Clan territory is divided into discrete named parcels of land, each of which has its own character based on the history of residence and production in that locale.

The special affinity between clansmen and place means that when individuals travel to foreign and so alien places, they are liable to be taken ill. Since contact, men have gone to coastal plantations where they occasionally died or had bouts of serious illness. Maring link the deaths and sicknesses to the hostility of the environment (including the presence of sorcery for which they possess no counter-magic). Medical rationality may observe that coastal environments are truly more hostile and unforgiving, especially to highland peoples.

But this is only part of what Maring mean, for disease and misfortune are diagnostic of the disharmony between clansmen and land, not the cause. So when illness strikes clansmen typically shift their settlement compound to a more auspicious site. The old houses are razed and new ones built on another territory usually in the same vicinity. Residence shifts seem especially to be common when an influenza epidemic breaks out.

The disorderly confluence of elements is not the only basis of illness and affliction. Maring recognize that in addition to social relations there are various natural diseases and ailments. The natural cycle is a perceived continuity between procreation, growth and development, old age, followed by death, decomposition and decay, leading to fertility and rebirth. This cycle is represented in Fig. 37.

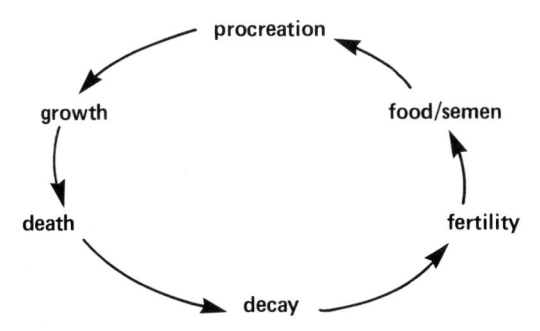

Fig. 37. The natural cycle.

The natural cycle represents the orderly and inevitable progression of elements. People's living arrangements, adherence to food and sexual taboos, and participation in ritual are conducted in terms of this cycle. Moreover, this cycle is seen to account for the continuity and perdurance of the clan in history.

CONCEPTS OF ILLNESS AND HEALTH

Social illness has the following form. An individual's or clan's behavior breaches norms regarding the proper relationship between categories of social beings or, what amounts to the same thing, between persons and land. Depending on the nature of the offence, this will invite the attack of ancestors, sorcerers or wild spirits. These attacks cause physical illness of some kind. Food may blockade a critical body canal, such as the windpipe, or a poisoned object may be implanted in a vital organ (especially the liver). The result is a physical/spiritual transformation of the person, as characterized by pain and a loss of *min* (implying a descent towards death).

Natural illness is associated with the development and the ageing process, including problems with individual organs, such as teeth decay or bowel problems suffered by older people. For the most part, natural illness is associated with stages in the life cycle - certain diseases common to infants or menstrual cramps for women. As long as an illness is consistent with the natural cycle, and within the more specific life cycle, it is not thought to be the result of sorcery or angry ancestors, or the fault of the patient (cf. Ngubane 1977). Sorcery trials, whose touchstone is intentionally motivated illness and misfortune, do not center on such diseases. Natural illness leads to the physical/spiritual decline of the patient as surely as social illness.

The general concept of illness is illustrated in Fig. 38.

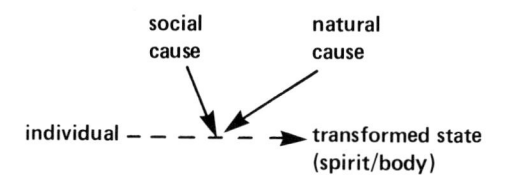

```
              social        natural
              cause         cause
                  \         /
                   \       /
individual — — — — ↓ ↙ — → transformed state
                              (spirit/body)
```

Fig. 38. Indigenous model of illness.

In general, an individual who contracts an illness undergoes a change in his internal state. This may be either a natural part of the inevitable cycle, or else a socially-induced transformation brought about by the intentional acts and intervention of spirits and sorcerers. Within this frame, health depends on two things: first, the harmony or balance (*kopla*) that an individual maintains within the social and cosmological order; second, an individual's personal strength and recuperative powers. People's strength and regenerative powers diminish as they become older, as does their resistance to disease (see Lewis 1976: 96–98).

For natural illness, people believe that Western treatments are probably superior and so they are seldom afraid to go to the health clinic or capitalize on the availability of Western drugs. By contrast, Western medicine is thought to have little effect on the cause of socially induced illnesses, although it can be quite effective in relieving symptoms and assisting the body's normal regenerative process.

MEDICAL CARE AND THE ANGLICAN MISSION

For the Maring, the hospital is to the Church as the deed is to the word. Their view is that truth is inalienable from action; no amount of preaching about Christ's powers is meaningful without concrete, observable acts of power (as concrete and observable are culturally defined). In this respect, the health center is more powerful than church services but less so than the tradestore.

The Anglican Church, like most mainstream churches in New Guinea, believes that providing medical services is part of its mission to serve the body which keeps the soul. This dovetails with a theme repeated time and again at evangelical conferences: traditional religions are based on fear whereas Christianity is rooted in love. The local view that ancestors will cause death and illness lends support to the idea of a religion of fear and trembling. Against this, the Church feels that is must spread the good news about Christ's love and show that it, too, can deal with illness.

The St. John's health center at Koinambe contains a small sick ward, an outpatient clinic, a maternity ward and an education room. The center serves a community of about 5000. It is run by a head nurse who supervises several junior nurses and a small staff of orderlies. Cases are treated first by aid post orderlies (APO) and then by the health center. In extreme circumstances, patients are flown to the provincial hospital in Mt. Hagen. The head nurse makes monthly visits to the aid posts in the region (walking about 100 kilometres) to conduct children's health clinics. As this suggests, the vast majority of people who are involved are mothers and their children.

During the late 1960s and early 1970s, a string of aid posts was established in most of the local territories. It is important to note that aid posts were established in terms of population densities rather than political boundaries. In some cases, two clan clusters who were opponents in the 1950s' wars and who currently oppose one another politically, were assigned one post, and the aid post was sited on the land of one of the clan clusters. This has led to situations in which a vanquished clan cluster has to visit an aid post on the land of their enemy (in some cases the APO is also from an enemy clan). The mission is only too aware of these political rifts but feels that the key to promoting a Christian spirit and to unifying the various groups, is overcoming old animosities.

Maring think of Western health care as a new inventory of practices rather than as an alternative system. They overlook its systematic aspect, conceptualizing it in the light of ethnomedicine which, indeed, is not a natural or bounded system (see Comaroff 1981: 367). By contrast, Western health workers and clergy view "traditional" and "modern systems" as diametrically opposed: the hospital fighting a battle for men's bodies just as the Church fights to redeem their souls. Like the Maring, Western health workers perceive all of medicine through the prism of their own system. Thus they imbue ethnomedicine with a systematicity and closure which it could never possess. They believe the Maring must choose between competing and alternative medical systems. In the eyes of mission educated Maring, more than the Anglican mission itself, this choice is a referendum on modernity.

THE EVOLUTION OF PLURALISM

Maring initially perceived Western medicine as part of the enormous, yet incomprehensible, powers of the West. They understood that biomedicine was strong but also very dangerous. Thus in the early years of contact, fear led people to avoid the aid posts and health center. During this era, Western medicine was not perceived as medicine, but as part of the conquering process at the hands of the Australians. Hospitals, examinations and policies to maintain health were not in the inventory of Maring practices.

This initial phase of contact gave way to a second phase in the early 1970s. Its central feature was the incorporation of Western medicine into the distinction between social and natural illnesses. Biomedicine was thus seen to specialize in promoting the body's natural regenerative powers. People felt that it was a greatly enhanced version of their own natural treatments, such as rubbing with nettles.

Clansmen soon began to see that they could use Western and ethnomedicine in complementary fashion. However, while the two forms of medicine were conceptually harmonized, they were still divided at the level of practice: for the local populace played no part whatsoever in administering Western medicine. It was presented as a foreign knowledge beyond their ability to manage or understand. The difference between simply receiving medical treatment and participating in its practice was inscribed in the social structure of medicine. The management of biomedicine had three tiers. At the top was a nurse from Voluntary Service Overseas of England (VSO). During the 1970s, there was a succession of VSO nurses who organized and directed the health center Under the VSO nurse were junior nurses, almost always from coastal areas where the Anglican mission had been operating for half a century. At the bottom of the hierarchy were local orderlies who did cleaning and carried heavy loads. The social hierarchy expressed the view that Westerners were more capable of administering biomedicine than coastal Papua New Guineas who in turn were more capable than Maring. Westerners, coastal New Guineans and Maring all shared this view which was objectified in levels of perceived competence (defined as length of medical training, knowledge of English, ability to understand Western forms of reasoning).

An important instrument of change were the patrols conducted by the VSO nurse. They moved the medical hierarchy from village to village, displaying the social order of medical care. More, the patrols were indoctrinations in Western medical values. For example, the responses demanded from mothers when their children were examined, presumed and required that the parent assimilated Western medical concepts. The grading of the health of children as well as questions as to the degree of health/sickness, viewed health and illness as existing on a continuum. This contrasted with the indigenous view that while there are various degrees of health and illness (i.e. those who are ill may improve or become worse; those who are healthy vary in strength), health and illness are discrete: people are either sick or healthy.

In the 1980s, medical care began to enter a new phase in which the social position of Maring with respect to biomedicine moved towards greater participation. Local aid post orderlies, especially in the Jimi valley, began to replace their coastal counterparts. In addition, the head nurse at Koinambe became a Papua New Guinean rather than a European, a point which greatly impressed many Maring.

SYMPTOMS OF CHANGE: A CASE HISTORY

The following case history gives a sense of the reality of social change as experience. It also illustrates key elements of the Maring approach to sickness and health in the context of modernization. The time is 1980 and the setting is the Kauwatyi clan cluster, the largest and most powerful Maring cluster both before and after contact. The Kauwatyi maintain a particularly ambiguous relationship with the Anglican mission. Due to the fact that they are land-poor, the Kauwatyi are leading exponents of modernization. Though they number about 20% of the population, more than half of the children attending the mission school are Kauwatyi. The Kauwatyi have invested their own money and labor in the construction of larger and more sophisticated facilities for the local APO. Nevertheless, Kauwatyi leaders fathom that the goals of the mission are a challenge to their authority and control. So in their desire to keep the mission at a distance, they have expelled the Anglican evangelist and do not actively participate in festivals and other ceremonies organized by the Church. The result is a continuing tension between embracing modernity – medicine and education especially – and maintaining a Kauwatyi identity.

Punt, a man of about 55, took seriously ill. He said that something was blocking his body's canals, causing fever, chills, slack skin and a loss of spirit. He withdrew from all social life into the recesses of his hut, feeling that the weakening of his body rendered his *min* or life-force susceptible to further attack from sorcerers and evil spirits.

Punt was in a state of physical and spiritual decline. His body was racked with fever and he worried that he was losing his hotness and dryness. He avoided washing as the cold, damp water would only accelerate the process. He sat by the fire inhaling smoke to help restore his heat/dryness and rubbed his arms and back with stinging nettles to produce heat and excite the flow of blood.

But preliminary treatment was ineffective and Punt became progressively sicker. He waxed hot and cold and appeared to be dying. His younger brother suggested the cause of the illness – ancestral anger over the failure to sacrifice pigs. They had withdrawn their protection leaving Punt vulnerable to attack by sorcerery. The brother then planned a sacrifice to the ancestor spirits to propitiate them. Some said the brother was anxious to make amends because he was party to the offensive action and was now gripped with fear that he would be next. In any case, the subclan prepared to sacrifice a pig to the ancestors.

Punt's son, who lives at Koinambe and works at the mission hospital, came back to the settlement to see his ailing father. He judged that earlier treatments, the rubbing with nettles and visits to the APO, had been ineffective. With scant ceremony or consultation he removed Punt to the Koinambe hospital. At the hospital, the nurse diagnosed the illness as cerebral malaria, and directed a junior nurse to begin treatment. But Punt's son objected, saying that because his father was dying he wanted the VSO nurse to administer the tablets herself. Later in the day, the nurse informed the Anglican priest that Punt was likely to die.

Punt's brother raved that he was furious with the ancestors. He noted that many clansmen were no longer making regular ritual offerings, and that, moreover, his previous sacrifices had produced little in the way of ancestral help. To darken matters, Christ was no help because he was unconcerned with sorcery. So now the ancestors were taking revenge. Stripped of protection, the man was an easy prey for sorcerers who coveted his pigs – pigs that should have been sacrificed and given to ancestors and affines.

The day following Punt's admission to the health center, a Kauwatyi shaman arrived with a small entourage. Shortly after arriving, he pronounced that a sliver of sorcerized bamboo had penetrated Punt's liver. While Punt was writhing on a small cot delirious, making unintelligible sounds, the shaman took a bamboo tube filled with bespelled leaves and other items, and worked a cure. The spell was not said in Maring but in bastardized Kalam, the language of the neighboring people.[4]

At the same time that Punt's brother was fetching a shaman Punt's son, a loyal churchgoer, was telling the Anglican priest about his father's plight. That same day the priest announced from the pulpit that there was a dying man at the hospital who needed their prayers. He told the congregation that only the intercession of God could save him. For three days Punt hung on. On the fourth, his fever started to subside and his recuperation began. The Anglican priest proclaimed a miracle from the pulpit and over the shortwave to other missions. He rejoiced that God had seen fit to show the Maring his power. The shaman told me that his magic dissolved the bamboo and stopped the sorcery.

ANALYSIS: RESPONSES TO ILLNESS

Here, as in numerous other instances, Maring patients make use of both forms of medicine, either separately or in tandem. While Punt's son favored Western therapy, he made no effort to halt the ethnomedical cure and indeed was present. The concept is that when someone is ill all sources of power must be tapped until they are cured. Throughout, treatment is cumulative. A failure of the preliminary therapy of stinging nettles led to a visit to the aid post which in turn led to hospitalization and employment of a shaman. This is the usual progression of local treatment nowadays, a change from earlier times when many fewer people used the hospital and the shaman was consulted first.

The cultural belief is that illness results from disruption of the body's functions. The agent may be spiritual, tangible, or the natural result of ageing, but the effects are invariably physiological. Sorcery harms by damaging the victim's tissues, circulatory systems and liver, just as enraged ancestors will disable limbs and knot internal organs. Similarly, pollution may cause burns or lead to physical dissolution.

The example also underscores the complementarity between Western and indigenous medicine. Maring think that treatment offered at the aid posts and health centers assists the body's natural processes. There is an analogical transfer of schemes from ethnomedicine to Western medicine. For instance, if an indigenous medicine relieves pain by causing the blood to rush, and a Western medicine better relieves the same pain, then the Western medicine must achieve its success by circulating blood more effectively than the indigenous one. Western medicine in general is conceptualized as a form of therapeutic magic which specializes in aiding the body's basic recuperative powers. It cannot, however, counteract the effects of sorcery or spiritual attack. The sorcerized bamboo sliver would cause death if not removed with techniques beyond the purview of Western medicine. This fosters the idea that if biomedicine cannot cure an illness then the illness must result from sorcery or malevolent spirits. In such cases the wisest course of action is to combine Western and indigenous treatments. So the malarial medicine was seen to strengthen the patient, a positive mobilization of power vested in the competence of Western medicine. The divination and magic was aimed at removing a continuous agent of death – the sliver of bamboo – thus eliminating an inevitable because unremedied cause of death (cf. Glick 1967).

The attitude of Punt, his brother, and the shaman capture the indigenous idea that illnesses are specific to individuals. There is not an entity – a given disease type – which attacks an individual, exhibiting its effects based on the physical state of the victim, the strength of the disease and other factors. Rather, illness is a specific transformation of an individual from a potentially identifiable cause. Within this framework, diagnosing the cause of the illness is less critical than the administration of treatment. In some cases, the initial cause of the illness (e.g. failure to make ritual sacrifices) is only divined after the patient has been treated (cf. Johannes 1980: 51). Similarly, the means of sorcery, its reasons, or how the bamboo sliver entered the liver are not relevant to treatment.

It is also worth noting that the position of the Anglican church contains a contradiction. On one hand, the Church as a representative of Western virtues extols the value of medicine and the health center. In so doing, the Church plays into the Western opposition between religion and healing. On the other hand, the Church wants to oppose the separation of the science of healing from the Word of God. Certainly the priest's claim that only God's hand could cure Punt seeks to reunite them.

Finally, it is important to observe that the use of Kalam and other foreign words, as well as the purchase of spells from other groups, is part of the cultural concept that social power and renewal — as exemplified in new alliances, new plant species, etc. — derives from outside sources. This view finds nothing strange in the fact that Western medicine was discovered to have power or that the health center is one with the Church. In the years immediately following pacification, people were scared of Western medicine because they mistrusted the power they knew it must possess.

THE POLITICS OF PLURALISM

It should not be ignored that the social organization of illness always fulfills a political function by defining the limits of health — the boundaries which differentiate healthy from sick people, the social limitations imposed on those who are ill, and the duties, responsibilities and privileges of health. But medical pluralism among the Maring touches the social polity in another decisive way.

The use of Western medicine and the uses made of it are part of social and political strategy. Older men, especially those who were leaders prior to pacification, still reject or quietly disregard Western medicine. They visit the aid post or hospital only under pressure from their sons and daughters. Needless to say, of all the categories of people who make use of the health center, those over fifty do so least and rarely in a non-critical situation.

The schemes of perception and motivation of the younger generation are evolving under different objective conditions from their elders — conditions being defined by the presence of Western medicine and modernizing forces generally. The younger generation, in following their inclinations and adapting to new conditions, adopts the implicit strategy of embracing Western medicine in order to differentiate itself from the senior generation. Many say, with an earnestness that is at once sincere and uncertain, that the essence of following the modern road is abandoning those aspects of tradition which conflict with modernity. Thus young men are much more likely to use the aid post and the hospital, to approach biomedicine with more confidence. It is young men who become aid post orderlies and who seek to capture the work opportunities offered by the hospital. More, because the use of and participation in Western medicine is a source of political strength for the younger generation, they are motivated to push for its success.

Maring big men say not only that they support biomedicine against the claims of traditional magic, but that they really have no choice. Thus, they help promote the renovation of aid posts and round up people for health clinics. From their point of view, they cannot but acknowledge the superiority of Western medicine since their only chance of harnessing biomedicine is to submit to it in order to make use of it (cf. Bourdieu 1977: 165). By endorsing biomedicine and accepting it on behalf of the clan cluster, they index and reinforce their claims to power in the modernizing world. It allows them to control the reproduction of medical practices. Hence big men insist on the status of intermediary, sometimes exercising their power in the village by helping the mission and sometimes exerting power over the mission by withholding their help in the village. Working within the cultural opposition between natural and social illness, and the parallel opposition between modernity and tradition, the use big men, young men or elders make of medicine expresses the interests of their group and also the interests of individuals operating within the specific logic of a given situation. For example, a young man may disparage ethnomedicine in the presence of other young men, especially in the context of the mission station or aid post; he may be sympathetic to ethnomedicine in the company of older men; and he may actively promote biomedicine as when, at the command of a big man, he organizes mothers for a monthly health clinic.

For Maring, the coexistence and validity of two forms of medicine is itself revolutionary. It inclines them to perceive the indigenous order as arbitrary, as one possible order among others and hence open to question, especially by young men who believe that abandoning ritual sacrifice and medicine are keys to securing the fruits of modernization. That ritual practice should be questioned is significant because as Rappaport (1979: 208–211) has argued, it is precisely the unquestionableness of ritual which allows it to hold the cosmic and social order in place. The major result is that there is now a wide diversity of opinions on medicine and modernity, ranging from senior men who hold fast to tradition to young men who eschew the powers of ancestors and sorcerers. In between are a great number who have found no clear hold on the truth.

THE DIMENSION OF MEDICAL CHANGE

The current political structure sanctions complementarity and reproduces it to the advantage of biomedicine. Illness is increasingly perceived as a problem for Western medicine. This change is taking place in terms of the relationship between the classification of and response to illness. On one hand, people are progressively classifying more instances of illness as part of the natural cycle. They are thus amenable to Western therapy and outside the scope of ritual and magic. For natural illness, there is no need to invoke ancestors or sorcerers or search for other causes. On the other hand, the successful treatment of an illness by Western medicine implies that the illness is natural rather than social.

The idea that the natural cycle is on the ascendency fits local concepts of modernity. Maring feel that the social cycle of war and peace was extinguished by pacification. Accordingly, the ancestors who presided over war, and who are themselves the spirits of clansmen who have died fighting, are less critical to the clan's well-being. In the same vein, relationships between affines, and thus allies, are declining in importance. Nowadays clans make marriages far and wide. Older men believe that they were emasculated by pacification, and that the distance between male and female cycles converges as one moves into the present.

The influence of Western medicine is, from the vantage of local healers, part of the overall weakening of Maring society which they have come to accept as inevitable. Their authority was based on a monopoly on competence: their ability to remedy serious illnesses. Today this monopoly has been doubly lost: once to Western medicine and once to the younger generation who have special competence in obtaining access to Western medicine. Young men can speak Pidgin, sometimes English, and know the way around the mission station "the way older men know the forest" (cf. Frankel 1980: 103–105). Few young men show an interest in learning indigenous healing practices. Many feel that diseases once attributed to sorcery and ancestral anger are now known to be natural diseases. As one young man put it: "We used to think that a sorcerer caused the illness, but now we know that illness just happens."

THEORIES OF ILLNESS IN NEW GUINEA

An objective of many analyses is to account for the presence of healing practices. This immediately raises the question as to their physiological and social efficacy: why healing succeeds even when local practitioners know little about scientific disease types or appropriate remedies. Theories about the existence of indigenous medical practices have operated along several complementary lines.

One thesis is that processes of natural remission generate healing on their own, independent of medical intervention. Many patients would recover whether or not they received treatment of any kind, although shamans as well as Western healers may claim credit. This thesis can be further supported with a recognition that cultural responses to illness can help to promote recovery. Greenwood (1981: 219) notes that from the perspective of biomedicine, the value of cultural response lies in its social acknowledgement of illness, restoration of ontological wholeness and creation of optimal conditions for natural recovery. Anthropologists can site medical studies conducted both in Western and non-Western societies to support this viewpoint. The elaborate, emotionally moving, ritual events which frequently surround curing strengthen this argument. Finally, analysts may reinforce both these views by noting that ethnomedical treatments can have pharmacological, nutritional or physiotherapeutic value. To cite a famous Maring example, feeding ritual pork to the sick may add quality protein to their diet at a critical time, helping to replace nutrients and to assist the body's natural defenses. Johannes (1980: 62) explains with respect to the Nekematigi of the Eastern Highlands:

As a placebo, pork is likely to be highly effective because of Nekematigi values and benefits about its salubrious qualities. Killing a pig for someone communicates to him not only the acknowledged seriousness of his condition but also the fact that others, who value his life, are doing something about it.

In addition, pork may function as a important dietary boost... Added dietary intake of high quality protein during times of stress or infection helps to restore physiological equilibrium by replacing lost nutrients and/or providing the excess necessary for the formation of antibodies and phagocytes.

Although all of these factors may contribute to the health of the patient, they are neither an explantation nor a description of ethno-medicine. Singularly or together, the views operate in terms of the functions of the practice: the creation of optimal conditions for recovery. But there is no door which leads from the functions of psychology or dietary habits to the structure of practice. The functions can engross the phenomena because they are abstract, but they cannot specify the determinate forms of ethno-medical practice.[5] This argument holds for the adoption of Western medical practices; nothing in the improved efficacy of biomedicine in treating certain types of illness can explain the structure and evolution of pluralism.

The scientific disease type is given an important part in medical anthropology because it is the point where biomedicine and ethnomedicine overlap. But the contrasts are more critical for the study of pluralism and the social changes it engenders. The review of social and natural illnesses illustrated how the nature of change moved along structural cleavages always there within the society. That diagnosis is based on the analogical transfer of schemes from one case to the next allows people to resolve problems similar in substance and shape. The various illnesses have a specific social form because they are produced and unified by a cultural sense of body, and because they serve similar practical functions. More than the desire to obtain a better standard of health, the current use of both ethno- and biomedicine is defined by social relations of power involved in the transformation from tradition to modernity.

NOTES

1. The paper is based on 21 months fieldwork among the Maring; four months in 1974 and sixteen months in 1979–1980. I would like to thank Sarah Keene Meltzoff, Roy Rappaport and Cherry Lowman for their suggestions and comments. To avoid confusion, I should note that I use Western medicine and biomedicine, and indigenous medicine and ethnomedicine, interchangeably.
2. For more detailed accounts of social organization, economy, and politics see Rappaport (1968), Lowman (1971), and LiPuma (1985b).
3. The relationship between categories on different axes will depend on their field of use. And a reading of the figure from the perspective of the concentric circles yields very different results. For instance, men exemplify culture in opposition to nature, yet are quintessentially wild and untamed in the context of warfare.
4. There is a view subscribed to by structuralists as well as positivists that a shaman does

not become great by curing his patients, rather he cures his patients because he has become a great shaman. The central idea is that the power of suggestion can assist recovery even if the works and words of the shaman hold no medical efficacy. The force of recovery runs from the social persona of the shaman to the psychology of the patient. However, I would argue alternatively that there is a dialectic between greatness and efficacy such that a shaman becomes great by curing just as he cures because he is powerful. To assign a logical priority to one aspect over the other is to flatten the indigenous concepts of time and efficacy, the successes which advance the career of a shaman and the failure which retard it.

5. See Sahlins (1976: 73–96) for a discussion of function and the role of instrumental logic in anthropological explanations.

LIST OF CONTRIBUTORS

Dr Bryant J. Allen, Department of Human Geography, The Research School of Pacific Studies, The Australian National University, GPO Box 4, Canberra, ACT 2600, Australia.

Dr John Barker, Department of Anthropology and Sociology, University of British Columbia, Vancouver, British Columbia, Canada V6T 2B2.

Professor Gilbert H. Herdt, Department of Behavioral Sciences, The University of Chicago, Committee on Human Development, 5730 South Woodlawn Avenue, Chicago, IL 60637, U.S.A.

Dr Michael W. Young, Department of Anthropology, The Research School of Pacific Studies, The Australian National University, GPO Box 4, Canberra, ACT 2601, Australia.

Professor Andrew Strathern, Department of Anthropology, Faculty of Arts & Sciences, University of Pittsburgh, Pittsburgh, PA 15260, U.S.A.

Dr Achsah Carrier, Department of Anthropology and Sociology, The University of Papua New Guinea, Box 320 University PO, Papua New Guinea.

Dr Carol Jenkins, Papua New Guinea Institute of Medical Research, PO Box 60, Goroka, Papua New Guinea.

Dr Paul Roscoe, Department of Anthropology, University of Maine, Stevens Hall, South Orono, MA 04469–0158, U.S.A.

Professor Ann Chowning, Department of Anthropology, Victoria University of Wellington, Private Bag, Wellington, New Zealand.

Dr David Hyndman, Department of Anthropology & Sociology, University of Queensland, St. Lucia, Queensland, Australia 4067.

Drs David R. and Dorothy Ayers Counts, Department of Anthropology, McMaster University, 1280 Main Street West, Hamilton, Ontario, Canada L8S 4L9.

Dr Edward LiPuma, Department of Anthropology, University of Miami, PO Box 248106, FL 33124, U.S.A.

REFERENCES

Alland, A.
    1970   Adaptation in Cultural Evolution. New York: Columbia University Press.
Allen, B.J.
    1976   Pangu or Peli: the Dreikikir Open Electorate. *In* D. Stone (ed.) Prelude to Self Government: Electoral Politics in Papua New Guinea 1972. Canberra: Australian National University Press.
    1983   A bomb, a bullet or the bloody flux? Population change in the Aitape Inland, Papua New Guinea, 1941–1945. Journal of Pacific History 18(4): 218–235.
AMMR
    Australian Methodist Mission Review
Armstrong, D.
    1983   Political Anatomy of the Body: Medical Knowledge in Britain in the 20th Century. Cambridge: Cambridge University Press.
AWMMS
    Australian Wesleyan Methodist Missionary Society: Annual Reports.
Barker, J.
    1985   Maisin Christianity: an ethnography of the contemporary religion of a seaboard Melanesian people. Ph.D. Dissertation, University of British Columbia.
Barth, F.
    1975   Ritual and Knowledge among the Baktaman of New Guinea. New Haven: Yale University Press.
Basso, E.
    1973   The Kalapalo Indians of Central Brazil. New York: Holt, Rinehart and Winston.
Bayliss-Smith, T. and R. Feachem (eds.)
    1977   Subsistence and Survival. London: Academic Press.
Bell, C.
    1973   Arboviruses. *In* C. Bell (ed.) The Diseases and Health Services of Papua New Guinea. Port Moresby: Department of Public Health.
Bell, C. (ed.)
    1973   The Diseases and Health Services of Papua New Guinea. Port Moresby: Department of Public Health.
Bhaskar, R.
    1979   On the possibility of social scientific knowledge and the limits of naturalism. *In* J. Mepham and D.H. Ruben (eds) Issues in Marxist Philosphy 3: Epistemology, Science, Ideology. Sussex: Harvester Press.
Bird, P.
    1972   School in the stars. Education Gazette. Port Moresby: Government Printers.
Black, F.
    1980   Modern isolated pre-agricultural populations as a source of information in prehistoric epidemic patterns. *In* N. Stanley and R. Joske (eds.) Changing Disease Patterns and Human Behaviour, pp. 37–56. London: Academic Press.
Black, F., F. Pinheiro, W. Hierholzer and R. V. Lee.
    1977   Epidemiology of infectious diseases. *In* Health and Disease in Tribal Societies. pp. 115–153. CIBA Foundation Symposium 49, Amsterdam: Elsevier.

REFERENCES

Blaxter, M.
    1978   Diagnosis as category and process: the case of alcoholism. Social Science and Medicine 12: 9–17.

BNGAR
    British New Guinea: Annual Reports.

Bodmer, W. and L. Cavalli-Sforza
    1976   Genetics, Evolution and Man. San Francisco: W. Freeman and Co.

Bourdieu, P.
    1977   Outline of a Theory of Practice. Cambridge: Cambridge University Press.

Bramwell, J.B.C.
    1948   Comment on a patrol report by R. Bell to Collingwood Bay, Sept. 3–20, 1948. National Archives of Papua New Guinea.

Braun, T.G.
    1967a   Experiences with retained placental tissues, Astrolabe Bay Area, 1930–1967. Papua and New Guinea Medical Journal 10(4): 111–116.
    1967b   37 years of obstetrical and gynaecological experience in New Guinea. Papua and New Guinea Medical Journal 10(4): 107–110

Brookfield, H. and D. Hart
    1971   Melanesia. London: Methuen

Brown, P.
    1978   Highland Peoples of New Guinea. Cambridge: Cambridge University Press

Brunton, R.
    1980   Misconstrued order in Melanesian religion. Man 15: 112–28.

Buchbinder, G.
    1973   Maring microadaptation: a study of demographic, nutritional, genetic and phenotypic variation in a Highland New Guinea population. Ph.D. Dissertation, Columbia University.
    1977   Nutritional stress and postcontact population decline among the Maring of New Guinea. In L. Creene (ed.) Malnutrition, Behaviour, and Social Organization, pp. 109–142. New York: Academic Press.

Buchbinder, G. and P. Clark
    1971   The Maring people of the Bismarck ranges of New Guinea: some physical and genetic characteristics. Human Biology in Oceania 1: 121–133.

Bulmer, R.
    1967   Why is the Cassowary not a bird? A problem of zoological taxonomy among the Karam of the New Guinea Highlands. Man 2: 5–25.

Bureau of Statistics n.d.
    1980   National Census, East Sepik Province, Preliminary Field Counts. Papua New Guinea Bureau of Statistics.

Burridge, K.
    1960   Mambu: A Study of Melanesian Cargo Movements and their Ideological Background. New York: Harper and Row.
    1965   Tangu, Northern Madang District. In P. Lawrence and M.J. Meggitt (eds) Gods, Ghosts and Men and Melanesia, pp. 224–249. Melbourne: Oxford University Press.

Carrier, J.G.
    1981   Labour migration and labour export on Ponam Island. Oceania 51: 237–55.

Cattani, J. et al
    1986   The epidemiology of malaria in a population surrounding Madang, Papua New Guinea. American Journal of Tropical Medicine and Hygiene 35: 3–15.

Chambers, R.
    1983   Rural Development. London: Longmans.

Chignell, A.K.
1911   An Outpost in Papua. London: John Murray
Chowning, A.
1977   An Introduction to the Peoples and Cultures of Melanesia. Menlo Park: Cummings.
1978   First-child ceremonies and male prestige in the changing Kove society. *In* N. Gunson (ed.). The Changing Pacific. Melbourne: Oxford University Press.
1982a Self-esteem and drinking in Kove. *In* M. Marshall (ed.) Through a Glass Darkly: Beer and Modernization in Papua New Guinea. Boroko, P.N.G.: Institute for Applied Social and Economic Research.
1982b Physical anthropology, linguistics and ethnology. *In* J. Gressitt (ed.) Biogeography and Ecology of New Guinea, pp. 131–168. The Hague: Juck.
1985   Infant feeding in Kove. *In* L. Marshall (ed.) Infant Care and Feeding in Oceania. New York: Gordon and Breach.
In press. Sorcery and the social order in Kove. *In* M. Stephen (ed.) Witch and Sorcerer in Melanesia.
Christian Mission in Many Lands
1977   Nupela Wokabnaut, Ukarampa, SIL Print.
Clarke, W.C.
1971   Place and People: An Ecology of a New Guinea Community. Canberra: Australian National University Press.
Comaroff, J.
1981   Healing and cultural transformation: the Tswana of Southern Africa. Social Science and Medicine 15B: 367–378.
Counts, D.A.
1980   Fighting back is not the way: suicide and the women of Kaliai. American Ethnologist 7: 332–351.
1983   Near-death and out-of-body experiences in a Melanesian society. Anabiosis 3: 115–135.
1984a Infant care and feeding in Kaliai. Ecology of Food and Nutrition 15: 49–59.
1984b Tamparonga: the "big women" of Kalijai. *In* J. Brown and V. Kerns (eds.) In Her Prime: Anthropological Perspectives on Middle-Aged Women. South Hadley, MA: J.F. Bergin.
Counts, D.R.
1976–77 The good death in Kaliai: preparation for death in western New Britain. Omega 7: 367–372. Reprinted *In* R. Kalish (ed.). Death and Dying: Views From Many Cultures. New York: Baywood Publishing Co. (1979).
Counts, D. and D. Counts
1974   The Kaliai lupunga: disputing in the public forum. *In* A.L. Epstein (ed.) Contention and Dispute: Aspects of Social Control in Melanesia. Canberra: Australian National University Press.
Counts, D.R. and D.A. Counts
1983–84 Aspects of dying in northwest New Britain. In P.H. Stephenson (ed.) Special Section: Dying in Cross-Cultural Perspective. Omega 14: 101–113.
Department of Public Health
1974   Papua New Guinea National Health Plan 1974–1978. Konedobu: Department of Public Health.
Dornstreich, M.
1973   An Ecological Study of the Gadio Enga (New Guinea) Subsistence. Ph.D. Dissertation, Columbia University.
Dosedla, H.C.
1974   Ethnobotanische Grundlagen der materielle Kultur der Mount Hagen-Stamme. Tribus, Veroff. des Linden-Museums, Stuttgart, 23: 155–74.

Economic and Social Commission for Asia and the Pacific/South Pacific Commission
    1982   Country Monograph Series No. 72: Population of Papua New Guinea, New York, United Nations.

Eggleton, M.
    1968   Report of Patrol to Wopkaimin Territory. Olsobip Patrol Report 4/1968–1969.

Engle, R.L. and B. J. Davis
    1963   Medical diagnosis: present, past, and future. Archives of Internal Medicine. 112: 512–519.

Erasmus, J.C.
    1952   Changing folk beliefs and the relativity of empirical knowledge. South Western Journal of Anthropology 8: 411–428.

Ewers, W.H.
    1972   Malaria in the early years of German New Guinea. Journal of Papua and New Guinea Society 6 (1): 2–21.

FAO/WHO Ad Hoc Expert Committee.
    1973   Energy and protein requirements. WHO Technical Report Series No.522. Geneva.

Feachem, R.
    1977   Environmental health engineering as human ecology: an example of New Guinea. *In* T. Bayliss-Smith and R. Feachem (eds.) Subsistence and Survival, pp. 129–182. London: Academic Press.

Feierman, S.
    1979   Change in African therapeutic systems. Social Science and Medicine, 13B: 277–284.

Firth, R.
    1959   Acculturation in relation to concepts of health and disease. *In* I. Galdston (ed.) Medicine and Anthropology. New York: International Universities Press.

Firth, S.
    1983   New Guinea under the Germans. Melbourne: Melbourne University Press.

Fitzgibbon, M.
    1981   Personal Communication.

Fortune, R.F.
    1932   Sorcerers of Dobu. New York: E.P. Duttun.
    1963   Manus Religion. Philadelphia: American Philosophical Society.

Foster, G.M.
    1977   Medical anthropology and international health planning. Social Science and Medicine 11: 527–534.

Foster, G. and B.G. Anderson
    1978   Medical Anthropology. New York: John Wiley and Sons.

Foucault, M.
    1973   The Birth of the Clinic. London: Tavistock.

Frankel, S.
    1980   "I am dying of man": the pathology of pollution. Culture Medicine and Psychiatry, 4: 95–117.
    1982   Family Health Services and the Organisation of Health Care in Tari: An Evaluation prepared for the Southern Highlands Project. Mendi: Southern Highlands Project.
    1984   Peripheral health workers are central to primary health care: lessons from Papua New Guinea Aid Post. Social Science and Medicine 19(3): 279–290.
    1986   The Huli Response to Illness. Cambridge: Cambridge University Press.

Freedman, L. and N. MacIntosh
   1965   Stature variation in western Highland males of east New Guinea. Oceania 35: 286–304.
Freudenburg, A.
   1976   The dialects of Boiken. In R. Loving (ed.) Surveys in Five P.N.G. Languages, Workshops in P.N.G. Languages. 16, Summer Institute of Linguistics, Ukarumpa.
Gajdusek, D.C.
   1957–66   uru Epidemiological Patrols from the New Guinea Highlands to Papua. Bethesda, MD: National Institutes of Mental Health.
   1963   Kuru. Transactions of the Royal Society of Tropical Medicine and Hygiene, 57: 151–169.
   1977   Unconventional viruses and the origin and disappearance of kuru. Science 197: 943–960.
Galdston, I. (ed.)
   1959   Medicine and Anthropology. New York: International Universities Press.
Galton, J.C.
   1880a   Further notes upon the Papuans of Maclay Coast, New Guinea I. Nature, Jan. 1: 204–206.
   1880b   Further notes upon the Papuans of Maclay Coast, New Guinea II. Nature, Jan. 8: 226–229.
Garner, P. and P. Giddings
   1985   Rural health centre use: variation with distance and disease. Papua New Guinea Medical Journal. 28(2): 105–108.
Garruto, R.
   1981   Disease patterns of isolated groups. In H. Rothschild (ed.) Bioculture Aspects of Disease, pp. 557–597. London: Academic Press.
Gewertz, D.
   1983   Sepik River Societies. New Haven: Yale University Press.
Gillies, E.
   1976   Casual criteria in African classifications of disease. In J. B. Loudon (ed.) Social Anthropology and Medicine, pp. 358–395. (ASA Monograph 13). London: Academic Press.
Glick, L.
   1967   Medicine as an ethnographic category: the Gimi of the New Guinea Highlands. Ethnology 6: 31–56.
Golson, J.
   1982   Agriculture in New Guinea: the long view. In D.Denoon and C.Snowden (eds.) A Time to Plan and a Time to Uproot, pp. 33–42. Port Moresby: Institute of Papua New Guinea Studies.
Gratten, M. et al.
   1981   Nasal carriage of pathogenic bacteria in Kalauna village, Goodenough Island. Papua New Guinea Medical Journal 24(3): 174–8.
Greenwood, B.
   1981   Cold or spirits? Choice and ambiguity in Morocco's pluralistic medical system. Social Science and Medicine 15B: 219–235.
Gunther, J.T.
   1972   Medical services, history. In Encyclopaedia of Papua and New Guinea, pp. 748–756. Melbourne: Melbourne University Press.
Haantjens, H. et al
   1972   Lands of Aitape-Ambunti Area. Melbourne: CSIRO.

Haiveta, C.
  1982	Men's participation in child health care in Maindroin vilage, Sissano, West Sepik Province. BA (Hons) thesis, University of Papua New Guinea, Port Moresby.
Hamnett, M. and J. Connell
  1980	Medical beliefs and practices in the North Solomons, a comparative study of the Evio and Siwai. *In* J. Connell (ed.) Traditional Medicine in Bougainville, pp. 39–68. Christchurch: Bouganville Special Publications.
  1981	Diagnosis and cure: The resort to traditional and modern practitioners in the North Solomons, Papua New Guinea. Social Science and Medicine 15B: 489–498.
Hannemann, E.F.
  1949	Village life and social change in Nadang Society. Unpublished manuscript.
Harding, T.G.
  1967	Voyagers of the Vitiaz Straits. Seattle: University of Washington Press.
Harvey, P. and P. Heywood
  1983	Nutrition and growth in Simbu. Report of the Simbu Land Use Project, Vol. 4. Port Moresby: Institute of Applied Social and Economic Research.
Hau'ofa, E.
  1981	Mekeo. Canberra: Australian National University.
Herdt, G.H.
  1977	The shaman's "calling" among the Sambia of New Guinea. *In* B. Juillerat (ed.) Folie, Possession et chaumanism en Nouvelle Guinee. (Special Volume) Journal de la Societe des Oceanistes 56–57: 153–67.
  1981	Guardians of the Flutes. Idioms of Masculinity. New York: McGraw-Hill.
  1983	Alcohol use and abuse and urban adjustment of Sambia male identity. *In* M. Marshall (ed.) Through a Glass Darkly: Beer and Modernization in Papua New Guinea, pp. 227–241. Boroko, P.N.G.: Institute for Applied Social and Economic Research.
  in press.	Sambia: ritual and gender in New Guinea. Case Studies in Cultural Anthropology. New York: Holt, Rinehart and Winston.
Herdt, G.H. and R.J. Stoller
  in press.	Sakulambei: an hermaphrodite's secret. An example of clinical ethnography. The Psychoanalytical Study of Society.
Hetzel, B. (ed.)
  1978	Basic Health Care in Developing Countries. Oxford: Oxford University Press.
Heywood, P.
  1985	National Nutrition Survey 1. Preliminary District Level Analysis of Length and Weight Data. Papua New Guinea Institute of Medical Research. Unpublished mimeo.
Hide, R. (ed.)
  1984	South Simbu: studies in demography, nutrition and subsistence. Report of the Simbu Land Use Project, Vol. 6. Port Moresby: Institute of Applied Social and Economic Science.
Hipsley, E. and N. Kirk
  1965	Studies of dietary intake and the expenditure of energy by New Guineans. South Pacific Commission Technical Paper No. 147. New Caledonia: Noumea.
Hornabrook, R. (ed.)
  1976	Essays on Kuru. Farrington, Berkshire: E. Classey Ltd.
Hornabrook, R.
  1977	Human ecology and biomedical research. *In* T. Bayliss-Smith and R. Feachem (eds.) Subsistence and Survival, pp. 23–62. London: Academic Press.

Howells, W.
1973   The Pacific Islanders. London: Weidenfeld and Nicolson.
Hughes, I.
1977   New Guinea Stone Age Trade. Canberra: Australian National University, Press.
Hwekmarin, L.J. Jamenam, D. Lea, A. Ningiga and M. Wangu
1971   Yangoru cargo cult 1971. Journal of the Papua New Guinea Society 5(2): 3–27.
Hyndman D.
1982   Biotope gradient in a diversified New Guinea subsistence system. Human Ecology 10: 289–309.
1984   Hunting and the classification of game animals among the Wopkaimin. Oceania 54: 289–309.
In press (a) Men, women, work and group nutrition among the Wopkaimin. In L. Manderson (ed.) Shared Wealth and Symbol: The Anthropology of Food in Southeast Asia and Oceania. Cambridge: Cambridge University Press.
In press (b) Ethnoscience of the mountain i.e: a guide for resource utilisation and preservation. In Theme 2: What Role for Traditional Science? New Ways for a Synthesis. 1984 Waigani Seminar, University of Papua New Guinea.
Janzen, J.M.
1978   The Quest for Therapy in Lower Zaire. Berkeley: University of California Press.
Jenkins, C., A. Orr-Ewing, and P. Heywood
1984   Cultural aspects of early childhood growth and nutrition among the Amele of Lowland Papua New Guinea. Ecology of Food and Nutrition 14: 26–275.
Jenkins, C. and P. Heywood
1985   Ethnopediatrics and fertility among the Amele of Lowland Papua New Guinea. In V. Hull and M. Simpson (eds.) Breastfeeding, Child Health and Childspacing: Cross-Cultural Perspectives, pp. 11–34, Kent: Croom Helm Ltd.
Jilek, W.G.
1982   Indian healing: shamanic ceremonialism in the Pacific Northwest today. British Columbia, Canada: Hancock House.
Johannes, A.
1976   Illness and Medical Care in a New Guinea Highlands Society. Ph.D. Dissertation, Northwestern University.
1980   Many medicines in one: curing in the eastern Highlands of Papua New Guinea. Culture, Medicine, and Psychiatry 4: 43–70.
Jolly, R. and M. King
1966   The organisation of health services. In M. King (ed.) Medical Care in Developing Countries. London: Oxford University Press.
Kelly, Father J.
1983   Personal communication from the Bundralis Parish priest.
Kettle, E.
1979   That They Might Live. Sydney, Australia: F.P. Leonard.
King, D. and S. Ranck
1982   Papua New Guinea Atlas. Bathurst, NSW: Robert Brown & Assoc.
Kleinman, A.
1980   Patients and Healers in the Context of Culture. Berkeley: California University Press.
Kopp, K.
1913   Zur Frage des Bevolkerungsruckganges in Neupommern. Archiv für Schiffs- und Tropen-Hygiene Band 17, N. 21.
Kroeger, A.
1983   Anthropological and socio-medical health care research in developing countries. Social Science and Medicine 17(3): 147–161.

Kulz, L.
1919 Zur Biologie und Pathologie des Nachwuchses bei den Naturvölkern der Deutschen Schutzgebiete (Biology and Pathology of the Children of the Aboriginals in German Protectorates). Deutsche Tropenmedizinische Zeitschrift 23 (Beiheft): 3–146.

Kunstadter, P.
1976 Do cultural differences make any difference? Choice points in medical systems available in northwestern Thailand. *In* A.M. Kleinman, et al. (eds.) Medicine in Chinese Cultures. Bethesda, MD: National Institutes of Health.

Landy, D.
1974 Role adaptation: traditional curers under the impact of Western medicine. American Ethnologist 1: 103–127.

Leach, J. and E. Leach (eds.)
1984 The Kula. Cambridge: Cambridge University Press.

Leonard, D.K.
1977 Reaching the Peasant Farmer: Organisation Theory and Practice in Kenya. Chicago: University of Chicago Press.

Lewis, G.
1975 Knowledge of Illness in a Sepik Society. London: Athlone Press.
1976 A view of sickness in New Guinea. *In* J.B. Loudon (ed.) Social Anthropology and Medicine, pp. 49–103. (ASA Monograph 13). London: Academic Press.
1977 Beliefs and behaviour in disease. *In* Health and Disease in Tribal Societies, pp. 227–241. CIBA Foundation Symposium 49, Amsterdam: Elsevier.

Limbrock, E.
1912–13 Buschreise ins Hinterland von Beukin. Steyler Missionsbote 40: 126–127, 142–143.

Lindenbaum, S.
1979 Kuru Sorcery: Disease and Danger in the New Guinea Highlands. Palo Alto, CA: Mayfield Publishing Co.

LiPuma, E.
1980 Sexual asymmetry and social reproduction among the Maring. Ethnos, 1–2: 34–57.
1982 The spirits of modernization: Maring concept and practice. *In* M. Marshall (ed.) Through a Glass Darkly: Beer and Modernization in Papua New Guinea. pp. 175–188. Boroko, P.N.G: Institute for Applied Social and Economic Research.
1985a Social and cultural factors which influence aggression. *In* J. Martin Ramirez and P. Brain (eds.) Agression: Functions and Causes, pp. 49–66. Sevilla: University of Sevilla Press.
1985b The Gift of Kinship: A Study of Maring Social Organization. In press.

Littlewood, R.
1972 Physical Anthropology of the Eastern Highlands of New Guinea. Seattle: University of Washington Press.

Loudon, J.B.
1976a Introduction. *In* J.B. Loudon (ed.) Social Anthropology and Medicine, pp. 1–38. (ASA Monograph 13). London: Academic Press.

Loudon, J.B. (ed.)
1976b Social Anthropology and Medicine. (ASA Monograph 13). London: Academic Press.

Lowman, C.
1971 Maring Big-Men. *In* R. Berndt and A. Lawrence (eds.) Politics in New Guinea, pp. 317–361.

1980 Environment, society and health: ecological bases of community growth and decline in the Maring region of Papua, New Guinea. Ph.D. Dissertation, Columbia University.

Macintyre, M. and M.W. Young
1982 The persistence of traditional trade and ceremonial exchange in the Massim. *In* R.J. May and H. Nelson (eds.) Melanesia: Beyond Diversity, I: 207–22. Canberra: Research School of Pacific Studies.

Maddocks, L.
1973 History of disease in Papua New Guinea. *In* C. Bell (ed.) The Diseases and Health Services of Papua New Guinea, pp. 70–74. Port Moresby: Department of Public Health.
1978 Papua New Guinea: Pari village. *In* B. Hetzel (ed.) Basic Health Care in Developing Countries, pp. 38–62. Oxford: Oxford University Press.

Malcolm, L.
1978 Papua New Guinea: the health care system. *In* B. Hetzel (ed.) Basic Health Care in Developing Countries, pp. 38–62. Oxford: Oxford University Press.

Marshall, A.J.
1938 Men and Birds of Paradise: Journeys Through Equatorial New Guinea. London: William Heinemann, Ltd.

Marwick, M.
1964 Witchcraft as a social strain-gauge. Australian Journal of Science 26: 263–68

May, R.J.
1982 The view from Hurun. *In* R.J. May (ed.) Micronationalist Movements in Papua New Guinea. Monograph No. 1. Department of Political and Social Change, Research School of Pacific Studies, Australian National University, Canberra.

Mayer, J.
1982 Body, psyche and society: Conceptions of illness in Ommura, Eastern Highlands, Papua New Guinea. Oceania 52: 240–260.

McArthur, M.
1977 Nutritional research in Melanesia: a second look at the Tsembaga. *In* T. Bayliss-Smith and R. Feachem (eds.) Subsistence and Survival, pp. 92–128. London: Academic Press.

McCarthy, J.K.
1963 Patrol in Yesterday: My New Guinea Years. Melbourne: Cheshire.

McDermott, W. et al.
1972 Health care experiment in many farms. Science 175: 23–38.

Mead, M.
1947 The Mountain Arapesh vol. IV. Diary of Events in Alitoa, pp. 233–415. New York: Museum of Natural History.
1968 [1956] New Lives for Old. New York: Dell.
1971 [1947] The Mountain Arapesh, Vol. III: The Stream of Events in Alitoa. New York: Natural History Museum Press.

Mendaris, G.R.
1969 Patrol Report, Tufi, 3/1968–69. National Archives of Papua New Guinea.

Mennis, M.
1974 History of Madang. Paper given at Madang Primary A School Inservice Training, August 21.

Mitchell, W.
1978 The Bamboo Fire. New York: W.W. Norton and Co.

Mitchell, W.E.
1978 On keeping equal: polity and reciprocity among the New Guinea Wape. Anthropological Quarterly 51(1): 5–16.

Moi, W.
1976 Growing up in Ambasi. Papua New Guinea Medical Journal 19: 14–18
Moir, J.
1982 Causes of Death in 72 Rural Villages of Madang Province. Paper presented at Papua New Guinea Medical Symposium, Lae.
Monckton, C.A.W.
1922 Taming New Guinea. New York: Dodd Mead.
Morauta, L.
1974 Beyond the Village: Local Politics in Madang, PNG. Canberra: Australian National University Press.
Morren, G.E.B.
1977 From hunting to herding; pigs and the control of energy in montane New Guinea. In T. Bayliss-Smith and R. Feachem (eds.), Subsistence and Survival, pp.273–316. London: Academic Press.
Morris, J.R.
1973 Managerial structures and plan implementation in colonial and modern agricultural extension. In D.K. Leonard (ed.) Rural Administration in Kenya. Nairobi: East Africa Literature Bureau.
Muhlenhard, E.
1980 Death of a Pioneer, Post-Courier, Friday June 20.
Muller, A.
1935–36 Drei Wochen auf Pferdesrücken durchs Steppenland. Steyler Missionsbote 63: 103, 106–107.
Munster, P.
1979 Makarai: A history of early contact in the Goroka Valley, New Guinea Central Highlands 1930–1933. M.A. Thesis, University of Papua New Guinea.
Nadel, S.
1954 Nupe Religion. London: Routledge and Kegan Paul.
Neel, J.
1977 Health and disease in unacculturated Amerindian populations. In Health and Disease in Tribal Societies, pp. 155–177. CIBA Foundation Symposium 49. Amsterdam Elsevier.
Nelson, H.E.
1971 The ecological epistemological and ethnographic context of medicine in a New Guinea Highlands culture. Ph.D. Dissertation, University of Washington.
Ngubane, H.
1977 Body and Mind in Zulu Medicine. London: Academic Press.
Nietschmann, B.
1973 Between Land and Water: the Subsistence Ecology of the Miskito Indians: Eastern Nicaragua. New York: Seminar Press.
NMGR: Nutrition Monitoring Group Report
1980 National Nutrition Conference, July 1980. Mimeo. Provincial Health Office, Alotau, Milne Bay Province.
North Fly Clinico-Epidemiological Pilot Study
1979a First Report of Teams 2 and 3. Medical School, University of Papua New Guinea.
1979b Second Report of Teams 2 and 3. Medical School, University of Papua New Guinea.
Oomen, H.
1971 Ecology of Human Nutrition in New Guinea: Evaluation of Subsistence Patterns. Ecology of Food and Nutrition 1: 3–18.

Osmers, D.
1981 Language and the Lutheran Church on the Papua New Guinea mainland. *In* H.J. Davies, D. Osmers, J. Lynch and S.A. Wurm (eds.), Papers in New Guinea Linguistics No. 21, Pacific Linguistic Series A No. 61. Canberra: Australian National University Press.

PAR.
Papua: Annual Report.

Parker, F.
1972 Local Government Survey. Ningerum Patrol Report 4/1972–1973.

Parkinson, A.D.
1973 Malaria in Papua New Guinea. Papua New Guinea Medical Journal 17(1): 8–16.

Parkinson, R.
1900 (translation by P. Swadling) People of the West Sepik Coast. Records of the National Museum and Art Gallery 7: 43 (1979).

Parkinson, R.
1907 (translation by N.C. Barry, M.S). Dreizig Jahr in der Südsee. Stutgart: Strecker und Schroeder.

Patrol Reports, Manus District Various years.

Patterson, M.
1974–75 Sorcery and witchcraft in Melanesia. Oceania 45: 132–60, 212–34.

Peters, W.
1959 Malaria control in Papua New Guinea. Papua New Guinea Medical Journal 3(3): 66–75.
1960 Studies on the Epidemiology of Malaria in New Guinea. Transactions of the Royal Society of Tropical Medicine and Hygiene 54: 242–260.

Philip, J.
1973 Ningerum Patrol Report 11 1972–1973.

Polgar, S.
1963 Health action in cross-cultural perspective. *In* H.E. Freeman et al. (eds.) Handbook of Medical Sociology. New Jersey: Prentice Hall.

Poole, G.
1981 Transforming 'natural' female ritual leaders and gender ideology among Bimin-Kuskusmin. *In* S. Ortner and H. Whitehead (eds.) Sexual Meanings. New York: Cambridge University Press.
1982 The ritual forging of identity: aspects of person and self in Bimin-Kuskusmin male initiation. *In* G. Herdt (ed.) Rituals of Manhood: Male Initiation in Papua New Guinea, pp. 95–154. Berkeley: University of California Press.
1984 Cultural images of women as mothers: motherhood among the Bimin-Kuskusmin of Papua New Guinea. Social Analysis 15: 73–93.

Pred, A.
1982 Social reproduction and the time-geography of everyday life. *In* P. Gould and G. Olsson (eds.) A Search for Common Ground, pp. 157–186. London: Plon.

Prins, G.
1981 What is to be done? Burning questions of our movement. Social Science and Medicine 19B: 175–183.

Radford, A.J.
1980 The inverse care law in Papua New Guinea. *In* N.F. Stanley and R.A. Joske (eds.) Man and the Evolution of Health. pp. 323–343. London: Academic Press.

Rajalakshmi, R. and C. Ramakrishnan
1969 Dietary and nutrient requirements for Indians. Plant Foods for Human Nutrition 1: 163–192.

Ram, E.R. and Datta, B.K.
  1976   A study on the utilization of primary health centre and sub-centre health services by the rural people of Miraj Taluka, Maharashtra. Indian Journal of Public Health 20: 134–143.

Ranger, T.O.
  1981   Godly medicine: the ambiguities of medical mission in south-east Tanzania, 1900–1945. Social Science and Medicine 15B 261–78.

Ransley, G.
  1975   Ningerum Patrol Report May–June 1975.

Rappaport, R.
  1968   Pigs for the Ancestors: Ritual and the Ecology of a New Guinea People. New Haven: Yale University Press.
  1979   Ecology, Meaning and Religion. Richmond, CA: North Atlantic Books.

Read, K.
  1955   Morality and the concept of the person among the Gahuku Gama. Oceania 25: 233–282.

Reid, J.
  1984   The role of maternal and child health clinics in education and prevention: a case study from Papua New Guinea. Social Science and Medicine 19(3): 291–303.

Roheim, G.
  1954   Cannibalism in Duau, Normanby Island. Mankind 4(12): 487–95.

Romanucci-Ross, L.
  1977   The Hierarchy of resort in curative practices: the Admiralty Islands, Melanesia. In D. Landy (ed.) Culture, Disease and Healing: Studies in Medical Anthropology, pp. 481–486. New York: Macmillan.
  1983   Folk medicine and metaphor in the context of medicalization. In L. Romanucci-Ross et al. (eds) The Anthropology of Medicine. Massachusetts: Bergin and Garvey.

Roscoe, P.B.
  1983   People and planning in the Yangoru Subdistrict, East Sepik Province, Papua and New Guinea. Ph.D. Dissertation, University of Rochester.
  1984   The impact of family planning services in rural Yangoru. Papua New Guinea Medical Journal 27(1): 16–19.
  1986   Maiyire: the emergence and development of a Sepik culture-bound syndrome. Ethnology 25(3): 181–193.

Rowley, C.D.
  1958   The Australians in German New Guinea 1914–1921. Melbourne: Melbourne University Press.
  1965   The New Guinea Villager: a Retrospect from 1964. Melbourne: Cheshire.

Russell, B.
  1931   The Scientific Outlook. New York: Norton.

Russell, D. and C. Bell
  1973   Leprosy. In C. Bell (ed.) The Diseases and Health Services of Papua New Guinea, pp. 185–190. Port Moresby: Department of Public Health.

Sack, P. and D. Clarke
  1979   German New Guinea: the Annual Reports. Australian National University Press, Canberra: Australia.

Sahlins, M.
  1976   Culture and Practical Reason. Chicago: University of Chicago Press.

Schiefenhovel, W.
  1982   Results of ethnomedical fieldwork among the Eipo, Daerah Jayawijaya, Irian Jaya, with special reference to traditional birthgiving. Medika 11(8): 829–43.

1983   Of body and soul – about the concept of man among the Eipo, Mek Language group, Highlands of Irian Jaya. Bikmaus 4(1): 87–93.

Schofield, F.D. and A.D. Parkinson
1963   Social medicine in New Guinea: beliefs and practices affecting health among the Abelam and Wam peoples of the Sepik district. Part 1. The Medical Journal of Australia 1(2): 1–8.

Schwartz, L.
1969   The hierarchy of resort in curative practices: The Admiralty Islands, Melanesia. Journal of Health and Social Behaviour 10: 201–209.

Schwartz, T.
1962   The Paliau Movement in the Admiralty Islands, 1946–1954. Anthropological Papers of the American Museum of Natural History 49: 211–421.

Scragg, R.F.R.
1968   Specialists and spraymen. Papua and New Guinea Medical Journal 11(2): 43–48.
1969   Mortality changes in rural New Guinea. Papua and New Guinea Medical Journal 12(3): 73–83.
1977   Historical epidemiology in Papua New Guinea. Papua and New Guinea Medical Journal 20(3): 102–109.

Sentinella, C.L. (transl.)
1975   Mikloucho-Maclay: New Guinea Diaries 1871–1883. Madang: Kristen Press.

Sinnett, P.
1977   Nutritional adaptation among the Enga. In T. Bayliss-Smith and R. Feachem (eds.) Subsistence and Survival. London: Academic Press.

Sinnett, P. and H. Whyte
1973   Epidemiological studies in a Highland population of New Guinea. Human Ecology 1: 270.

Skamene, E., P. Kongshaun and M.Landy
1980   The Genetic Control of Natural Resistance to Infection and Malignancy. London: Academic Press.

Sorenson, E.
1972   Socio-ecological change among the Fore of New Guinea. Current Anthropology 13: 349–383.

Sorenson, E. and D. Gajdusek
1969   Nutrition in the Kuru region. 1. Gardening, Food Handling and Diet of the Fore people. Acta Tropica 26: 281–330.

Stanhope, J., R. Sturt and D. Russell
1968   An outbreak of leprosy in a previously unexposed population of eastern New Guinea. Transactions of the Royal Society of Tropical Medicine and Hygiene 62: 700–711.

Stocklin, W.
1984   Toktok. Am Rande der Steinzeit auf Neuguinea. Hallein: Burgfried-Verlag.

Strathern, A.J. (ed.)
1982   Inequality in New Guinea Highlands' Societies. Cambridge: Cambridge University Press.
1984   A Line of Power. London: Tavistock.

Strathern, M.
1975   No Money On Our Skins: Hagen migrants in Port Moresby. N.G. Research Bulletin No. 61. Port Moresby and Canberra: Australian National University Press.

1980   No nature, No culture: The Hagen Case. *In* C. Macormack and M. Strathern, (eds.) Nature, Culture and Gender, pp. 174–222. Cambridge: Cambridge University Press.

Strauss, H. and H. Tischner
1962   Die Mi-Kultur der Hagenberg Stamme. Hamburg: Cram Verlag.

Sturt, R.J.
1972   Infant and toddler mortality in the Sepik. Papua and New Guinea Medical Journal 15: 215–226.

Sturt, R.J. and M. Stanhope
1968   Mortality and population patterns of Angugunak. Papua and New Guinea Medical Journal 11(4): 111–117.

Swadling, P.
1984   How Long have People been in the Ok Tedi Impact Region? National Museum Record No. 8. Boroko: Papua New Guinea National Museum.

Thomas, J.
1976   Interpreation of social profiles of production in Tsembaga Maring, Simbae Valley, Eastern Highlands, New Guinea. Oceania 47: 21–35.

Thrift, N.J.
1983   On the determination of social action in space and time. Environment and Planning D: Society and Space 1: 23–57.

Tietjen, A.M.
1984   Infant care and feeding as beginnings of socialization among the Maisin of Papua New Guinea. Ecology of Food and Nutrition 15: 39–48.

Townsend, P.
1969   Subsistence and social organization in a New Guinea society. Ph.D. Dissertation, University of Michigan.

Townsend, P., S. Liao and J. Konlande
1973   Nutritive contributions of sago ash as a native salt in Papua New Guinea. Ecology of Food and Nutrition 2: 91–97.

Trompf, G.
1983   Independent churches in Melanesia. Oceania 54: 51–72

UNDP Project PNG 82/002
1983   Profile and Planning Study for Subsistence Food Production. Port Moresby: Department of Primary Industry.

United Nations
1983   Marital Status and Fertility: A Comparative Analysis of World Fertility Survey Data for Twenty-one Countries. ST/ESA/SER.R/52. New York: Department of International Economic and Social Affairs.

Valentine, C.A.
1965   The Lakalai of New Britain. *In* P. Lawrence and M. Meggitt (eds.) Gods, Ghosts and Men in Melanesia. Melbourne: Oxford University Press.

Venkatachalam, P.
1962   A Study of the Diet, Nutrition and Health of the People of the Chimbu Area (New Guinea Highlands). Monograph No. 4. Port Moresby: Department of Public Health.

Vines, A.
1970   An Epidemiological Sample Survey of the Highlands, Mainland and Islands Regions of the Territory of Papua and New Guinea. Port Moresby: Department of Public Health.

Wagner, R.
1972   Habu. Chicago: University of Chicago Press.

Ward, R.G. and D.A.M. Lea (eds.)
1970   An Atlas of Papua and New Guinea. Port Moresby: Longmans.

REFERENCES

Wark, L. and L.A. Malcolm
   1969   Growth and development of the Lumi child in the Sepik District of New Guinea. Medical Journal of Australia 2: 129–136.

Watson, E.J.
   1968   The village medicine man and the health worker. Papua and New Guinea Medical Journal 11(4): 130–132.

Webster, E.M.
   1984   The Moon Man. Melbourne University Press.

Wedgewood, C.H.
   1934   Sickness and its treatment in Manam Island, New Guinea. Oceania 5(1): 64–79.

Welsch, R.
   1982   The Experience of Illness among the Ningerum of Papua New Guinea. Ph.D. Dissertation, University of Washington.

Welsch, R.L.
   1983   Traditional medicine and western medical options among the Ningerum of Papua New Guinea. In L. Romanucci-Ross (ed.) The Anthropology of Medicine: From Culture to Method. New York: Prager.

Wigley, S.
   1973   Tuberculosis. In C. Bell (ed.) The Diseases and Health Services of Papua New Guinea, pp. 179–184. Port Moresby: Department of Public Health.

Williams, F.E.
   1930   Orokaiva Society. London: Oxford University Press.
   1976   [1941] The natives of Lake Kutuba. In The Vailala Madness and Other Essays, pp. 161–302. London: C. Hurst and Co.

Williams, Jnr., R.B.
   1984   The heart's worst enemy. The Sciences, Sept.–Oct. 1984.

Wolf, E.
   1966   Peasants. New Jersey: Prentice Hall.

Woodham, A.
   1968   How the international biological programme can help. Plant Foods for Human Nutrition 1.

Woods, C.
   1977   Alternative curing strategies in a changing medical situation. Medical Anthropology 3 (1): 25–54.

Wookey, S.
   1973   The nutritional state of the population of Papua New Guinea. In C. Bell (ed.) The Diseases and Health Services of Papua New Guinea, pp. 96–130. Port Moresby: Department of Public Health.

Worsley, P.
   1968   The Trumpet Shall Sound. London: Paladin.

Young, J.
   1981   Non-use of physicians: methodological approaches, policy implications, and the utility of decision models. Social Science and Medicine 15B: 499–507.

Young, M.W.
   1971   Fighting with Food. Cambridge: Cambridge University Press.
   1977   Bursting with laughter: obscenity, values and sexual control in a Massim society. Canberra Anthropology 1(1): 75–87.
   1980   Anthropology of the Dobu Mission. Canberra Anthropology 3(1): 86–104.
   1981   Children's illness and adult's ideology: patterns of health care on Goodenough Island. Papua and New Guinea Medical Journal 24(3): 179–187.
   1983a   "The best workmen in Papua": Goodenough Islanders and the labour trade, 1900–1960. The Journal of Pacific History 18(2): 74–95.

1983b Magicians of Manumanua: Living Myth in Kalauna. Berkely: California University Press.
in press (a). "The worst disease": the cultural definition of hunger in Kalauna. *In* L. Manderson (ed.), Shared Wealth and Symbol: Food, Culture and Society in Oceania and Southeast Asia. Cambridge: Cambridge University Press.
in press (b). Skirts, yams and sexual pollutions: the politics of adultery in Kalauna. *In* L. Manderson (ed.), Gender, Substance and Subsistence.
in press (c). Like father, like son: filial ambivalence and the death of fathers in Kalauna. *In* G. Appel, N. Mada and M. Singarimbun (eds.), Choice and Morality (Essays in honour of J.D. Freeman).
in press (d). Suffer the children: Wesleyans and the D'Entrecasteaux. *In* M. Jolly and M. Macintyre (eds.), Christianity and Colonialism: Transformations of Family and Household in the South Pacific.

YPR 2/48-49
Yangoru Patrol Report No. 2 1948-49. The National Archives, Port Moresby.
YPR 3/48-49
Yangoru Patrol Report No. 3 1948-49. The National Archives, Port Moresby.
YPR 5/48-49
Yangoru Patrol Report No. 5 1948-49. The National Archives, Port Moresby.
YPR 5/49-50
Yangoru Patrol Report No. 5 1949-50. The National Archives, Port Moresby.
YPR 3/55-56
Yangoru Patrol Report No. 3 1955-56. The National Archives, Port Moresby.
YPR 1/61-62
Yangoru Patrol Report No. 1 1961-62. The National Archives, Port Moresby.
YPR 2/61-62
Yangoru Patrol Report No. 2 1961-62. The National Archives, Port Moresby.
YPR 4/61-62
Yangoru Patrol Report No. 4 1961-62. The National Archives, Port Moresby.
YPR 7/61-62
Yangoru Patrol Report No. 7 1961-62. The National Archives, Port Moresby.

Zelenietz, M. and S. Lindenbaum (eds.)
1981 Sorcery and Social Change in Melanesia. Social Analysis 8.

Z'graggen, J.
1975 The languages of the Madang District. Papua New Guinea. Pacific Linguistic Series B No. 41. Canberra: Australian National University Press.

Zigas, V. and R. Rodrigue
1972 Problems Facing Malaria Eradication Program in the Territory of Papua and New Guinea. Tropical and Geographical Medicine 24: 95-99.

INDEX OF SUBJECTS

abscess 288
acceptance of change 24, 56
agnatic ideology 131
aid post 23, 25, 79, 122
    community response to 102
    Goodenough Island 124
    orderly 6, 7, 61, 62, 73, 102, 160, 220, 235, 238–241
        attitudes to 80
        position in community 81, 161
        resistance to shamans by 104, 107
        Sambia use of 20, 105
        Sambian 101
            problems of 103
Amele 181–188
    at time of early contact 182
    attitude to Western doctor 193 ff.
    current health status of 196
    description of 181
    German rule of 185
    social life of, pre-contact 183
    spiritual beliefs 184
    village life of, in 1880s 183
ancestral ghost 76
    Russian naturalist as 182
anger (popokl) 147
animal, ethnoclassification of, Wopkaimin 257
    food supply 267
ante-natal clinic 73
anthropometry, Wopkaimin 272

Bakonabip houses 252
belief change 111
    continuity of, Western medicine and 69–93
    reinterpretation 195
birth control 194
body, mechanical model of 168
Bolubolu health center, map 127
Braun, Theo, doctor to Amele people 181–198
bush spirit 76

care, quality of 162
cargo cult 28, 159, 237

Catholic Church, power of 177
change, acceptance of 24
child care 130, 235
    death, in Torricelli foothills 39
    deformed 285
    health clinic 59
    mortality 40, 200
    retarded 286
    spacing 60
childbearing risk 40
childhood inoculation 234
children, care of 8
choice 25
Christian prayers, healing effect of 143
Christianity, in Ponam 158
coconut 228
Collingwood Bay 69
    exploration of 70
    medical services in 70
colonial change 19
    medical officer 40, 56
    medicine, public health and 46
colonizers, microparasites of 12
communicable disease, indigenous 13
community health, standards of 65
complementarity 292
compliance 21
contagion, control and 51
    understanding of 52
contract labor 9, 10
control, contagion and 51
    loss of, in epidemic 52
conversion 32–33
cult house 252
    leader 256
curers, foreign (to Kove) 232
custom 18
    different views of 2

death, attitude to 41
    cause of adult 78
demography of Amele 196
dependency 21, 24
depopulation 186
diagnosis 172, 224
    among Yangoru Boiken 203 ff.

and treatment, failure of 165
  as empirical science 174
diagnostic technique, shaman 100
diet and gender 274
  and gender, Wopkaimin 255
  effect of custom on 15
  gender, health and 17
  health, and gender 249–275
  in Mount Hagen 145
dietary pattern, Wopkaimin 262
disease causation, spiritual 149
  classification of, Lusi 283
  environments and patterns of 10
  etiology, Kove 222
    Yangoru Boiken 201
  in Torricelli foothills 38
  introduced by foreigners 12
  pattern 271
    geographical variation of 14
  present-day attitudes to 241
  treatment, contemporary 243
diseases of Amele 185
  Kalauna 118
  Wopkaimin 271
divination ritual 291
Divine punishment 229
dokta 95, 233
  as agent of role change 110
  competition of, with traditional healers 109
  visits to, in Sambia 106
dream, as diagnostic and etiological aid 224
dysentery 43, 44, 50, 52

earthquake 48
eating as cultural phenomenon 264
environment, adaptation to 10
epidemic 72
  in Torricelli foothills 41
  post-contact 27
  short-lived 52
epidemiology, of Goodenough Island 116
ethnomedicine modification 201
European belief in sorcery 236
European contact, response to medical care and 19
evangelization 50

fertility rates of Amele 197
fish-eye magic 288
fishing 269
  equipment 228

food avoidance, gender-based 263
  ethnoclassification 267
    Wopkaimin 256
  prohibition 15, 120
  taboo, inherited 183
foreign substance, theories of 232
frambesia 40
funerary custom, Amele 184
  Kove 222

Gnau, understanding of contagion 53
gender and diet 274
  and diet, Wopkaimin 255
  and health 270
  diet, and health 249–275
  difference in health treatment 131
    in nutrient allocation 270
  health difference 18
German measles 46
ghost 170
  as accuser of sorcery 290
  as agent of disease 289
glasman 60
Gnau response to epidemic 52
goldfield 10
Goodenough Island 115–139
  map 123
  modern health facilities 122
government officer 9, 71
  village view of 9
gumema 85

healer as sorcerer 120
  local, Sambian 98
healer, Maisin 79, 83
    diagnostic techniques of 84
  prestige of local 118
  technique of local 119
healing ceremony 100
  prayer and 83
  psychological aids to 152
  technique, Maisin 72
  traditional, among Sambia 97
health and gender 270
health care, access to and availability of 25
  delivery of 64
    delivery of, decentralization of 65
  future implications 64
  in Mount Hagen 141–154
  organization of 1
  present-day patterns of 58
  recent deterioration 73
health center, attendance as function of

INDEX OF SUBJECTS

distance from 210
Goodenough Island 123
Ponam 161
records 124
travel to 57, 121
health, gender, and diet 17, 249–275
health service, accessibility to and quality of 26
Ponamian use of 175
health worker, baffling activities of 22
heil tultul 7, 47, 48, 62
hematology, Wopkaimin 272
hospital admission, fear of 237
reasons for 121, 126, 133
Goodenough Island 123
image of 142
Ponam 163
strangeness of 25

ideological change 112
ideology, illness and 115–139
illness as misfortune 86
cause and treatment of 58, 74
complementary responses to 305
explanation of 26, 29
ideology and 115–139
Kalauna attitude to 117
Marin 297
patterns of response to 1
Sambia attitude to 97
social context of 4
spirit and 29
theories of, in New Guinea 308
traditional ideas 3
infant care, in Mount Hagen 144
mortality 7, 194
infanticide 230
infection, in Torricelli foothills 35–68
influenza 45, 53
innovation 53

Kalauna epidemiology 124
people 117
Kaliai health center 280
Kaliai Lusi 277–294
Kaliai see also Lusi
Kam Basin, map 250
Kandoka village 278
kerosene 231
kiap 47
Koinambe health center 301
Kove, bodily cleanliness 222
description of 217

diet of 221
diseases in 226
missions to 218
present-day attitudes of 241
sanitary conditions 222
traditional medicine 221

latrine 145
hygiene of 55
liklik dokta 47
living conditions, in Torricelli foothills 38
Lusi, diseases of 282
Lusi *see also* Kaliai
traditional care 280

magic, in Torricelli foothills 38
magician, shaman versus, as healer 101
Maisin, description of 70
economic advancement of 70
medical beliefs and practices of 69
pluralistic attitude to health care of 87
response of, to health problems 86
malaria, among Amele 185
control 200
return of 146
male nutritional privilege 268, 269
Maring 295–310
clans of 299
cosmology of 298
description of 296
diseases of 297
maternal and child health clinic 164, 200, 220
service 8
maternal health clinic 59
maternity service 162
mechanical failure of body 167
medical aid provision to Kove 219
care, Amele need for 188
payment effect on 279
change 19
scope of 307
innovation 3
pluralism 141–154, 199
practice and theory in Kove 217–247
traditional 4
record, Kalauna 125
service, in Collingwood Bay 71
treatment, complementarity in 277–294
medicine, religion and 28
traditional 81
Sambian 99
white man's, as real 21

Melanesian people 254
menstrual blood poisoning 289
microparasites, of colonizers 12
mining camp 9
miracle, Christian, or sorcery? 304
misfortune 58, 74
    Amele 183
    illness as 86
    in Torricelli foothills 35–68
    Maisin 71
        etiology of 75
    Maring 297
    survey of 77
mission 303
    status of 178
missionary 9, 10, 50, 71
    as agent of change 20
    attitude to healers 72
    food taboo introduced by 229
    health care and 22
    Kove resistance to 229
    solution to Amele problem 187
moral transgression as causative agent 225
mortality pattern 40
Mount Hagen 141–154
    lack of primary health care in 144

natural cycle, Maring 299
New Guinea, ecology of 11
    flora and fauna of 12
    geographical variety of 10
    German colony 183
    theories of illness in 308
ngarivali 281
nurse patrol 122
nutrient requirement, Wopkaimin 258
    status, Wopkaimin 259
    supply 266
        Wopkaimin 258
nutrition 14
    new crop introduction and 228
nutritional education 239
    requirement 265
    return from animal, Wopkaimin 259
    status 266

obstetrics 193
outpatient treatment, reasons for 128, 131

Papua New Guinea 5
Papua New Guinea, archaeology of 11
    colonial administration of 8, 9
    colonial powers in 6

    local analogues to medicine 3
    map of vi
    nutritional status of population 16
    pre-contact 2
    public helath standards in 66
patrol officer, health care and 22
perinatal care 132, 239
person, concept of 23
personal hygiene 145
physiology, Ponamian 166
plant remedy 142
    decline in use of 143–144
plantation 9, 10
pluralism 30, 31, 32, 142
    evolution of, among Maring 302
    in Mount Hagen 151
    politics of 306
pneumonia 53
poison sorcery 76
poisoning 231
Ponam, pre-Christian 157
    Western medicine in 155–180
popokl 141, 148, 152, 153
populaton control 146
pragmatic change 113
prayer, healing and 83
priest, duties of, in sickness 82
    versus shaman as therapist 304
primary health care, lack of, in Mount
        Hagen 144
protein and undernutrition 16
    women's access to 18
psychological aids to healing 152
public health, colonial medicine and 46
    education 235
    measure 24
    provision, in Ponam 160
public hygiene, enforced 55
    hygiene measure 23

reinterpretation 201
religion, medicine and 28
resistance 55
ritual 142
    in traditional medicine 143
rivalinga 281
role change 110
rule 18
rural health center 103

sacred shrub 252
sacrifice 149
sago working 269

INDEX OF SUBJECTS

Sambia, description of 96
   doktas and shamans among 95–114
   household survey of 105
sanguma sorcery 53, 54
sanitary conditions, Kove 222
Second World War 50, 158, 190
self-diagnosis 224
shaman 95, 98
   aid post orderly resistance to 104
   magician versus, as healer 101
   recourse to, in Sambia 99, 106
   versus priest as therapist 304
shamanistic healing 103
sick person, behavior of 119
sickness, Amele 183
   as punishment 159
   causes of 169
   divine 171
   earthly 169
   etiology and changing response to, Maisin 90
   Maisin etiology of 75
   Western treatment of casual 77
   wrongdoing and 150
sik nating 202, 206, 211
sista 233
smallpox 41–43, 52
   vaccination 234
social change 303
   illness, Maring 300
societal origin of illness 281
Society of the Divine Word (SVD) 50
sorcerer 53, 74, 87, 183, 223, 242, 287
   confrontation of 85
   ghost identifies 291
   healer as 120
sorcery 53, 74, 87, 183, 223, 242, 287
   acceptance of, by administrators 65
   attacks based on envy 225
   bundle, Yangoru Boiken 206
   declining importance of 230
   Maisin 71
   or Christian miracle? 304
   poison 76
soul as origin of life 166
   loss as cause of illness 167
South Seas Evangelical Mission (SSEM) 50
spirit attack 147
   crazy 170
   illness as affliction of 166
   illness and 29
suicide 231

surgery 163
   attitudes to 150
sweet potato 12 .
systematization, perils of 4

taboo 15, 18, 263
tatami 75, 76
therapy, availability of 209
thermometer, as diagnostic instrument 173
tinea 40
tinea imbricata 222
tokweli 118
Torricelli foothills 25–68
   description 37
   disease and living conditions in 38
   map 36
   spirits inhabiting 38
totemism of Amele 184
totoruga 85
traditional healing in Goodenough Island 117
traditional medicine, of Kove 221
   specialists in 225
treatment, traditional ideas 3
Trichothanses worm 145
tropical ulcer 40
   ulcer, Urat treatment of 56
tubrculosis 289
Tumam, quarantine practices of 52

undernutrition, protein and 16
Urat response to epidemic 52

venereal disease 72
   etiology of 202
victim, protection of 85
village health services, development 5
   health worker 7
   hygiene 71
   life, aid post orderly attitude to 62
   sickness 78
village sickness 89, 90

Wailaga hospital admissions, geographical spread 133 ff.
   map 133
weight gain, of child 17
West New Britain, map 279
Western chemical poison 231
   medical help, accessibility of 212
   medicine, breakdown of belief in 236
      continuity of belief and 69–93
      decline in use of 176

early experience of 181–199
in Ponam 155–180
introduction to Ponam 157
misunderstanding of 104
Ponamian interpretation of 168
practitioners of 233
sceptical attitude to 237
woman, care of 8
  protein access of 18
  work of 17, 18
Wopkaimin 249–275

parishes, map 251
population 252 ff.
wrongdoing, sickness and 150

Yagaum hospital 191
yam exchange 44
Yangoru Boiken 199–215
  description of 199
  early acquaintance with Western medicine 200
  health improvement of 212
yaws, treatment of 57

The Culture, Illness, and Healing Book Series

Editors

Margaret Lock and Allan Young

Leon Eisenberg and Arthur Kleinman (eds.), *The Relevance of Social Science for Medicine*, 1981, x + 422.

Arthur Kleinman and Tsung-yi Lin (eds.), *Formal and Abnormal Behavior in Chinese Culture*, 1981, xxiv + 436.

Carolyn Fishel Sargent, *The Cultural Context of Therapeutic Choice*, 1982, xii + 192.

Anthony J. Marsella and Geoffrey M. White (eds.), *Cultural Conceptions of Mental Health and Therapy*, 1982, xii + 414.

Noel J. Chrisman and Thomas W. Maretzski (eds.), *Clinically Applied Anthropology*, 1982, viii + 438.

Robert A. Hahn and Atwood D. Gaines (eds.), *Physicians of Western Medicine*, 1985, ix + 346.

Ronald C. Simons and Charles C. Hughes (eds.), *The Culture-Bound Syndromes*, 1985, xv + 516.

L. L. Langness and Harold G. Levine (eds.), *Culture and Retardation*, 1986, xv + 212.

Craig R. Janes, Ron Stall, and Sandra M. Gifford (eds.), *Anthropology and Epidemiology*, 1986, ix + 350.

John G. Kennedy, *The Flower of Paradise*, 1987, xii + 268.

Nancy Scheper-Hughes (ed.), *Child Survival: Anthropological Perspectives on the Treatment and Maltreatment of Children*, 1987, x + 396.

Sjaak van der Geest and Susan Reynolds Whyte (eds.), *The Context of Medicines in Developing Countries*, 1988, xiii + 394.

Margaret Lock and Deborah Gordon, *Biomedicine Examined*, 1988, viii + 542.

Stephen Frankel and Gilbert Lewis, *A Continuing Trial of Treatment*, 1989, v + 334.